A Lift *for* Living

Herman Kroeker

1 Peter 1:8

A Lift for Living

by Herman Kroeker

Essence PUBLISHING

Belleville, Ontario, Canada

A Lift *for* Living
A Daily Devotional

ISBN: 1-896400-04-3

Essence Publishing is a Christian Book Publisher dedicated to furthering the work of Christ through the written word. For more information, write: 103B Cannifton Rd., Belleville, ON, Canada K8N 4V2. Phone: 1-800-238-6376. Fax: (613) 962-3055. Email: essence@intranet.on.ca

Printed in Canada
by

Essence
PUBLISHING

ACKNOWLEDGEMENTS

The author would like to acknowledge the kindness of authors and publishers who generously granted permission to use extracts from their copyrighted publications in this devotional book.

An earnest attempt has been made to locate the authors of all copyrighted selections used in this book. Where we have failed in this, we beg your indulgence. Should we succeed in locating any further copyright owners, acknowledgement will be given.

PREFACE

During the years that I was involved in radio ministry, *Springs in the Valley* and *Consolation* by Mrs. Charles E. Cowman became the first devotional books in my Christian experience. Early in my pastoral ministry, my devotional life took on the form of (as I put it) living with Bible characters. I nibbled through the book of Job and a commentary on Job for about 1 1/2 years, and the concept of living with Bible characters or authors of books became the source of my devotional life, and it has remained so ever since.

I will list just a few authors and books, not in any particular order, that aided me in my personal devotions over the years. I recall spending a year with Spurgeon in his *Morning and Evening* devotional book. F.B. Meyer was another author I appreciated. I spent three years going through his *Daily Homily* along with my Amplified Bible. Meyer chose one verse from every chapter in the Bible and then wrote a brief homily about it. *Daily Readings* by Wm. E. Sangster, *Renewed Day by Day* by Tozer, *Every Day With Jesus* by George Duncan, *Through the Year* with William Barclay, *Awake My Heart* by Sidlow Baxter, *My Utmost For His Highest* by O. Chambers, *Daily Bible Readings* with Andrew Kuyvenhoven, *Giant Steps* by W. Wiersbe, *Your Father Loves You* by James Packer and *Daily Delights* by Pauline Spray were among the other books that kept me fresh in my devotional life.

Currently, while beginning to write this book, I am reading the book, *Amazing Grace* by K.W. Osbeck, the Stories of 366 Hymns. These have enriched and blessed my life immensely. Of course, the Bible is always open along with all the helps mentioned above. That is the ultimate devotional book!

What I am seeking to do in writing this book is to share all the radio messages that I've written and used over a period of 17 years, as well as the short messages that were used on Cable

TV and the spots used on "Dial-a-Meditation." Some will be short and others a little longer. But I hope that all will bless your life in some way.

The beginning of this adventure started early in my retirement from the ministry. At the age of 68, after 40 years of ministry, I finally purchased a computer with the help of my son, Clifford. It has always been my desire to leave something for the next generation — my children and grandchildren — and it is my hope that this book will be something from which they can grow and learn.

I have done my very best to credit the material that I have borrowed for this book. Many of the poems and quotations that I have used, however, have been gleaned from my radio ministry, and were often sent in by listeners, making follow-up difficult. So I apologize for any works that have not been given proper credit.

To my wife Irene, my children and grandchildren, family and friends who have encouraged me in my ministry, I dedicate this book.

Herman Kroeker

INTRODUCTION

There is no substitute for sitting at the feet of Jesus. Remember what Jesus said to Martha in Luke 10:42: *"...Only one thing is needed... Mary has chosen what is better...."*

A private devotional life grows out of a daily quiet time.
— Waldo Wiebe

If we spend 16 hours a day dealing with the tangible things and only five minutes a day trying to find God, it's no wonder that the tangible things of this world are 200 times more real than the spiritual.
— Dean Inge

Many believers admit that private devotions are one of their greatest difficulties. Living in a busy world keeps them from having time alone with God. You may ask, "Why should I spend time alone with God?" The answer is because God *desires* our fellowship! He *yearns* for His children; and He has given us His Word as our guide, our inspiration, our compass, our armour and our source of comfort. He wants to give us a "lift for living" each day!

How do we go about doing this? First of all, we need to find a place (Matt. 6:6). We need to shut *out* distractions and be shut *in* with God. We need to come seeking — desiring spiritual food and spiritual fellowship. We should come silently, ready to hear, with a heart open to God. We can come with sheer delight, knowing that we are entering His presence. David said in Psalm 38:9 (KJV), *Lord, all my desire is before Thee.* Desire is the soul of prayer (Ps. 21:2). Desire without words may be the truest, highest kind of praying (Rom. 8:26).

When you come to read the Word, plan your Bible reading. Never be in a hurry. Remember that it is quality, not quantity that counts. When you look at a passage of Scripture, look for a command to obey, a promise to claim, an error to avoid or correct, an example to follow or a special lesson to remember.

A strong healthy devotional life will cause you to grow in your faith and in your fellowship with God. You will find cleansing, peace, joy, renewed energy, and life! And you will have something to share with others. May God bless you richly as you seek Him in your private devotions.

The following is one of my favourite devotional poems:

THE SECRET

I met God in the morning
  When my day was at its best,
And His presence came like sunrise,
  Like a glory in my breast.

All day long the Presence lingered,
  All day long He stayed with me
And we sailed in perfect calmness
  O'er a very troubled sea.

Other ships were blown and battered,
  Other ships were sore distressed,
But the winds that seemed to drive them
  Brought to us a peace and rest.

Then I thought of other mornings,
  With a keen remorse of mind,
When I too had loosed the moorings,
  With the Presence left behind.

So I think I know the secret,
  Learned from many a troubled way:
You must seek Him in the morning
  If you want Him through the day!

— Ralph Spaulding Cushman

A Lift *for* Living

The following books are currently available from Essence Publishing:

Ask at your local bookstore or use our convenient order form.

Setting the Captives Free by John Visser ***106pp, $9.95***
Practical and biblical help in learning how we can be effectively used of God to make a difference in a hurting world. Includes Study Guide. Excellent for group study!

To Have and To Hold by John Visser. . . . . ***99 pp, $7.50***
Biblical Reflections on Marriage. Chapters include: God's Idea of Marriage; Living Happily Ever After; So, You're Single; Divorce & Remarriage; and more. Includes Study Guide. Excellent for Marriage Preparation Classes and married couples seeking to improve their marriage.

A Voice Behind You by Sheila White . . . . ***112 pp, $9.95***
This is a prophetic word to the Church by an anointed woman of God. It examines the present state of the Church and calls her towards her full destiny in Christ.

Handling Stress by John Visser . . . . ***112 pp, $9.95***
To live is to experience stress. Some people cope very well with stress while others do not. This book discusses causes and symptoms of stress in today's world and gives practical advice on how to handle it.

And the Pink Snow Fell by Rev. Ray Cross. . . . ***100 pp, $14.95***
This is the story of the Port Hope, ON, gas explosion of November 1993 and the huge impact it had on one of the families living adjacent to the site of the explosion. Contains many photographs. Excellent for grief therapy!

Protestant Church Growth in Korea by Dr. John Kim . . ***364 pp, $24.95***
The Korean Church is one of the fastest growing churches in the world today. In this book, the author offers some insights into why this is so and examines some of factors that have influenced this growth.

Binder of Wounds by Sini Den Otter . . . . ***(Feb., 1996)***
A medley of meditations describing some of the author's experiences as a hospital chaplain. Inspirational and honest, this book hopes to encourage believers in their daily struggles and give practical insights into caring for others.

For more information or to place an order,
please contact your local Christian Bookstore
or:

PUBLISHING

103B Cannifton Road
Belleville, ON K8N 4V2
Phone (613) 962-3294; Fax (613) 962-3055
1-800-238-6376

A convenient Order Form is available on
the next page.

January 1   THE NEW YEAR!

Everybody likes new things: new cars, new houses, new clothes, new shoes, new tools, new books! Fresh starts appeal to each one of us. We like new beginnings!

For example, there is something delightful about blotting out dirty fingerprints with a fresh coat of paint. Add new curtains, clean wall paper and a set of new furniture to this, and living takes on a fresh meaning. Everything is new and clean. Along with redecorating, many of us would also like to have a fresh start in other areas of our lives. A fresh start in business might lead to a much better position. A new beginning at school might make a big difference in our education. A chance to start over in our marriage relationships might alter the whole outlook on life. In fact, some of us would like to get rid of the past entirely and start all over again.

Somehow the New Year seems to offer us a fresh start. It seems to say, "Forget the past! Begin again! Resolve to do better!" It sounds so easy. We make resolutions, have good intentions, but all too soon it proves to be an exercise in futility. There is a way to have a new start, though — a fresh new beginning that covers over the old soiled past. Here is His Word: *Therefore, if anyone is in Christ, he is a new creation, the old has gone, the new has come* (2 Cor. 5:17). Here is a fresh start unconditionally backed by God's word. God desires to reveal Himself as a Person. He did that in the Person of His Son Jesus Christ. God gave His Son to bring us back to Himself. Faith in Him secures salvation — a new beginning!

As a new person in Christ, you will begin to enjoy His Word and His presence. You will meet and gain new friends. Worship and fellowship with believers will strengthen your faith. Faith needs nourishment! You will have the Holy Spirit to guide you (John 16).

Go with God!

> *Read: 2 Corinthians 5:17-21; Matthew 7:13-14;*
> *John 14:1-3; Hebrews 13:8*

January 2   FOOTPRINTS!

Before us lies a new year like a field of fresh fallen snow. Untrodden! Untouched! Unblemished! God has given us a new opportunity for purposeful, meaningful living; a new field in which to stamp our footprints.

1. Footprints remind us of the need for direction. Often we walk carelessly and aimlessly with no sense of where we're going. Surely a believer's life should be marked by direction. We should be conscious of daily leading by the Lord Himself. Israel enjoyed this privilege (Exod. 40:36-38). Along the journey of life we need guidance. Implicit trust brings infallible guidance (Prov. 3:5-6).

2. Footprints remind us of our future destination. Heaven is our home! Like a compass pointing to the magnetic north, the set of our soul should be heavenward (Col. 3:2). The more comfortable we are here, the fainter will be our desire to be up there. Every believer ought to have a healthy tug toward heaven, like the tug on the string of an airborne kite. In *Pilgrim's Progress*, Pilgrim set his back on the City of Destruction and set out for the Celestial city. Decision decides destiny! Do you know where you are going? Have you made reservations (1 Peter 1:4)?

3. Footprints remind us of the need for decision. Throughout the year, we will make decisions large and small. Some will be far-reaching; some will influence our lives and the lives of others. *But be sure to fear the LORD and serve Him faithfully with all your heart; consider what great things He has done for you* (1 Sam. 12:24).

> Sensitivity God demands — *be sure to fear the Lord.*
> Service God desires — *serve Him faithfully.*
> Sincerity God decrees — *with all your heart.*

John Wesley is to have said, "Lord, deliver me from being half a Christian." We should have the same desire.

Decision rests with each of us! Joshua 24:15b proclaims, *But as for me and my household, we will serve the Lord.* Ruth says to her mother-in-law, Naomi, in Ruth 1:16-17, *...Don't urge me to leave you or to turn back from you. Where you go I will go, and where you stay I will stay. Your people will be my people and your God my God. Where you die I will die, and there I will be buried....* Elijah, in 1 Kings 18:21, asks, *...How long will you waver between two opinions?* May the New Year bring to us direction, destination and decision to have a closer walk with Jesus Christ and a life of surrender to His Father.

Read: Deuteronomy 11:8-25

January 3   A NEW YOU FOR A NEW YEAR!

How about a new you for a new year? *Therefore, if anyone is in Christ, he is a new creation; the old has gone, the new has come!* (2 Cor. 5:17).

The corruption of human nature requires the new birth. Romans 1 reveals the total depravity of man. No one can enter heaven without the experience of the new birth. *...Jesus declared, "I tell you the truth, no one can see the kingdom of God unless he is born again"* (John 3:3). Evil is so inwrought into man's constitution and habits that he needs to be spiritually reconstructed in order to see as God sees, feel as God feels and act as God wills. Our old nature is totally corrupt.

The heart is deceitful above all things and beyond cure. Who can understand it? I the LORD search the heart and examine the mind, to reward a man according to his conduct, according to what his deeds deserve (Jer. 17:9-10). The change to be effected is so radical and so complete that no human means can avail to bring it about. The work of the Holy Spirit is mighty and mysterious. Through the instrumentality of the Word of God this is accomplished. *He chose to give us birth through the word of truth, that we might be a kind of firstfruits of all He created* (James 1:18). *For you have been born again, not of perishable seed, but of imperishable, through the living and enduring word of God* (1 Peter 1:23). The new birth is, therefore, of the will of God, of the mercy of God and for the glory of God. Often it is described as a new heart: *I will give you a new heart and put a new spirit in you; I will remove from you your heart of stone and give you a heart of flesh. And I will put my Spirit in you and move you to follow my decrees and be careful to keep my laws* (Ezek. 36:26-27).

There is no part of the believer's life from which this newness should be absent. His speech, character, acts, plans, purposes and desires are to become new. This newness also furnishes a test. The proof of your conversion is continuance. There must be a decided change. This new nature that you receive from God is bent to the will of God. You will want to do His will.

Unless we are new creatures in this world, we shall not be new creatures in the next. How about a new you for a new year?

Read: John 3

January 4 MAKING A DECISION — NEW YEAR

Here we are at the threshold of a brand new year! We say it that way because that's the term most commonly used in everyday language. We talk about a brand new house, a brand new car, a brand new bicycle and so on. When something is new it is *brand* new!

New Year's resolutions are the subject of conversation during the closing days of the year. Do we make them in order to break them? Personally, I do not put too much faith in making New Year's resolutions.

People talk about turning over a new leaf, thinking they might do better in the coming year. Turning over a new leaf and intentions have much in common: They never get much done. These things will not change your life!

Let's be very frank! Only Christ can and will give you a change of heart and mind. Only Christ will give you a new outlook on life and make life worth living. Only Christ can give you the assurance and security for what lies ahead. Jesus Christ fits into every circumstance of life! The song writer says, "With Christ in the vessel, I can smile at the storm."

Have you ever found yourself in a watchnight service? Did you say, "I'll start a life with Christ soon, maybe in the New Year" or "I'll raise my hand and go forward in another meeting"? It is a sad fact that many have heard the gospel often yet continue to put off or refuse God's gift of salvation. Do you know how I know that you should make a decision? The Holy Spirit is faithful. He is working in your heart right now. He is offering you something better for your sin-burdened soul. How could you refuse God's gift of salvation? It is full and free to everyone. Today is God's day! *Today, if you hear His voice, do not harden your hearts* (Heb. 3:7-8).

I still recall how I dreaded hearing the invitation of a pastor or an evangelist: "Come, give your life to Christ." I kept putting it off; I'll do it tomorrow. Not until the age of fifteen, away from home, listening to a radio broadcast, did I kneel and make a decision for Christ. I was saved, and I knew it! How do I know? *He who has the Son has life; he who does not have the Son of God does not have life. I write these things to you who believe in the name of the Son of God so that you may know that you have eternal life* (1 John 5:12-13). Start the New Year living for Him!

Read: Deuteronomy 30:11-20; 31:8; 1 John 5:12-13

January 5   GO FORWARD

Then the LORD said to Moses, "Why are you crying out to me? Tell the Israelites to move on [go forward (KJV)]*"* (Exod. 14:15). This text is connected with the wonderful deliverance of the children of Israel from the land of Egypt. Scarcely had they left the land, when Pharaoh again hardened his heart and pursued them to bring them back to bondage and slavery. The spot where he overtook them was near the Red Sea. Before them was a watery sepulcher; behind them a powerful enemy. Escape seemed impossible! God said to Moses, "Go forward, move on!"

Like the children of Israel, who were on their way to the promised land, believers are on their way to heaven. Satan, our enemy will pursue us! He will do his level best to bring us back into bondage and the slavery of sin. The believer is encouraged to "go forward," to "move on." A believer must not stand still.

1. We must go forward in Christian graces: *For this very reason, make every effort to add to your faith goodness; and to goodness, knowledge; and to knowledge, self-control; and to self-control, perseverance; and to perseverance, godliness; and to godliness, brotherly kindness; and to brotherly kindness, love* (2 Peter 1:5-7). Life must be different! We cannot play the chameleon! We have an example to follow. *To this you were called, because Christ suffered for you, leaving you an example, that you should follow in His steps* (1 Peter 2:21).

2. We must go forward in Christian growth: Move on in faith; faith must grow! (Rom. 10:17). Move on in love; love must increase! (1 Thess. 3:12) (That is where good deeds come in — see Titus 2:14). Move on in prayer! (1 Thess. 5:17) (That is where devotions and fellowship with the Lord take place). Move on in building relationships! (Eph. 5:25) (Our homes need the atmosphere of love and affection). Move on in obedience, obeying the Word of God (1 Peter 1:22). For all this we have Jesus! We have the Holy Spirit to guide and to teach, to lead and to comfort us (John 16:13).

The examples of the Old Testament saints are an incentive for us to "go forward" and to "move on." Noah, Abraham, Moses, Joshua and Caleb went forward. Our motto could, and should be, "Go Forward!"

Read: Hebrews 11:1-29; 12:1-2

January 6 THE NEW YEAR — 3D's

The land you are entering to take over is not like the land of Egypt, from which you have come, where you planted your seed and irrigated it by foot as in a vegetable garden. But the land you are crossing the Jordan to take possession of is a land of mountains and valleys that drinks rain from heaven. It is a land the LORD *your God cares for; the eyes of the* LORD *your God are continually on it from the beginning of the year to its end* (Deut. 11:10-12).

How good are you at predicting the future? Can you qualify as a crystal gazer? If you were invited to witness a preview of the coming year, would you accept it?

Looking at the text above, I want to ask, "What will the future be like?"

1. It will be different! Different from the past. It will not be like Egypt. Israel had to learn to welcome change. In the year ahead there will be changes. Life is dynamic! Stagnation means death! We must find keys to unlock doors of new opportunities.

2. It will be difficult! Ahead are the mountains and the valleys. New opportunities spell new responsibilities. Mountains are meant for climbing. Caleb welcomed the idea (Josh. 14:12). Why should we detour from difficulties?

3. It will be dependable! The Lord cares for the land, and the eyes of the Lord are upon it from the beginning of the year to the end. We know who holds the future! Amen! He is dependable!

Tomorrow will be guided and guarded by God. We have a Divine, Wise Commander. Go into the New Year with God! Be optimistic!

"Put your hand in the hand of the Man of Galilee."

Read: Hebrews 11:8-10 (We are a pilgrim people!)

January 7 PONDER THE PATH (Part 1)

Ponder the path of thy feet, and let all thy ways be established (Prov. 4:26, KJV). *The steps of a good man are ordered by the* LORD: *and He delighteth in his way* (Ps. 37:23, KJV). Other translations read: *Watch the path; Consider well the path; Make level paths.*

Most of us are afflicted with eye trouble. We are shortsighted. We refuse to look ahead to see where our path leads. We don't stop to think! We seem to live under the impression that we can live as we like and still escape the consequences of that kind of living and attitude. Most of us would like to arrive at a successful destiny in life. We would like to achieve. We would like to arrive at a goal. We have a goal, but so many things distract us.

Some of us shy away from the path of self-discipline and self-denial. Sometimes we're like a child, preferring a penny now in preference to a nickel tomorrow. We are like the student who chooses an easy course that requires little effort, to the more meaningful course that requires rigid self-discipline. Many young people make a tragic mistake in selecting a marriage partner when they follow the romantic impulse of the moment, instead of taking the long look concerning what marriage really involves. Many yield to high-pressure advertising and find themselves on a financial precipice. Life would be so much different if each of us would *ponder the path of our feet*. THINK! Give consideration to the outcome of your attitudes, ambitions and actions.

Moses wrote a song one day and they [Israel] were to sing all forty-three verses (Deut. 32:1-43). He makes a forecast of their future, but sadly, Israel does not discern (Deut. 32:28-29). It's too bad Israel did not know Psalm 39:4 at that time: *Show me, O LORD, my life's end and the number of my days; let me know how fleeting is my life.* All of us could profitably join David and pray. *Teach us to number our days aright, that we may gain a heart of wisdom* (Ps. 90:12).

Read: Deuteronomy 32:1-43

January 8   PONDER THE PATH (Part 2)

Begin today with the prophet Haggai, who repeatedly urged the people in his day: *Now this is what the LORD Almighty says: "Give careful thought to your ways"* (Haggai 1:5,7).

Life is precious! We have only one life! There is the urgency of today! Our destiny is wrapped up in the decisions of today! The Lord weighs the motives of our heart (Prov. 16:2,3). Let Him establish the thoughts by which you decide the course of your life.

The Word of God is always a safe guide for our feet (Ps. 119:105). The word of God will speak words of correction, counsel, commendation and comfort. We must read it in order to do it! Let's bring in Jeremiah! *This is what the LORD says: "Stand at the crossroads and look; ask for the ancient paths, ask where the good way is, and walk in it, and you will find rest for your souls. But you said, 'We will not walk in it'"* (Jer. 6:16). Israel had come to the point where they were not ashamed; they did not even know how to blush anymore (Jer. 6:15). Jeremiah would say: "STOP! LOOK! and LISTEN!" Take a good long look! The Paraschauer duet used to sing, "Two paths lie before you; which one will you take?" It is so true. We are constantly on the march or on the move from the cradle to the grave. Our hearts like muffled drums are beating. We are standing in the way! Ask where the good way is and walk in it.

All roads are not good. Some roads are bad. The path of sin leads to slavery. The path of faith leads to life. Many have walked the path of faith (Heb. 11). Our parents, our pastors and our peers have walked that path. The path of loyalty to Christ is good. The path of personal and family devotions is good. The path of church attendance is good. The path of love and obedience is good. One must get on the road with an attitude of dedication and determination to follow through in faithfulness to God.

Jesus said, "I am the way." He is the way out of the wilderness of sin. He is the way through an uncertain tomorrow. He is the way into the family of God. He is the way to the home of our heavenly Father. Would you read the verses that arrested me when I became a believer? *"Enter through the narrow gate. For wide is the gate and broad is the road that leads to destruction, and many enter through it. But small is the gate and narrow the road that leads to life, and only a few find it"* (Matt. 7:13,14).

Are you on the path that leads to life?

Read: Proverbs 4:26; Psalm 37:23

January 9   ZIGZAG PATH

History and experience seem to point to the fact that God's line for us is not usually a straight line, but a winding zigzag path. Joseph Parker, the English preacher used to say, "The round-about way may be the nearest."

Back in Exodus 13:17, God did not lead them by the way of the land of the Philistines, even though it was the closest. God led the people around by the way of the wilderness. Why? Because the people needed disciplining and molding as a nation. By way of the wilderness, they were trained slowly for the great task at their journey's end. We also are aware that God, who chose the route, also chose the leader. God, who disciplined the people, also disciplined the man who led them.

Over the Apennines mountains, there is a wonderful railroad. It passes through forty-three tunnels in less than seventy miles. There are magnificent outlooks, but every few minutes, a tunnel. The road has been built to carry the traveller to his destination by the shortest way; anyone getting off at the first station because he or she did not like tunnels and starting into the mountains to find another path, would almost surely become lost.

Can we not believe the same thing of God's way? His way may lie through tunnels, but it is the best and safest road. Along the way there are glorious prospects. There are places full of beauty. There are outlooks of love and mercy. This ought to reconcile us to some intervals of darkness. Do not be afraid of the winding way if God turns you into it. Travel the road He points out to you.

> We climbed the height by the zigzag path
>   And wondered why — until
> We understood it was made zigzag
>   To break the force of the hill.
>
> A road straight up would prove too steep
>   For the traveler's feet to tread;
> The thought was kind in its wise design
>   Of a zigzag path instead.
>
> It is often so in our daily life;
>   We fail to understand
> That the twisting way our feet must tread
>   By love alone was planned.
>
> Then murmur not at the winding way,
>   It is our Father's will
> To lead us home by the zigzag path,
>   To break the force of the hill.

— Anonymous

Travel the road He points out to you!

Read: Deuteronomy 8:1-5

January 10   HURRY KILLS

Along highways, most of us have seen the sign that says, "HURRY KILLS," at one time or another. This sign is really saying, "Slow down and live!"

Indeed, we are in a hurry so much of the time. Our friends may pass along the street and say, "Hey! What's the hurry?" "Where are you going?" "Where's the fire?"

Some time ago, Psalm 23:2 became very precious to me. *He maketh me to lie down in green pastures....* (KJV). There are times when a Christian needs to lie still, like the earth under a spring rain, letting the lesson of experience and the memories of the Word sink down to the very roots of his life and fill the reservoirs of his soul. Days when hands are not busy are not always lost, any more than rainy summer days are lost because they keep the farmer indoors.

The Good Shepherd makes us lie down in green pastures.

There are times when people say they are too busy to stop, or times when they think they are doing God a service by going on. Now and then God makes such a one "lie down." When we've been driving through the pastures so fast that we haven't noticed how green they are, God decides it's time to slow us down.

Many a man has had to thank God for some such enforced season of rest, in which he first learned to meditate on the Word and to wait upon the Lord. You see, the soul cannot be hurried.

> *God is not in a hurry; dear!*
>   *The work He chose for you*
> *Can wait, if He is giving you*
>   *Another task to do*
> *Or, if He call you from your work*
>   *To quietness and rest,*
> *Be sure that in the silence*
>   *you may do His bidding best.*

— Edith Hickman Divall

Remember the hymn:

> *Not so in haste, my heart!*
>   *Have faith in God and wait:*
> *Although He linger long*
>   *He never comes too late.*

— Bayard Taylor

Read: Psalm 23. He makes me lie down....

January 11   INSTANT PRAYER

If radio's slim finger can pluck a melody
From night, and toss it over a continent or sea;
If the petaled white notes of a violin
Are blown across a mountain or a city's din;
If songs, like crimson roses, are culled from thin blue air —
Why should mortals wonder if God hears prayer?

— Ethel Romig Fuller

From the well-known account of feeding the five thousand, I quote part of Matthew 14:19: *...And looking up to heaven, He gave thanks and broke the loaves....*

Stonewall Jackson was once asked what he meant when he used the expression, *Instant prayer.* "I will give you," he said, "my idea of it for illustration, if you will allow it and not think that I am setting myself up as a model for others." On being assured that there would be no misjudgement, he went on to say: "I have so fixed the habit in my mind, that I never raise a glass of water to my lips without a moment's asking of God's blessing. I never seal a letter without putting a word of prayer under the seal. I never change my classes without a minute's petition on the students who go out and those who come in."

"And don't you sometimes forget this?" the inquirer asked.

To this Stonewall Jackson replied, "I think I can say that I scarcely do; the habit has become almost as fixed as breathing."

That's beautiful! Instant prayer — prayer as fixed as breathing.

Frequently, in the gospels, we are told that Jesus looked heavenward. It was as though the Master was always looking up for His Father's smile, direction and benediction; for the assurance that what He was engaged in was in the line of His Father's purpose; and for the needed power to act and wisdom to speak.

And isn't this the way that we shall meet the needs of those around us? Our little bit (five loaves and two fish) will not go far in a crowd, but if we bring what we do have to Him, place it in His hands and look up to heaven for His help, we shall be able to give and give again. This habit can only be maintained by those who are in continual fellowship with Him.

E.M. Bounds has written: *Prayer to God the noblest exercise, the loftiest effort of man....*[1] Let prayer be as fixed as breathing in our lives.

Read: Psalm 55:6-17

23

January 12   IF ONLY!

Have you ever heard the statement, "IF ONLY!"?

If only my circumstances and my environment were different; if only so and so were easier to live with; if only I had the opportunities, the advantages that other people have; if only that insurmountable difficulty, that sorrow, that trouble could be moved out of my life; then how different I would be.

If only! This seems to be the feeling and attitude of Martha in John 11. The account of the dying and resurrection of Lazarus brings us to what Martha said: "Master, if only you had been here, my brother would not have died. If you'd only been here!"

Paul harboured these thoughts, as well. He wanted the thorn in his flesh to be removed, and yet it was allowed to remain.

A certain gentleman had a garden which might have been very beautiful had it not been for a huge boulder in the middle of it which reached deep under the soil. He tried to blast it with dynamite, but in the attempt only shattered the windows of his home. Being self-willed, he used one harsh method after another without success. After his death, the heir, perceiving the hopelessness of trying to budge the boulder, set to work converting it into a rock garden covered with flowers, ferns and vines. Visitors to the garden commented on its unsurpassed beauty. The owner could never quite decide which gave him the greater happiness: the harmonious aspect of his garden, or the success in adapting himself to the thing that was too deep to move. So, the unsightly boulder which could not be removed, proved to be the most valuable asset in the garden when left in the hands of one who knew how to turn its defects into things of beauty.

God often plants His flowers among rough, rocky places. With Paul, we remember God said, *My grace is sufficient for you.* In that insurmountable difficulty, that sorrow and trouble, God is sufficient. Draw upon the resources of heaven each day. Take into this day the thoughts of 1 Corinthians 12:9-10. God is with you; that is all you need. His power shows up best in weak people. The hardships and difficulties need not be removed; rather, the more I can depend on HIM!

Read: Romans 8:28-29

CIRCUMSTANCES

Try to find the minor prophet Habakkuk.

How irrational it seems: *Though the fig tree does not bud and there are no grapes on the vines, though the olive crop fails and the fields produce no food, though there are no sheep in the pen and no cattle in the stalls, yet I will rejoice in the LORD, I will be joyful in God my Saviour* (Hab. 3:17-18). How irrational it seems!

When all goes well, we can be joyful. But have we not had some complaint in adverse circumstances? We would have great respect for the man who did not complain. Let's bring this closer to home and translate what Habakkuk said into current experience. Instead of flocks and herds, use profits; instead of figs and olives, read credit balances; for farming and its terms, use business and its terms; for the Chaldean invasion (the nation coming against Israel) (Hab. 3:16), use the economic blizzard that is sweeping our world, and then see where you stand.

Now you could read: *Though there shall be no balances and securities, and all dividends shall be passed, and though I be reduced to utter poverty, yet I will rejoice in the LORD.* You say that's impossible! Yes, apart from the Lord helping us, we could not do it. Life cannot be a solo affair — it's a duet. We need Another!

If life were a solo, it would mean a tragic breakdown. A duet means harmony — namely, life-linked to the Lord, to His purposes and to His power. By having Jesus, you have everything. By having God in your life, you lose nothing.

We are indeed a pilgrim people. As such, we look up. Though the road may be dusty and the journey long, look up. Look up in early morning when the sun comes over the horizon, out of the shadows of the night. Look up at noon when the resting spot is still ahead. Look up when you see the evening star. Listen; inner peace comes by trusting God in every experience. Looking to God in times of trouble doesn't guarantee a change of circumstances, but finding answers in them does bring inner freedom and rest.

The minor prophet found his strength where we should find our strength. He says, *The Sovereign LORD is my strength; He makes my feet like the feet of a deer, He enables me to go on the heights* (Hab. 3:19).

We have the resources of heaven for all our circumstances.

Read: Habakkuk 3:17-19

There are days when we ask, "Is life worth living?" The response to that may vary.

Ask the doctor and he'll say, "That depends on the liver."

Ask the economist and he might say, "That depends on the living and the social conditions around us."

Ask the Christian and he'll say, "That depends on the life."

Let me say this: Every man needs something in which he can invest his life. The apostle Paul comes with the word, *For to me, to live is Christ....* (Phil. 1:21). To live is Christ! Christ makes life worth living!

Christ makes life worth living because:

1. He gives you a conscience you can live with. Into the conscience must be put the content of the mind of Christ. Otherwise it is an incompetent conscience. And the mind of Christ is found in the Word of God.

2. He gives you a creed you can live by. Oliver Wendall Holmes said, "It is faith in something that makes life worth living."

3. He gives you a cause to live for. Wm. Sangster, the Methodist minister, said, "I am not satisfied to live. I want something to live for."

4. He gives you a company you can live with. The best company in the world is the Church of Christ. To belong to the company of believers is a great experience. In Christ there is a bond that binds us together.

5. He gives you a consummation you can live toward. Wm. Penn said one day, "The true end of life is to know the life that never ends."

Life is in a Person. That Person is Jesus Christ. He said, *"I am the way, the truth and the life"* (John 14:6). In Him was life and the life was the light of men. He wants to live in your life. Ultimately, no life is worth living that is not in right relationship with God through faith in Jesus Christ.

Life is a journey to be taken but once! We are in this life to prepare for the next. The true end of life is to know the life that never ends. Take these thoughts into your life today.

Read: John 14:1-6

26

January 15   MOUNTAINS CROSSABLE

It may be that you have heard or even sung the chorus:

Got any rivers you think are uncrossable?
Got any mountains you cannot tunnel through?
God specializes in things thought impossible,
He does the things others cannot do.

— Oscar Eliason

In Isaiah 49:11, God says, as He speaks of restoring Israel, "*I will turn all My mountains into roads, and My highways will be raised up.*" God is preparing a way! He always is!

Mountains suggest difficulties. These mountains of difficulties may well be His stepping stones. Do not try to tunnel under them, squeeze through them, nor run away from them. Difficulties may strengthen your faith or bring you into the promises of God. You can trust God — even in the dark. We are safer *with* Him in the dark than *without* Him in the sunshine. At the end of every gloomy passage beams the heavenly light. At the end of the road we may discover that our most profitable experiences were gained on the very road from which we shrank in dread. God goes before us; He will turn all His mountains into roads. Be patient! Read Proverbs 3:5-6.

Often darkness fills the pathway of the pilgrim's onward track,
And we shrink from going forward — trembling, feel like going back:
But the LORD, who plans so wisely, leads us on both day and night,
Till at last, in silent wonder, we rejoice in Wisdom's light.

Though the tunnel may be tedious through the narrow, darkened way,
Yet it amply serves its purpose — soon it brings the light of day:
And the way so greatly dreaded, as we backward take a glance,
Shows the skill of careful planning: never the result of chance!

Is your present path a tunnel, does the darkness bring you fear?
To the upright, oh, remember, He doth cause a light to cheer.
Press on bravely, resting calmly, though a way you dimly see,
Till, at length, so safely guided, you emerge triumphantly.

Trust the Engineer Eternal, surely all His works are right,
Though we cannot always trace them, faith will turn at last to sight;
Then no more the deepening shadows of the dark and dismal way,
There for ever in clear sunlight, we'll enjoy "the perfect day."

— Selected

We need to trust Him even when we cannot trace Him!

What! Nothing to eat today! Why?

In the Jewish religion, there was one day in the year that was a compulsory fast, and that was the Day of Atonement (Lev. 16). The stricter Jews, however, made it a regular practice, fasting for two days every week, on Mondays and Thursdays. It is to be noted that fasting was not as serious as it sounds, for it lasted from 6 a.m. to 6 p.m. and after that normal food could be eaten.

There are very good reasons why a man might fast. He might deny himself the things he likes for comfort, for the sake of discipline; to be certain that he is the master of them and not they of him; to make sure that he never grows to love them so much that he can't give them up. He might deny himself his comforts and his pleasant things, so that, after self-denial, he might appreciate them all the more. One of the best ways to learn to value our homes is to be away from them for a time, and one of the best ways to appreciate God's gifts is to do without them for a time. These are good reasons for fasting.

Fasting is not to call attention to our own goodness. It is not for self-display. It is not to call the attention of God to our piety. To be of value, fasting must not be the result of ritual. It must be the expression of a feeling in the heart. It must not be mere convention, but a genuine way of expressing a need of the heart.

Christ came with a new message, a message of light and life. The disciples were enjoying His company when the question arose, *"How is it that we and the Pharisees fast, but your disciples do not fast?"* The answer Jesus gave was, *"The time will come when the Bridegroom will be taken from them; then they will fast"* (Matt. 9:14-15).

The discovery of Christ and the company of Christ is the key to happiness. Fasting has significance if it brings me closer to Him. I will fast only if this fosters my spiritual well-being. This need not come in the form of legislation, but mutual agreement. Paul gives the examples of fasting taking place in a marriage relationship (1 Cor. 7:5), and as a special need within the ministry of the church (Acts 14:23). It must be a spiritual means to a spiritual end; a means by which the Spirit may control the body, so as to fashion it into its noblest purpose — in some sense, the likeness of Christ and service for Him. An observance is only acceptable when it is the natural outcome of the life of him or her who offers it. There is no telling what the Lord will do for you if you fast ...*to your Father, who is unseen; and your Father, who sees what is done in secret*.... (Matt. 6:18).

Could you make a day like this meaningful in your life?

Read: Matthew 6:16-18; 9:14-20

January 17   PRAYER

Prayer to God the noblest exercise, the loftiest effort of man....[2] These are the words of E.M. Bounds. Would to God we did more prayerful praying. God commits Himself into the hands of those who pray. Today we want to remember four little words, the words of Jesus, "Enter into your closet." Apostolic men, saintly men and women, heroic servants of God have prayed without ceasing. If Francis of Assisi knew how to do battle among men, it was because he loved to pray. John Welsh spent eight hours out of the twenty-four in communion with God, therefore he was equipped and armed and dared to suffer. David Brainard rode through the American woods praying and so fulfilled his ministry in a short time. John Wesley came out from seclusion (out of the closet) to change the face of England. Andrew Bonar did not miss the mercy seat and his fellowship with heaven, and that made him a winsome Christian. Adoniram Judson won Burma for Christ through unwearied prayer. Let me say it again: God commits Himself into the hands of those who truly pray.

I am sure we can say, such was the habit of those who wrought nobly for God. *Prayer to God the noblest exercise, the loftiest effort of man*.... If we are to attempt and achieve great things for God we must pray. Enter into your closet wherever that may be and wait upon God. For Moses, his closet was in the silent desert. In serene solitude, he kept his vigil. Paul, the fiery warrior of the Cross of Christ, learned the lessons God had in mind for him in the desert under Arabian skies. And for David, the hills and the desert became his sanctuary. There his heart sought fellowship with God.

Enter into your closet — you are not alone. God is there! Seek His face in prayer. Just to be there in His presence is prayer.

What do you believe about prayer? Answer that in your own heart.

Read: Matthew 6:5

January 18   MAJESTY, TENDERNESS, STRENGTH

Some interesting thoughts flood our minds from the pen of the minor prophet Micah.

Three things from Micah 5:4 that will make our hearts rejoice: What majesty, what tenderness and what strength is HIS!

1. What majesty! It says here, *He will stand.* He will stand amid all the swirling waves of change, the shifting quicksands of time and the drifting clouds of revolution. He will stand unchangeable and unmoveable. He will stand with His flock which He gathers around Him out of the storm and tempest. The majesty that mantles Him is the majesty of the Name of Jehovah, the glory that He had with the Father before the world began.

2. What tenderness! It says here, *He will shepherd His flock.* Isaiah the prophet says, ...*He gathers the lambs in His arms* (40:11). He is the Prince of Peace. He makes peace. He does His work calmly and tenderly. He laid the foundation of peace by yielding His life to death on the cross without resistance or complaint.

3. What strength! What strength is His! *He will stand and shepherd His flock in the strength of the LORD, in the majesty of the name of the LORD, His God.* Strong with the original strength of Deity. Strong with the acquired strength of perfect obedience. Strong with strength that comes from prevailing over His foes.

My friend, His strength is ours. He loves us. He bears the infirmities of the weak. He does not seek His own. This ONE is our peace. He made peace through the blood of His cross. He is the Prince of Peace to loyal and loving hearts. He pours into our heart His peace, a peace which the world cannot give, nor take away.

What majesty! What tenderness! What strength! He stands and He feeds His flock. Are you one of His sheep?

Read: Micah 5:2-5; Isaiah 40:10-11

January 19   TOOL CHEST

A tool chest is always a fascinating thing. Today, there are tools that are very versatile and designed to do more than one thing. There are tools for all sorts of things: tools for carpenters, tools for mechanics, tools for electricians, etc.

Did you know there was a tool chest in the Bible? I have always enjoyed the tool chest mentioned in 1 Corinthians 1:26-29.

I like to think of the tools God chooses. I notice that not many influential are chosen; not many powerful, not many of high and noble birth are chosen. Did you notice the selection? God chose the foolish to put the wise to shame. God chose the insignificant, the things that are nothing, that He might bring to nothing the things that are. Do you know why? So that no man could have pretense for glorying and boasting in His presence. The thing is this, we must not be faint-hearted because we are consciously poor tools or instruments. The main question is the mastery of Him who uses the instruments.

Once Paganini, standing before a vast audience who had come to hear his greatest sonata, broke string after string on his violin. All hope of continuing his performance seemed to be destroyed. Then the artist held up his violin; one string and Paganini — but on that one string he made the first complete manifestation of his greatness. It may have been a poor violin, but in the artist's hands, it made sweet music.

It is said that Gainsborough, an artist, longed also to be a musician. He bought instruments of many kinds and tried to play them. He was so charmed one day by a great violinist, that he bought a violin. He thought that if he had the instrument, he could play too. He soon learned that the music was not in the violin, but in the master who played it.

So do not be discouraged because you have so little ability you can call your own. Think of God's tool chest; think of yourself as an instrument in God's hand. Think: one talent and God. Greatness is not required. Be encouraged! Be available!

Read: 1 Corinthians 1:26-29

January 20   DON'T QUIT!

Deep indeed is the world's debt to people who would not quit.

Suppose Columbus had not sailed. Having said that, can't you hear the words, "Sail on, sail on."

Suppose Anne Sullivan, discouraged, had lost hope for Helen Keller. I am sure these names bring back memories of great achievements. Suppose Louis Pasteur, searching for a cure for rabies, had not said to his weary helpers, "Keep on." The important thing is not to leave the project.

One day Jesus said, "...*No one who puts his hand to the plow and looks back is fit for service in the kingdom of God*" (Luke 9:62). Our prayer should be: "Keep me from turning back." Out there in the real life, many a race is lost at the last lap. Many a ship is washed on the reefs outside the final port. Many a battle is lost on the last charge. Pray again, "Lord, keep me from turning back."

What hope have we of completing the course upon which we have embarked? What hope do we have? The hope we have is that He is able to keep us. We must be willing to stand with Him, to trust Him. Do not quit.

Remember! There was something you were trying to do: win a friend; restore a prodigal; save a Sunday School class. For a long time, you held that purpose persistently in mind, and you gave yourself to earnest and diligent endeavour. You persevered in spite of obstacles. You were patient under temptation to impatience. You refused to be discouraged, though reasons for discouragement were many and obvious. But there came no results from your efforts and at last you gave up the struggle. Suppose that some day, when it is all too late, you find out that when you quit the work, you were just on the verge of accomplishment — could you forgive yourself for quitting?

There is always, and for all of us, the danger of stopping too soon. Let's bring in Paul, who wrote, *Let us not become weary in doing good, for at the proper time we will reap a harvest if we do not give up* (Gal. 6:9).

Deep indeed is the world's debt to people who would not quit!

Read: Galatians 6:1-10; Luke 9:57-62

January 21   FOOD FOR MY SOUL

We are living in a day when we are constantly asking, "What are our priorities?" "What are the things that we should pursue first?" "What are some of the things that should be paramount?" Some answers come from reading good authors. Some answers come from being exposed to people with high standards. I believe there is room to learn from each other.

As a believer, I began to see that my first priority was to attend to my soul, to have my soul happy in the Lord. I will confess that usually my concern was to serve the Lord in the church, to see how I might set the word of God before His people and how I might benefit them. I began to see that my own soul needed nourishment first. I saw that the most important thing was to give myself to the Word of God and to meditate on it. This is how my heart is encouraged, comforted, warmed and instructed. Food for my soul! My heart desired to be brought into communion with the Lord.

Psalm 119:162 became very real to me: *I rejoice at Thy word, as one that findeth great spoil* (KJV). Food for my soul!

My meditation invariably turned to thanksgiving and intercession. But I still continually kept before me the fact that food for my own soul was the object of my meditation.

There were times when my mind would wander, but gradually being nourished by the truth of God's word, I was brought into fellowship as with a Friend. A Friend that I could talk to. A Friend who sticketh closer than a brother. Begin to relish in the things of God's word. Food for your soul, that's the secret!

Find the source of your peace in Psalm 119:161-168.

January 22   SILENT COMMUNION!

The life of Joseph has always filled my life with intrigue. From the coat of many colours, to the courage of meeting and confronting his brothers, this has thrilled me more than once. I love the story of Joseph!

What I really enjoy is the way he made himself known to his brothers. In Genesis 45:1b, we read, *So there was no one with Joseph when he made himself known to his brothers*. There are feelings and experiences too tender and too sacred for the public gaze. Joseph could not reveal himself to his brothers in the presence of Egyptian attendants. *"Have everyone leave my presence"* is the word. No one was allowed to interfere with the demonstration of Joseph's love. A person can hardly stop reading the account in Genesis 45. What a moment when he said, *"I am Joseph... Come close to me... I am your brother, Joseph, the one you sold into Egypt... God sent me ahead of you to save your lives...."*

So there was no one with Joseph when he made himself known to his brothers. Let me make an application.

This is also true with Christ revealing Himself to us. Not in the busy market place, not in the social circle, not even in a crowded church service do we come into a close touch with Jesus Christ. In the hour of silent communion, when the door is shut, when the world is excluded, in the hush of silence there comes the fullest expression of His love and grace. It is then that we see, with the clearest vision, the glory of our Lord and Saviour. We hear most distinctly that still small voice that enriches our lives. Someone has said, "No public feast with Him can compensate for the loss of the private interview." Look at Matthew 6:6. Make time to be alone with God! It was Robert Murray McCheyne who said, "A calm hour with God is worth a whole lifetime with man."

> *I met God in the morning*
>> *When my day was at its best,*
> *And His presence came like sunrise,*
>> *Like a glory in my breast.*
>
> *All day long the Presence lingered,*
>> *All day long He stayed with me,*
> *And we sailed in perfect calmness*
>> *O'er a very troubled sea.*
>
> *Other ships were blown and battered,*
>> *Other ships were sore distressed,*
> *But the winds that seemed to drive them*
>> *Brought to us a peace and rest.*
>
> *Then I thought of other mornings,*
>> *With a keen remorse of mind,*
> *When I too had loosed the moorings,*
>> *With the Presence left behind.*
>
> *So I think I know the secret,*
>> *Learned from many a troubled way:*
> *You must seek HIM in the morning*
>> *If you want HIM through the day!*

— Ralph Spaulding Cushman

No public feast with HIM can compensate for the loss of the private interview.

Read: Genesis 45:1-28

January 23   WASTE

A parable from nature! The subject of waste is most familiar. We are indeed a wasteful people. Even in Christ's day, the disciples were disturbed when, in the home of Simon, a woman broke the bottle of costly perfume and poured it over Jesus' head. Some of the disciples grumbled, "Why this waste?" (Mark 14:4).

There is nothing that seems more strange than the waste of nature. The showers fall and sink into the ground and seem to be lost. The rain comes down from the sky and doesn't return; the earth absorbs it and the rivers run into the sea. All this seems like waste — is it?

Helen Steiner Rice has represented, in a poetic parable, a little raindrop trembling in the air, questioning the Creator whether it should fall upon the earth or linger in the beautiful cloud. "Why should I be lost and buried in the dirty soil? Why should I disappear in the dark mud, when I may glisten like a diamond or shine like an emerald in the rainbow?" "Yes," the Creator agreed, "but if you fall into the earth, you will come forth with a better resurrection in the petal of a flower, in the fragrance of a rose, in the hanging cluster of the vine."

So at last the timid raindrop drops one tear of regret and disappears beneath the soil. It is speedily drunk by the parched ground; it is gone from sight, apparently out of existence. But wait! The root of yonder lily drinks in the moisture; the rose absorbs its refreshing draught; the far-reaching rootlet of the vine has found a source of life. In a little while that raindrop comes forth in the blossom of the lily, in the perfume of the rose, in the purple cluster of the vine, and it meets once more the Creator and answers back its glad acknowledgement: "Yes, I died, but I have risen and now I live in a higher ministry, in a larger life."

Why shouldn't we pour out our love, like a rush of a river wasting its waters as it moves on? Why shouldn't we scatter our lives like the showers of summer? Why this waste? Jesus said, *Leave her alone... why are you bothering her? She has done a beautiful thing to me... She did what she could... What she has done will also be told, in memory of her.*

The hymn writer has written: "Let me lose my life and find it Lord in Thee.*"

Read: Mark 14:1-9

January 24   AS THE EAGLE

Are you a bird watcher? Then this is for you. I suppose Moses had time to watch the birds during the time he was in the wilderness looking after sheep. I am not surprised that his messages were filled with illustrations from nature. Perhaps the Lord arranged this display to enrich his ministry and to give him lessons to learn.

As an eagle stirreth up her nest... so the LORD (Deut. 32:11-12, KJV). The habits of eagles provide real interest. The destruction of a nest is a prelude to lessons in flying. The offspring must prepare for the future. They must learn to fly. Unless they are pushed over the precipice they will never have the courage to go it alone.

1. How strange are the ways of God! Sometimes, through misfortune or through unfavourable circumstances, God is teaching us lessons we need to learn.

2. How watchful are the ways of God! *As an eagle... fluttereth over her young... so the LORD....* Ruthlessly, the mother bird pushes her chick over the edge of the precipice. Watching every move, she hovers over the falling eaglet, ready to rescue instantly should danger threaten. God is never far from His children. Wisdom and affection are manifest in every action. The hymn writer says, "Standing somewhere in the shadows, you'll find Jesus."

3. How careful are the ways of God! *As an eagle... spreadeth abroad her wings... so the LORD....* Frantically, the falling eaglet tries to arrest the downward rush, its wings thrashing the air. The mother bird follows and, at the right moment, her broad wings spread out to form an aerial landing-stage for her chick. Amid the dangers of life, the faithfulness of God remains unchanging.

4. How reliable are the ways of God! The dependability of God is beyond question. Happy are the people who trust in His care.

5. How capable are the ways of God! *As an eagle... beareth them on her wings... so the LORD....* The youngster was carried to safety up into the heights only to be thrown into mid-air again. Slowly, but surely, the eaglet would learn to fly.

In the Christian life, we were meant to fly. It's life on the wing! The highest life comes from the disciplines of God. May we be mindful of His presence today!

As an eagle... so the LORD! How strange, how watchful, how careful, how reliable and how capable are the ways of God.

Read: Deuteronomy 31:1-12a

January 25   CHARIOTS OF GOD

The chariots of God are tens of thousands and thousands of thousands (Ps. 68:17). This reminds me of another verse in Psalm 104:3: *...He makes the clouds His chariot.* Rehearsing a bit of

Israel's history, the minor prophet wrote about how the Lord rode before them (in the Red Sea experience) upon chariots of victory and deliverance (Hab. 3:8).

The chariots of victory! Many times they don't look like chariots of victory. They look instead like enemies, sufferings, trials, defeats, misunderstandings, disappointments; these come to roll over us and crush us.

But they are chariots! They are circumstances in which we may rise to heights of victory, for which we have been longing and praying. The circumstances of life are the opportunities. God's chariots are controlled by spiritual forces and they triumph over all hindrances. Our spiritual eyes may not always see them, but they are all around us. Remember how Elisha's servant saw the mountains full of horses and chariots after his eyes were opened (2 Kings 6:17)? Elisha's prayer was, *"O LORD, open his eyes so he may see."* What about you and me? If our eyes were open today, we would see our homes, our places of business and our streets filled with the chariots of God. God's protection! God's watchcare! There may be that unhappy relationship in your home. It may be that kind of relationship that will bring to you heavenly patience.

It's the daily happenings of life, the misunderstandings, the disappointments and the losses — these are the conflicts that lead you to victory in your life (James 1:2-4,12). Somewhere in the trial His will must be hidden; and you want to accept His will and hide yourself in His loving care. In this way, you will find yourself riding with God in a way you never thought you could. Words cannot express the glorious places to which your soul will rise and be encouraged. Travel with God!

God moves in a mysterious way His wonders to perform;
He plants His footsteps in the sea, and rides upon the storm.
—William Cowper

Psalm 104:3 says, *He makes the clouds His chariot and rides on the wings of the wind.* Learn to live in His presence every day!

Read: Psalm 104

January 26   THE OLD VIOLIN

Read 2 Corinthians 5:17 and Ephesians 2:10. You are God's opportunity in your day! *"You must go to everyone I send you to"* were God's words to a young prophet named Jeremiah (Jer. 1:7).

Have you ever heard of Stradivarius? Stradivarius was the famous old violin maker whose violins, nearly two centuries old, are almost worth their weight in gold today. George Eliot wrote a poem entitled, "Stradivarius" in which Stradivarius said:

> *"If my hand slacked,*
> *I should rob God — since He is fullest good,*
> *Leaving a blank instead of violins.*
> *He could not make Antonio Stradivari's violins*
> *Without Antonio."*

You are God's opportunity in your day. He has waited for a person just like you. There is no one just like you. If you refuse Him, then God loses His opportunity which He sought through you, and He will never have another for there will never be another person on earth just like you. You are God's opportunity in your day.

> *Bring to God your gift, my brother,*
> *He'll not need to call another, you will do;*
> *He will add His blessing to it, and the two of you will do it;*
> *God and you.*
>
> — R.E. Neighbour

We need to learn the purposes of God and let Him use us as His instruments. I believe He wants to use you and He wants to use me. I desire, with Paul, to be a vessel unto honour — like the violin in the hands of Stradivarius; the violin in the hands of the Master.

THE TOUCH OF THE MASTER'S HAND

> *'Twas battered and scarred, and the auctioneer*
> *Thought it scarcely worth his while*
> *To waste much time on the old violin,*
> *But held it up with a smile:*
> *"What am I bidden, good folks," he cried,*
> *"Who'll start the bidding for me?"*
> *"A dollar, a dollar;" then, "Two!" "Only two?*
> *Two dollars, and who'll make it three?*
> *Three dollars, once; three dollars, twice;*
> *Going for three" — But no,*
> *From the room, far back, a gray-haired man*
> *Came forward and picked up the bow;*
> *Then, wiping the dust from the old violin,*
> *And tightening the loose strings,*
> *He played a melody pure and sweet*
> *As a caroling angel sings.*

The music ceased, and the auctioneer,
With a voice that was quiet and low,
Said: "What am I bid for the old violin?"
And he held it up with the bow.
"A thousand dollars, and who'll make it two?
Two thousand! And who'll make it three?
Three thousand, once, three thousand, twice,
And going, and gone," said he.
The people cheered, but some of them cried,
"We do not quite understand what changed its worth."
Swift came the reply:
"The touch of a master's hand."

And many a man with life out of tune,
And battered and scarred with sin,
Is auctioned cheap to the thoughtless crowd,
Much like the old violin.
A "mess of pottage," a glass of wine;
A game — and he travels on.
He is "going" once, and "going" twice,
He's "going" and almost "gone."
But the Master comes, and the foolish crowd
Never can quite understand
The worth of a soul and the change that's wrought
By the touch of the Master's hand.

— Myra Brooks Welch

January 27   BESIDE STILL WATERS

"Slow down and live!" So many slogans have surfaced to lessen the pace of life. One of the more drastic expressions is, "Life is a rat-race." Everybody is in a hurry! I want to ask if this ceaseless chase is really worth while. Does it pay? Why this hurry which has become a part of our lifestyle? Must we be forever driven like a herd in a stampede? Is there no escape from this feverish haste that is manifest in all walks of life?

Let's pause! Is it possible for a believer to make his active life restful? All of us know the words of Psalm 23: *He leads me beside quiet waters* [waters of quietness]. This is the promise of the Good Shepherd. I believe that you can carry the atmosphere of quietness into the work place. This hurried life is not what the Shepherd intended. We run ahead of our Shepherd instead of letting Him lead us beside quiet waters. We need to follow the Shepherd at the rate He prescribes. Our hurried lives would take on dignity and deeper worth if we stayed in step with the Good Shepherd.

Many great men and women in and out of the Bible have known times of silence and rest, a time of being alone with God! Abraham was alone with God. Moses was with Him in the quietness and stillness of the desert. Much of their training was in the school of silence. *It takes time to be spiritual; it doesn't just happen.* That is a good sentence sermon.

Some of us smile at the things we've read. In the deep jungles of Africa, a traveler was making a long trek. Coolies had been engaged from a tribe to carry the baggage. The first day, they walked rapidly and went far. The traveler had high hopes of a speedy journey. The second morning, these jungle tribesmen refused to move; they just sat and rested. On inquiry as to the reason for this strange behaviour, the traveler was informed that they had gone too fast the first day, and they were now waiting for their souls to catch up with their bodies.

I believe this whirling rushing life needs a balance. If we were more docile (disposed to being taught) we should be more restful. Let's learn what it means to rest! Let's learn to follow the Shepherd. *He leads me beside quiet* [still] *waters, He restores my soul.* Make the Shepherd Psalm yours today! The green pastures, the quiet waters are for you!

Read: Psalm 23; Isaiah 26:3

January 28   PRAYER AND PATIENCE

Waiting is difficult! None of us really likes to wait. We are always in a hurry. To be delayed drives us up the wall. Oh, we hear the phrase, "Patience is a virtue," but who has patience? Sometimes we act like children. We want it *now*, whatever it is.

We are so quick to think that delayed answer to prayer means that prayer is not going to be answered. Dr. Stuart Holden has said, "Many a time we pray and are prone to interpret God's silence as a denial of our petitions, whereas, in truth, He only defers their fulfillment until such time as we ourselves are ready to cooperate to the full in His purposes. Prayer registered in heaven is prayer dealt with, although the answer still tarries."

The account of the raising of Lazarus brings some of this to mind. Jesus loved Martha and Mary and Lazarus. When He heard that Lazarus was ill, He stayed two days longer in the place where He was. He simply delayed His visit to their home. We also read, *See how He loved him!* He loved, yet lingered. There is the discipline of delay. Faith is trained to its supreme mission under the discipline of patience. The man who can wait for God's time, knowing that He edits his prayer in wisdom and affection, will always discover that He never comes to man's aid one minute too soon or too late. God's delay in answering the prayer of our longing heart is the most loving thing God can do. He may be waiting for us to come closer to Him, fall at His feet and abide there in trustful submission. He wants us to have the greater blessing in His time. The poet writes, *O wait, impatient heart, as winter waits the spring.* It is said that it takes years for the aloe to blossom, but every hour is needed to produce the delicate texture and the resplendent beauty of the flower. God never hastens, and He never tarries!

> *Not so in haste, my heart!*
> *Have faith in God and wait:*
> *Although He linger long*
> *He never comes too late.*
>
> *Until He cometh, rest,*
> *Nor grudge the hours that roll,*
> *The feet that wait for God*
> *Are soonest at the goal.*
>
> *Are soonest at the goal*
> *That is not gained by speed.*
> *Then hold thee still, my heart,*
> *For I shall wait His lead.*

—Bayard Taylor

Keep on watching, waiting and praying! He loves you, that's why He lingers!

Read: Luke 11:1-7, 32-36

January 29   THE PAUSE THAT REFRESHES

The "Pause that Refreshes" has become a way of life for many people. I am not so sure about the pause that refreshes in the dimension that I want to share. "Rest pauses" contribute to the finer music of life. Do we really become quiet? Quiet hearts are as rare as radium. We need to be led daily by the Divine Shepherd into green pastures and beside quiet waters. The pause that refreshes! We are losing the art of meditation. Jesus Himself withdrew into a desert or mountainside to pray and to be with His Father. Inner preparation is necessary for outer service. For this, we have the example of our Lord.

We have yet to learn the power of silence. Not in the college or academy, but in the silence of the soul, do we learn the greater lessons of life and become rooted in spiritual inwardness. The geologist says that certain crystals can only come to their perfect form in stillness. In the undistracted moment, men and women are in touch with God and things eternal. The tension of life and the increasing distractions of the world demand a time of silence and the quiet hour. All of us need a lift for living!

"Come away to some lonely spot and get a little rest" are words of the Master. Our Maker knew the importance of rest and the quiet hour. I hope that we find that spot every day. Discover the fellowship of silence. In such moments good things begin to happen in our lives. In every life there is a pause that is better than the onward rush. To stand still is better than hewing and stewing and doing. There is a hush that is better than a lot of chatter. Being still is better than sighing or crying.

God's good word to every heart is, *"Be still, and know that I am God"* (Ps. 46:10). God desires to work in your life. The pause and the hush are there for a purpose, like a rest in a measure of music. Be silent and let Him mold your life. Take your Bible today and take a break. THE PAUSE THAT REFRESHES!

Read: Psalm 62:1-8

January 30   ONE DAY AT A TIME

There is a secret in the Bible that all of us need to learn. I know that I will keep on learning the secret as the days of the year come to me: the secret of living one day at a time. In Matthew 6:34, Jesus said, *"Therefore do not worry about tomorrow, for tomorrow will worry about itself. Each day has enough trouble of its own."* Some of you will remember the devotional book, *Springs in the Valley*, by Mrs. Charles Cowman. Her words on this subject have been a great blessing to me and I have shared them often. She wrote:

"There are two golden days in the week, upon which, and about which, I never worry — two care-free days, kept sacredly free from fear and apprehension.

"One of these days is Yesterday; yesterday, with all its cares and frets, all its pains and aches, all its faults, mistakes and blunders, has passed forever beyond my recall. I cannot undo an act that I wrought; nor unsay a word that I said. All that it holds of my life, of wrong, regret and sorrow, is in the hands of the Mighty Love... Save for the beautiful memories — sweet and tender — that linger like the perfume of roses in the heart of the day that is gone, I have nothing to do with Yesterday. It *was* mine! It *is* God's!

"And the other day that I do not worry about is Tomorrow; tomorrow, with all its possible adversities, its burdens, its perils, its large promise and poor performance, its failures and mistakes, is as far beyond my mastery as its dead sister, Yesterday. It is a day of God's... Tomorrow *is* God's day! It *will* be mine!

"There is left for myself, then, but one day in the week — Today. *Any man can fight the battles of Today! Any woman can carry the burdens of just one day! Any man can resist the temptations of Today!* O, friends, *it is when we wilfully add the burdens of those two awful eternities — Yesterday and Tomorrow... that we break down.* It isn't the experience of Today that drives men mad. It is the remorse for something that happened Yesterday; the dread of what Tomorrow may disclose.

"These are God's days! Leave them with Him!"

Therefore, I think and I do, and I journey but one day at a time! That is the easy way. That is Man's Day. Dutifully I run my course and work my appointed task on that Day of ours. God... takes care of Yesterday and Tomorrow.

— Bob Burdette

"Tomorrow is God's secret — but today is yours to live."[3]

The Bible says, *As your days so shall your strength be*. Live by the day!

Read: Matthew 6:25-34

January 31   JESUS DREW NEAR

All of us enjoy the account of Luke 24:13-35. Two men walking the Emmaus road are saddened by their Master's death. Another overtakes them as they walk. A stranger falls in step with them and joins them in conversation. They earnestly talk of what's on their heart and their hearts are strangely warmed. When they reach Emmaus they want the stranger to stay and share their simple fare. As He breaks the bread, they know it's the Lord.

Let me emphasize verse 15: *Jesus Himself came up and walked along with them.* I am wondering if we have the desire in our hearts that He might overtake us in the path of life. I think we do. Along our way of sorrow we would like His radiant light to shine, and, when the load is heavy, for Him to come and warm the heart and ease the load. We would like Him to walk with us along our Emmaus road, sometimes the lonely road.

Jesus never sends a man ahead alone. He clears the way and then softly calls, "Follow Me." Let's go on together, you and I. He knows it well, the valley road of disappointment, the steep path of temptation, down through the rocky ravines and slippery gullies. He knows the narrow path of pain and the path that leads to victory. He knows the common-place daily routine. He knows each road. He will walk with us in everyday paths. The only safe way to travel is with Him.

After a long, trying march over the perilous Antarctic mountains and glaciers, a South Pole explorer said to one of his men, "I had the curious feeling on the march that there was another Person with us." Another Person, He is ever there to walk with us, side by side with those who trust Him. Remember the song: "Put your hand in the hand of the Man of Galilee." He is a very present help in time of trouble. Jesus Himself drew near and went with them. He is with you today.

Read: Luke 24:13-35

February 1   AS THE DEER PANTS

Some of you will recognize this Psalm from the very first three words: *As the deer pants* [longs] *for streams of water, so my soul pants for You, O God* (Ps. 42:1). My soul thirsts for God, the living God. My heart needs you. No part of my being needs YOU like my heart. My hunger can be satisfied by daily bread. My thirst can be quenched with fresh water. My coldness can be warmed by a household fire. My weariness can be relieved by restful sleep. We could go on to name other gifts that satisfy our being, but no outward thing can satisfy the heart.

The fairest scene will not beautify my soul. The richest music will not make harmony within. A breeze may clean the air, but no breeze can cleanse my soul. This world has not provided for my heart. Earth was never meant to satisfy the human heart. It has provided for my eye, it has provided for my ear, it has provided for my touch, it has provided for my taste, it has provided for my sense of beauty, but it has not provided for my heart.

So the cry continues. *As the deer pants for streams of water, so my soul pants for You, O God.* Our hearts cry out, "Provide for my heart, O Lord. Give it wings; earth has failed to give it wings."

The answer comes from the same author: *I lift up my eyes to the hills — where does my help come from? My help comes from the LORD....* (Ps. 121:1-2). The real answer lies in knowing Jesus Christ personally. The invitation is to come to Calvary. Contemplate the agony of our Lord, where He tasted death for every man. In Christ you will find an answer for your heart. He will be a source of strength. He will be a shelter in the time of storm. He will direct your heart with its doubts. He will calm your soul in conflict. He will give you rest. He is the voice in the solitude of life.

Read: Matthew 11:28-30

February 2   ATONEMENT

It has been said that "every true preacher of the gospel strings all his pearls on the red cord of the Atonement."

— Dr. T.L. Cuyler

Martin Luther preached the doctrine of the atonement and Europe awoke from slumber. Calvin never ignored or belittled the atonement. Spurgeon, the prince of preachers, thundered this glorious message into the ears of peer and peasant. John Bunyan made the cross the starting point to the Celestial City. Moody's key message was Calvary.

The great apostle Paul wrote, *For I resolved to know nothing while I was with you except Jesus Christ and Him crucified* (1 Cor. 2:2). In Galatians 6:14, Paul continues, *May I never boast except in the cross of our Lord Jesus Christ, through which the world has been crucified to me, and I to the world.*

The apostle John says, *He is the atoning sacrifice for our sins, and not only for ours, but also for the sins of the whole world* (1 John 2:2). To sum up, we would have to say, *He Himself is the atonement.*

Hymn writers have taken up the themes in "In the Cross of Christ I Glory" and "Beneath the Cross of Jesus I fain would take my stand." Have you ever personalized the second verse of that last hymn just mentioned?

Upon the cross of Jesus mine eyes at times can see
The very dying form of One who suffered there for me.
And from my smitten heart, with tears, these wonders I confess:
The wonder of His glorious love, And my unworthiness.

— Elizabeth C. Clephane

One day Napoleon, after conquering almost all of Europe, put his finger on the red spot on the map that represented the British Isles and said, "Were it not for that red spot, I would conquer the world." The Enemy of our soul, Satan, would say that about the place called Calvary where Jesus shed His blood for you and for me.

Calvary covers it all! He Himself is the Atonement!

Read: Leviticus 16 (The Day of the Atonement)

February 3   GOD'S WILL

F.B Meyer has told the story of how, when crossing the Irish Channel one dark starless night, he stood on deck by the Captain and asked him, "How do you know Holyhead Harbour on so dark a night as this?" The captain replied, "Do you see those three lights on ahead? Those three lights must line up behind each other and when you see them lined up like that, you know the exact position of the mouth of the harbour."

That introduces the subject of the will of God in my mind.

When we want to know God's will, there are at least three things which line up. There is the inward impulse, the Word of God and the trend of circumstances. There is, first of all, God in the heart, impelling you forward; there is God in the Book, corroborating whatever He says in the heart; and finally, God in our circumstances. These three are an indication of His will.

Should we not say to each other, "Never start until these three agree?" We may want to recall the words of our Saviour, who said, *"For I have come down from heaven not to do my own will but to do the will of Him who sent me"* (John 6:38). He came to do the Father's will. May our desire be no less than to do His will.

When we are not quite certain if we are to turn to the right or to the left, isn't it a blessing when a sign looms into sight? If there were no signs, we would wander miles astray in the wrong direction when we didn't know the way. Most of us have experienced this in our travels. I am glad that God has set His signposts on life's strange and winding roads. He leads our footsteps along paths that often twist and turn. In some form or another, He guides us. It may be through a book we read, a song we sing, or a word from a trusted friend. When we're at the crossroads and decisions have to be made, though the track is unfamiliar, rest assured: There is bound to be a signpost on the way.

> *He's helping me now this moment,*
> *Though I may not see it or hear,*
> *Perhaps by a friend far distant,*
> *Perhaps by a stranger near,*
> *Perhaps by a spoken message,*
> *Perhaps by the printed word,*
> *In ways that I know and know not,*
> *I have the help of the LORD.*

Wait on Him today and believe that He has a messenger along the road with direction and the help we need.

Read: 1 Thessalonians 5:18

February 4   SILENCE!

"Silence is a great peacemaker!" Longfellow said those words.

Another great sentence sermon is, "Silence is golden!" I am sure you've heard it or even read it.

Solomon, the wise man in the Scriptures, said, *There is... a time to be silent and a time to speak....* (Eccl. 3:7b).

Have you ever talked to God and said, "Let me no wrong or idle word, unthinking say; set a seal upon my lips just for today"? Some good advice may be: Keep still! When trouble is brewing, keep still. When slander comes your way, keep still. When your feelings are hurt, keep still. Yes, keep still — at least until you recover from your excitement. Things look different through an unagitated eye.

Did you ever write a letter and send it on its way and then wish you had not mailed it? It may be that there was a time when you wrote a letter and then waited. You kept it in your pocket until you could look it over again without agitation. Then you discovered it was not necessary to send it at all. In fact, you learned to keep silent and the letter was destroyed.

Time works wonders! Wait till you can speak calmly and then perhaps you will not need to speak. Silence is the most powerful thing conceivable sometimes. It is strength in its grandeur; it is like a regiment ordered to stand still. To plunge in is twice as easy.

Nothing is lost by learning to keep still. An unknown author writes:

> *Lord, keep me still,*
> *Though stormy winds may blow,*
> *And waves my little bark may overflow,*
> *Or even if in darkness I must go,*
> *Yet keep me still, yet keep me still.*
>
> *Lord, keep me still,*
> *And may I ever hear Thy still small voice*
> *To comfort and to cheer;*
> *So shall I know and feel Thee ever near.*
> *And keep me still, and keep me still.*

There is a prayer in Psalm 141:3 that my English teacher made us aware of: *Set a guard over my mouth, O Lord; keep watch over the door of my lips!*

Remember: Silence is a great peacemaker! — *Longfellow*

Read: Psalm 39:1; 46:10a

February 5   GOD WAITS

Usually we are called upon to wait, to wait upon the Lord. You know the words of David in Psalm 62:1: *My soul finds rest in God alone.*... Then out of Isaiah 30:18, we read that the Lord waits; the Lord earnestly waits, looking and longing to be gracious to you. In the context here, we discover that as long as Israel tried to help themselves, sending ambassadors to Egypt and seeking an alliance against the invader, God could do nothing for them. He could only wait until they returned to simple reliance upon Himself. They were opposed to the idea of simple trust in God. It seemed impossible to believe that if they simply rested on Him, He would do better for them than all their strenuous efforts. And all the while, God was waiting till they were reduced to such a condition that He could step in and help.

Isn't this just like we are? It is long before we learn the lesson of returning and finding rest, quietness and confidence. Like Israel, we'll trust in our own strength and material resources. We will try to do it all by ourselves. We will meet perplexing problems, we'll try to overcome complicated circumstances, we'll run backward and forward, and we'll flurry and get all excited. Think of all the doors you have tried to open, only to find them closed. All the while, God is waiting to be gracious to you, waiting till you come to the end of yourself; waiting till, like a spent struggler in the water, you cease from your own efforts and cast yourself upon His strong and loving arms.

God is waiting in the silence for a heart that He can fill.

It is in returning and in trusting that you can find rest for your soul. You can be set free from your own pursuits and efforts.

Go with Isaiah 30:15 into this day: *This is what the Sovereign LORD... says: "In repentance and rest is your salvation, in quietness and trust is your strength...."*

Read: Psalm 62

February 6   WHEN GOD WANTS TO DRILL A MAN

We are living in a day when people all around us react quickly to things that happen to them. The first reaction you hear is, "Why did this happen to me? What did I do to deserve this?" I believe we are in the making. *Please be patient with me, God isn't finished with me yet.* God is at work in our lives!

The Sculptor, our Maker, is grinding and chiseling, and the chips may fill the air. He has an image in mind that He wants to produce in your character. A poet has written,

When God wants to drill a man,
And thrill a man,
And skill a man,
When God wants to mold a man
To play the noblest part;
When He yearns with all His heart
To create so great and bold a man
That all the world shall be amazed,
Watch His methods, watch His ways!
How He ruthlessly perfects
Whom He royally elects!
How He hammers him and hurts him,
And with mighty blows converts him
Into trial shapes of clay which
Only God understands;
While his tortured heart is crying
And he lifts beseeching hands!
How He bends but never breaks
When his good He undertakes;
How He uses whom He chooses,
And with every act induces him
To try His splendor out —
God knows what He's about.

— Selected

It was Goethe, a German theologian, who said, "Life is a quarry, out of which we are to mold and chisel and complete a character." In the same vein, I have read about a piece of wood who was bitterly complaining because it was being cut and filled with rifts and holes. He whose knife was cutting into it did not listen to this complaining because he was making a flute out of the wood he held in his hands. He said to this piece of wood, "Oh, you foolish piece of wood. Without these rifts and holes, you would merely be a stick forever, a bit of hard wood with no power to make music or be of any use. These rifts that I am making, which seem to be destroying you, will change you into a flute, and your music will cheer the hearts of men. My cutting is the making of you. You will be valuable and a blessing in the world."

A classic from the Bible is David. He would never have sung his songs had he not been sorely afflicted. His afflictions made his life an instrument into which God could breathe the music of His love to soothe the hearts of men. Haven't we all enjoyed the Psalms?

God is at work in your life! He may be whittling away in your life and making for Himself an instrument that He wants to use. Let the Sculptor touch the keys of your life and make you a vessel unto honour, set apart, so that Christ Himself can use you for His glory and highest purpose.

Read: 2 Timothy 2:20-21; Psalm 119:65-72

February 7   INSTRUMENTS

As a child in a Vacation Bible School, I was taught a short chorus that still comes to mind when I think of the things God uses:

> *Shamgar had an oxgoad, David had a sling,*
> *Dorcas had a needle, Rahab had some string;*
> *Samson had a jaw-bone, Aaron had a rod,*
> *Mary had some ointment, but they all were used of God.*

Of course, there were others and other things. The Bible says that God chose the weak things of the world to shame the strong, that no one can ever brag in His presence (1 Cor. 1:27-28).

Using only a trumpet blast, the smash of lighted pitchers and a shout by 300 men and Gideon, God delivered Israel from the seven-year yoke of the Midianites. I always enjoy the account in Judges 6-8; a trumpet, a pitcher and a torch.

Only a sling and a stone, sent with unerring precision by David and directed by God, slew the giant Philistine, put to shame the skeptical armies in Israel and vindicated God's honour. That familiar account is known to us from our youth. The lesson is this: Under the control of God, ordinary instruments become extraordinary! God moves in to heighten our power. He is the source! Amos was just a herdsman, but inspired and directed by God, he became a great prophet. God turns His people into warriors and vessels. It happened to Peter. It happened to Paul. We are all in need of more power, more courage and more wisdom than we actually possess.

Whatever God has called you to do — do it! One of my teachers used to say, "God's commandments are His enablings." It was Charles Finney who said, "When God commands you to do a thing, it is the highest possible evidence that we can do it."

Remember again the choice of God's instruments. He has chosen the weak things. We need to be thrown upon Him to find our resources in Him. Moody is to have said often, "Give your life to

God; He can do more with it than you can." God will never take advantage of you. God's will for you means your fullest happiness.

Read: 1 Samuel 17:46-51; 1 Corinthians 1:26-30

February 8 SOMEONE I LOVE WENT HOME TODAY

I borrow the words of Solomon when he first became king in the place of his father, David: *I do not know how to go out or come in.* It was part of the prayer he made for an understanding heart to rule his people (1 Kings 3:6-15, RSV).

I do not know how. Isn't this the response that comes from our hearts at times? How can I face the future without my loved one? *I don't know how.* It is better for you not to ask what no one can answer. *Let the day's own trouble be sufficient for the day* (Matt. 6:34, RSV). You will never need God's help and comfort more than now. Tomorrow's burden will come soon enough, but then today's burden will have been lifted before the new one comes.

Let me now borrow the words of 2 Peter 2:9: *...The Lord knows how....* Place the *I know not how* alongside of *the Lord knows how.* I know, you've been thinking that you could bear today's burden if it were not for the dread of tomorrow, and you are right. So, just bear today's burden faithfully, and if tomorrow's load is to crush you, let it do that tomorrow, not today. It's the piling up of future sorrow upon the sorrow of the present that brings us to the breaking point.

[God's] *grace is sufficient....* (2 Cor.12:9)! *The Lord knows how*! Having touched upon the thought, "How can I face the future without my loved one," I would like to share these lines that have touched my own life.

Someone I love went home today,
Went home to God.
I cannot say how I can live the years
Until I see his face again, how to fill the empty days.
I only know, yes, know, that someday I shall go to him,
And hear his voice again, and touch his hand.
Till then, my chart upon this lonely sea,
Those last faint words he spoke to me,
"Dear, keep the home together, and the children in school."
Sacred command, my task until the prize is won —
His smile, his words, "Beloved, well done."

Someone I love went home one day,
Went home to God,
He did not say how long He would be gone,
Nor when He would be coming back again.
I only know that He has gone to make a place for me.
Some dawn or evening light He'll come for me.
Till then there is a task that He has set for me.
To preach the word, be consecrated to His cause.
Spend strength and purse until that wondrous prize is won.
His tender words, "Beloved, well done."

Read: Romans 8:28-39

February 9   TIME

What is time? Time is the period during which an action or a process continues. Time is a measured duration. We think of a life-time. We could think of a prison sentence as a measured duration. Time is also the allotted, the appointed, the fixed hour for some-thing to happen. Time comes to us in seasons; there is summer-time, wintertime, springtime, and so on. Time also has to do with a rate of speed, as well as rhythm. Time has to do with the finite (having definable limits), as contrasted with the infinite, when time shall be no more.

A word about the stewardship of time — the right use of time. We are a time-conscious people; we are creatures of time. The Bible exhortation is "Redeem the time." The right use of time is the important thing.

1. The right use of time is secured by realizing the brevity of life. *Teach us to number our days aright, that we may gain a heart of wisdom* (Ps. 90:12). True biblical wisdom is indeed the outcome of the biblical injunction: "*The fear of the Lord — that is wisdom, and to shun evil is understanding*" (Job 28:28). We need to honour, acknowledge and seek the ways of God in our lives. We are in this life to prepare for the next, and therefore, the right use of time is to realize that life is brief and our preparation to meet God is important.

2. The right use of time is secured by youthful, loyal devo-tion. *Remember your Creator in the days of your youth, before the days of trouble come and the years approach when you will say, "I find no pleasure in them"* (Eccl. 12:1). Loyal devotion now, while you are young. Give Him the best years of your life. An elderly man said to me one day, "You got to cut the stick while the knife is sharp." This same man said, "If only I had given my life to God while I was young." Remember God now!

3. The right use of time can be secured by subordinating earthly duties to heavenly duties. That is, spiritual interests should be paramount. Jesus said, *"Seek first His kingdom... and all these things will be given to you as well"* (Matt. 6:33). Paul said, *...Time is short* (1 Cor. 7:29). Spiritual interests come first. Get married, yes; rejoice, yes; use this world's goods, yes; but spiritual things come first. We get so tangled up with the tangible that we fail to realize that these things lack permanence. Things perish!

4. The right use of time is secured by serious living. *See then that you walk circumspectly* [cautiously], *not as fools, but as wise, redeeming the time, because the days are evil* (Eph. 5:15-16, KJV). This is a call to careful, cautious, prudent living. Webster says, a fool is a dupe, a simpleton; he tampers and wastes time. We have all heard the expression, "Just fooling around." I hope life holds more for you than just fooling around. Life is serious!

Read: Ecclesiastes 3:1-12

February 10   FELLOWSHIP WITH GOD!

"Where are you?" The Lord God called to the man and the woman who hid themselves in the garden (Gen. 3:8-9). Where are you? God came in the cool of the day to have fellowship. That's an appropriate time! We need His hand upon our pounding hearts. We need His peace to calm our souls. What the breath of evening is in summer, fellowship with God will be for your soul. See to it that you are not so absorbed in yourself or your business as to miss the appointed time or appointed place.

F.B. Meyer chose this verse for his daily homily and he wrote, "The question tells me that God misses His child." The few moments of fellowship will mean so much to you and it means a lot more to God. Love, God's love, craves for fellowship! As the musician craves for his instrument, as the deer pants for the water brook, as the mother longs to hear the babbling of her child, God longs for the free outpourings of His child in prayer; He misses them when they're withheld and is jealous when they are fitful and intermittent.

The question, "Where are you?" tells me that God seeks His child. He did not wait till Adam found his way back to His side.

God hastened in search of him. He comes to seek you. You've with-held yourself from the hour of prayer — He's missed you! The heart of God must mourn with sorrow for our loss. We miss out when we miss meeting Him! God's love craves for fellowship. He misses it!

How does that make you feel? I can hear you say, "Is God really interested in me?" Yes, He is! This first question put to man, "Adam, where are you?" is every indication of what you have just read. God keeps an inventory of His children. Your name, your residence, your circumstances, your occupation — all is known to Him. God calls to help us. As free moral agents, we need to respond to His love. Today, God calls us through His Word. His Word is Divine. Spend some time in His Word today. God desires your fellowship.

Read: Psalm 139

February 11   HURRY DOWN, ZACCHAEUS!

Posters and bumper stickers say things like, "Slow down and live!" and "Bring them back alive!" The first slogan is the one to which I wish to speak today. Let me introduce a question and sug-gest a paradox: What is the cure for Hurry? The answer is, more Hurry — hurry *away* from the wrong goals, *towards* the right goals.

There is the speed of a brook that hurries down to the sea. There is the speed of a bird in flight. Have you ever felt like David in Psalm 55:6? *"Oh, that I had wings like a dove! I would fly away and be at rest...."* There is the speed of wind as it travels around the world. Let me present a proposition: The best way to slow down your pursuit of the material life is to speed up that of your spiritual life.

You all know the story of Zacchaeus, the little man who ran ahead and climbed a tree in order to see Jesus (Luke 19:1-10). The Saviour knew he spent much of his life in a hurried pursuit of gain. All of us are aware that this is an inadequate ideal. Christ slowed him down by inviting him to hurry. The word was, "Hurry down, I must stay in your house today." In his passing hurry, Zacchaeus suddenly felt the need to slow down. He wanted to see a Man who was not in the pursuit of possessions. In his own way, he was asking ultimate questions: "What is the meaning of life?" "Who am I?" "Where did I come from?" "Where am I going in such a hurry?" What can I do with this life of mine between the cradle and the grave?"

Christ slowed Zacchaeus down by inviting him to hurry down. Hurry down and welcome the Man who is the answer. Zacchaeus, the dwarf became Zacchaeus, the desirous. His desire was to see Jesus, and Jesus' desire was to meet him. The stage was set for a thrilling experience. Meeting in that home meant a great discovery. He discovered how little men can suddenly grow tall. All men are apt to increase in stature when they respond to Christ. You can see now that you can cure hurry with hurry if you change the goal. The goal is Christ! Hurry to Christ! This little man must have summed it all up in the words, "He sees me, He knows me, He loves me, He wants me — so, He can have me." He turned his heart and his home over to Jesus Christ.

Read: Luke 19:1-10

February 12   SEE WITH YOUR EYES SHUT

Vision is a wonderful thing! To have eyes to see is a blessing! But vision is also a bewildering thing, and one has difficulty understanding the various ramifications of a man's sight. Some people who have excellent eyes succeed in seeing nothing. Others who are blind are able to see a lot. Queer, but true! Many things can hinder our vision: a cataract, a fog or a piece of dirt; even a dizzy faint can plunge a man into blackness. This is not surprising. But when a blind man can succeed in identifying objects, and recognizing at a distance what others cannot see close at hand, ordinary explanations seem inadequate.

Let me mention blind Bartimaeus who excelled in these qualities. He could see with his eyes shut. Bartimaeus sat by the wayside begging, but his hearing was good. He heard Jesus was passing by. Suddenly his idea of life changed. Up to that moment, his primary interest had been to increase his earnings. A crowd always brightened his prospects. Suddenly, he lost all interest in monetary gains and thought only of the nearness of Jesus. The great Healer was within calling distance and that meant the chance of healing. He began to cry out, *"Jesus, Son of David, have mercy on me."* His inward vision increased moment by moment, and, realizing that he had no time to lose, he appealed loudly to the Saviour. He was very wise, for Christ was on His way out of Jericho. He knew that if he waited, the Master would soon be out of earshot and his opportunity would be gone. Desperately, he lifted his voice, determined not to be passed by.

What do we learn? It is never safe to postpone to a later date something that demands urgent attention. Bartimaeus knew it was a case of "now or never," and he refused to be silenced by the critical crowd. For a blind man, his eyesight was very good indeed!

Jesus stopped and called him forward. Bartimaeus obeyed, received his sight and followed Jesus. I am sure his soul hunger was satisfied in fellowship with the Saviour.

He could see with his eyes shut! *Fellowship* demands *followship!*

Read: Mark 10:46-52

February 13   HEARTS FOUND IN THE BIBLE

Looking up these references can be part of an evening on Valentine's Day! Use a number of translations.

1. *A Broken Heart* — Psalm 34:18.
2. *A Clean Heart* — Psalm 51:10.
3. *A Glad Heart* — Psalm 4:7.
4. *A Merry Heart* — Proverbs 15:13.
5. *A Perfect Heart* — 1 Kings 8:61.
6. *A Pure Heart* — Psalm 24:4.
7. *A Rejoicing Heart* — Psalm 105:3.
8. *A Righteous Heart* — Proverbs 15:28.
9. *A Tender Heart* — Ephesians 4:32.
10. *A Sound Heart* — Proverbs 14:30.
11. *An Understanding Heart* — 1 Kings 3:11-12.
12. *An Upright Heart* — Psalm 7:10.
13. *A Wise Heart* — Proverbs 10:8.
14. *A Willing Heart* — Exodus 35:5.
15. *A Deceitful Heart* — Proverbs 12:20.
16. *A Blind Heart* — Ephesians 4:17-18.
17. *A Crooked Heart* — Proverbs 17:20.
18. *A Foolish Heart* — Proverbs 15:7.
19. *A Perverse Heart* — Proverbs 12:8 [warped].
20. *A Proud Heart* — Proverbs 16:5.
21. *A Sick Heart* — Proverbs 13:12.

February 14   YOUR HEART!

Your heart is your life! It is amazing what your heart can do. Everyday it works to lift a man 1,000 feet in the air. Everyday it pumps 2,400 pints of blood. Everyday it supplies a highway of veins about 60,000 miles long. Your heart is pictured as your life, your mind, your will and your affections in the Bible. The Bible describes our hearts as sinful, wicked and restless (Isa. 57:20-21).

Proverbs says, *My son, give Me your heart* (23:26).

1. The Petition comes from God. God the Father calls you, "My son." He made you! He gave you life! God the Son invites you to give Him your life. He loves you! He gave Himself for you! God the Holy Spirit desires that you give your life to Jesus. He convicts you of sin. He shows you that you need Jesus. He converts you! He calls you to believe in Jesus. Do you know why these Three make this petition? There is something They want to do for you.

2. The Petition is for our benefit. God wants to enlighten your heart (John 1:9). Our hearts were darkened! God wants to pardon your heart (Isa. 55:7). God wants to keep, guard and guide your life (Phil. 4:7). Surely you will not give your heart [life] to Satan. He will only destroy, pollute and ruin your life.

3. The Petition may be granted today! You can give your heart to the One who asks for it. Give your heart [life] to Jesus and believe. He loves you and died for your sins. Your sins have been forgiven on the cross (Rom. 5:6). Believe Him! Receive Him! (John 1:12). Give Him your heart [life] willingly, with all the love you have in it. He knows how much you love Him! David says in Psalm 119:10, *I seek You with all my heart*. Give your heart [life] to Jesus immediately. *Today, if you hear His voice, do not harden your hearts....* (Ps. 95:8). Now is the accepted time! Now is the day of salvation. Tomorrow may be too late!

Moody is to have said, "Give your life to God; He can do more with it than you can." You can make heaven happy today! There is joy in heaven over one sinner that repents (Luke 15:7,10).

Read: Proverbs 4:23; 23:26; Psalm 119:11

February 15   TWIN ANGELS!

There are mothers who are always tidying up after their children. The little ones have a good time, leaving the house in confusion and disorder. Mother comes behind to pick up the toys, mend the torn garments and make everything neat and tidy .

F.B. Meyer reminded his readers about twin angels that follow us and pick up the pieces. From Psalm 23:6, those familiar lines,

Surely goodness and mercy shall follow me all the days of my life (KJV). We are well-escorted, with the Shepherd in front and these twin angels, Goodness and Mercy, behind. That is a beautiful thought! How often we leave the house of our lives in confusion and disorder. We make mistakes, say the wrong things, work half-heartedly and keep the rooms of our lives pretty untidy. It is good to know that two such angels follow close upon our tracks as we go through life. They come to untangle the knots, prevent us from ill advice and put kind thoughts into our actions. They also protect us. *Surely goodness and mercy shall follow me all the days of my life.*

As mothers who are always tidying up after their children, as the ambulance corps goes over the battlefield, as love puts the most tender construction on word and act, so the love of God follows us. His goodness imputes to us the noble motive, though the act itself has been a failure. His mercy forgives, obliterates the traces of our sins from His heart, undoes their ill-effects as far as possible toward others, and treats us as if we had never transgressed.

We need not fear the future. God's angels do not tire. The Enemy may seem to have obtained permission to sift you; Satan may give you a rough time. But remember again: *Surely goodness and mercy shall follow you all the days of your life*. The Shepherd goes before — follow Him! The twin angels follow to pick up the pieces. Every provision and protection is made for us in knowing the Good Shepherd.

Read: Psalm 23

February 16   AS A HEN... JESUS CALLS!

Artists can paint pictures from domestic scenes that last a lifetime.

Jesus painted some word pictures that we still read in the New Testament. A broken bottle-skin, a patched garment, a handful of girls attending a wedding feast, a sower going out to sow and many other subjects never to be forgotten.

Let us look at the picture painted in Matthew 23:37: Jesus is weeping over a city that rejected Him. Hear His words: *"How often I have longed to gather your children together, as a hen gathers her chicks under her wings, but you were not willing."* The way a hen gathers her chicks under her wings! Think a moment! Who hasn't heard the cluck of the hen when danger threatens her brood. She is quick to detect the danger and she is ready to protect her chicks.

Often, the rush of life drowns the call of Jesus to come under His wings for rest and protection. I understand from reading that the hen has a variety of calls, some six or eight different sounds. Jesus also calls us for different purposes: sometimes to draw us near for fellowship, sometimes to feast on the truths of His word, sometimes to hide in the shadow of His wings to rest and sometimes to abide in Him until some dreaded evil passes. Are we hearing the calls? Think of the trouble, the trials and the temptations we often face. Jesus cares! He knows what we face. He called you — did you hear Him? Maybe we didn't want to hear. Who can enumerate the many, many times when we have been summoned by Jesus to draw near, but would not. He says, "...*you were not willing.*

Does the rush of life drown out the call?

Let us take time to realize that there is safety in Jesus Christ. There is shelter under His wings! May this never-to-be-forgotten picture remind us that Jesus calls! Jesus cares!

Read: Matthew 11:28-29; 23:37-39

February 17   SOMETHING SOLID

I would like to write about something solid today! The question may come to your mind, "Is there anything solid in this changing, rather unstable world?" How do we find stability in a troubled world? We are more aware than ever before that those in government cannot guarantee stability. We seem to be threatened and tortured by ill health, highway tragedy, unemployment, broken homes and moral corruption. Our newspapers are full of violence and death. War continues even though peace treaties are signed. Nations can't get together. Nothing seems solid or stable.

Today, let's look at some lessons from a ROCK. Four times, Moses mentioned a Rock in the song he wrote before he died (Deut. 32). Paul picks up on that theme in 1 Corinthians 10:4 and says, *...and that Rock was Christ.*

In Christ, there is stability! My faith is in Jesus Christ! The foundations are unshakable. *For other foundations can no man lay...* (1 Cor. 3:11, KJV). Once I was part of a troubled, unstable world. Today, I stand in Christ! He is stable! Once I was building on the sand, now I'm on the Rock (Matt. 7:24-27). Can you sing with conviction, "On Christ the solid Rock I stand, all other ground is sinking sand"?

In Christ, there is strength! In the Lord is everlasting strength. In Isaiah 28:16, the Lord says, *"I lay... for a foundation a stone, a tried stone, a precious corner stone, a sure foundation....* (KJV). We boast of our strength and forget how frail we really are. In Christ, there is strength to live the Christian life. Christians around the world testify, "The Lord is my strength and my song."

In Christ, there is singing! *Sing for joy, O heavens... shout aloud, O earth... Burst into song, you mountains... for the Lord has redeemed Jacob....* (Isa. 44:23). Those who know Christ can well sing.

In Christ, there is satisfaction. *For He satisfieth the longing soul, filleth the hungry soul with goodness* (Ps. 107:9, KJV).

In Christ, there is standing. This is described in Psalm 40:2: *He set my feet upon a rock and gave me a firm place to stand.*

In Christ, there is shelter. There is good hiding in Him! *...He will keep me safe in His dwelling; He will hide me in the shelter of His tabernacle and set me high upon a rock* (Ps. 27:5). Many a stormbeaten soul has found peace and security in Christ the Rock.

In Christ, there is safety! Spiritual safety! The assurance of faith. Safe am I in the hollow of His hand.

By faith you will find a resting place; something solid for your life.

Read: 1 Corinthians 3:10-11; Psalm 1

February 18   A SENSE OF VALUES

Do you have a good sense of values? Do you know what is really worthwhile? Are there standards that you cherish? We all like to think that we know what's worthwhile and of real value.

God too, has a sense of value, which is different from ours. God relegates the great things of earth to a place of insignificance. He lifts the unattractive to a place of importance. God does things differently!

The world in which we live is a treasure house of beauty. Our Creator gave His best when He fashioned it. This planet is one of many. On this earth we find immeasurable riches. There is mineral wealth: gold, silver, diamonds, etc. There are harvests, with provisions of food to eat. There is the splendor of the forests and their value in building material. There is the freshness of flowers and the scent they give. Oh, the beauty of the earth!

None of this is compared to the value of one soul. Jesus said, *"What good is it for a man to gain the whole world, yet forfeit his soul?"* (Mark 8:36). Christ had a unique sense of values! From

God's viewpoint, man is His crown creation. Man was made in the image of God. Psalm 8:4 always comes along to bless my heart: *What is man that you are mindful of him, the son of man that You care for him?* God lifts the unattractive to a place of importance!

Christ became man that He might redeem man. In the sight of God, the reconciling death of Christ equalled the need of those who believe. We have to exclaim, "How great was the value of His sacrifice!" Paul talks about the unfathomable riches of Christ in Ephesians 3:8. Believers are His prize possession in Ephesians 1:18! We are of great value to God! Aren't you amazed at the love and grace of the Lord Jesus Christ?

Read: Psalm 8; Ephesians 2:1-10

February 19   CAPACITY FOR GOD

The words of Augustine, "Thou hast made us for Thyself, and the heart is restless until it rests in Thee," are as contemporary, or up-to-date, as ever. Man has the capacity for God! Man is greater than the changes around him; he has eternity in his heart (Eccl. 3:11). We have the capacity for the Eternal and Infinite. As the seashell sighs for the ocean, so our hearts cry out (though sometimes inarticulately) for God, the living God. God made man in His own image, and nothing more surely attests to the greatness of our origin, than those faculties of the soul which enable us to conceive, enjoy and yearn for God.

There came a day in the life of Solomon when he drifted from God. He plunged his life into pleasure and laughter; into building and planting; into pursuits of science and learning. He says in Ecclesiastes 2:10-11, *I denied myself nothing my eyes desired;* and then later, *Everything was meaningless, a chasing after the wind* .

Nothing can satisfy us but God! We were made for Him! The heart, as Augustine has said, must be forever restless till it finds rest in God. The seashell sighs for the ocean from where it came.

We have no need to envy those who prosper in this world, yet leave God out and have no hope. *All his days, his work is pain and grief; even at night his mind does not rest* (Eccl. 2:23). If we are to avoid inward anguish, we must learn to take God into our lives.

We need to come to Him who has the words of eternal life. We need to come to Him, who is the Bread of Life. He that comes to Him will never hunger; he that believes will never thirst. We have the capacity for God. He put that into our heart. He longs to satisfy that yearning in your life. The word is *"Come!"* (Matt. 11:28-30).

Read: Ecclesiastes 2:1-11; 3:11

February 20   YOUR CALLING, YOUR WORK!

We lightly speak of a man's occupation as his *calling*, and we fail to realize the significance of the phrase. Our faculty, desire and circumstance constitute a call. There may be a distinct vocation in the merchant's office, the tradesman's shop or in the work of a domestic servant, as well as in the church itself. One man is called into the ministry, another to be a lawyer, others to work in all manners of workmanship. God does the placing! Believe, each day as you go to work, that God has called you to the task before you. He will give you the strength, wisdom and grace to do your work right. If you must leave your work, wait for God to open another door. He sees and knows all, even the motives that prompt our work.

In building the Tabernacle, Israel's portable place of worship, God called men to work in all areas of craftsmanship. There was great variety in the contributions made, from precious jewels and cloth to wood and goat's hair. The completed structure was a monument to the united gifts, handcrafts and gems of all the people. In all, there was the unity of the spirit, plan and devotion. So, in the church and in the world, there is work for each of us to do. It may be a very humble part in a factory, like minding the lift, stoking the furnace, or fetching materials; but there is a place for each of us. God prepares the work for the workers, and the worker for the work!

Whenever God gives us a task to fulfill, it's because He sees in us the ability for its happy accomplishment in cooperation with Himself. It's a mistake to turn back daunted by difficulty or even opposition. You can bring your resources and powers to Him. Willing hearts were summoned to bring their offerings to the Lord.

The maker of a musical instrument knows best how to develop its waiting music, and He who created us can make the most of us. Let's yield ourselves to Him. We may differ from all others in the special character of our work; but it matters not, so long as God effects through us, His purpose in creating us.

Read: Exodus 31:1-11; Romans 12:1,2

February 21   **WEATHERVANES**

The word, *weathervane,* or weathercock, is not found in the Bible, but there is a text that suggests it: *Then we will no longer be infants tossed back and forth by the waves, and blown here and there by every wind of teaching and by the cunning and craftiness of men in their deceitful scheming* (Eph. 4:14).

In Scotland, a weathercock is recognized for what it is. In England, it is known as a *vane.* A vane is a flat surface, attached to an axis, that moves with the wind. Many of us have seen them in forms of arrows or roosters (I understand the rooster was the original form), and we now have all kinds of things, like windmills, banners and flags, to show us the direction of the wind.

Today, I'm speaking to you as a weathervane: a person who can't make up his mind. We have all met people like that — they face one way one minute and whirl around the next. They are never settled. May I suggest a few "don'ts" about weathervanes?

1. Don't be a weathervane in small things. Let me illustrate: Children are classic in this; they have some spending money so they go to a store to buy candy. But they stand there looking at the candy counter for ages because they can't make up their mind. The girl at the counter is almost frustrated as she waits. Make up your mind! Decide! In trifles, it is better to decide wrongly, than never to decide at all. That may sound strange, but it cures the problem of indecision. Learn to make a decision!

2. Don't be a weathervane in the big things. For instance, don't be undecided about what you are going to be when you grow up. Remember the days when you wanted to be a nurse, a doctor, a bus driver, a mechanic, a storekeeper, a taxi-driver, a teacher, a farmer and whatever else? There comes a day when you decide. As a believer, you can think and pray about these decisions. Just take a good look at your interests, your talents and your abilities — decide! God will guide a sincere seeker.

3. Don't be a weathervane in the biggest thing of all. What do I mean? Don't be undecided about following Jesus Christ! Do not be half-persuaded, thinking it would be fine to be a Christian, and then holding back. Do not tell yourself, "Christ is my Master to serve," and then whisper in your heart, "What if service means giving up all my fun?" You can only truly enjoy yourself when you decide to follow Jesus. Being a believer means real joy, peace and contentment. You do not have to give up anything, except the love of sin and evil. You are responsible for your life — your social, moral, mental and spiritual life. Read the Book inspired by God, which can feed your soul, show you the Saviour and give direction to your life. Decide! Decide to be a responsible person today!

Read: Ephesians 4:14-24

February 22   ENJOY THE LITTLE THINGS!

How many things are there that you really enjoy? If you can't do things you would enjoy, try enjoying the things you can. There is fun in little things. Henry Jacobson, who wrote the Adult material for Scripture Press years ago, compiled a list of some of the things he enjoys, and I have gleaned from that and made my own list.

I want to share some of my favorite things. Look for joy in the commonplace things within reach. Make your own list, too.

- *Reading a well-written book*
- *Spring cleaning the garage*
- *A cheery "Hi!" from a grandson*
- *Using a pencil that's just been sharpened*
- *Turning off the sound on a TV commercial*
- *Sleeping in on a rainy Saturday morning*
- *A wool blanket in a cold bedroom on a winter night*
- *Sitting in the shade in the summertime*
- *Driving a car, especially through colourful fall countryside*
- *Opening a letter from a friend*
- *Taking off a necktie, and changing into casual clothes*
- *Typing with a new ribbon*
- *A long-distance phone call from a friend*
- *Eating left-overs that are well prepared*

Yes, there is big fun in little things. Did you list some of your own? *Who despises the day of small things?* (Zech. 4:10). We should never take life for granted, even the everyday routine. We need to look for little things that we can enjoy, and enjoy them! Life will become a lot more interesting. [God] *richly provides us with everything for our enjoyment* (1 Tim. 6:17). He wants us to delight in all that is wholesome and good. Life is full of small, enchanting pleasures. Like finishing another devotional for this book.

Enjoy going to church on Sunday! Take someone with you — you'll be the richer for it!

Read: Zechariah 4:1-14

February 23   TOUCHING SHOULDERS WITH YOU!

Man is a social being! We need each other!

You might be surprised if, all at one time, certain people were left out of your life. We need each other! Others are important.

A songwriter has written:

> Others, Lord, yes others,
> Let this my motto be,
> Help me to live for others,
> That I might live like Thee.

There is a poem, sent to me by a radio listener, that I cherish:

TOUCHING SHOULDERS WITH YOU!

There's a comforting thought at the close of the day,
When I'm weary and lonely and sad,
That sort of grips hold of this crusty old heart
And bids it be merry and glad.
It gets in my soul and it drives out the blues,
And finally thrills through and through.
It's just a sweet memory that chants the refrain
I'm glad I touched shoulders with you!

Did you know you were brave, did you know you were strong?
Did you know there was me leaning hard?
Did you know that I listened and waited and prayed
And was cheered by your simplest word?
Did you know that I longed for a smile on your face,
For the sound of your voice ringing true?
Did you know I grew stronger and better because
I had merely touched shoulders with you?

I am glad that I live; that I battle and strive
For the place that I know I must fill;
I'm thankful for sorrows, I'll meet with a grin
What fortune may send good or ill;
I may not have wealth, I may not be great,
But I know I shall always be true;
For I have in my life, that courage you gave,
When once I touched shoulders with you!

Is your life touching other lives? Happiness comes upon you unawares while you are helping others. Happiness is like perfume: You can't spray it on others without getting some on yourself. It all may begin with a smile. Smile! It's worth a million dollars and doesn't cost a cent.

Read: Romans 15:1-7

February 24   HOW TO MAKE LIFE WORSE

Life is problems! The other day I read something about making life worse than it is. Some of us go through life thinking that we are victims of our circumstances. Attitudes play a noble part in all of this. You can make life worse by having an attitude that expects any change to be for the worst. The very expectation helps bring it about.

Let me list a few things that make life worse than it is:

1. Pessimism. Do you surrender to pessimism? Pessimism helps produce the conditions it fears, giving an atmosphere of defeat. It is where you think defeat is certain and there's nothing you can do.

2. Worry. Worry is the interest you pay on trouble that never happens. Worry undermines, strangles and cripples your trust and confidence in God. He who trusts does not worry; and he who worries does not trust.

3. Anxiety. This fear is a mixture of desire and dread. Anxiety is like sand in a machine, grinding and destroying. Anxiety piles tomorrow's load on top of today's, and few are able to carry the load.

4. Defeatism. Losing the will to win. Giving up the struggle.

Why don't we ask, "Why make life worse than it is? Why not make it better than it is?" No, not by yourself, but by the grace of God. Be sure of your personal commitment to Jesus Christ, be sure your sins are forgiven and be sure your faith is on the unfailing promises of God's Word. Then, in the power of His grace, go out to make life better for yourself, your family, your church and your community.

Read: Matthew 6:25-34

February 25   FEAR

Fear — a life-long enemy!

It seems the fight against fear is almost as important as the battle for faith. Fear is our life-long enemy and it may well demand our life-long enmity. "Say this for me," a man once wrote, "He fought his fears."

The word *fear* appears more than 400 times in the Bible. The words *fear not*, about 118 times. It is often found in our daily conversation. "I'm afraid," says a statesman, "of what the future holds." A college girl phones her bank and says, "I'm afraid I've overdrawn my account." "I am afraid of what this pain may mean," are the words of a patient to his doctor. Some have said, "I'm afraid of fear; the emotion itself is destructive."

Now you should read the passage in Matthew 14:22-32.

Fear in Jesus' disciples brought out some of His most memorable words. Ten words were flung into a storm by night (actually, it was very early morning): *"Be of good cheer; it is I; be not afraid."* (Matt. 14:27, KJV).

Jesus emphasized courage and cheerfulness as a cure for fear. *"Be of good cheer."* He also underlined companionship with Himself as a cure for fear. In the storm, He said, *"It is I."* Circle that in your Bible! We have His promised presence. We need to practice His presence on a daily basis. Christ Himself is the door to fearlessness. Martyrs, missionaries and believers all over the world have testified to the contagion of His courage.

Then, Christ provides confidence as a cure for fear. *"Be not afraid."* Confidence is the conviction of adequacy. We need to say that Jesus Christ is adequate.

Whatever the storm, He is adequate! It may be true that in the storm of this world we are fearful about our health, our children, our finances and the evil in all its forms. Let's take those ten words into today: *Be of good cheer; it is I; be not afraid.*

Cheerfulness, companionship and confidence in Him is the cure.

Read: Matthew 14:22-32

February 26   GET UP AND GET GOING!

I like the story of the little boy walking along with his mother, all dressed up for a special party. Little boys are full of life and energy. This little fellow was romping around, jumping here and there. His mother warned him, "Be careful, settle down! You are going to fall and get all messed up." Sure enough, the boy did fall down into a muddy place. His mother stopped, looked at him, and said, "Now, what are you going to do?" With amazing composure in such a situation, the little boy replied, "I'm going to get up!"

Who hasn't found him or herself in a similar situation? Life can be rough! There are a few "downers." We tumble, fall and fail! Life does hold some daring adventures. Think of the inventors, reformers, builders of industry or some other pioneering persons. Would they have made a contribution if they had been afraid to fail, fall or risk? The secret of their success may well be characterized by the little boy. "I'm going to get up." That could be the first step to recovery. Nothing is accomplished if, after the first tumble, we stay down. Many a scientist has risen to triumph from the ashes of mistakes. Thomas Edison had hundreds of experimental failures, but he did not stay in defeat. He got up and moved on. A good football player falls forward, determined to gain every foot possible. In addition to that, he gets up and goes on. Life is filled with examples of those who get up and get going.

"Get up and get going" is the good word today. The battle-scarred apostle Paul says, *I press on... straining toward what is ahead* (Phil. 3:12-14). Peter made a great comeback. For all of us, there is opportunity to get up and get going.

Read: John 21:15-19

February 27   THE ABILITY TO THINK

The realm of our thoughts is a most fascinating one. It is the gift of our great Creator. The operation of millions of tiny cells in the human brain lifts man into a sphere where he stands alone among creatures in his ability to THINK.

Our thoughts can transport us to places where we have never been. They are a magic carpet that can bring back the experiences of the past or the great scenes of history. By them, we visit the Garden of Eden, the Holy Land, cities like Rome, London, Paris, Zurich in the Alps and other places in the world.

Our thoughts, with such fascinating power, also bring us in touch with the Eternal — for here we share in His likeness. How it enriches our lives! What marvels it unfolds! What beauty it holds!

The mind can also be an area of life that is filled with terrors. It often calls up fears, both real and imaginary. It musters up moments of great anxiety and days of troublesome worries.

You can begin to see the powers of Thought! Thoughts are the material with which we work. Before any deed is done, it is conceived in thought. Before a large building is constructed it has been seen in the mind of an architect. Thoughts can also be an influence for evil. Before we commit a sin, we have first had sinful thoughts. Thoughts are important, *for as he thinketh in his heart, so is he* (Prov. 23:7, KJV). The more I think of this, the more I need to apply the redemptive work of Christ to my life.

There are avenues of faith that we all should travel which will help balance our view of life. A beautiful example of all this is found in the words of Paul, in the letter to the Philippians: *Whatever is true, whatever is noble, whatever is right, whatever is pure, whatever is lovely, whatever is admirable — if anything is excellent or praiseworthy — THINK about such things* (Phil. 4:8). Think! This is positive thinking at its best.

I'm indebted to the book, *The Art of Christian Living*, by Ralph Heymen, from which I will be gleaning for the next few days.

Read: Philippians 4:5-9

February 28   HEALTH IS WHOLENESS

Do you have a healthy attitude toward life? Is it fair to say that people have a hard time getting better physically when they harbour "unhealthy attitudes"? We are all aware that mind and feelings have a tremendous influence upon our lives.

The term *heart* is used often in the Scriptures, many times in figures of speech. It is considered the very center of life. Proverbs 4:23 says, *Above all else, guard your heart, for it is the wellspring of life*. Out of the heart flow the springs of life. Figures of speech are interesting in that they tend to indicate our perceptions of things. For instance, we give the idea that the mind influences the body by speaking of a person that annoys us as "getting under our skin." Or, the people whom we resent a great deal give us a "pain in the neck." You have heard the expression, "he makes me sick." When we hear something that thrills us, like a beautiful piece of music, it "sends shivers up and down our spine." The scratching of a fingernail on a blackboard "gives us a chill." Something that we find disgusting is said to "turn our stomach." We are very much aware that emotional tensions express themselves in many ways.

All strong emotions are accompanied with bodily reactions: When we have sorrow — we weep; when we are joyful — we laugh; when we are ashamed — we blush; when we have fear — our heart beats faster; and so on. I am sure you have heard the statement, "Health is Wholeness."

70

Jesus used the term, *"...that they may be made whole."* God wants us to be healthy, whole people. To be really healthy, we need healthy thoughts, healthy emotions and healthy values in life. Peace of mind and contentment are important. Both are priceless! When love dominates the mind, there will be a warm glow of tenderness and happiness in the human heart. The attitude of reverence and worship will also have a wholesome effect upon your life. It's Halverson who says, "Man in Christ, is man at his best." I need ANOTHER to help me live this life. That "ANOTHER" is JESUS.

Read: Philippians 4:10-20; Isaiah 26:3

February 29   THE COLOUR OF YOUR THOUGHTS

The psychology of colour is a wide and complex field. Some colours are warm, others are cold. Some are cheerful, some are somber. There are shades of blue which we would never use in our hospital rooms. We would never think of dressing a nurse in a bright red uniform. Such colours would have a disturbing effect.

Common usage also expresses the fact that colour influences our human spirit. A person is said to be "blue" when he or she is depressed. We describe others as being "green with envy." The coward is said to be "yellow." The anarchist is red. White is associated with purity. An ancient philosopher once said, "The soul is dyed the colour of its thoughts."

Is there a colour to our thinking? There are people whose thoughts are grey. They always bring out the gloomy side of life. Their thoughts seem to flow in a gloomy mood and they have usually lost their sense of humour. Others are perennially tinged with green. They are envious and jealous of others, living in suspicion. They rarely have a good word for others. Then, the conversation of still others makes you think their minds are black — black with sordid stories, profane remarks and suggestive statements. You feel sorry for those who have to listen to them. What about the thoughts with varying shades of blue? These are full of worries, anxieties and fears. They're almost certain that things will go wrong.

By now you may be wondering if you can determine the colour of your own thoughts. That depends entirely on what you put into your mind. If you fill your mind with drab and lowly things, the furnishings of the chamber of your mind will be drab. If you fill your mind with rich and noble thoughts, the chamber of your mind will be richly furnished. Good books, good music, the beauty of nature, the wonders of science can turn your thoughts towards God.

Your personal faith in Jesus Christ will help you to put the proper colour into your life. Paul says in Romans 13:14, ...*Put on the Lord Jesus Christ....* Again today, Philippians 4:8 could be so very applicable.

Read: Colossians 3:5-17

March 1   FELLOWSHIP

The more I think and pray about the low spiritual state of many Christians, the deeper my conviction becomes that the reason for this is that they don't realize the need for daily fellowship with God.

This is the first thing I need in my life — daily fellowship with the Father. It's like breathing! I have no power of my own to maintain my spiritual life. I need to receive new grace from God. I need fellowship with Him! This cannot happen through a hasty prayer or a superficial reading of a few verses. I must take time — quietly and deliberately — to come into His presence. It was David who said, *Be still before the LORD and wait patiently for Him* (Ps. 46:10). Most of us long for a better life, but so few of us realize the importance of giving God time each day.

Parents take pleasure in their children and enjoy their fellowship. God desires to have fellowship with us. Take time! Believe in this personal fellowship! He is a living Person in heaven who thinks of us each day and longs to reveal Himself. He desires for us to bring Him our love and devotion each day. As you learn to spend time alone with Him, you will find the secret of true happiness, and experience His presence with you.

Prayer in fellowship with Jesus cannot be in vain. Jesus said, *"But when you pray, go into your room, close the door and pray to your Father... Then your Father, who sees what is done in secret, will reward you"* (Matt. 6:6). May I encourage you to practice a daily devotional life? It will grow on you. You will learn to love it!

Prayer in secret will be followed by the secret working of God in your heart.

You all know the hymn by William D. Longstaff:

> *Take time to be holy, the world rushes on;*
> *Spend much time in secret with Jesus alone.*
> *By looking to Jesus, like Him thou shalt be;*
> *Thy friends in thy conduct His likeness shall see.*

Read: Acts 4:13; 1 John 1

March 2   CHARACTER IS WHAT YOU ARE....

Someone said in my hearing one day, "Character is what you are when you are alone." To this I want to add, "Secrecy as to character is impossible." Let me illustrate this with a brief story I once read.

As he was hurrying along the street, a business man dropped a dime out of his pocket. A boy of honest character picked it up, and, realizing that the man was unaware that he had dropped it, ran after him and gave him the dime. Impressed, the man asked for his name and address. Later when the boy graduated from high school, the man offered him a position which involved the handling of large sums of money. He was sure of a boy who could be trusted to return a dime.

In a hundred small and undramatic ways, we let the world know what manner of persons we are. Secrecy as to character is impossible! From my collection of poetry, I share this bit of prose:

> *You tell on yourself by the friends you seek,*
> *By the very manner in which you speak,*
> *By the way you employ your leisure time,*
> *By the use you make of dollar and dime.*
>
> *You tell what you are by the things you wear,*
> *By the spirit in which you your burdens bear,*
> *By the kind of things at which you laugh,*
> *By the records you play on the phonograph.*
>
> *You tell what you are by the way you walk,*
> *By the things of which you delight to talk,*
> *By the manner in which you bear defeat,*
> *By so simple a thing as how you eat.*
>
> *By the books you choose from the well-filled shelf,*
> *In these ways and more, you tell on yourself.*
> *So really there's no particle of sense*
> *To keep up with false pretense.*

Character is what you are when you are alone. Be yourself! Be honest! Let your life be the real thing. This is what people want to see today. Two Bible characters come to mind immediately: Joseph and Daniel. You should read their account.

Read: Daniel 1; Genesis 39. The Lord was with them!

March 3   FACING YOUR CRITICS

The way we accept criticism is a real test of character. All of us have our share of criticism in a life-time. We can learn from our critics because our knowledge is limited.

An artist knows his paintings. A shoemaker knows his leather. The carpenter knows his wood, and the seamstress knows her cloth.

The question I would raise today is: How do we face our critics?

1. We can face our critics with an open-minded attitude. Be willing to listen! You may learn a few things. In other words, "Be teachable!" Don't cut yourself off from a means of growth and improvement.

2. Face your critics honestly. Find out whether it was given with good or evil intention; whether in love or in hate. Ask yourself, "Is it true? Do I really have the fault that is mentioned?" Accept criticism as a part of being human. It is only natural that we do not do all things well.

3. Face your critics with a sense of humor. Humor helps us look at ourselves with a sense of detachment. Laugh at yourself at least once a day. Don't take yourself too seriously. Constructive acceptance of criticism will make it serve as a stepping stone rather than a stumbling block. Constructive criticism can be very helpful. It can be the means of encouragement to improve. We are not perfect, but we are improving!

I would like to add some words from the pen of William Barclay: "There are some people who have a very highly developed faculty of criticism. They see faults much more easily than they see virtues, and they find it much easier to criticize than to praise. There is one principle of criticism which we should always observe: No man has the right to criticize any other man, unless he is prepared to do the thing better himself, or unless he is prepared to help the other man to do it better."

The "wet blanket" is not the flag to fly. Make it your aim to encourage those who are doing their best.

Read: 1 Thess. 2:15; Acts 7:52; Heb. 11:32-40; 2 Chron. 36:16

March 4   FORGIVENESS

Let's begin with a Bible verse today: *Forgive as the Lord forgave you* (Col. 3:13b). Nothing sours life more than an unforgiving spirit.

Mrs. Cowman in *Springs in the Valley*, tells this story:

"A custom far out in the African bush, which has no equivalent in this part of the world, is *"Forgiveness Week."* Fixed in the dry season when the weather itself is smiling, this is a week when every man and woman pledges him or herself to forgive any neighbor any wrong, real or fancied, that may be a cause for misunderstanding, coldness or quarrel between the parties.

It is, of course, a part of our Christian living that a man should forgive his brother. But among recent converts, and even older brethren, this great tenet is, perhaps naturally, apt to be forgotten or overlooked in the busy and burdensome life. *"Forgiveness Week"* brings it forcibly to mind. The week itself terminates with a festival of happiness and rejoicing among the native Christians."[4]

I'd like to be among these native Christians. Is it too much to suggest that in this supposedly more civilized part of the world a similar week might be instituted? We sing, "Nothing between my soul and the Saviour" — what about nothing between my brother and sister in Christ? *Ah, listen, let grudges die! When God forgives, He forgets!*

God loves to pardon! In the New Testament the word is *forgiveness.* Pardon is the act of a Sovereign; forgiveness is the act of a Father. God pardons gloriously (read Neh. 9:17). God pardons abundantly (read Isa. 55:7). Then read those words in Psalm 32 that bless my soul: *Blessed is the man whose sins are forgiven.*

The word to all of our hearts today is Ephesians 4:32: *Be kind and compassionate to one another, forgiving each other, just as in Christ God forgave you.* That is the measure of our forgiveness!

Read: Psalm 32:1-11

March 5   SMILE!

A cheerful look brings joy to the heart, and good news gives health to the bones (Prov. 15:30).

Have you ever considered the value of a smile? It costs nothing, it enriches those who receive it, it takes but a moment and the memory lasts for a long time. A smile creates happiness in the home, fosters goodwill in business, brings cheer to the discouraged and sunshine to the sad. What I like about a smile is that it cannot be bought, begged or borrowed. It is only valuable when it is given away. A smile is worth a million dollars and doesn't cost a cent. So, if you see someone without a smile today, give them one of yours. Did you know that a smile means the same in any language?

Let's add another verse today: *A cheerful heart is good medicine* (Prov. 17:22). Have you ever felt so gloomy that you thought you'd never laugh again? Then it didn't take long and you did laugh again. Did you know that it began with a smile and then you broke into laughter?

Laughter is a sign of health! We all need a good sense of humour. You have heard it said, "Laugh at yourself at least once a day." Most of us take life too seriously.

God gave us laughter to use as an outlet for our emotions. How often the irritations of life can be resolved in moments of cheer and pleasantry. Tensions can be broken when there is a burst of laughter. This can take place in our homes, at work or even at school.

As a believer in Jesus Christ, I have a joy that runs deep, and a humour that faith makes possible. Jesus often said, *"Be of good cheer."* Smile! It's worth a million dollars and doesn't cost a cent.

Read: Proverbs 15:13,30; 17:22; John 15:11; John 16:33

March 6   BREATH!

What is it that you do 18 times a minute, 1,080 times an hour, and about 25,000 times a day, yet rarely notice?

The answer is, you breathe!

Twenty-five thousand gifts a day! A measured gift of life from the hands of God.

Your lungs are among the most important parts of your body. They furnish your blood with oxygen, and they carry away carbon dioxide and water. A few moments without breathing and you lose consciousness — a minute or two longer could prove fatal.

To whom are we indebted for the blessing of respiration? Job 12:10 says, *In **His** hand is the life of every living thing, the breath of all mankind.* The Lord gives us those twenty-five thousand gifts a day so that we in turn might honour and glorify Him with our lives (Eph. 1:12).

He also gives us the gift of eternal life through faith in Jesus Christ. Today we all owe Him a prayer of thanks. Don't save your breath when it is time to breathe a prayer of thanks. The last verse of the last Psalm says, *Let everything that has breath praise the LORD.*

Read: Psalm 150

March 7   SAY IT!

A word aptly spoken is like apples of gold in settings of silver (Prov. 25:11). A word in season, how good it is.

Try and capture two words today: "SAY IT." This is a lesson I'm still trying to learn.

You have a friend and for some reason you love him or her very much. Have you ever said so? They would like you to — say it! A friend has helped along the way, and your heart is filled with gratitude — say it! Some joy comes to your friend and you rejoice with him or her — say it! Your friend succeeds in a job well done and you are proud of him or her — say it! A friend wins a game and you are glad — say it! Illness may have taken the glow out of life and you would share their sorrow — say it! A word of sympathy would lighten the load — say it!

Remember, a word aptly spoken... how good it is!

A personal word, a telephone call, a postcard, a letter, a telegram and only a few minutes. Your friend will be encouraged. Your life will be the better for it. You may add to the joy. You may lighten the load. You may brighten the road, if only you would take time to SAY IT !

Say it to someone today!

Read: Proverbs 25:11; Ephesians 4:25; Colossians 4:6

March 8   RELAXATION AND CONTENTMENT

Let me put the two together. Reader's Digest, years ago, had an article entitled, "The Art of Relaxation." The author brought up the rocking chair, saying it should be brought back into our homes again. Can you picture mother, knitting in hands, sitting in a rocking chair? Was there not a bit of contentment there as well? Learning to relax is both an art and an attitude. It depends on my attitude toward life as a whole. Learn to enjoy life. Life is meant to be enjoyed! Take time to think of the pleasant things in life. There is so much we can enjoy. The sunrise and the sunsets are absolutely free.

In our highly commercialized society, we are driven by the desire for things, as if things satisfy. It seems we have allowed the material world to dominate us. We see this restless striving for things. Things lack permanence! There is more to life than making a living. There is a spiritual dimension we often neglect.

Have you not enjoyed the invitations of Christ? *Come to Me... and I will give you rest* (Matt. 11:28). How good to rest and relax in the Lord. Paul says, *I have learned the secret of being content in any and every situation....* (Phil. 4:12). Through Jesus Christ, I can learn contentment. Through Him, I can conquer the pressures and the tensions of life.

Contentment is to know the Saviour! Find rest and relaxation in the Lord!

Read: Matthew 11:28-30; Philippians 4:10-12

March 9   FRIENDSHIP

A friend loves at all times (Prov. 17:17).
The poet says,

> *Love makes people friendly,*
> *Love makes people smile;*
> *If you show a little love,*
> *Today will be worthwhile.*

We all need support, companionship and the feeling of personal worth. From a poster at a camp-site, I share this:

> *When the roses lose their fragrance*
> *And the world seems at an end,*
> *When the day has lost its gladness,*
> *What a blessing is a friend!*
>
> *One who takes you as he finds you*
> *Caring not who is to blame;*
> *One who knows all your shortcomings,*
> *But who loves you just the same.*
>
> *Heaven sends a gift each morning,*
> *Of a bright new day to spend,*
> *What a joy it is to share it*
> *With God's greatest gift — a friend.*

Proverbs 18:24b says, *..There is a friend who sticks closer than a brother.*

Would you sing the hymn, "What a Friend we have in Jesus"?

Read: John 15:13-17

March 10   THE ART OF FRIENDSHIP

It is important to cultivate the art of friendship! We all need to discover the price of being a friend. A friend is loyal in spite of the cost. There are far too many fair-weather friends.

The story of the "Praying Hands" is for me one of the best illustrations.

Albrecht Durer, a renowned painter, had a true friend. When they were young men, both interested in art, it was decided that Durer would paint while his friend would work to support him. It took many years for the artist to make a name for himself, and by that time his friend's hands were calloused and hardened by toil. To express his thanks to his friend, Durer painted a picture of these hands, and it became his most famous work of art. It was a tribute to a friend who was willing to pay the cost of friendship.

All of us have enjoyed seeing those praying hands on pictures, posters and postcards. We need others to stand by our side to help us, to give us support, and to be our companions in time of need.

It is important to cultivate the art of friendship! Try to find some within the context of the church. Believers should always be your best friends. Having said that, there is always room to have other friends within our society.

Read: Proverbs 4:10-27; Run with the right crowd!

March 11   CULTIVATE FRIENDSHIP

To have a friend, be a friend! Cultivate friendship! Friendship withers when you neglect to cultivate it. I think you will enjoy what an unknown author has written:

> *To laugh a bit and joke a bit*
> *And grasp a friendly hand;*
> *To love a bit and scold a bit*
> *And know they'll understand;*
> *To tell one's secret hopes and fears*
> *And share a friendly smile;*
> *To have a friend and be a friend*
> *Is what makes life worthwhile!*

The J.B. Phillips paraphrase of Romans 12:17 goes like this: *Take a real interest in ordinary people.*

Take an interest in helping someone. These things help us to have wholesome attitudes; like the lady who said, "I have so many friends that I never get a chance to be lonely."

Companionship with Jesus can be very helpful too!

Read: Romans 12:9-21

March 12   **CAST DOWN!**

Housework often seems futile. By the time the dishes are done and the kitchen cleaned, it's nearly time to get another meal. Hours are spent in cooking and baking. We sit down to the table and in half an hour what is there to show for all our labour? There are more dirty dishes. We scrub floors and dust and wonder where all the dirt comes from. Often we say, "What's the use!"

You may be cast down, troubles may surround you. We blunder on and make mistakes. Financial setbacks come and we throw up our hands. It seems as if life is problems!

So, you've had some down days; David did too. David had this feeling, as he talked to himself: *Why are you so cast down O my soul? Why so disturbed within me?* He is deeply troubled. But notice, immediately he adds, *Put your hope in God... I will yet praise Him* (Ps. 42:5). He senses the presence of God!

God sees us; He knows us, He understands us, He hears us, He cares for us and He loves us. The Scriptures support us. Go with Psalm 46:1 today.

Read: Psalm 139; Psalm 33:18-22

March 13   **MOODY?**

All of us swing in our moods! We have our highs and lows. The weather plays a part many times. Cloudy days get to us. The feeling brings gloom into our hearts and minds. Then someone who meets you or calls you on the phone has a home remedy. I can hear them say, "When you're down — get busy!" Now it may be true that "busy hands" can do much to get our minds back into a normal mood.

Constructive thinking and putting ourselves to work can be an emotional tonic. All is not lost and all is not hopeless in the world in which we live. Hope is the dominant characteristic of the Christian spirit and experience. Our hope is built upon the faithfulness of God, upon His promises and upon the atoning work of the person of Jesus Christ. Faith and trust are the two elements we need to exercise. Trust Him for your down days!

David, the author of most of the Psalms, had his moody moments. I recommend that we read Psalm 42 for today!

Read: Psalm 42

March 14   LITTLE TATERS!

Some of us remember when small potatoes could be purchased inexpensively. Many families often ate "little taters." Some of you have too. Mom used to scrub them and cook them with "jackets on." They tasted delicious with creamy milk gravy. We really enjoyed them. They were tiny, but the size did not lessen their flavour.

What am I trying to say? Big things in life do not always give us the most enjoyment; nor the big gifts the greatest blessing. Good things come in small packages!

There is the question I borrow from the minor prophet, *Who despises the day of small things?* (Zech. 4:10). I hope we never despise the day of little things. That "cup of cold water" that Jesus spoke about shall not lose its reward. The smiles we give, the prayers we say for friends and loved ones shall not go unrewarded. We can look for the best in others and do acts of kindness when the opportunity is given. Remember — a few "little taters" or "a cup of cold water."

Little things in life bring us enjoyment!

Read: Zechariah 4:8-14; Matthew 10:40-42

March 15   A GREETING CARD!

Little things bring us moments of real enjoyment and pleasure. On a shopping bag from a stationery store in the city of St. Catharines, Ontario, I saw these words:

A GREETING CARD CAN:

Warm a heart, hold a hand, lend an ear, pat a back, light up a face, tickle a funny bone, dry an eye, surprise a child, woo a sweetheart, toast a bride, welcome a stranger, wave a good-bye, shout a bravo, blow a kiss, mend a quarrel, ease a pain, boost a morale, stop a worry and start a tradition.

Isn't that terrific! A greeting card can do that in any season of the year. I hope we will never despise the day of little things.

Maybe after reading the above, you may put a little more thought to promote warmth in sending a card. What about scribbling something around the edges, the empty spaces on a card. It may be something you underline in parts of the script in a card. A double line will give it emphasis. That would be so much better than just a bare signature. Lines like, *Your friendship is deeply appreciated* or *Wishing you the finest joy! Sincerely yours because of Jesus*, can add a blessing.

Read: Mark 9:33-41—The best club to belong to!
B.Y.B.T.C.= Because You Belong To Christ!

March 16   SALTY

Holidays and birthdays are big events for children. Our children anticipated coming events with joy and impatience. How often they said, "We can hardly wait." They mark up calendars, crossing off the days one by one until that special day arrives.

Now it is true, special events make life interesting. We all know that most of life is made up of just plain living and rubbing elbows with our fellow man. What really counts are our attitudes, our kind thoughts, our comforting words and our gracious deeds.

Christianity is always something very practical. The Christlike life ought to permeate all of our daily living. A pinch of salt seasons the contents of a dish. Foods are flat and tasteless without it. Salt is important! Christians are important! Our very lives as believers should improve the flavour of our surroundings.

Jesus spoke to His audience one day with the words, *"You are the salt of the earth... You are the light of the world"* (Matt. 5:13,14). We need to make people thirsty for the good news of Jesus Christ.

Would you determine today to let your light shine — daily and on special days?

Read: Matthew 5:13-16

March 17   SOMETHING BEAUTIFUL

We can be beautiful people! Each of us are "tailor-made" by God. We are all different, just like our faces. We are designed by God for a special purpose. This reminds me of the answer to the question in many catechisms. What is the sole purpose of man? The sole purpose of man is to glorify God and enjoy Him forever. We were made for God, to love Him, to praise Him, to serve Him, to live in fellowship with Him and to do His will.

The practical outworking of all this is that God needs Christians to be living channels — channels of blessing.

A Christian is:

> *A mind through which Christ thinks,*
> *A heart through which Christ loves,*
> *A voice through which Christ speaks,*
> *A hand through which Christ helps.*

"Tailor-made" for God! Think about that today!

Read: Psalm 149:1-4 ; 2 Timothy 2:19-21; Ephesians 1:12

March 18   QUAKER LADY COMPLEXION

We live in a day of cosmetics! We want to look good and feel good and smell good. So we put on make-up and deodorant, and dress in fine clothes. The desire to look beautiful is there!

An elderly Quaker lady with a beautiful complexion was asked one day, "What kind of cosmetic do you use?" She replied, "I use:

> *for my lips, truth;*
> *for my voice, prayer;*
> *for my eyes, pity;*
> *for my hands, charity;*
> *for my figure, uprightness; and*
> *for my heart, love."*

This prescription can be filled without expense. The best is this: The supply will increase with continued use.

Gloria Gaither writes and sings:

> *Something beautiful, something good;*
> *All my confusion He understood;*
> *All I had to offer Him was brokenness and strife,*
> *But He made something beautiful of my life.*

Read: 1 Corinthians 13 — Living Letters; Isaiah 57:15

March 19   GETTING EVEN!

The following may sound like something that happens in your home: "He hit me first," accuses one child, tearfully. Mother asks, "And with that one hit, he blackened your eye, bloodied your nose, tore your shirt and rolled you in the mud?" "Well, no," comes the admission, "that happened after I knocked him down."

The natural tendency is to strike back. The Scriptural admonition is, *See that none of you repays evil for evil....* (1 Thess. 5:15, RSV). Bloody noses, black eyes, and torn shirts can be healed or mended, perhaps leaving a memory that is of future benefit.

However, any attempt to get even usually results in broken relationships and a guilty conscience. We need to harbour a forgiving spirit not a revengeful attitude. David refused to take revenge when Saul was at his mercy. Jesus says, *"Love your enemies, do good to those who hate you"* (Luke 6:27). Our prayer should be, "Lord, help us to remember that You love others just as much as You love us."

Read: Romans 12:17-21

March 20   "SECOND MILE"

Our inspiration today is illustrated by the story of a small boy who was sent by his mother to pick a quart of raspberries. He did not like picking raspberries, but his mother had spoken, so he made his way slowly and reluctantly toward the raspberry patch. Then, a happy thought came to his mind: Why not pick two quarts and surprise his mother? Suddenly, a new motivation of love dissolved his strong dislike for picking berries. He could hardly wait to see the surprise on his mother's face when he showed her the extra quart!

The power of a new affection. Paul taught this in Colossians 3. Jesus taught it in the Sermon on the Mount. It's the "second mile" that counts. So often we have the opportunity to love the unlovely, to bless those who strike back or misuse us. The extra mile is not easy at times, but it is Christ-like.

Is God getting some extra mileage out of you? Check Mark 9:41.

Read: Matthew 5:40-48

March 21   "THINGS"

The world today places a great emphasis on "things." We want things to make life more enjoyable. Our newspaper ads, the mail, the media are all bringing their influence into our homes. Win a vacation, win a car, win another gadget, and life promises a good time. We seem to be conditioned to want "things."

Don't get me wrong; possessing things is not wrong, as long as they do not possess *you*. The question may well be asked, "Is acquiring 'things' our primary purpose in life, or is there a greater purpose?" There is a spiritual dimension we often forget and even neglect. We need a proper balance between those things that make life more enjoyable and those things that enrich our spiritual life. Spiritual things ought to be paramount!

I have often said, "Things lack permanence; things do not satisfy!" Earth was never meant to satisfy the human heart. A life filled with generosity and good deeds has spiritual value (Titus 2:14). Most of all, our commitment to Jesus Christ has eternal value.

As you read Luke 12:13-21, you will see a man who built his barns: **1. Too Narrow** — for himself;
                    2. Too Low — leaving God out;
                    3. Too Short — for this life only.

Go with verse 15 today!

March 22   LITTLE THINGS

Little things are important! Little things make people happy! Again, that verse in Zechariah 4:10 intrigued me, as well as encouraged me. Little things! We don't have to make headlines, although there is room for that. But it's the little things that can make life so worthwhile and all of us can do it.

Tucked in a corner of a children's publication were these lines:

LITTLE THINGS

A smile is such a little thing,
As is a word of praise,
But each of them can warm a heart
And make a happy day.

A helping hand, a kindly deed,
Or just a friendly wave
Could lighten someone's burden,
Could fill another's need.

These are all just little things,
As we go along our way;
But little things are big things
If they brighten someone's day.

— Myrtle E. Shafer

I enjoyed that when I read it. Let's be open to what it says.

Read: John 6:1-15 (Remember the leftovers?)

March 23   **LONELINESS**

This world is a busy place. People are rushing from place to place. Our highways are crowded with the flow of traffic. Many feet beat upon the sidewalks of our cities and towns. There are always people and more people. In that same crowd are people who are alone. There is possibly no feeling that is more disheartening than that of loneliness. The songs that are sung are songs of loneliness.

There is a cure for loneliness! That cure is in Jesus Christ! Jesus said, *"...I am with you always...."* (Matt. 28:20). That's good to know! I suppose King David had moments of loneliness; I depict that from Psalm 142. He says in verse 4, *Look to my right and see, no one is concerned for me... no one cares for my life.* That's how we feel sometimes. No one cares for my life. Then I read how he called upon God. David knew that God cares.

Perhaps we should celebrate the care of God in our lives a little more than we do. God sees us. He knows us, He hears us and He understands us. You are NOT alone!

Read: Psalm 142

March 24   **JIGSAW PUZZLES**

There is something fascinating about jigsaw puzzles! Once you start putting one together, you just can't leave until that one other piece is found — or maybe you stay till *every* piece is in place!

When you empty a box of puzzle pieces, you see a jumbled mess of cardboard shapes. But as these pieces are put together, they become a beautiful picture. We all know there are some great picture puzzles; we have some in our home.

I think many times our very own lives seem like a puzzle. We wonder how things will turn out. For those who believe in God, there is an assurance that things will work out. The Author of our faith, Jesus Christ, is fitting all the pieces together in a perfect picture or pattern even as we wonder. Sooner or later, we see the pieces of our life fall into place just like a puzzle picture. He will complete the picture in His own time. He understands! He cares! Paul assures us in the Word, *...He who began a good work in you will carry it on to completion until the day of Christ Jesus* (Phil.1:6).

Read: Romans 8:28-39

March 25   STRAIGHTEN UP!

May I reflect a little bit today? I'm reminded of a teacher I once had who would say to her pupils, "Straighten up! Sit up straight!" She would even exhort us to walk straight — practice with a book on our head. I still recollect those words many times in a day — Straighten up!

I'm wondering if that thought doesn't come to our minds when we see people with stooped shoulders. I think I sense a reason for that (why some have stooped shoulders). It may all be summed up in one word: "ANXIETY." Proverbs 12:25 says, *An anxious heart weighs a man down, but a kind word cheers him up.*

Many people are troubled with heavy hearts. Today the words of Jesus are most suitable: "Do not be anxious, do not worry" (Matt. 6:25-34). The word from 1 Peter 5:7 is one you all know, *Cast all your anxiety on Him because He cares for you.* Cast the weight you are carrying on Him. Straighten up! You don't have to have stooped shoulders. Jesus Christ has promised rest and comfort for those who are weighed down with care. Release your load! With Him you can walk straight and upright.

Read: Luke 13:10-17

March 26   LOOKING UP!

Stop! Look! Listen!

All three words are familiar. We've been taught to honour them at certain places when we travel. It's the word, "LOOK," that I want to emphasize today. Actually, J.D. Carlson has coined the phrase, "Keep looking up!" as a conclusion to his daily radio broadcasts.

Let's see this in contrast to something I read:

A young man once found a five dollar bill while walking down the street. From that time on, he never lifted his eyes when walking. In the course of the years, he accumulated 29,516 buttons, 54,172 pins and 12 cents. While doing this, he got a bent back and a miserable disposition. He lost the glory of the sunlight, the sheen of the stars, the smile of friends, tree blossoms in the spring, the blue sky and the entire joy of living.

How foolish! Listen! How often we keep our eyes on human temporal things. Would the words, "Keep looking up!" not be helpful for all of us? We need to look up in worship to God. We need to look up to Jesus. Hebrews 12:2 is the good word today: *Let us fix our eyes on Jesus....* And Hebrews 13:8: *Jesus Christ is the same yesterday and today and forever.*

Read: Psalm 121: "I will lift up my eyes...."

March 27   INCH BY INCH

Our inspiration today has its roots in a little chorus we used to sing in Vacation Bible School:

Got any rivers you think are uncrossable?
Got any mountains you cannot tunnel through?
God specializes in things thought impossible,
He does the things others cannot do.

— Oscar Eliason

Rivers and mountains may suggest difficulties and sometimes opposition. We all have them. We are the people who look ahead and gaze at that river or mountain and say, "How am I ever going to get over that? How shall I face all that lies ahead?"

Someone has said, "Yard by yard, life is hard; inch by inch, life's a cinch."

Today, I'd like to encourage you to keep to the present "little inch" that is before you, and do the things in that little moment that are possible. The mountains — the big things— and the rivers — the seemingly impossible— can be passed over in the same way. When you come to them, you will have the strength to face them. To one of the tribes in Israel, Moses wrote, *...Your strength will equal your days* (Deut. 33:25). In the New Testament, we read: *"Nothing will be impossible for you"* (Matt. 17:20).

Read: Psalm 37:1-7,23

March 28   GRATITUDE / ADVERSITY / PAIN

Today I talked to someone who was in pain. There is so much we could say and share about the ministry of pain. There is so much of it! But let's talk today about our attitudes toward pain. One I'd like to mention is the attitude of *gratitude*! The apostle Paul comes to my mind. He wore the garment of gratitude in all of his hardships, heartaches and hurts. This man writes from prison where it is damp and cold, *...Give thanks in all circumstances, for this is God's will for* *you in Christ Jesus* (1 Thess. 5:18). *...Always* [give] *thanks to God... for everything, in the name of our Lord Jesus Christ* (Eph. 5:20).

I read of an invalid who said, "Today I've experienced the most exquisite pleasure that I have ever had in my life; I was able to breathe freely for five minutes." Having read that, I was thankful that breathing comes easily to me. We take so many things for granted.

We must also learn to reflect upon the spiritual benefits received from adversity and trials. An old Scottish prayer book contains a beautiful expression of praise that emphasizes the value of our trials. It says that through difficulties, our souls are enriched by the fuller experience of God's love, a more childlike dependence on His will, and a sympathy for the suffering and sad.

Whether life is pleasant or difficult, let's look for reasons to give thanks. We can find them all around us. Conscious gratitude will enrich life's pleasures and sweeten its pains.

Read: Psalm 13 — A prayer for help in trouble.

March 29   TESTS

As children in school, we often had "tests." If I paid attention in class and kept up the assignments, the tests were easy; but if I didn't pay attention, they were hard.

As adults, we also have "tests." If you wish to drive a car, you must pass the driver's test. To work for the government, you must pass civil service tests. Doctors, lawyers, teachers, nurses, mechanics must all pass the tests of their disciplines.

As believers in Jesus Christ, we too face "tests." James 1:2 says, *Consider it pure joy... because you know that the testing of your faith develops perseverance.* If we were to follow through in James 1, we would see several "tests." What follows has been gleaned from the Dake's Annotated Reference Bible.

> **The test of faith** (vs. 5-8)
> **The test of humility** (vs. 9-11)
> **The test of endurance** (vs. 12)
> **The test of temptation** (vs. 13-16)
> **The test of appreciation** (vs. 17)
> **The test of the new birth** (vs. 18)
> **The test of Christian living** (vs.19-21)
> **The test of obedience** (vs. 22-25)
> **The test of pure religion** (vs. 26-27)

The test of your faith is precious. See 1 Peter 1:7.

How do you and I face the "tests"? Do we give in immediately or do we endure with patience? Do we trust instead of worry? Will I pass the "test"? Be encouraged that we have an anchor and an advocate in Jesus Christ. In knowing HIM, we have a resource person, and we have the Holy Spirit who walks alongside to help.

Read: James 1

March 30 HARVESTS AND BREAKFASTS

I shall never forget some of the breakfasts my mother made during harvest time back in Saskatchewan. They were the kind that stuck to your ribs. They were no "juice and toast" affairs. There were fried eggs, sausages and potatoes, with home-made bread and butter and jelly to top it off. Those breakfasts were designed to last us until noon. We had hours of pitching bundles and hauling grain. What we needed to start the day was a nourishing breakfast!

Spiritually speaking, we need a good breakfast! Today, especially, our faith needs the nourishment of the Word of God. I would be remiss if I didn't repeat: Faith needs nourishment!

The Christian life is no "namby-pamby" experience. We know we have an Enemy. His subtle attacks move in upon us from every side. He would destroy, discourage and defeat our efforts as believers.

I don't know how you feel, but I need the Word of God to help me in my daily life. I need a substantial spiritual breakfast! I need the guidance of God.

Peter calls us to make every effort to add to our faith. There's a thrilling verse in Psalm 107:9: *...He satisfies the thirsty and fills the hungry with good things.*

When did you last have a good spiritual breakfast?

Read: 2 Peter 1:3-11; Hebrews 4:12; James 1:22-25

March 31 WHAT PLEASES GOD?

For a motto in 1981, I chose Ephesians 5:10: *And find out what pleases the Lord.* I have seen that verse many times since then, most recently, in the little devotional booklet, ANCHOR (Haven of Rest) written by Earline Kline from Boise, Idaho. I borrow the headings used during the month of January, 1992. I hope you enjoy looking up Bible verses — it's a good exercise.

EXPLORING WAYS WE CAN PLEASE GOD:

1. *Having Faith* — Hebrews 11:6
2. *Obeying* — 1 Samuel 15:22
3. *Loving each other* — John 15:12
4. *Giving Thanks* — Hebrews 13:15
5. *Singing to the Lord* — Psalm 92:1
6. *Seeing myself as God sees me* — Micah 6:8
7. *Being truthful* — Psalm 51:6
8. *Denying myself* — Matthew 16:24
9. *Having a servant spirit* — Philippians 2:5-7
10. *Giving to others* — Philippians 4:18
11. *Living in the Spirit* — Romans 8:4
12. *Being separate* — 2 Corinthians 6:17
13. *Living honestly* — Proverbs 11:1
14. *Loving God* — Matthew 22:37
15. *A living sacrifice* — Romans 12:1
16. *Loving my enemies* — Matthew 5:44
17. *Being salt and light* — Matthew 5:16
18. *Practicing hospitality* — Romans 12:13
19. *Giving cheerfully* — 2 Corinthians 9:7
20. *Taking in the Stranger* — Matthew 25:35
21. *Having compassion* — Romans 12:15
22. *Praying in secret* — Matthew 6:6
23. *Forgiving* — Ephesians 4:32
24. *Bearing much fruit* — John 15:1-8
25. *Finding contentment* — Hebrews 13:5
26. *Submitting to authority* — Romans 13:1
27. *Being joyful* — Philippians 4:4
28. *Being an encourager* — 1 Thessalonians 5:14
29. *Spending time alone with God* — Psalm 5:3
30. *Worshipping* — Psalm 100:4
31. *Above all, Love* — 1 Corinthians 13:13

(Used by permission)

How long did it take to look up all the verses?

April 1   **A LETTER FROM JESUS!**

Most of us enjoy receiving letters! Could we imagine a written letter in the mail from the Lord Jesus? The person who wrote this one sure did. It was written in a poster format (author unknown).

DEAR FRIEND:

I just had to send a note to tell you how much I love you and care about you. I saw you yesterday as you were walking with your friends. I waited all day hoping you would want to talk with me also. As evening drew near, I gave you a sunset to close the day and a cool breeze to rest you. And I waited. But you never came. It hurt me, but I still love you because I am your friend.

I saw you fall asleep last night and I longed to touch your brow. So, I spilled moonlight on your pillow and your face. Again I waited, wanting to rush down so that we could talk. I have so many gifts for you. But you awakened late the next day and rushed off to work. My tears were in the rain.

Today you looked so sad, so all alone. It makes my heart ache because I understand. My friends let me down and hurt me so many times, too. But I love you. Oh, if you would only listen to me. I really love you. I try to tell you in the blue sky and in the quiet green grass. I whisper it in the leaves on the trees and breathe it in the colors of the flowers. I shout it to you in the mountain streams and give the birds love songs to sing. I clothe you with warm sunshine and perfume the air with nature's scents. My love for you is deeper than the oceans and bigger than the biggest want or need in your heart.

If you only knew how much I want to help you. I want you to meet my Father. He wants to help you, too. My Father is that way, you know. Just call me, ask me, talk with me. I have so much to share with you. But, I won't hassle you. I'll wait because I love you.

Your Friend, Jesus

April 2   **SINCERELY YOURS**

Have you ever written a letter to Jesus? Would it read like the one Gary Chapman wrote? This has blessed my heart every time I've read it. It, too, comes from a poster.

SINCERELY YOURS

As I take my pen to write to you a letter,
Knowing even now you know what's on my mind,
And I think perhaps it might make me feel better
If I see myself here written in a line.

And as I pause, I see a phrase I took for granted
And it leaps out as I see it written there;
And as the truth of it begins to become planted,
These two words have now become my heartfelt prayer:

Sincerely Yours.

Lord, I sign my life to You,
Sincerely Yours,
With a strong and earnest wish
To be the best that I can be at what I am,
Without a thought for me.

Lord, teach me now to be
Sincerely Yours,
Without a proud or selfish line;
Sincerely Yours,
Now until the end of time.

Please make my life
Become a letter You can keep
And never throw away;
I'll write until the day that I become
Sincerely Yours.

Sincerely Yours

April 3   AN EASTER MEDITATION IN POETRY

This is suitable for the Easter season and seems to be designed for the homemaker.

"Are you ready for Easter?" A friend of mine phoned,
Last week, when the snow twirled around.
"Have you cleaned the house and painted the walls?
Have your drapes been aired and pressed?
Have you baked your 'goodies,' that delicious bread,
And painted the children's eggs?

Have you purchased that hat — an Easter must,
Or, what have you done these days?"
I hung up the phone and forgot what she said;
But the question I just couldn't shake:
"Are you ready for Easter?" I repeated again,
Now what does it really mean?

I left all my mending, my mopping and work;
I went to the Book of all Books.
I read it in Matthew, in Mark and in Luke,
The story of Christ — how He rose.
And there I met Jesus, as Mary of old,
Saying, "Woman, why weepest thou?"

"I'm not ready for Easter," I simply confessed,
"There still is so much I should do."
And then I beheld Him with eyes that were opened
And all I could say was, "He lives."
I sank on my knees in my simple, small kitchen
And felt a new fervor to pray.

New joy filled my heart; a new light lit my pathway,
New peace just flooded my soul.
I suddenly felt new help from above;
New courage to face all my trials,
New strength for the day,
And a new understanding for all those around me was given.

New hope for the future, new grace for my sins.
On my lips I found a new song,
New love for my Saviour, and new consecration,
New loyalty came to its own.
New life, everlasting, because Jesus lives
Was mine, to have and to hold.

And as I arose, I was ready for Easter,
For THAT is what EASTER gives!

Think of it: new joy, light, peace, help, courage, strength,
understanding, hope, grace, love, loyalty, a song and new life. Are
you grateful?

Read: John 20:19-23

95

April 4   THE BLOOD OF HIS CROSS

Read Colossians 1:15-23.

...By making peace through His blood, shed on the cross (Col. 1:20) — one of the most wonderful statements about the character of our Lord Jesus Christ.

Two questions:

1. What does the blood of His cross mean? The blood of HIS cross must be distinguished from the blood of every other cross. The blood of those who were crucified with Christ avails nothing. It was HIS cross! All that He was in His holy humanity, in His divine dignity, glory and honor was sacrificed there. He gave Himself for us! The blood of Christ shed for our sins is what stands for all that Christ Himself is before God in our behalf. It is the value that God sets on it!

2. What has the blood of His cross secured? It has laid the basis by which God can righteously justify the ungodly.

a. *Through the blood of His cross there is propitiation.* He Himself is the atoning sacrifice or covering for our sins, and not only ours, but for the sins of the world (1 John 2:2).

b. *Through the blood of His cross there is redemption.* It is a ransom price paid for the sinner. He gave Himself to purchase our freedom from all iniquity. You are bought with a price! This is true for everyone who is by grace a child of God (1 Cor. 6:19-20).

c. *Through the blood of His cross there is forgiveness.* In Him, we have redemption through the blood, the forgiveness of our sins (Eph. 1:7). The blood of His cross is the ground of God's complete and eternal forgiveness.

d. *Through the blood of His cross there is peace.* This is not a peace made with God, but a God-made peace! God made peace through His blood which was shed upon the cross. This is peace with honor! This is peace that the world cannot give. He is our peace!

e. *Through the blood of His cross we have reconciliation.* We have been brought near. We were far away from God! Sin and rebellion drives the soul away from God. Love for the Lord Jesus as our sacrifice for sin, brings us near to God. We are now His friends; we've been reconciled.

Have you taken advantage of this blood-bought freedom? Are you finding peace and rest in the Lord Jesus?

Prayer: Thank You, Lord, for saving my soul!

April 5   THE PURPOSE OF THE CROSS

Grace and peace to you from God our Father and the Lord Jesus Christ, who gave Himself for our sins to rescue us from the present evil age, according to the will of our God and Father (Gal. 1:3,4).

What are those special privileges and blessings that have been bought by the blood of His cross?

1. Christ died for us to purchase our freedom from sin. Titus 2:14 says, ...[Jesus] *gave Himself for us to redeem us from all wickedness and to purify for Himself a people that are His very own, eager to do what is good.* The precious blood of Jesus delivers us from all iniquity. Jesus sets us free!

2. Christ died for us to reconcile us to God. *For Christ died for sins once for all, the righteous for the unrighteous, to bring you to God* (1 Peter 3:18). We never could have known the infinite love and mercy of God had His Son not been sent to suffer and die for the ungodly. Jesus brings us to God!

3. Christ died for us to rescue us from this present evil world. As long as we are in the body, we shall be exposed to the influences and cross-currents of this present evil age. *The ways of this world...* [are] *at work in those who are disobedient* (Eph. 2:2). Christ died to save us from this poisonous atmosphere. One of the petitions of our Lord in His prayer of John 17:15 was, *"protect them from the evil one."* Think of the three Hebrews in the fiery furnace (Dan. 3). The ever-present cross is an ever-present protection from the evil of this world. We overcome by the Blood of the Lamb!

4. Christ died for us to be our Lord. ...*Christ died and returned to life so that He might be the Lord of both the dead and the living* (Rom. 14:9). He redeemed us by His blood that He might be Lord of our lives! What a privilege to belong to Him! If Christ is your Redeemer, then He also is your Lord. Only those alive unto God will own Him as their Lord! Those who die in their sins will confess Him as Lord at the throne of judgement. Philippians 2:11 says, ...*Every tongue* [will] *confess that Jesus Christ is Lord, to the glory of God the Father.*

Are you a blood-bought believer? Is your name recorded in the Lamb's book of life? Have you made reservations?

Read: Galatians 1:1-10

April 6   THREE APPEARINGS

The three appearings mentioned in Hebrews 9:24-28 give us three aspects of salvation.

1. The past: *...He has appeared once for all... to do away with sin by the sacrifice of Himself* (9:26b). Redemption for fallen man. He spanned the gap between fallen man and God. Christ died as a sacrifice for sin. He has reconciled a guilty world to God, and procured peace of conscience for the believer. The efficacy of the atonement extends over all the past. Its saving influence has been retrospective. The Old Testament saints lived under the shadow of Calvary. Christ's atonement has opened the door of mercy to the world. He is the propitiation for the whole world (1 John 2:2).

2. The present: *He entered heaven itself, now to appear for us in God's presence* (9:24b). He ascended into heaven as our eternal high priest. His presence in heaven is a perpetual and prevalent intercession. On the basis of His own finished work, He introduces each believer to the Father, and acts as an Advocate before the throne. He lifts up His nail-pierced hands and pleads for mercy for us. This has been a personal blessing for me. Christ, at the right hand of the Father, is making intercession for us (Heb. 7:24-25).

3. The future: *And He will appear a second time... to bring salvation to those who are waiting for Him* (9:28b). He will appear to bring salvation and to complete the redemption of His people.

At His first coming, He paid the ransom price for our redemption. At His second coming, He shall receive the final installment of His purchased possession. Our High Priest still tarries in the heavenlies, filling it with the fragrant incense of His intercession. Believers expect Him to come soon!

Are you looking for the appearing of the glory of our Great God and Saviour Jesus Christ? What attitude do you take in relation to His coming? Will He come to deliver you into everlasting life? Will you be ready when He comes? He appeared the first time to put away sin; He now appears in the presence of God for us; and He will appear the second time to complete our salvation. *...We wait for the blessed hope — the glorious appearing of our great God and Saviour, Jesus Christ* (Titus 2:13).

Read: Hebrews 9:24-28

April 7 THE OFFENSE OF THE CROSS

The Weymouth translation of 1 Corinthians 1:22-24 says, *The Jews demand miracles, and Greeks go in search of wisdom, while we proclaim a Christ who has been crucified, to the Jews a stumbling block, to the Greeks foolishness, but to those who have received the call, Christ the power of God and the wisdom of God.*

If we are faithful to the truth of God as revealed in the cross of Christ, it will be an offense and a stumbling block to those who are trying to be saved by their works. The cross of Christ can never be anything besides a stumbling stone in the way of those who refuse to be saved by grace alone.

Why is the cross of Christ a stumbling block? When the divine mystery of the cross of Christ is not understood, it is looked upon as a misfortune or a martyrdom. Some can be very religious and see nothing attractive in the cross of our Lord and Saviour. They rather shun it! It is an offense to them because there is no place for it in their heart and life. Many today would have a Christ without the cross; but the cross and the Christ, in the gracious purpose of God have been eternally nailed together. There is now no Christ but the Christ who was crucified. The cross of Christ is a stumbling block to those who are satisfied with a religious life. If we want to follow Him fully, we must be willing to be identified with Him.

To whom is the cross of Christ a stumbling block? Paul preached Christ crucified, to the Jews a stumbling block, to the Greeks foolishness. They are typical and representative classes. The first stands for religious works; the second for the worldly wise. Neither the proud religionist, nor the worldly wise can possibly pass the cross without being affected in some way by it. It knocks the feet from the legalist and pricks the bubble of the fleshly wise.

The cross of Christ is God's dynamic power in operation for the salvation of the world. It takes the power of God to save! The preaching of the cross is the power of God to those who believe.

> *A crossless Christ my Saviour could not be.*
> *A Christless cross, no refuge were for me.*
> *But, O, Christ crucified, I rest in Thee.*

Read: 1 Corinthians 1:20-24

99

April 8   CALVARY!

Read Luke 23:33-43.

1. Calvary was a place of guilt (vs. 33). The passerby counted possibly three crosses. He was numbered with the transgressors. We see the Redeemer dying *for* sin, one thief dying *to* sin and one thief dying *in* sin. ONE was not guilty! The other two were both guilty and both dying. One of these two is in heaven today. *He said, "Jesus, remember me when You come into Your kingdom." Jesus answered him, "...Today you will be with Me in paradise"* (Luke 23:42-43).

2. Calvary is a place of compassion (vs. 34). The seven sayings from the cross begin here. *"Father, forgive them, for they do not know what they are doing."* Today you and I have the forgiveness of sin.

3. Calvary was a place of derision (vs. 35) (confusion). Rulers derided (sneered) at Him: *"He saved others; let Him save Himself...."* Others, yes others — you and me! Cords of love bound Him to the cross and one strand was fastened to me.

4. Calvary was a place of testimony (vs. 38). Written in three languages, Aramaic, Latin and Greek, were the words: "THIS IS THE KING OF THE JEWS." Absolutely true! But it does reveal the natural enmity of the human heart (John 19:19-22).

5. Calvary was the place of salvation (vs. 42-43). The penitent thief's request is granted: *"Today you will be with Me in paradise."* Two things were not tied: His heart and His mouth. The word is, *That if you confess with your mouth, "Jesus is Lord," and believe in your heart that God raised Him from the dead, you will be saved* (Rom. 10:9-10).

6. Calvary is a place of death (1 Cor. 15:3-4). Christ died for our sins. He bore our sins in His body on the tree (1 Peter 2:24). In Adam we all die, in Christ we are made alive (1 Cor. 15:22).

Every time we hear the gospel, we are in our hearts honoring Him or dishonoring Him. We were born to make a decision! Have you decided to follow Jesus? Would you identify your life with His?

Kneel at the cross; Christ will meet you there.

April 9   GETHSEMANE

Today, we want to dwell with the Lord Jesus in Gethsemane. This was His last memorable visit to the garden. The saving interests of a dying world, and the eternal honor of His holy Name are now to be cast into the crucible.

1. Gethsemane was a place of solemn loneliness. He was withdrawn from His disciples about as far as you can throw a stone. The disciples were there sleeping in spite of the repeated command to "watch and pray." It was alone that the Saviour prayed in dark Gethsemane; yes, all alone.

2. Gethsemane was a place of prayerful resignation. This cup was enough to crush into nothing an ordinary mortal. Christ knew its terrible contents. He knew the holiness of God and the heinousness of sin. This was the hour of agonizing prayer. Our Lord's faith, patience and fidelity in the work He had undertaken was never put under a fiercer trial than while under the fiery darts of the wicked one in Gethsemane (Heb. 5:7).

3. Gethsemane causes us to reflect! Think of the cruel betrayal! Do we give Jesus the Judas kiss when we give Him the lips of profession and deny Him a heart of love? His was a heart of love! Even in this hour, He healed the cut off ear, the undoing of Peter's revenge. What self-forgetting love was His! What do we know about sacrifice? What do we know about agonizing prayer? Do we have the interests of a dying world in mind? Or are we troubled about ourselves?

Miss Amy Carmichael, a staunch veteran of the cross, said this: "We, who follow the Crucified, are not here to make a pleasant thing of life; we are called to suffering for the sake of a suffering sinful world. The Lord forgive us our shameful evasions and hesitations. His brow was crowned with thorns; do we seek rosebuds for our crowning? His hands were pierced with nails; are our hands ringed with jewels? His feet were bare and bound; do our feet walk delicately? What do we know of travail, of tears, of heart-break or being scorned?"

> *Lord, when I am weary with toiling,*
> *And burdensome seem Thy commands;*
> *If my load should lead to complaining,*
> *Lord, show me Your hands,*
> *Your nail-scarred hands, Your cross-torn hands.*
> *Saviour, show me Your hands.*

Read: Mark 14:32-41

The finished work on Calvary is very important! At Calvary, all humanity became divided. You are today either saved or lost, a believer or an unbeliever.

With three words, the Lord Jesus ended His work and suffering on the cross. He laid down His life. Through these words, the Saviour declared a truth so wonderful that Satan has tried ever since to hide it from mankind. Millions don't realize that salvation is a finished and complete work, and they are still striving to attain it. People do so many things to gain favour from God. They keep the golden rule, keep the commandments, go to church, get baptized, give to charity and so on. There is nothing wrong with these acts in themselves, but if we substitute them for the finished work on Calvary, then we err. Satan's way is DO. God's way is DONE. God's word says that works have no part in earning salvation.

When these three words were spoken at Calvary, all His sufferings were finished. He was rejected, criticized, scorned, mocked, threatened, misunderstood, despised, opposed, captured, bound, beaten, spat upon, slapped, abused, pierced with thorns on His head and nails in His hands. Christ suffered!

Prophecy was fulfilled and finished. All that had been foretold through the prophets had happened: Jesus' coming, His birthplace, His rejection and His death. Every detail of the Word was fulfilled. He had met the requirement of God to be the Saviour of men, He had made full atonement; nothing else was needed. The sin question was settled; you and I must settle the Son question. The gift of God is eternal life through Jesus Christ our Lord.

Religion is what man does for God; salvation is what God does for man. Religion says, "Something in my hand I bring;" salvation says, "Nothing in my hand I bring — simply to the cross I cling." Religion is trusting in a work we do; salvation is trusting in a work that has been done. Religion depends upon our behaving; salvation depends upon our believing. Religion says we must act our best; salvation says we must accept God's best. Religion depends on the sufficiency of character; salvation depends on the sacrifice of the cross. Religion is striving for a better attainment; salvation is secured through a perfect atonement.

Do you have religion or salvation? Trust the finished work of Christ.

Read: John 19:28-37

Man travels all over the world to visit the tombs of famous men: Washington's tomb in Mt. Vernon; Abraham Lincoln's tomb in Springfield, Illinois; Napoleon's tomb in France; King Tut's tomb in Egypt and those of many other kings, leaders and religious pillars. It is known that an Arab has one life-time goal: To make a pilgrimage to Mecca to see the tomb of the prophet Mohammed. Whenever you go to these tombs, you often see a sign that says, "Here lies the body of...." Did you ever realize that Christians have no place anywhere in the world, no tombstone or monument of any kind anywhere on the earth where it says, "Here lies the body of Jesus"? Christians have an empty tomb. Christ Jesus is not dead — He is alive!

There is resurrection assurance! The Bible declares, [Christ] *has risen* (Matt. 28:6). The Christ of the Scriptures must die, be buried and rise again. That Jesus was indeed the Christ was proven by His resurrection from the dead (Rom. 1:4). This is no myth, but a fact established by many infallible proofs (Acts 1:3).

There is resurrection hope! Upon this foundation, the resurrection of Christ, the Spirit-taught apostle builds the whole structure of the Christian faith. The death of Christ will avail us nothing if He is not risen and accepted by God in our behalf. He died for our sins, but He must also be raised and exalted at God's right hand in order for forgiveness to be preached in His name. If Christ be not raised, there is no hope for man.

There is a resurrection body! It will not be the same body sown in the grave (1 Cor. 15:37). It will be a God-given body, pleasing to Him (vs. 38). It will be an incorruptible body, incapable of death, disease or decay (vs. 42). It will be a body like unto His own glorious body; we shall be like Him (1 John 3:2). It will be a spiritual body! (1 Cor. 15:43-44).

There is a resurrection mystery! We will not all sleep, but we will all be changed; in a moment, in the twinkling of an eye, the dead shall be raised and we (those living at the time) shall be changed. What a glorious prospect! What cause for rejoicing! There is a resurrection song! The resurrection leads to a great incentive for all believers (1 Cor. 15:58).

The resurrection is a day of triumph. Because He lives, we too shall live!

Read: 1 Corinthians 15

103

April 12   RESURRECTION!

Easter is the greatest day on the Christian calendar! The resurrection is at the very heart of Christianity. It is not just something tacked on as an appendix to the faith. It is not just one part of Christianity that we take or leave. It is the very heart of Christianity. Without it, Christianity would not exist. Christianity would have no message if Christ had not risen. The resurrection is so essential that it became the very expression of the ultimate power and purpose of God.

With the Apostle Paul, the resurrection was the expression of his mission (1 Cor. 15). For him, the empty tomb was essential. Here is a man who spoke of a new life; a man who spoke of Christ as having the power to change lives. Paul's own life was a testimony to the power of the risen Christ.

Christmas speaks of a beginning, but Easter speaks of a fulfillment. Christmas made it possible for God to come to man, but Easter made it possible for man to go to God. I believe that the worship and the work of the church testify to the importance of Easter in the believer's life. Sunday worship commemorates the resurrection of Christ. We read, *...on the first day of the week.* Christian baptism shows forth the death, burial and resurrection of Christ (Rom. 6:3-6). The Lord's Supper commemorates the death and resurrection of Christ *...until He comes.* A Christian funeral speaks of life, hope, reunion and eternity with the Lord.

Through the experience of the resurrection, Jesus left the limitations of time and geography and became our eternal contemporary. He now lives! He is with us today in the person of the Holy Spirit. We have His promised presence! His love is evident, His will is revealed, His power is shared and His promise is, "I am with you always." The empty tomb makes all of this authentic and authoritative. I like things said in a nut-shell. Make it brief! Come to the point!

Read: 1 Corinthians 15:3-4 , 12-22 (Here it is in a nut-shell.)

April 13   THE RESURRECTION OF CHRIST

The resurrection of Christ is:

1. *The greatest fact of history* — Acts 1:3
2. *The greatest evidence of Christianity* — Romans 1:4
3. *The greatest exhibition of God's power* — Ephesians 1:18-20

4. *The greatest truth of the gospel* — 1 Corinthians 15:3-4
5. *The greatest reality of faith* — 1 Thessalonians 4:14
6. *The greatest assurance of coming glory* — 1 Cor. 15:20
7. *The greatest incentive to holiness* — Romans 6:9-12

How do I know that Christ is risen?
  What proof have I to give?
He touched my life one blessed day,
  And I began to live.

How do I know He left the tomb
  That Easter long ago?
I met Him just this morning,
  And my life is all aglow.

How do I know that endless life
  He gained that day for me?
His life within is proof enough
  Of immortality.

How do I know that Christ still lives,
  Rich blessings to impart?
I know it's true because He lives,
  And reigns within my heart.

Read: 1 John 5:12-13

April 14   BECAUSE HE LIVES!

An aged verger (a caretaker of a church building) of Winchester never tired of telling the story of how the news of Wellington's victory over Napoleon reached England.

News of the history-making battle came by a sailing vessel to the south coast and by a semaphore being wig-wagged overland toward London. (Semaphores are signals given by flags or lanterns). On top of Winchester Cathedral, the semaphore began to spell out the eagerly awaited message: "Wellington - defeated..." and then a dense fog settled oppressively over the land. The semaphore could no longer be seen, and the sad, heart-breaking news of the incomplete message went on to London: "Wellington - defeated." It was not long and the fog lifted, and again the signalling semaphore on top of the Cathedral became visible, spelling out the complete message of the battle: "Wellington - defeated - the - enemy." Now the message was all the more glorious because of the preceding gloom. Like a prairie fire, the joyful news spread across the land and lifted the spirits of the people to a plane of gratitude: "Wellington defeated the enemy!"

Long years ago on a lonely hill outside the city gate, the sinless Son of God gave Himself in a vicarious death upon a cruel cross for the sin of the world. Amos predicted the awesome scene as darkness covered the earth (Amos 8:9). Luke speaks of darkness about noon-time (Luke 23:44-45). As He died, the darkness deepened for His followers. To them, Calvary meant but one thing: "Jesus - defeated." During the three days of His entombment, things were dark and dismal. The three days dragged to their close, then suddenly the darkness lifted. The gloom-dispelling news turned to gladness on Easter Sunday morning. The glad news of Christ's resurrection dispelled the lingering fog of doubt and gloom from the hearts of Christ's disciples. He was alive!

The risen Christ is now seated at the right hand of the Father in heaven making intercession for us. He gives this victory-bringing invitation: *Let us then approach the throne of grace with confidence, so that we may receive mercy and find grace to help us in our time of need* (Heb. 4:16). He lives, death holds no fear for the believer (Ps. 23:4). He brought life and immortality to light through the gospel.

Is the living, loving Christ your Saviour?

Read: Matthew 28:1-10

April 15   THE ASCENSION OF CHRIST

The advent of Christ and the ascension of Christ complete the Christian calendar. Without the ascension, faith, discipleship and ministry are impoverished.

Four questions surface to relate the historical facts:

1. When did the ascension take place? (Acts 1:3). Forty days after the resurrection.

2. Where did the ascension take place? (Acts 1:12; Luke 24:50-53). In the vicinity of Bethany from Mount Olivet.

3. How did the ascension take place? (Acts 1:9). A cloud received Him up out of their sight. I would have enjoyed seeing this!

4. Why did the ascension take place? Several answers surface:

a. *Jesus, who went before us, has entered on our behalf. He has become a High Priest....* (Heb. 6:20). *...He entered the Most*

Holy Place once for all by His own blood, having obtained eternal redemption (Heb. 9:12). ...When [He] *offered for all time one sacrifice for sins, He sat down at the right hand of God* (Heb. 10:12). *He entered heaven itself... to appear for us in God's presence* (Heb. 9:24).

b. Jesus went to prepare a place for us (John 14:1-3). Is He building and paving streets? No, He is there interceding for us. Satan is accusing us before God daily (Rev. 12:10). Christ pleads our case and cause in the presence of a Holy God. He is our Advocate! For this I have been thankful throughout my Christian experience.

c. Jesus went so that He could send the Holy Spirit. *It is for your good that I am going away. Unless I go away the Counselor will not come to you; but if I go, I will send Him to you* (John 16:7). The Lord Jesus was limited on earth as a Person. He could not be everywhere, so He sent the Holy Spirit who could. The Holy Spirit would take the things of Christ and make them real to us. The Holy Spirit would also guide and teach us in the truth of the Word (John 16:13).

Is Jesus Christ real in your life?

Read: Luke 24:50-53; Acts 1:1-11

April 16   TAKE A BREAK

It's amazing what a cup of steaming hot tea can do for a tired individual. When things pile up and nerves begin to fray, put on the kettle, sit down and leisurely drink that hot cup of tea; it may help you to relax and rest. We have all had our souls drained, dried out and devastated at times. When the day is turbulent, when stress and perplexities mount up, where do you go?

What I am going to say is not new: You can have hope and assurance through reading the word of God; you can exchange distress for composure through quiet meditation. Coming to God in prayer can bring inner strength. Take time to sense His presence. Draw near! Heaven's resources are unlimited and never run dry.

Some of us remember the gasoline shortage days. When we pulled up to the pumps the attendant would say, "There's no more gas available, the pump is dry." Listen, God is available! God is also knowable! You can know Him through faith in Jesus Christ. For this, we should be deeply grateful. His resources never run dry! Every day we are faced with situations that call for His strength and sustaining grace.

Go with 2 Corinthians 12:9 today. God's grace is sufficient!

"God's grace keeps pace with whatever we face."

Read: Psalm 63:1-8

April 17   KEEP UP THE UPKEEP

Have you ever heard the slogan, "Keep up the upkeep"?

Maintenance is a big item today! We're always asking, "Does your furnace need repair? What does it cost to heat your home? Do the shingles on your roof need replacing? Is the siding in good condition? Will the paint last another year?"

Clothes, too, require constant upkeep — washing, ironing, dry-cleaning and mending. If one is to look neat and attractive, clothing needs careful maintenance.

Cars are a constant expense. Oil changes, grease jobs, wheel alignments, motor tune-ups are all required to keep the car running in good order. Maintenance is the word!

Let me quickly add, our spiritual lives need constant attention (maintenance), as well. As a pastor for many years, I've discovered that believers neglect their salvation (Heb. 2:3). Again, reading God's word and prayer are important! Fellowship with believers is important. I *need* the fellowship of believers in my life! So keep up the upkeep — the maintenance of your soul!

He who would maintain a strong character, free from the rust of monotony and the decay of carelessness, must be constantly active along helpful lines. To support that sentence sermon, read Titus 2:14; 3:8; 3:14.

Read: Hebrews 4:1-11

April 18   LOVE IS OLD

Brand new shoes are good, but old ones can be better, especially for walking, shopping or hiking. Old houses have a certain something that new ones don't; memories that give them a friendlier atmosphere. Maybe that's why antiques prove so fascinating to us. Old things seem to be surrounded with old dreams, old loves and old memories.

Here's where I want to bring in the thought of LOVE. Love is old too! It's as old as God Himself! ...*God is love* (1 John 4:8). Made in His image, we are capable of loving and being loved. One day Jesus said, *"Love one another"* (John 13:34). It's a new commandment, but it's old too. About those words, "Love one another," a little girl is to have said, "I am one, you are another." Let me list a few things about love:

LOVE IS...

Slow to suspect — quick to trust,
Slow to condemn — quick to justify,
Slow to offend — quick to defend,
Slow to expose — quick to shield,
Slow to reprimand — quick to forbear,
Slow to belittle — quick to appreciate,
Slow to demand — quick to give,
Slow to provoke — quick to help,
Slow to resent — quick to forgive.

—Author unknown

Love makes the world go round smoothly!

Read: 1 Corinthians 13 — the greatest is Love!

April 19 TIRED OF DOING GOOD?

Do you ever get tired of eating? You'd think people would, seeing they do it three times a day, every day. That's 1,095 meals a year, and 10,950 meals in ten years. It's strange that we never get tired of food, even when we eat the *same* foods for 20 to 50 years or more. For example — potatoes. How many times have you eaten potatoes in some form or another during your lifetime?

Listen! Likewise, we should not get tired of "doing good." The Bible says, *Let us not become weary in doing good* (Gal. 6:9). This includes loving others and serving sacrificially. I read something the other day that made me think. It said, "Ten rules for getting rid of the blues." Are you ready for the answer? "Go out and do something for someone else, and repeat it nine times." Your inspiration may well come to you as you do something for someone else. When you are good to others, you are always best to yourself.

"I shall pass through this world but once. Any good, therefore, that I can do, or any kindness that I can show to any human being, let me do it now. Let me not defer or neglect it, for I shall not pass this way again" (author unknown).

Let me add the words of John Wesley: "Do all the good you can, by all the means you can, in all the ways you can, in all the places you can, at all the times you can, to all the people you can, as long as ever you can." Never get tired of doing good!

Read: Romans 2:9-13; Galatians 6:9; Colossians 3:24

April 20   PATIENCE!

Our inspiration today has its roots in the thought of patience. Often you've heard it said, "Patience is a virtue." John Dewey said, "The most useful virtue is patience."

It's part of a homemaker's work to replace buttons. We all know that the washing machine is responsible for taking some buttons off. Many are pulled off because Nathan or James does not take time to unbutton his clothes. In haste and impatience, the garment is given a yank and off pop the buttons.

Patience is the ability to idle your motor when you feel like stripping the gears. We may smile at the following poem:

Patience is a virtue, possess it if you can,
Seldom in a woman, never in a man.

It takes patience to get along with people. We are all different, but we must be patient — with children, with parents, with friends, with administrators, with employees, with store clerks and even with ourselves. We can be so impatient!

"For this I have Jesus" were the words on our fridge for a long time. Again, I have to say, "I need Another in my life to help me to be patient with people."

I like the words in Luke 21:19 (KJV): *In your patience possess ye your souls.* Lord, help me to be patient!

Read: Luke 21:19; Romans 5:1-5; 1 Thessalonians 1:4

April 21   THE MASTER'S MANUAL

Did you ever have trouble with a product that others had no problem with, and you wondered why? Finally somebody asked, "Did you read the directions?" You hadn't, but you do, and the problem is solved. Directions are helpful!

The directions we need in our material world are almost always necessary. The directions we need in our spiritual life are *always* necessary. Having a spiritual sense of direction is very important. If we read God's word with an open mind, ask for God's guidance and seek to know Him and His will, we can receive help and direction. So many times we need counsel, comfort and even correction. I would encourage you to be informed, be instructed and be inspired.

The Psalmist says it best: *I have hidden Your word in my heart that I might not sin against You* (Ps. 119:11). The Word keeps us from sin. The Word becomes the GOVERNMENT OF GOD. It governs my life!

Your word is a lamp to my feet and a light for my path (Ps. 119:105). The Word is a light to follow. The Word becomes the GUIDANCE OF GOD. It's a path to walk on!

I rejoice in Your promise [word] *like one who finds great spoil* (Ps. 119:162). The Word brings joy into my life! The Word becomes the GLADNESS OF GOD. It is a delight to read!

If you lose a sense of meaning and direction in life, read the MASTER'S MANUAL. We have a choice to make.

Read: Psalm 119:1-8

April 22   COMPASSION

There are various ways of stretching ground beef. This "know how" comes in handy when you're on a small budget or when company drops in unexpectedly. It doesn't take much meat to make goulash or a nice casserole. You may be thinking about Hamburger Helper. A little ground beef goes a long way.

Something else will go a long way! A little compassion will go a long way towards making life happier for others. All around us are people who are in need. Many are yearning for a compassionate word, a sympathetic look or a helping hand.

Several times in the gospels, we read of Jesus, who was moved with compassion. His great heart of love reached out to people with deep need. We ought to feel this Christ-like compassion towards others today. H.W. Beecher said, "Compassion will cure more sins than condemnation."

The well-known story of the Good Samaritan suggests three attitudes that are relevant:

1. The robber says, "What's yours is mine — I'll take it."
2. The Priest and Levite say, "What's mine is mine—I'll keep it."
3. The Samaritan says, "What's mine is yours — I'll share it."

The man who showed compassion is the example to follow. A little compassion goes a long way!

Read: Matthew 9:36; 14:14; 15:32; 20:34;
1 Peter 3:8; Luke 10:25-37

April 23   CLOSED FOR THE SEASON

With the passing of summer, days become cooler and autumn days glide into winter. As the tourist trade diminishes, "CLOSED FOR THE SEASON" signs appear in many places. Novelty shops, fruitstands, motels and even some business establishments put them up. They may add, "See you in spring." That's how things go with the passing seasons.

Aren't you glad the Lord never "CLOSES UP SHOP"? The doors to His kingdom are always open. His "WELCOME" mat is never withdrawn. In fact, the Bible shows us His hands being stretched out to all who pass by. Psalm 136 declares with repetition, *His love endures forever.* He is available day and night and is never "CLOSED FOR THE SEASON."

His eyes are open to my needs; His ears are open to my cries and His arms are outstretched for me to come to Him. He knows all about me. He hears me. He sees me. He understands me. He knows my thoughts. We are never out of His thoughts. He is never "CLOSED FOR THE SEASON!"

Come to Him in a prayer today — Psalm 139:23,24.

Read: Psalm 139

April 24   ABRAHAM, A TYPE OF THE FATHER

He who did not spare His own Son, but gave Him up for us all — how will He not also, along with Him, graciously give us all things? (Rom. 8:32).

I am sure there is an allusion to Abraham in this verse. In Christ, God gave us everything! Let me suggest briefly at least eight ways in which we can see Abraham as a type of the Father.

1. In the uniqueness of his love for Isaac. We are aware of the circumstances connected to the promise of a son. Isaac was the object of Abraham's special love. *"Isaac, whom you love"* are the words God spoke (Gen. 22:2).

2. In the costliness of his sacrifice. *"Take your son...* [and] *sacrifice him...."* Costly! The son of his old age, in whom lay all the hope of the divine promise.

3. In his readiness to make the sacrifice. There is no hesitation on Abraham's part. Abraham got up and went, even though this strange request contradicted all he knew about God.

4. In his preparation and foresight. The wood, the fire and the knife; the three day journey, with that lump in his throat; the sight of the place in the distance. So Calvary was seen afar off, divinely prepared *before the creation of the world* (Eph. 1:4).

5. In his intense suffering. How gladly Abraham would have given anything, even his own life. We can only imagine what was in his heart and on his mind. So it was with the Father at Calvary!

6. In that his sacrifice revealed his heart. [Abraham] *believed the Lord* (Gen. 15:6). We see his supreme love for God! At Calvary we see the supreme unveiling of the heart of God. *This is how God showed His love among us: He sent His One and only Son into the world that we might live through Him* (1 John 4:9).

7. In that his sacrifice was in response to a call. The voice of God called Abraham to make the sacrifice. A divine necessity! Abraham was led to the highest height of faith and fellowship. Our heavenly Father gives in response to a call — the call of human need. We need a Saviour! The Lord will provide — Jehovah Jireh!

8. In that his sacrifice had wonderful results. Abraham received his son! The blessing continued, *"...and all nations on earth will be blessed, because you have obeyed me"* (Gen. 22:18).

When we think of Jesus, God's Son, think of the results: *...Bringing many sons to glory* (Heb. 2:10). When we get to Revelation 7:9-12, it's a number no one can number. God spared not His Son! Abraham spared not his son!

Read: Genesis 2:1-19

April 25   BIBLE INVITATIONS

From my Vacation Bible School days, these invitations were used for an opening exercise, as well as for an invocation at an evangelistic week at the Chapel in Orillia:

1. *Come to me; hear me, that your soul may live* (Isa. 55:1-3). Incline your ear! Put your hand to your ear! Man lost his spiritual life by listening to the Tempter's voice. We get life again by listening to the voice of God.

2. *Come and see!* (John 1:43-49). Philip said, *We have found Him....* Nathaniel had one interview with Christ and his skepticism was gone. We need to come into personal contact with Jesus Christ.

3. *Come and drink* (Isa. 55:1; John 7:37). *If any man...* It's not a select few. People are thirsting for satisfaction. Thank the Lord God for the well of salvation (Isa. 12). With joy you may draw from the well. Spiritually-speaking, you will never thirst again.

4. *Come and dine* (John 21:9-13). Are you hungry? He can give you your daily bread. He fed Israel in the wilderness for forty years with angel's food — manna from heaven! Jesus is the Bread of Life.

5. *Come and rest* (Matt. 11:28-30). Restlessness is all over the world today. Where can we find rest? There is no peace for the wicked. This rest is not for sale. Jesus said, *"I will give you rest."* Every weary soul may have rest.

6. *Come and reason* (Isa. 1:18). Verses 16 and 17 precede this invitation. When we repent, He will reason. When we cease to rebel, He will reason. The moment you are willing to forsake your sin, God will meet you in grace. He offers peace and pardon.

7. *Come to the marriage* (Matt. 22:1-10). Who wouldn't feel honoured by a great wedding invitation! You would want all your friends to know. This is a real invitation! The feast has been prepared at great cost. It cost God His Son! Will you come?

8. *Come, inherit the kingdom* (Matt. 25:34). Think of a poor man possessing a kingdom. This is not fiction! This is real! There is an inheritance! It's reserved in heaven for you (1Peter 1:4). The word is, *Seek first His kingdom* (Matt. 6:33).

9. *Come up hither* (Rev. 11:12). The two witnesses are called up into heaven. These are end times. We are to lift up our heads for our redemption is drawing near. The Church is waiting! One day when the trumpet sounds, we'll be caught up to meet the Lord.

10. *Whosoever will, may come* (Rev. 22:17). One day, God said to Noah, "Come, you and your family into the ark." That is what he did. You have a choice to make. You may accept the invitation or you may reject it.

The choice is yours! Why not say, "I will!"

April 26   REMEDIES FOR STRAIN

Our choice of attitudes is so important! Our minds need fuel to feed on. Our inspiration has its roots in Philippians 4:8. Here is some good advice; let your mind dwell on six specific things:

1. On things that are true — not unreal, far-fetched dreams, but things that are real and valid.

2. On things that are honorable — not cheap, flippant, and superficial, but things worthy of respect.

3. On things that are right — not critical, negative, unjust and wrong.

4. On things that are pure — not carnal, smutty and obscene, but wholesome and clean.

5. On things that are lovely — not argumentative and defensive, but agreeable, attractive and winsome.

6. On things of good report — not slander, gossip and put-downs, but things that build up, encourage and lift.

Think on these things!

From the above passage, something additional:

TEN REMEDIES FOR STRAIN — Philippians 4:1-13

1. Stand firm in the Lord (vs. 1)
2. Work in harmony in the Lord (vs. 2) — *agree... in the Lord*
3. Rejoice in the Lord always (vs. 4)
4. Do not be anxious about anything (vs. 6) — *pray*
5. Let the peace of God guard your heart and mind (vs. 7)
6. Set your mind on good things (vs. 8) — *think*
7. Practice what you have learned from fellow believers (vs. 9)
8. Learn to be content (vs. 11)
9. Face all circumstances and situations (vs. 12) — *do not run*
10. Do everything through Christ who gives you strength (vs. 13)

April 27   THE WORLD IS MINE

I am always amazed at how poetry gives expression to the deep-felt needs of people. I would suppose that they were written out of some real-life experience. Dr. Tennyson Guyer has written the following:

Today upon a bus I saw a girl with golden hair;
She seemed so glad, I envied her, and wished that I were half so fair;
I watched her as she rose to leave, and saw her hobble down the aisle.
She had one leg and wore a crutch, but as she passed — a smile.
Oh, God, forgive me when I whine;
I have two legs — the world is mine.

Later on, I bought some sweets. The boy who sold them had such charm,
I thought I'd stop and talk awhile. If I were late, 'twould do no harm.
And as we talked he said, "Thank you, sir, you've really been so kind.
It's nice to talk to folks like you because, you see, I'm blind."
Oh, God, forgive me when I whine;
I have two eyes — the world is mine.

Later, walking down the street, I met a boy with eyes so blue.
But he stood & watched the others play; it seemed he knew not what to do.
I paused, and then I said, "Why don't you join the others, dear?"
But he looked straight ahead without a word, & then I knew, he couldn't hear.
Oh, God, forgive me when I whine;
I have two ears — the world is mine.

Two legs to take me where I go,
Two eyes to see the sunset glow,
Two ears to hear all I should know,
Oh, God, forgive me when I whine;
I'm blest, indeed, the world is mine.

Let me add these lines in keeping with the above:

Whenever you are discontented with the life you lead,
Just take the time to look around and to my phrases heed.
You'll find that you are better off than many others who
Must struggle up the road of life the self-same way as you.
Although your cross seems heavy there is no need to frown
For others carry so much more beneath their troubled crown.

Read: 2 Corinthians 2:7-10
I grumbled because I had no shoes until I met a man who had no feet.

April 28   GOSPEL ACCORDING TO YOU

Envision three boys selling apples at a train station while people are waiting to board the train. Someone asks, "Johnny, why is it that you always sell more apples than the rest? What's your secret?" "Well," replies Johnny, "I just polish an apple till it shines good and bright, and then I bite into it and let the juice run down my chin. The passengers see for themselves what good apples I have and they want to buy them."

The greatest advertisement of the gospel of Jesus Christ is found in the lives of Christians who exemplify, in their daily lives, the love, joy, humility, integrity, generosity, unselfishness, courage, faith and hope they have within. Like juicy apples, Christianity speaks for itself. As Johnny said, "Let them see for themselves."

> *There's a sweet old story translated for men,*
> *But writ in the long, long ago*
> *The Gospel according to Mark, Luke and John —*
> *Of Christ and His mission below.*
>
> *Men read and admire the Gospel of Christ,*
> *With its love so unfailing and true.*
> *But what do they say, and what do they think,*
> *Of the gospel "according to you"?*
>
> *'Tis a wonderful story, that gospel of love,*
> *As it shines in the Christ-life divine;*
> *And, oh, that its truth might be told again*
> *In the story of your life and mine!*
>
> *Unselfishness mirrors in every scene;*
> *Love blossoms on every sod;*
> *And back from its vision the heart comes to tell*
> *The wonderful goodness of God.*
>
> *You are writing each day a letter to men;*
> *Take care that the writing is true;*
> *'Tis the only gospel that some men will read —*
> *That gospel according to you.*

— Author unknown.

Read: Matthew 5:13-16

April 29 WATCH ME — FOOTPRINTS IN THE SAND

Children love the attention of their parents. "Watch me," a tiny tot insists. If mommy or daddy is not watching, they'll come and turn your head toward them. They want you to watch. Children also want to be watched when they run outside in the dark to bring in a toy or something left in the yard.

117

All of us need comfort — the comfort that our Heavenly Father is watching. *From heaven the LORD looks down and sees all mankind; from His dwelling place He watches....* (Ps. 33:13,14). Every activity is noted, everything that happens to us is known. He realizes our many limitations and infirmities. He knows about the daily burdens, the trying circumstances, the monotonous tasks and the overwhelming problems that confront us continually. He knows! He sees! He cares!

FOOTPRINTS

One night I dreamed a dream.
I was walking along the beach with my Lord.
Across the dark sky flashed scenes from my life.
For each scene, I noticed two sets of footprints in the sand,
one belonging to me, and one to my Lord.
When the last scene of my life shot before me
I looked back at the footprints in the sand.
There was only one set of footprints.
I realized that this was at the lowest and saddest times of my life.
This always bothered me
and I questioned the Lord about my dilemma.
"Lord, You told me when I decided to follow You,
You would walk and talk with me all the way.
But I'm aware that during the most troublesome times of my life
there is only one set of footprints.
I just don't understand why, when I needed You most,
You leave me."
He whispered, "My precious child,
I love you and will never leave you,
never, ever, during your trials and testings.
When you saw only one set of footprints
it was then that I carried you."

(Copyright © 1964 by Margaret Fishback Powers)

Read: Psalm 139

April 30   **LOOKING UP!**

When you go to certain homes, you'll see mottos on the wall in certain rooms. I like mottos, they are good reminders. One nicely embroidered motto that I've seen said, "KEEP LOOKING UP."

That motto became very important to a man once when he was lost on a lake. In his distress, he began to pray "looking up". A star caught his eye, and with his eye on that star he rowed his boat home.

This idea of "looking up" is mentioned and even taught in the Scriptures (Ps. 121). *Look and live* was the word to Israel in Numbers 21:4-9.

An unknown author has written:

> *If you want to be*
> *Distressed, look within;*
> *Defeated, look back;*
> *Distracted, look around;*
> *Dismayed, look ahead;*
> *Delighted, look up;*
> *Delivered, look to Christ.*

Jesus is the source of strength, encouragement and delight. Looking unto Jesus, the Author and Finisher of our faith, is the good word in Hebrews 12:2.

> *Turn your eyes upon Jesus,*
> *Look full in His wonderful face;*
> *And the things of earth will grow strangely dim;*
> *In the light of His glory and grace.*

— Helen H. Lemmel

Read: Psalm 121

May 1   SHARE YOUR COURAGE

Robert Louis Stevenson said, "Keep your fears to yourself, but share your courage." I like that! We all need courage and we all need to share our courage with others. We need the courage of convictions, the courage to stand up for what is right and the courage to face unpleasant situations.

Bible characters come to my mind very quickly. Daniel was courageous in his prayer life (Dan. 6:10). He was courageous in the lion's den (Dan. 6:22). God was with him! Shadrach, Meshach and Abednego were courageous in the fiery furnace (Dan. 3). They would not bow, they would not budge and they would not burn. David was courageous in facing Goliath (1 Sam. 17). The size of the giant did not dismay him. Esther was courageous and risked her life for her people. Stephen was courageous while facing death by stoning (Acts 7). Peter and John were courageous when thrown into prison (Acts 4).

These men and women trusted God! How often God has spoken in His Word, *Be strong and courageous* (Deut. 31:7). My motto for 1984 was, *He goes before in '84. He is mine in '89.*

Wm. Cowper writes:

> *Ye fearful saints, fresh courage take,*
> *The clouds ye so much dread*
> *Are big with mercy and shall break*
> *With blessings on your head.*

Read: Joshua 1

May 2   TRUST

Have you ever thought about how trusting we are? We trust our lives to the hands of a doctor. We trust our children to nurses in the hospital. We drive on our highways and trust other drivers. We trust our life savings to people in the bank. Every day we are trusting people for the safety of our lives, our loved ones and our possessions.

Now here is the question: Why are we so reluctant to trust the Lord? Why do we find it so difficult to believe in Him? Why do we hesitate to take Him at His word?

I want you to know that I am glad I am learning to trust Him. He is my Saviour! Thousands down through history have trusted Jesus Christ, and they have not been disappointed.

Proverbs 3:5-6 says, *Trust in the Lord with all your heart and lean not on your own understanding; in all your ways acknowledge Him, and He will make your path straight* [or direct your path.]. From this passage, I share the following homily:

1. Trust in the Lord — that's the *object* of our trust

2. With all your heart — that's the *measure* of our trust

3. Lean not on your own understanding — that's the *warning*

4. In all your ways — that's the *occasion* of our trust

5. He will direct your paths — that's the *promise*

Implicit trust brings infallible guidance!

Trust, lean and acknowledge — that's my part. Directing our path — that's God's part.

Go today with Psalm 40:4: *Blessed is the man who makes the LORD his trust.*

Read: Psalm 40; Proverbs 3:1-8

May 3   **FORGIVENESS**

All of us enjoy an early morning sunrise — the sun rising slowly from the other side of the world, pushing back the dawn to give us a new day. A new beginning! What a comforting thought!

Each morning, we have the privilege of beginning afresh. This is our opportunity to do better than we did yesterday. So often we make mistakes. In our weak moments, we give less than our best. We mess things up in our relationships with others. We sin, we stray and we become discouraged.

We need forgiveness! It can restore a broken relationship.

Forgiveness is man's deepest need and highest achievement.

— H. Bushnell

He who cannot forgive others breaks the bridge over which he must pass himself.   — George Herbert

The Christian life involves forgiveness. There was a day in my life when I accepted the forgiveness of God. Today I rejoice at the words spoken by David: *Blessed is he whose transgressions are forgiven, whose sins are covered* (Ps. 32:1). Every day can be a new beginning. The slate can be wiped clean. [God's] *compassions never fail. They are new every morning* (Lam. 3:22-24).

Read: Psalm 32; Psalm 51. He who forgives ends a quarrel!

May 4 — A GOOD EAR!

Have you got a good ear?

A mother usually has a good ear. Her ear is constantly tuned for the cry of her child. She listens for the tiniest whimper in the middle of the night. A mechanic's ear is tuned to the sound of a motor, and he's not satisfied until the motor runs smoothly. A music teacher's ear is tuned to hear chords and harmonies.

We could go on and on to say things about hearing. A workman tunes his ears for the noon whistle; a child never fails to hear the recess bell at school.

How are your ears tuned? Do you hear only the pessimistic side of everything or do you hear the sounds of optimism? Do you hear the sounds of happiness and joy around you? Are we open to hear the notes of cheer, of hope and of faith? Are we open to the voice of God?

David's prayer would be good for us today: *Let me hear joy and gladness* (Ps. 51:8).

Read: Matthew 13:1-9; 18-23

DIVINE SERVICE

In a kitchen somewhere in Scotland, I understand there is a motto carved in wood by a kitchen sink that says, "DIVINE SERVICE DONE HERE THREE TIMES A DAY." "Just a minute," you say, "You mean washing dishes, keeping the house, sweeping the floors, ironing clothes and wiping runny noses are divine tasks?" Yes, they are. God has not despised the day of little things (Zech. 4:10). It isn't the the size or the glamour of the tasks that counts, it's our willingness and our attitude. The word is, "Whatsoever you do, do it heartily as unto the Lord." A cup of cold water given in the name of Jesus shall not go unrewarded (Mark 9:41). Peeling potatoes and sweeping walks can be glamorous tasks done in the spirit of service. So, if you are at home today with a lot of little things to do, think of the motto, "DIVINE SERVICE DONE HERE THREE TIMES A DAY." That tells me I had something to eat today and I should be grateful.

Read: John 13:1-16

May 5   WHEELBARROWS AND BURDENS

We don't buy wheelbarrows for their looks, but for their usefulness. Once in a while, we may see them on front lawns filled with flowers to decorate the yard, but for the most part, a wheelbarrow is used to carry burdens — heavy loads like cement, sand, dirt and whatever. Wheelbarrows and Christians have something in common. We are called to *carry each other's burdens* (Gal. 6:2).

It is so easy to overlook the troubles of our neighbors. We fail to sympathize with the fellow next door. There are burdens we can help to bear. A word of cheer, comfort and encouragement can really lighten the load. Acts of love would be so helpful! How about praying for someone today? It is said, "A praying man can never be a useless man." Have a good day!

Read: Galatians 6:1-10

WORDS

It's fun to read humorous signs in different stores. Have you ever read this one: "Even a fish wouldn't get into trouble if she kept her mouth shut"? Here is another: "The reason a dog has so many friends is because she wags her tail instead of her tongue." Do these lines tell the truth? Whether we like to admit it or not, much of our trouble is of our own making — with words. Another sign I read in a barber shop once: "Lord, help me to keep my big mouth shut until I know what I'm talking about, and sometimes even then."

A careless word may kindle strife. A cruel word may wreck a life. A brutal word may smite and kill. A gracious word may smooth the way. A joyous word may light the day. A timely word may lessen stress. A loving word may heal and bless.

There is a beautiful prayer in Psalm 141:3: *Set a guard over my mouth, O LORD; keep watch over the door of my lips.*

Read: Matthew 12:36,37; Psalm 39:1-13

May 6   FORGETFUL/RETURN

There is one thing everyone has in common — bills. Each month the postman brings them. They remind us that there is something we owe. It is almost impossible to forget that we have debts. The mail reminds us. The postman doesn't let us forget.

This reminded me that we often forget the Lord. With our temporal demands and the pace of living today, we forget or even neglect the spiritual dimension of living. Our faith gets weak and flabby. Then God, in His mercy, may remind us, often through a series of frustrations or trials, to look to Him for fellowship, strength and support. Someone wrote a prayer and said, "Remind me always to depend on You, Lord, for strength and support." The hymn writer, W.W. Walford says in "Sweet Hour of Prayer,"

In seasons of distress and grief,
My soul has often found relief;
And oft escaped the tempter's snare,
By thy return, sweet hour of prayer.

"Return" is the call of God to His people over and over again in Deuteronomy 30:1-3. Returning brought blessing in 2 Chronicles 6:36-39. Return in repentance and you will find rest says Isaiah 30:15. ...*The LORD longs to be gracious... and show you compassion* (Isa. 30:18). John the Baptist, Jesus and the Apostles called people to repent and return (Matt. 3:1,2; 24:17; Acts 2:38). If you ever forget, there is room to return!

Read: Deuteronomy 6:4-12; 8:11,14,19; 32:18

May 7   THE "D's" FOR PARENTS

1. Children deserve to be desired. Unwanted children hurt! Children want to be accepted for who they are. Boy *or* girl! Parents should never say to their children, "I wish you were a boy instead of a girl," or vice versa.

2. Children deserve the devotion of their parents. Affection and devotion are necessary for the well-being of our children. As sunshine is to the plant, so is love to children.

3. Children deserve the discipline of their parents. Disciple your children! Lead them to Jesus! Teach your children! *Discipline your son, for in that there is hope; do not be a willing party to his death* (Prov. 19:18). *These commandments that I give you today are to be upon your hearts. Impress them on your children. Talk about them when you sit at home and when you walk along the road, when you lie down and when you get up* (Deut. 6:6-7).

4. Children deserve to be developed (Prov. 22:6). We need to meet the needs of our children mentally, socially, physically and spiritually. We need to support them in their education, their choice of friends and their worship.

5. Children deserve the defence of their parents. This involves practical integrity and the practice of godly principles. Example is always best! Living by example, loving by demonstration and listening. Listen to your children! Model your faith! Give them an example to follow and you will defend your children.

6. Children deserve to be dedicated to the Lord. Children are teachable, trusting and tender. Children are a reward in what they are, in what they do and in what they become. Children are the gift of God. Children need a God-centred home!

God is the Founder, Defender and Preserver of the Family! The hymn writer says, "God give us Christian homes."

Read: Psalm 127

On a tombstone in Butler's Burying Ground in Niagara-on-the-Lake, are these words:

> *My dear children, think on God and His commandments*
> *And He will think on you;*
> *Observe your youth, don't lose no time,*
> *Lest God should take you in your prime.*
> *Therefore, in time, serve God above*
> *And in this world, fix not your love.*

May 8 MOTHER'S KISSES FOR BRUISES

Children are amusing! When they fall and bruise a knee or scratch an arm, how quickly they run to Mother. As soon as she has kissed the injured spot, the pain vanishes and the tears stop falling. Then the child skips away to play. What healing and consolation is found in a mother's kiss! How valuable! A.B. Alcott said, *Where there is a mother in the home, matters speed well.*

Where do you go when there are burdens and bruises, when everything goes wrong, when life is difficult and the pain shows on your face? Where do you go? I know there are some who indulge in self-pity. Others, I know, find their consolation in prayer. I'd like to suggest the practice of the closet prayer time which is mentioned in Matthew 6:5. In the secret closet, you'll find comfort, courage, strength and sustaining grace. There you can bring your injuries to Him in prayer, like the child whose bruises have been healed by a mother's kiss.

Most of us know the hymn, "What a Friend we have in Jesus." I choose these lines for today:

O, what peace we often forfeit, O, what needless pain we bear,
All because we do not carry everything to God in prayer.

— Joseph Scriven

The invitation to come still stands! Go with Matthew 11:28-30!

F.B. Meyer said, "Even the faintest whisper is like drumbeats in the ears of our God."

The secret of prayer is prayer in secret!

Read: Matthew 6:6-13

May 9   MOM'S HOME!

Memories are a wonderful thing!

Memories are engraved early in life. I suppose I'm speaking mainly to mothers today. Mothers, you are important! Your thoughtfulness is engraved on your children.

Take yourself back: A fire glowed in the big kitchen stove, a plate of hot buttered toast greeted you as you tossed your school books on the floor. Just bread toasted to a golden brown? NO, much more than that — Mom was home. Mom was home and watching for you as you rounded the corner of the street or jumped off the school bus. Mom was home and ready to hear the stories of your day while they were fresh on your mind. And she listened!

Contrast that with the poor children in many homes today — poor because their mothers are not at home. A child dawdles home in no hurry at all. Why? Because nobody is home anyway. Sadly, the film of childhood cannot be rewound for a second run. Good memories require time, unselfishness and understanding, but they are worth it! What kind of memories will warm the hearts of your children? Think of your delight in later years when your son and daughter recall, "Mom, it was great coming home from school! You were there! I saw you ironing in the front window."

Ironing or warm toast, they spell the same: MOM'S HOME! Mother had time to teach us to sing, to pray, and to listen. Later, we came to know the Saviour she loved and served at home. If God has given you a family, then yours is the greatest task in the world. Greater than making the national laws or ruling somewhere. As the home, so goes the nation. *Take* your children to Sunday School and church, don't *send* them. Be an example; it will pay big dividends in fruitful memories and fruitful lives.

Read: Proverbs 31:10-31

May 10   MOTHER

Someone has said, "The three greatest words in the English language are "mother," "home" and "heaven."

On Mother's Day, we honour our mothers! The word "mother" should bring back memories. One of my favorite poems is:

MY ALTAR

I have worshiped in churches and chapels,
I've prayed in the busy street,
I have sought my God and found Him
Where the waves of His ocean beat;
I have knelt in the silent forest,
In the shade of some ancient tree,
But the dearest of all my altars
Was raised at my Mother's knee.

I have listened to God in His temple,
I've caught His voice in the crowd,
I have heard Him speak where the breakers
Were booming long and loud;
When the winds played soft in the tree tops,
My Father has talked to me,
But I never heard Him clearer
Than I did at my Mother's knee.

Somehow we know that our Mothers' prayers follow us! Today we should embrace the latter part of Proverbs 1:8: *...Do not forsake your mother's teaching.*

Read: Proverbs 1:1-19

May 11   BELIEVE AND PRAY

What a marvelous subject for an artist to paint: An old woman with silvered hair, hot tears flowing down her cheeks, her worn hands busy over a washboard in a room of poverty — praying!

Praying for her son, John; John, who ran away from home in his teen years to become a sailor; John, who, it was now reported, had become a very wicked man. His mother was praying that her son might be of service to God. Again, what a marvelous subject for an artist's brush! A mother, her tears and a wash-board.

This mother believed in two things: The power of prayer, and the reformation of her son. While she scrubbed, she continued to pray. Perhaps the words of the Saviour, *"Only believe,"* inspired her. And God answered her prayer by working a miracle in the heart of John Newton. The black stains of sin were washed white in the blood of the Lamb. Oh, the chemistry of God! *"Though your sins are like scarlet, they shall be as white as snow,"* says the Lord.

The wash-tub prayers were heard! John Newton, the drunken sailor, became John Newton, the sailor-preacher, the author of the hymn "Amazing Grace." His life touched other lives. Among them was Thomas Scott, who used both his pen and his voice to lead many unbelieving hearts to Christ; among them was William Cowper, who wrote, "There is a fountain filled with blood, drawn from Immanuel's veins; and sinners, plunged beneath that flood, lose all their guilty stains." This song has brought many to Jesus, who died on Calvary. Because of the wash-tub prayers, the chain of events continued. Many a life was influenced for good. William Wilberforce, the great Christian statesman, unfastened the shackles of thousands of British slaves. All this resulted because a mother took God at His word and prayed that her son's heart might become as white as the soap-suds in the wash-tub.

Concerned parents may be encouraged today. Pray for your children! The good word today is "Believe and Pray!"

Read: 1 Thessalonians 5:16-24

May 12   **MOTHER!**

We all have the best mother! On this point, there is no room for argument. Although we cannot trace Proverbs 31:10-31 to one particular woman, we no doubt have a very high standard — an ideal mother. Inspiration was needed to paint this portrait. The standards are high, but we are to reach out to them. Let's look at this portrait of a mother:

1. Her price — Inestimable! Her worth is far above jewels, more valuable than precious stones. Her worth cannot be estimated by any material object, however costly. Her price? There is no price!

2. Her pursuit — His best interest! The interest of her husband is her interest. She will do him good. She is not wasteful in good times or in bad times. She works willingly at domestic affairs. She is a real homemaker and she finds pleasure in doing it. She enjoys her work. Her presence of mind speaks of industry. She is industrious and she plans while she works. She thinks and acts with prudence and discretion. She is satisfied to work, knowing that work around the house is legitimate and healthy. See in all these verses, the expression of energy. She knows how to meet the needs of the poor, the needs of the family and her own personal needs. Remember when mother would send a package for those in the neighborhood. Remember how she sensed the needs of others. She also advanced the reputation of her husband. She advanced his interests and increased his influence. That was her pleasure.

3. Her praise — Influential! The law of love and kindness are regulated by love in the heart. She opens her mouth in wisdom and the teaching of kindness is on her tongue. The things she talks about make sense. She looks well to the ways of her household.

4. Her power — Inspirational! *Charm is deceptive, and beauty is fleeting; but a woman who fears the Lord is to be praised* (Prov. 31:30). The foundation of all excellence is the fear of the Lord. Beauty of soul is more important than outward appearance. Lifelong actions speak for themselves.

What a picture! What a portrait! Mothers, yours is a great task. Remember, "The hand that rocks the cradle, rules the world."

Read: Proverbs 31:10-31

May 13   LOVE NEEDS NO LANGUAGE

Four little words caught my attention the other day, as I was reading a book: "LOVE NEEDS NO WORDS." Children sometimes ask, "What language will we speak in heaven?" The language that we speak seems to be the best. Everyone thinks his or her language is the best! What if I said, "There will be no need for words in heaven, for heaven is a place of universal love."

Let me bring that down to where we live every day. Love needs no language — a twinkle in the eye, the pressure of a hand, a small gift and flowers speak for themselves. You know what I mean! Living unselfishly, serving cheerfully and sharing willingly is the most eloquent language. "Love needs no words!"

LOVE IS:

The spring from which the saints are enriched in the household of God;
The sphere in which the saints move in the presence of God;
The soil in which the saints are planted in the garden of God;
The subject in which the saints are instructed in the school of God;
The spirit by which the saints are characterized in the family of God;
The substance by which the saints grow in the church of God;
The street along which the saints travel to the city of God;

Moody has written the following about the fruit of the Spirit:

Joy is love exalted,
Peace is love in repose,
Long-suffering is love enduring,
Gentleness is love in society,
Goodness is love in action,
Faith is love on the battlefield,
Meekness is love in school,
Temperance is love in training.

Read: John 13:34; Galatians 5:22-23

May 14   PSALM 119 — Psalm of the Word of God

There are twenty-two, eight-verse sections or divisions headed up by the Hebrew alphabet in Psalm 119. You may find this outline helpful when you read this psalm. Trust that you will gain insight!

1. *Aleph* — Blessings of the Word of God (vs. 1-8)
2. *Beth* — Cleansing by the Word of God (vs. 9-16)
3. *Gimel* — Enlightenment by the Word of God (vs. 17-24)
4. *Daleth* — Sustaining power of the Word (vs. 25-32)
5. *He* — Prayer for its Blessing (vs. 33-40)
6. *Waw* — Salvation by the Word (vs. 41-48)
7. *Zayin* — Comfort in the Word of God (vs. 49-56)
8. *Heth* — Satisfaction by the Word (vs. 57-64)
9. *Teth* — Chastening power of the Word (vs. 65-72)
10. *Yodh* — Righteousness of the Word (vs. 73-80)
11. *Kaph* — Source of Hope (vs. 81-88)
12. *Lamedh* — Eternity of the Word (vs. 89-96)
13. *Mem* — Source of Wisdom and Knowledge (vs. 97-104)

14. *Nun* — Source of Light and Joy (vs. 105-112)
15. *Samekh* — Source of Security (vs. 113-120)
16. *Ayin* — Source of Confidence (vs. 121-128)
17. *Pe* — Guidance by the Word (vs. 129-136)
18. *Tsadhe* — Character of the Word (vs. 137-144)
19. *Qoph* — Source of Strength (vs. 145-152)
20. *Resh* — Source of Deliverance (vs. 153-160)
21. *Sin & Shin* — Source of Peace (vs. 161-168)
22. *Taw* — Prayer for its Blessing (vs. 169-176)

(Gleaned from Dake's Annotated Reference Bible)

May 15 **SPENDING TIME IN THE WORD**

Let's look at Psalm 119 to see the benefits of spending time in the Word of God. According to this psalm, the Word:

1. *Establishes my way* (vs. 1-5)
2. *Purifies my life* (vs. 9-110)
3. *Gives me counsel* (vs. 24)
4. *Reveals everything false in me* (vs. 29)
5. *Produces reverence for God* (vs. 38)
6. *Increases my courage* (vs. 43)
7. *Comforts me in affliction* (vs. 50)
8. *Keeps me clean* (vs. 61-62)
9. *Teaches me discernment and knowledge* (vs. 66)
10. *Makes me resourceful* (vs. 79)
11. *Cultivates patience* (vs. 87)
12. *Keeps me spiritually revived* (vs. 93)
13. *Accelerates my understanding* (vs. 98-100)
14. *Creates a joyful heart* (vs. 111)
15. *Sustains me when I feel helpless* (vs. 116)
16. *Enables me to honour what is right* (vs. 128)
17. *Helps me walk in the truth* (vs. 133)
18. *Surrounds me with delight in difficulty* (vs. 143)
19. *Develops a discipline for prayer* (vs. 147)
20. *Rescues me when defenseless* (vs. 153-154)
21. *Fills me with great peace* (vs. 165)
22. *Draws me back when I go astray* (vs. 176)

(Taken from a radio broadcast, "Insights for Living," by Charles Swindoll)

Read: Psalm 138:2b

May 16　FELLOWSHIP WITH JESUS EVERY DAY

All of nature depends on hidden resources. The great trees send their roots down into the earth to draw up water and minerals. Rivers have their sources in the snow-capped mountains. The most important part of a tree is the part you cannot see, the root system.

The most important part of a Christian's life is the part that God sees. He sees the heart! Unless we draw upon the deep resources of God by faith, we will fail against the pressures of life. We are living in tough times. We need to say, as Paul did, *I can do everything through Him who gives me strength* (Phil. 4:13). I keep saying, "I need Another to help me in my daily life. I need the resource of the Word of God." The word for us today is this: "Fellowship with Jesus every day." You will have some hidden resources!

Read: Psalm 1

STRENGTH IN STRUGGLES

Those of us who are growing older (and all of us are!) find it amusing to turn back the pages and recall some of the things we did. Some of them were foolish, some were very daring and others, very immature. I'll let you fill in for yourself. As time went on, we did grow up! Maturity comes with time and experience! We have been told that experience is the best teacher. Often it is the most difficult. The school of "Hard Knocks" was good for us. It was a time in our spiritual life when God put some steel into our souls. We cringe from trials and hardships, but they can be profitable to us, providing we take the proper attitude toward them.

There is strength in struggles! Take a moment today to reflect upon Joseph. Look at Psalm 105:17-19. God put fibre into the soul of Joseph while in prison. The making of the man!

Read: Psalm 119:67,71

May 17　　IRONING OUT WRINKLES

One of the household chores is ironing. "Ironing — I hate it!" you say. But just a minute! Would you *really* want to be without your steam iron? With it, creases and wrinkles can be removed quickly and easily from otherwise untidy-looking clothes.

I have mentioned something about trials and struggles. Today, a word about pressures. We all have pressure of some kind or another in our lives. But God is in the process of refining His people, and He uses pressure to do that. He is removing wrinkles in our Christian experience. The work of grace continues to iron out creases in our character. The things we face are all matched by His grace, wisdom, strength and love. Someone prayed one day, "Lord, make me wrinkle free."

This reminds me of a poem:

> *When God wants to drill a man,*
> *And thrill a man,*
> *And skill a man,*
> *When God wants to mold a man*
> *To play the noblest part;*
> *When He yearns with all His heart*
> *To create so great and bold a man*
> *That all the world shall be amazed,*
> *Watch His methods, watch His ways!*
> *How He ruthlessly perfects*
> *Whom He royally elects!*
> *How He hammers him and hurts him,*
> *And with mighty blows converts him*
> *Into trial shapes of clay which*
> *Only God understands;*
> *While his tortured heart is crying,*
> *And he lifts beseeching hands!*
> *How He bends but never breaks*
> *When his good He undertakes;*
> *How He uses whom He chooses,*
> *And with every act induces him*
> *To try His splendor out —*
> *God knows what He's about.*

— Selected

A certain Mr. Knapp said, "Lord, continue the chiseling and grinding." Paul speaks about a church without spot or wrinkle (Eph. 5:27).

Read: Romans 5:1-5; 8:29,29; Galatians 4:19

May 18   CALL ON GOD — Matthew 7:7

When the telephone bill arrived, the statement on the inside wasn't exciting, but the message on the outside of the envelope was interesting. It read, "Lonesome... feeling sort of blue? Here's the very thing to do: Call that loved one far away. Presto! Everything's OK."

Today I am trying to say, "Make a call!" Call on God! The best "blues"-chaser in the world is prayer. When you are blue, the sky is dark and mountains of trials loom before you, contact heaven. A quartet used to sing, "Just a little talk with Jesus makes it right."

The first Bible verse I ever memorized was Matthew 7:7: *"Ask and it will be given to you; seek and you will find; knock and the door will be opened to you."*

ASK — start with a request. It could be something UNKNOWN. We need *wisdom*.

SEEK — have an earnest desire. It could be something UNSEEN. We need *to search*.

KNOCK — some doors don't seem to open. It could be something UNYIELDING. We need *persistence* while waiting for the answer.

Give God a call today!

Read: Isaiah 55:1-7; 59:1

May 19   THE WEAVER — Romans 8:28-29

Remember the words, "Open your mouth wide and take this — it's good for you." That's what Mother said when passing out the cod liver oil — that liquid bottled "sunshine." The taste was horrible and we'd gulp it down as quickly as possible. But Mother knew what was good for us, despite what we thought.

What God does is for our good, too! We do not always recognize God's dealings with us. We want a life of ease and blessing. We fail to see that sometimes it takes the bitter to produce the sweet. God knows what is best for us. He has a time for everything and He will give us what we need. God knows best!

THE WEAVER

My life is but a weaving
Between my Lord and me,
I cannot choose the colors,
He worketh steadily.

Oftimes He weaveth sorrow,
And I in foolish pride
Forget He sees the upper,
And I, the underside.

Not till the loom is silent
And the shuttles cease to fly,
Shall God unroll the canvas
And explain the reason why.

The dark threads are as needful
In the Weaver's skillful hand
As the threads of gold and silver
In the pattern He has planned.

Read: Romans 8:28-29 today!

May 20   EFFORT

It takes effort to be either good or bad. We have to work at being grumpy; we have to work at being joyful; we have to work at creating the atmosphere of our surroundings. I have often said, "Everything we do demands effort!"

Much depends on the attitude we assume at the beginning of the day. If we crawl out of bed gloomy, you can be sure of a pessimistic outlook on the whole day. Say you start the day joyfully with a song, even a prayer, or sincere praise to the Lord; living can be exciting. Determination plays a big part in the amount of gloom or gladness we will have.

Everything we do demands effort!

I will praise the Lord all my life... as long as I live (Ps. 146:2). Start your day with gladness!

ABSORB THE FLAVOUR!

Did you know that we absorb the flavour of the atmosphere in which we live? Or, as I put it, "We take on the colour of our environment." Someone else has said, "It's funny how cucumbers change flavour." It is the brine in which they are soaked that makes the difference.

Likewise, people take on the mannerisms and habits of those with whom they associate. Am I speaking to a "cucumber"

Christian who is absorbing the flavour of the world? I want to encourage you to become more Christ-like by becoming saturated with the Word and prayer. Then, share your relationship and create a Christ-like flavour around you, as well. The world around us needs a Christ-like fragrance!

Take a look at 2 Corinthians 2:15. Have a good day.

May 21   THE DEVOTION OF A DOG

The devotion of a dog is incredible! Dog stories intrigue me. Their obedience and friendly nature is just fascinating.

The story is told of a dog named Monday, who stayed near a train station until his master returned from the war. Although he grew old and stiff with rheumatism, Monday didn't leave. Few human friends could be as devoted as that.

Life would not seem worthwhile without someone to care for us. Somehow the burdens ease and the cares diminish when we are with those who love us. Friendships bring sunshine into our lives. Sad to say, however, is that our friends and loved ones often fail. Let me recommend Someone we can depend on at all times. His name is Jesus! Jesus never fails!

Go with Proverbs 8:24 today!

WANT AD — SOMEONE TO LOVE ME

Have you ever seen a want ad which read. "Wanted — someone to love me"? We advertise for everything else — help, houses, cars, furniture and jobs. But, have you ever read one that said, "Wanted — someone to love me"?

There are those who say, "No one loves me, no one cares about me, no one wants me." I want to say to those people, "You are wrong! God loves you, God cares for you and God wants you." All are wanted by Him! His love knows no difference in race, creed or social standing. All are wanted!

God loves you! We need to respond to that love in simple faith — faith in the person of His Son Jesus Christ.

Never get tired of John 3:16.

May 22   **EMERGENCIES**

Unexpected company at mealtime can create embarrassment unless you have a reserve of food on hand. Some homes have a special cupboard for emergencies.

Emergencies arise in the lives of all of us. As believers, we can be prepared by cultivating a sense of God's presence. We can achieve inner serenity by learning to rely on God's Word and His promises.

Practice the presence of God in your life and then, when emergencies arise, you will know He is there to help.

God is... an ever-present help in trouble (Ps. 46:1).

Trust Him, even if you cannot trace Him!

GOD POLISHING

The longer I live as a Christian, the more I realize that God is in the process of polishing His people.

The sculptor sees the possibilities secreted within the rough exterior of the stone. He looks at stone a little differently than you and I do.

So it is with the Lord. He looks at humanity far differently than most of us do. He sees beneath the exterior and knows what each individual can become with His help. He knows just what is needed to bring out the true beauty of the soul. God may use some experiences (like fine or coarse sandpaper) to polish His child. Some experiences may be heart-breaking or humiliating, but great things come to those who allow God to polish their character.

Read Ephesians 2:10 today!

May 23   **SLOW ME DOWN**

I wouldn't be a bit surprised if I walked into your kitchen and found your fridge all covered with signs, slogans and pictures. On one fridge was the slogan, "Slow down and live." That is what many of us need to do. Some things can wait. Life is too short to rush about madly. We need to slow down!

The desire for improvement is legitimate, but are we not over-anxious and over-burdened with the demands of this temporal life? Spiritual things are paramount! Spiritual attainment is more important than material abundance. Our prayer should be in keeping with the following:

SLOW ME DOWN, LORD — SLOW ME DOWN

Ease the pounding of my heart by quieting my mind,
Steady my hurried pace.
Give me calmness amidst the confusion of my day.
Break the tension of my nerves with soothing music
That lives in my memory.
Help me to know the magical restoring power of sleep,
Teach me the art of taking minute vacations,
Of slowing down to chat with a friend,
To read a book, to look at a flower.
Remind me each day of the fable of the hare and the tortoise,
That I may know that there is more to life than speed.
Let me look upward toward the branches of the towering oak,
And remember that it grew great and strong
Because it grew slowly...
SLOW ME DOWN, LORD — SLOW ME DOWN.

Have you read the teaching of Matthew 6:25-34 lately?

May 24   FOOD FOR THE BODY AND SOUL

Each morning, our family is grateful for what we have termed, "Food for the body and food for the soul." Each day, we begin with reading a small devotional, known as "Daily Bread," written by the Radio Bible Class. With that we have our raisin bran, coffee and toast. Our bodies need nourishment! We would not miss our breakfasts, dinners and suppers, would we? Our bodies require these for health and strength.

Our souls, our spiritual man, needs nourishment too. I am saddened to see believers spiritually starved. Do you think you can live the Christian life without the Word of God and without prayer? A good motto on your fridge door would be, "Never neglect the Word."

Go with Psalm 119:16 today!

CALORIES!

Diets! What a frustrating suggestion!

It takes a lot of self-discipline to sit down at a table filled with calorie-loaded food, and refuse the gravy, the dressing, the pies or cake, and just nibble celery sticks and carrot curls instead.

Spiritually speaking, you never have to count calories. The Lord's table is spread with many blessings. There is the gift of eternal life, through faith in Jesus Christ. There is rest for the weary, strength for the weak, solace for the sad, protection for the threatened, comfort for the lonely and courage for the fearful. The table is spread! I am surprised that many people deliberately pass up all these good things. Here is one time you do not have to diet.

I remember as a boy, having a pastor come into our classroom at school and say, "Boys and girls, you can never learn too much about the Lord Jesus." I have never forgotten that, and I believe now that he was right. Spiritually speaking, you *never* have to count calories.

Go with Psalm 119:57. You are my portion, O Lord!

May 25   SEE THE BEST...

A boy is full of curiosity! Give him an alarm clock and before you know it, wheels and springs are everywhere. Some of us find delight in tearing things apart. We haven't changed, have we?

Have you ever thought how quickly we tear people apart, how quickly we see what's wrong with the other fellow? It is so easy to criticize. When you are eager to criticize, just stop a moment and put yourself in that person's place. Reflect on his or her difficulties. Reflect on the situation they are in. You really don't know until you walk in his or her shoes. That's a good way to tame the tongue. Always see the best in others!

Today you must read 1 Corinthians 13:4-8.

THE LIGHT OF THE WORLD

All of us enjoy light! Light does a number of things: It warns, like a lighthouse on the shore. It warms, like a fireplace in a home. In this setting, light is cheerful! Lights regulate traffic in our city intersections. Light reveals beauty. Without light, we would have no radiance from the sapphire or diamonds. Light is also the emblem of joy in the Scriptures.

Of Jesus, it is said, *In Him was life, and that life was the light of men* (John 1:4). He Himself said, *"I am the light of the world"* (John 8:12). He said of us, *"You are the light of the world"* (Matt. 5:14). Can you see yourself as a light? Does my life have a warm cheerful influence on others around me? Do I reflect a Christ-like character?

Read: Matthew 5:14-16. REFLECT HIM!

May 26   CHRIST TO VARIOUS OCCUPATIONS

From time to time, we need to "talk turkey." Say it as it is! Jesus Christ requires our attention! A roll call of the world's workers supports what I have said.

To the artist, He is the One altogether lovely.
To the architect, He is the Chief Cornerstone.
To the astronomer, He is the Bright and Morning Star.
To the baker, He is the Bread of Life.
To the biologist, He is the Life.
To the builder, He is the Sure Foundation.
To the doctor, He is the Great Physician.
To the educator, He is the Great Teacher.
To the farmer, He is the Sower.
To the florist, He is the Rose of Sharon.
To the geologist, He is the Rock of Ages.

What is Jesus Christ to you? Is He your Lord and Saviour?

Go with Hebrews 13:8 today.

May 27   PROPOSITIONS: IF HE....

Have you ever been truly challenged? Then read this all the way through! I have found no other reasonable alternative!

If God didn't make me,
I don't know who did.
If Jesus Christ can't bring me to God,
I don't know who can.
If He doesn't carry me safely through death,
I don't know how I'll ever get out of this world alive.
If Christ was not who He claimed to be,
I have no explanation for how He did what He did.
If He does not keep His word, then I don't know
who I can trust when it comes to the subject of God.
If He did not pay for my sins,
then I am as good as dead.

If I cannot be accepted into heaven on His good name and mercy,
I certainly will not get there on my own.
If He did not rise from the dead, I don't know why
the disciples were willing to die for their claim that He did.
If He can't rescue me from the controlling power
of my own selfishness, I don't know who can.
I have found every reason to trust Jesus Christ
for the answers to life's ultimate questions.
I have trusted HIM! He has changed my life!

Read: John 6:37 for today.

May 28   AIM HIGH, FIGHT SHY, LIVE NIGH

Wing Commander Gregson, an Anglican padre in the air force, shared some words that I shall never forget. They were very helpful during my short military career. Here is what he said:

"AIM HIGH, FIGHT SHY, LIVE NIGH AND SAY WHY!"

Follow my brief homily on these words:

AIM HIGH — *And find out what pleases the Lord* (Eph. 5:10). That is a noble aim in life. *Find out what pleases God.* You have His Word to discover His will. See Hebrews 11:3,6.

FIGHT SHY — *Be self-controlled and alert. Your enemy the devil prowls around like a roaring lion looking for someone to devour. Resist him, standing firm in the faith....* (1 Peter 5:8,9). *Resist the devil, and he will flee from you* (James 4:7). Do not give the enemy any room.

LIVE NIGH — *Come near to God and He will come near to you* (James 4:8). *Abide in Him, and He will abide in you* (John 15). Practice His presence daily! Sing, "Close to Thee."

SAY WHY—*I am not ashamed of the gospel, because it is the power of God for the salvation of everyone who believes* (Rom. 1:16). *For it is with your heart that you believe and are justified, and it is with the mouth that you confess and are saved* (Rom. 10:10). The evidence of the new life lies in 2 Timothy 2:19: *The Lord knows those who are His, and everyone who confesses the name of the Lord must turn away from wickedness.*

I am sure you appreciate, as I did, the words of a padre who loved the Lord. Write them on the memory of your mind.

AIM HIGH, FIGHT SHY, LIVE NIGH, SAY WHY!

May 29   THE BLAZING LAMP OF THE FAITHFUL!

Be faithful unto death (Rev. 2:10). There is the call to be faithful in 1 Corinthians 4:2, as well.

Upon the fly-leaf of a Bible, a friend found these words: *When my life is past, how glad I shall be that the lamp of my life has been blazed out for Thee. I shall not mind whatever I gave, of labour or money, one sinner to save. I shall not mind that the way has been rough; that Thy dear feet led the way was enough. When I am dying, how glad I shall be that the lamp of my life has been blazed out for Thee.*

Faithfulness has ever been the royal road of many believers. What a remarkable chapter is Hebrews 11! It has been referred to as the "Westminster Abbey of the Bible." Read it to discover the record of men and women who were faithful unto death. They allowed nothing to dim the light of the blazing lamp of loyalty. Their constant refrain was, "By faith, by faith, by faith." They sealed their testimony with their blood. Church history has chilling stories of our forefathers suffering indescribable agony as their bodies were tied to stakes and burned. Perhaps we are not called to wear the martyr's crown, but we must adorn the martyr spirit.

> They climbed the steep ascent to heaven,
> Through peril, toil, and pain.
> O God, to us may grace be given,
> To follow in their train.

Faithfulness is something we owe to God. Are we as faithful to Him as we ought to be?

Faithfulness is something we owe to each other as fellow believers. We certainly need, in the Church today, a baptism of love and a commitment to be faithful to each other.

Faithfulness is a debt we owe to the world at large. Why? The existence of the Church depends upon evangelism. The world seems to pass the church door untouched, unreached. Are we serving the Lord fully where He has placed us? He desires faithfulness in the little things of life. Jesus said, *"He who is faithful in a very little is faithful also in much"* (Luke 16:10, RSV). The former is always the guarantee of the latter. By being faithful in the small, unnoticed things of life, we develop the character and strength that enables us to be faithful in the greater things

Read: Galatians 5:22-23. To be faithful means to be "full of faith."

142

May 30   WONDERFULLY MADE

Nothing shows the marvelous greatness of God's creation more than the human body. Every 24 hours, you perform the following functions: Your heart beats 103,680 times; your blood circulates through your entire body 3,756 times and travels 168 million miles; you breathe 23,000 times and inhale 438 cubic feet of air; you digest 3 1/4 pounds of food; you assimilate over half a gallon of liquid; you perspire 2 pounds of water and generate 450 tons of energy; you use 750 muscles and 7 million brain cells. And all this is done automatically, whether you are awake or asleep!

Small wonder that David exclaims, *I am fearfully and wonderfully made* (Ps. 139:14). Who keeps all this going? What maintains this human machinery? David realized it is God, for he says, *I will praise Thee.*

Have you ever thanked God for making you? For giving you health? For giving you the ability to feel, think, and be productive? God deserves praise, for we are wonderfully made.

Every cell in our body proclaims the greatness of our Maker.

Read: Psalm 139:13-18

STICKING!

Let's allow the postage stamp to teach us a lesson. I want to coin a word today: "Stick-to-it-iveness!" Are you able to stick to it?

There was a little postage stamp, no bigger than your thumb,
But still it stuck right on the job until its work was done.
They licked it and they pounded it, till it would make you sick.
But the more it took a licking, why the tighter it would stick.

So friend, let's be like the postage stamp,
In playing life's rough game,
And just keep on a-sticking,
Though we hide our heads in shame.

For the stamp stuck to the letter
'Till it saw it safely through,
There's no one could do better
Let's keep sticking and be true.

Read: Proverbs 6:6; 1 Kings 11:28. Be industrious!

A SMILE!

A smile is a curve that can set a lot of things straight!

A smile costs nothing, but gives much. It enriches those who receive, without making poorer those who give.

It takes but a moment, but the memory of it sometimes lasts forever.

None is so rich or mighty that he can get along without it, and none so poor but that he can be made rich by it.

A smile creates happiness in the home, fosters good will in business, and is the countersign of friendship.

It brings rest to the weary, cheer to the discouraged, sunshine to the sad, and it is nature's best antidote for trouble. Yet it cannot be bought, begged, borrowed, or stolen, for it is something that is of no value to anyone until it is given away.

Some people are too tired to give you a smile.

Give them one of yours, as none needs a smile so much as he who has no more to give.

Read: Proverbs 15:13, 30; 17:22

PRAYER OF ST. FRANCIS

Lord, make me an instrument of Thy peace;
Where there is hatred, let me sow love;
Where there is injury, pardon;
Where there is discord, union;
Where there is doubt, faith;
Where there is despair, hope;
Where there is darkness, light;
And where there is sadness, joy.

O Divine Master, grant that I may not so much seek
To be consoled, as to console;
To be understood, as to understand;
To be loved, as to love;
For it is in giving that we receive;
It is in pardoning that we are pardoned,
And it is in dying that we are born to eternal life.

Read: Matthew 5:1-10

June 1   BROKEN PIECES!

A heart is never at its best till it be broken, for till it be broken we cannot see what's in it. From a song by the Gaither Trio, I have gleaned these words:

JUST PLACE THE BROKEN PIECES
AT THE SAVIOUR'S FEET!

Have you failed in life's battles,
To accomplish your plans?
Is your heart heavy laden,
Do you fear the Lord's command?
Do you feel that no one loves you,
And there's just no use to try?
Bring your cares to Jesus,
Your sorrow, He'll satisfy.
Now you may feel that there's no hope —
Broken hearts just cannot mend,
Ah, though you're torn in many pieces,
Christ can make you whole again.
Storms of doubt blow all directions,
But don't you be afraid;
He can make the corrections,
He made a body out of clay.
So pick up those broken pieces,
And bring them to the Lord;
Pick up the broken pieces,
Trust in His holy Word.
He will put them all back together,
He'll make your life complete;
Just place the broken pieces
At the Saviour's feet.

Read: Psalm 51:17; Isaiah 57:15; 66:2

June 2   GARDENS AND WEEDS

Gardens and flower beds are nice to admire, but they take a lot of work. Weeds, unfortunately, have no respect for gardens, nor do insects. So, we pull weeds and spray plants to try and grow healthy and beautiful gardens. Does that remind you of something?

In our lives, there are weeds such as doubt, insecurity, inferiority, unbelief, hatred and fear, that often take root. These adversaries of the soul also have no respect for the people they afflict. We need to "pull" them out in the name of Jesus and "spray" against them to try and create holy and beautiful people in God's sight.

It's easy to think that no one else suffers from trials and temptations, and no one else is attacked by the adversities which buffet us, but be encouraged — the trial of your faith is precious to God.

Go with 1 Peter 1:7 today!

COOPERATION

Jack Sprat could eat no fat,
His wife could eat no lean;
And so between them both you see,
They licked the platter clean.

That's cooperation! Mr. and Mrs. Sprat knew the secret of cooperation. It's a secret we all must learn.

We must learn to cooperate with the Lord! God can give us peace of mind when our minds are stayed on Him (Isa. 26:3-4). God can give us guidance when we delight in His ways (Ps. 119:105). God can give us real joy when we keep singing His praise (Ps. 100). God can give us forgiveness when we confess and give up our sins (1 John 1).

If we truly want God's blessing to rest upon us, we cannot go our independent ways. We must COOPERATE with God!

Read: Proverbs 3:5-6

June 3   THE ROCK OF AGES

Material things are fast getting the better of a majority of people. Many people are building their hopes upon this life. Material things have blinded them, and therefore, they cannot see the things pertaining to spiritual life. Things of this world lack permanence.

Paul speaks of a Spiritual Rock. From Israel's history, he says, *...And* [all] *drank the same spiritual drink, for they drank from the same spiritual rock that accompanied them, and that Rock was Christ* (1 Cor. 10:4). The Lord Jesus is the Rock of Ages. A rock speaks of security and safety.

The Lord's our Rock, in Him we hide, a shelter in the time of storm;
Secure whatever ill betide, a shelter in the time of storm.

— Ira D. Sankey

There is no other Rock sufficiently strong or enduring on which to build the edifice of life. *For no man can lay any foundation other than the one already laid, which is Jesus Christ* (1 Cor. 3:11).

Many are building upon the foundation of human goodness. The Scriptures tell us, *"There is none that does good, not even one..." for all have sinned and fall short of the glory of God* (Rom. 3:12,23).

Many are building upon the foundation of self-righteousness. They go about establishing their own righteousness and will not submit to the righteousness of God.

Many are building upon the foundation of good works. We are told again, *It is by grace you have been saved, through faith... not by works, so that no one can boast* (Eph. 2:8-9). We have all enjoyed the old hymn, "Rock of Ages," written by Augustus M. Toplady:

Not the labors of my hands can fulfill Thy law's demands;
Could my zeal no languor know, could my tears forever flow,
All for sin could not atone; Thou must save, and Thou alone.

Be wise! Build your life on the Rock! (Matt. 7:24-27). When the storms of life come, as they surely will, you will have a solid foundation. Do not be foolish! A house built on sand cannot and will not stand. David's testimony is so good: *He lifted me out of the slimy pit, out of the mud and the mire; He set my feet on a Rock and gave me a firm place to stand* (Ps. 40:2). An evangelist in Hyde Park answered a heckler one day, saying, "On Christ the solid Rock I stand, all other rocks are sham rocks."

Do you cherish the Lord Jesus, the Rock of Ages, the Rock of your salvation?

Read: Deuteronomy 2:4,15,18,30,31.
The Rock is mentioned five times in a hymn that Moses wrote.

June 4   THE GOOD SHEPHERD

The image of the Good Shepherd powerfully appeals to the hearts and lives of people of all ages. There is only one Good Shepherd! He came to lay down His life for the sheep. By the sacrifice of Himself, we have redemption, even the forgiveness of sin. Christ's love is clearly seen in this act of giving His life. *Greater love has no man than this, that he lay down his life for his friends* (John 15:13). He gave His life a ransom for many (Matt. 20:28). Did you notice, Jesus says, *The reason my Father loves me is that I lay down my life....* (John 10:17)? He lay down His life for the salvation of all who would enter in at the door of the sheepfold.

The thought of false shepherds should strike us today. There are so many hired hands — false shepherds and false cults. I would encourage Christian workers and fellow pastors to feed the flock. Do not scatter the sheep! Care for the sheep! The Good Shepherd knows His sheep and His sheep know Him. His sheep hear His voice! Every soul who would follow the Good Shepherd must individually hear His voice. Have you heard the voice of the Good Shepherd? Can you say today, "The Lord is MY Shepherd"? Paul says, *I know whom I have believed* (2 Tim. 1:12).

A little boy had memorized the passage, "The Lord is my Shepherd," on his five fingers. The story goes on to say that the boy drowned, and when they found him, his other hand was clenched on the finger which to him meant "MY." In that moment of time, he knew the Lord was his Shepherd. You have all heard of the little girl who said, "The Lord is my shepherd, what more do I want?" She had her all in Jesus! Implicit trust! Do you have a restful dependence on the Good Shepherd?

Notice for a moment that Christ said, *"Other sheep I have; them also I must bring."* Here we see His love for every tongue and every nation. This present time is the time of bringing in the "other sheep." Here's where we come in — with our concern for the sheep that are lost. We all know that the wolf (Satan) finds pleasure in destroying sheep. Satan loves to hinder and to side-track. He wants you to put off your decision. How different from the Good Shepherd. The Good Shepherd cares for the safety of His sheep. He is able! There is keeping power in the blood of the Lamb! We have His promise and His Word, *"I am with you always"* (Matt. 28:20). Let us conclude with the grand thought — His sheep shall be gathered into one flock; there will be one flock and one Shepherd.

Read: John 10:11-18

148

June 5 **MAN AT HIS BEST**

What difference does it make whether or not a man takes God seriously? After all, isn't religion a "take it or leave it" proposition?

Sure, a man can get along without God! What's it like? Like getting along without his health; like getting along without an arm or a leg, or without sight or hearing. Of course a man can get along, but he'll never be the man he could be. A four engine airliner can limp along on two or three engines, but what a difference when all four engines are giving their full thrust.

Man was made for fellowship with God. To be in tune with reality and in harmony with life, we must be in touch with God. To be out of fellowship with God is to be mal-adjusted, like a fish out of water, or a bird without a wing.

Man in Christ is man at his best. — Halverson

Read John 3:16 today!

NO FAILURE IS FINAL

Most of us by now have heard the words, "No failure need be final." Try and try again! Never give up! Does your favourite cake always turn out? Doesn't it fail sometimes? Of course it does! Do you throw away the recipe? Of course not!

Often it's our own fault — we put in too much flour, or we don't beat the eggs enough, or whatever. When we make mistakes, we shouldn't throw up our hands and scream right away. Don't be discouraged! Every individual makes mistakes. If your favourite cake doesn't turn out — try again.

In our spiritual lives, we blunder too; but aren't you glad we can turn to the Lord and be forgiven when we admit our sin?

Go with 1 John 1:9 today.

June 6 **GOLD OR GOD**

Let me suggest a quick illustration of greed. Nothing is greedier than the beach along the lake or seashore. The waves come and go, but the thirsty sand is never satisfied.

A greedy man or a covetous man is like the sandy beach; the more he has the more he wants. May I make a quick comparison?

Gold will buy pleasure and entertainment;
   God can give abiding joy and happiness.
Gold will buy books for intellectual pursuits;
   God can give peace of mind.
Gold will buy musical instruments;
   God can put music in your heart.
Gold will buy the finest raiment;
   God can clothe you with the garment of righteousness.
Gold will buy fine homes and furniture;
   God can prepare mansions in heaven.
Gold will buy temporal comforts;
   God gives you eternal bliss.
Gold will buy fleeting satisfaction;
   God can give you the gift of contentment.

Take Romans 6:23 for today! The gift of God is eternal life!

Read: Luke 12:15

"GET AT IT!"

Dishes, dishes, dishes — there are always dishes to do. It's a task we never completely escape. It's a chore most people detest. The worst part of any task is the "getting at it." Once you begin, it's almost fun to see the dishes clean and shining, and in their place again.

Apply that principle to your prayer life. Prayer is essential to the believer's life. We need to commune with God. Our problem is "getting at it." When we take the first steps, we enjoy talking to God. We find that our burdens are lifted, our needs met, and people prayed for. So whatever the task, "Let's get at it." Do it heartily!

Go with Colossians 3:23 today!

June 7   **THE STATE OF A SINNER**

The parable of the Prodigal Son! The circumstances of this parable set forth the riches of God's grace. There is room for repentance and returning to God. The younger son is the prodigal whose character and case are designed to represent that of a sinner.

1. A sinful state is a state of departure from God. Sinners flee. Sinners get as far away from God as they can. The world is the far country in which they take up residence.

2. A sinful state is a spending state. The prodigal wasted his substance with riotous living. In a little time, he spent all! He associated with those who helped him spend what he had.

3. A sinful state is a wanting state. When he spent all, his friends left him. A famine made things even worse. Willful waste brings woeful want. He is dry, barren, wretched and miserably poor.

4. A sinful state is a state of perpetual dissatisfaction. He satisfied his hunger with the husks the pigs ate. It was poor provision! Isaiah asks, *Why labour* [for] *what does not satisfy?* (Isa. 55:2).

5. A sinful state is a state of death. *"This my son was dead."* A sinner is dead in trespasses and sin, destitute of spiritual life, without God and without hope in this world (Eph. 2:1,12).

6. A sinful state is a lost state. *"This my son was lost."* Lost to everything that was good. Lost to all honour and virtue. Souls that are separated from God are lost souls. Think of it — lost!

The Bible says, *"For The Son of Man came to seek and to save what was lost"* (Luke 19:10). *While we were still sinners, Christ died for us* (Rom. 5:8). *The blood of Jesus Christ purifies us from all sin* (1 John 1:7).

The word today is "Repent and return!" Have you been forgiven?

Read: Luke 15:11-24

June 8   THE PRODIGAL'S RETURN

God is mindful of every individual. The return of sinners is pleasing to God. He will abundantly pardon!

Several questions emerge from the account in Luke 15.

1. What was the occasion of his return and repentance? *When he was in want, he came to himself.* Often men are brought to their senses through severe circumstances. How vain the things of this world are! The world has no comfort when a soul is under the guilt of sin. No man can give us what we need. We need Jesus.

2. What was the preparative for his return and repentance? *He reasoned with himself.* It was consideration! He reflected upon his condition. His thoughts ran home where the hired servants had bread enough. His thinking led him to conclude, "I will arise and go to my father." True repentance is rising and coming to God. We must make a break with sin and turn to God.

3. What was his proposal and what does he prepare to say? *"I have sinned against heaven and in your sight, father."* This he planned to tell his father. He acknowledged that he had forfeited all the privileges of the family. *"I am no longer worthy to be called your son, make me one of your hired servants."* It becomes sinners to acknowledge themselves unworthy to receive any favour from God. The prodigal acted upon his consideration. He struck while the iron was hot. He did not wait for a more convenient season.

That is how we must come! Acknowledge God our Father, who is holy. Acknowledge that He is mindful of us. Acknowledge that God loves us! God in grace and mercy is ready to forgive when sinners repent and turn to Him.

Have you been running away from God? Did you know that Jesus stands at the door of your life knocking, waiting to enter? (Rev. 3:20). You must open the door! God bids you to return! See the father's love as he ran and embraced and kissed his son. The ring, the robe and the roast were all part of the celebration of his return.

Read: Luke 15:11-24

June 9   THE BREAD OF LIFE

Bread companies have advertised their bread with this slogan: "You can play one hour of hockey on one slice of bread." That's how much food value it contains.

After feeding the five thousand, Jesus makes the declaration, *"I am the Bread of Life."* The Bread of Life is better than natural bread. We all know where bread comes from (originally, I mean, not the bakery); it comes from a grain of wheat which comes from the ground. It satisfies the physical body. The loaves and fishes satisfied the multitude, and they wanted to make Him a King who would continue to provide daily bread. They wanted natural bread!

When Jesus makes the statement, *"I am the Bread of Life,"* there seems to be some argument and misunderstanding. True, Moses had given them manna in the wilderness, but the Father had given true bread from heaven. The true bread of God gives life to the world. The manna only had timely worth, only for a day. To eat manna did not make them live forever. Jesus declared, *"I am the Bread of Life. He who comes to me will never go hungry."* The Bread of Life is the best bread! Through faith we may partake of it.

This bread satisfies the soul! Many believers testify to that fact! Those who daily find their nourishment from Jesus do not find it difficult to understand. Natural bread is only for a very short time. This bread, the Bread of Life, gives you eternal life!

This Bread is for everyone! We must come as an individual and take for ourselves. No one else can do this for you. You benefit as you eat for yourself. No one else can eat your breakfast for you. God is asking you in simple faith to receive Jesus, The Bread of Life and He will give you eternal life.

There is an eternity ahead! Have you eaten of this life-giving bread?

Read: John 6:25-59

June 10 THE LIGHT OF THE WORLD

Jesus did not go about as a sight-seer. He went about doing good. The blind man was to Him a more interesting sight than buildings or scenery. Some striking features are recorded in John 9.

1. Blindness. A man born blind. He was not blind because he or his parents had sinned, but rather so that the work of God might be displayed. The Son of God would show His miraculous power. (Like in the case of Lazarus, the glory of God would be seen in raising him from the dead — John 11.)

2. Deliverance. The blind man's eyes were anointed with mud made with spit. Then he was told to go and wash in the pool of Siloam. There was no virtue in the mud, the spit, the pool or the washing. The eye-opening power lay in his obedience to the word spoken by Him who said, *"I am the Light of the world."* He went, he washed and he came back seeing! The man was not responsible for being blind, but he was responsible for accepting or rejecting the Word. If he had despised the means, he would not have been obedient to the word, "Go wash!" He would have remained blind. It is when we believe and obey that we come back seeing. There is no excuse for spiritual blindness today.

3. Testimony. The blind man took no credit for himself in the matter, and he was not ashamed to tell all he knew about it — and that was not much. In answer to the question, "How?" he answered, "A man called Jesus made mud, put it on my eyes and told me to go wash it off in a pool. I washed and I came back seeing." A little later he testifies to the assurance. It was real! *"One thing I know, I was blind but now I see."* This is the evidence that a man is in the light of Christ, and that he is a new creature. In this new power of vision, he has the witness in himself. There is a joyful ring about this, "I KNOW!" It is the confidence born of experience. It is a sure sign that his new Master is Jesus, when he fearlessly pleads with others to become followers of Christ, as well.

Jesus came as a light, that, through Him, the world might be saved. Whosoever believeth will not walk in darkness! It is as real and free as the light of the sun. As the Light of your life, confess Him! Be committed to the Lord Jesus Christ! Walk in the Light!

Read: John 9

June 11   I AM THE DOOR

I marvel at the simplicity of the gospel! The metaphor before us is full of meaning. There may be a door to a barn, a house, a palace, a fortress, a dungeon, a church, a torture chamber and a royal treasury. A door may be of material as weak as wicker, or as strong as oak, iron or brass. A door may be opened by a latch which a child may lift, or it may be secured by bolts and bars that may resist the blow of a battering ram. A door may always be open so that every passerby may enter, or it may be locked so that only those with the key may enter. A door presumes a "within" and a "without."

The spiritual state of sinful man is pitiable and distressing. Apart from God, no true good is accessible to man. The *way* to God, then, is of vital importance. Christ announces Himself to be such a *way*. He is the Door! He is the Way! When Christ left heaven for earth, He left the door ajar and opened a new and living way for man to enter. He said, *"I am the way and the truth and the life. No one comes to the Father except through Me"* (John 14:6). He also said, *"I am the Door of the sheep."* The door admits the sheep to go in and out and find pasture (John 10:7, RSV). Sheep need food! The soul of man needs nourishment. Several years ago, an elderly man confessed to me that through the daily routine of life, he had become spiritually starved. He had not taken the time to go in and out and find pasture. Blessings may be obtained by going in. Christ is the door.

Christ gives life to the full (John 10:10). *No eye has seen, no ear heard, no mind has ever conceived what God has prepared for those who love Him* (1 Cor. 2:9). Go in and find pasture!

By means of a simple metaphor, *"I am the Door,"* Christ placed Himself between the whole human race and true blessings. Christ is most attractive and worthy, and when we enter there is no disappointment. He is the door and must be acknowledged as such. There is one condition for all: *"...If anyone enters by Me, he will be saved"* (John 10:9, RSV). We must come by Jesus Christ! Jesus is the way to heaven! The door is open today. Your opportunity is today! Think of it for a moment — are you on the inside or the outside? Enter in by faith in Jesus Christ.

Read: John 10:11

June 12   I AM THE TRUE VINE

For those who live in the Niagara Peninsula, the fruit belt of Ontario, the simple metaphor of John 15 will be well understood. This has been called the "fruit chapter." Jesus Christ is the True Vine! He was true to God, to His own nature, to His environment and to the sons of men. As a Vine, He is true to those who are associated with Him. We are the branches. Christ is our life and the source of our fruitfulness.

God is at work in this chapter as the gardener, the vine-dresser. He shows us that He cares and that there must be a vital connection between the branch and the vine. A vital connection is essential to the continuance of life. Any branch that does not bear fruit, He takes away. Unfruitfulness is not abided. In many instances, worldliness is the cause of unfruitfulness. (See the parable of the Sower and the Seed, and read Matthew 13:22). God is at work pruning His branches. There is a reason! *...The Lord disciplines those He loves....* (Heb. 12:6)! Out of every affliction, God has a purpose. His purging has purpose — more fruit!

The key to the chapter is "abiding." It means to stay, to dwell, to remain. Are you abiding in the True Vine like that? Abiding is essential for fruitbearing! A true disciple of the Vine bears much fruit. The sap of the vine to the branch is what the Spirit of Christ is to the believer. *The fruit of the Spirit is love, joy, peace, patience, kindness, goodness, faithfulness, gentleness and self-control* (Gal. 5:22-23). When the Holy Spirit has control of our lives there will be the fruit of a Christ-like spirit. To abide in Him is to abide in His Word, His will, and His work. God works in us to both will and do His good pleasure. Prayer is important! If we are too busy to pray, we are too busy! Take time! Fellowship with Jesus every day! We expect fruit to be on the vine; God expects fruit to be in our lives. Are you in Christ? Is there the evidence of fruit? The results are twofold: The Father is glorified and discipleship is proven. See John 15:8.

Fruit is the natural outcome of a faithful following of Jesus Christ. Life lived in Christ and for Him is the God-glorifying life.

Read: John 15:1-8

June 13   THE MAN WITH THE WITHERED HAND

Many of the miracles of Christ suggest some principles that we all need to follow.

Observe three simple questions:

1. Where was the Saviour?
2. Whom did He meet?
3. What did He say?

The Lord Jesus was in the synagogue, a place of instruction. He taught in the presence of Scribes and Pharisees. Our attention is drawn to the man with the withered hand. Others were there to observe, and many held no sympathy with Jesus' ministry. Christ was in a fault-finding crowd. Some were men with withered hearts! They had come to accuse, to see if He would heal on the Sabbath.

What did the Saviour say? To the man with the withered hand, he said, "Stand up in front of everyone." This wasn't easy. Anyone who is handicapped or deformed doesn't usually want the whole world to see. The other word of command soon after was, "Stretch out your hand." This was impossible! He had never raised his hand before; it was limp and powerless. In obedience, however, he did stretch out his hand and it was restored. Remember, "God's commands are His enablings." This man expected Jesus to heal him.

Let me make an application. Adam put forth his hand and took of the forbidden fruit, and immediately his spiritual hand was withered. All his sons are born with a withered hand. All are helpless and lost in sin. But we may be restored through simple faith in Jesus Christ. For some, it may mean standing up and being counted, even among friends and loved ones. Others may need to make a clean break. Maybe some habit is keeping you from coming to Christ. Hear again, "God's commandments are His enablings." The Holy Spirit is faithful, and He will put His finger on the very thing that's keeping you from coming. Reach out in faith to Jesus Christ today!

Read: Mark 3:1-6

June 14   THE EARLY MINISTRY OF CHRIST

Do you have a testimony in your home town? It may be easy to testify away from home where no one knows you, but what about your home town?

He [Jesus] *went to Nazareth, where He had been brought up, and on the Sabbath day He went into the synagogue, as was His custom. And He stood up to read* (Luke 4:16).

Would you be prepared to say a word or even read in a worship service? Is it your custom to go to church on the Lord's Day? Jesus' custom was to go into the synagogue on the Sabbath day. Catch the phrase, *as was His custom.* I believe it is very important to attend church on Sunday. God has incorporated the one-in-seven day of rest, the day of worship. We need the fellowship of believers to strengthen us. We need the ministry of the Word to feed our soul. You need the Church and the Church needs you!

At the synagogue, they gave Jesus the scroll of Isaiah, a book full of Messianic prophecies. The word He read was fulfilled that very day. He had appeared to begin His early ministry. Here, before their very eyes, was the one able to fulfill the promise of Isaiah 61:1,2. He was anointed for this ministry that we see lined up in the word of prophecy — to preach the gospel to the poor and to heal the broken-hearted. Many times His words were words of comfort to the poor. His followers were mainly the common-place people. They heard Him gladly!

Men and women and boys and girls need spiritual healing. Sin has caused so much of our heartache and hurt. People seek deliverance! Jesus Christ is the only one who can set you free! Are you enslaved to sin and Satan? Come to Christ, He can set you free! The time is now! Today! *...It is time to seek the LORD* (Hos. 10:12).

Read: Luke 4:16-27

June 15   THE CLEANSED LEPER

The "I will's" of Christ are actually promises. They are given so that we might act upon them. God's Word is true and it is directed to us. The Lord Jesus is merciful! Wherever the Presence of the Lord Jesus Christ is, there is the power of God.

Before us today is the account of the leper who was cleansed. Notice his miserable condition! His disease has reached its final stage; he was full of leprosy. Leprosy in the Scriptures is representative of sin. Like sin, this loathsome disease works its way in slowly; and its course is irresistible and deadly. It poisons the blood, and the whole physical being becomes polluted. Sin affects the heart! A man living in sin is a man dead to God.

From this condition, there is a ray of hope. This leper was inspired when his eyes saw Jesus. Seeing Jesus will never fail to awaken hope in a darkened, sin-crushed heart. Here was a Man full of compassion, and he, the leper, full of leprosy. Hear his prayer, *"Lord, if You are willing You can make me clean."* This leper fell on his face! He took a humble position! This petition brings out the man's one burning desire — to be made clean!

The Lord Jesus reached out His hand and touched him, saying, *"I am willing — be clean!"* Immediately, the leprosy left him. Here was the touch of the Master's hand! The healing touch! The cleansing touch! He speaks, He touches and it is done!

After his cleansing, there comes the commission: *"Go show yourself to the priest and offer the sacrifices... for your cleansing...."* Indeed, a testimony of that which happened to him. Every soul that is saved should be a testimony of God's saving grace.

Have you been cleansed by the blood of Jesus Christ? Are you washed in the blood of the Lamb? Would you be free from your burden of sin? There is power in the blood!

Read: Luke 5:12-16

June 16   A SOLDIER'S FAITH

In this Roman centurion, we see a thoroughly practical man. Even Jesus marvels at this man's simplicity and greatness. *"...Say the word, and my servant shall be healed. For I myself am a man under authority, with soldiers under me. I tell this one, 'Go,' and he goes; and that one, 'Come,' and he comes. I say to my servant, 'Do this,' and he does it"* (Luke 7:8).

This man had learned to take a command. He believed the Great Commander had but to speak and it would be done. His servant was sick and about to die — at the point of death. Is this not the picture of everyone under the power of sin? And is this not a dangerous condition? The centurion came, not for himself, but for his servant. When he heard of Jesus, he sent for Him. His servant must have been dear to him. How much concern do we have for

158

those who are lost and sin-sick? How cold we sometimes are to those who have a need. We miss out because there is no concern.

This man had a good reputation. His prayer was a humble one; he says, *"I do not deserve to have you come under my roof."* This man had faith: Just *"say the word, and my servant will be healed."* Faith always has to do with the WORD. God's word cannot fail! The centurion placed himself right into the picture. He too had others set under his authority who followed his commands. He set an example of good "soldiership"!

God will always answer the cry of faith in due time. The Lord Jesus marvelled at this man's faith. I am reminded of William Carey, the missionary to India who said, "Attempt great things *for* God, expect great things *from* God." Sometimes we limit God! *Without faith it is impossible to please God, anyone who comes to Him must believe that He exists and that He rewards those who earnestly seek Him* (Heb. 11:6).

I would encourage you to take hold of God's Word like this centurion. God has not made it difficult for us to believe!

Read: Luke 7:2-10

June 17   COMMENDATION

A story is told of a lady, an excellent cook, who unexpectedly had to serve a pie she considered a failure. Her guest commended her for the pie she had baked.

A few days later, the same person came to eat with the family again. This time the lady knew she was coming and she diligently put out her best. To her surprise, the guest made no mention of the dessert she served. Overcome with curiosity, the lady asked her guest why she had so lavishly praised the inferior pie but made no mention of her dessert this time. The reply was, "The one tonight spoke for itself; the other one needed praising."

Often it's the people we least suspect who need a word of commendation. An encouraging word may be all that's needed to save another from defeat. A bit of praise may be all that's needed to spur one on to nobler deeds.When you've paid someone a visit, you've heard the words. "I'm glad you came, you made my day." Years later you still recall the warmth of those words.

When our spirits are low, it is easy to lose heart. We want to throw in the towel! Discouragement and doubt are like poison and we all need encouragement! And the good thing is, anyone can do it! When you notice a job well done, say so! Express appreciation — make a phone call, send a card.

...How good is a timely word (Prov. 15:23b).

Read: Proverbs 16:23 and Philippians 4:13

June 18   PARENTHOOD

Mothers have the greatest privilege, the greatest task and the greatest influence in the world! Only eternity will reveal their job for what it is and give the proper credit. What a tragedy that so many women will miss this opportunity of being the mothers for God and sacrifice the greatest gift — parenthood — for the pleasures and ease of a fleeting, empty age. If we continue to allow the home to degenerate, and our children to be spiritually neglected, history can only repeat itself. The downfall of nations, in every case, has been preceded by the breakdown of the home. Oh, the heartache and the heart-break that could be avoided if mothers and fathers would perpetuate a family altar in the home, with the Bible as the textbook and the person of Christ as the centre.

At its best, parenthood is a tremendous responsibility. Words cannot measure the length and breadth and depth and height of that solemn position of parenthood. It will always be by the grace of God that our children will grow up to follow the Lord. Children, as you know, receive their first concepts of God from their parents. Parents personify and establish the authority of God before their children. Have we taught our children what the Bible calls "the fear of the Lord?" Or has this been a missing note? *The fear of the Lord — that is wisdom....* (Job 28:28). Children who have not come under authority at home, find great difficulty submitting to God's authority. Parents who have their children in control, spare themselves and their children many family pains and heartaches. The Scriptures are plain: *Fathers... bring* [your children] *up in the training and instruction of the Lord* (Eph. 6:4). This responsibility requires divine guidance. What a trust! What a guardianship! Only God's grace is sufficient for these things.

Has God given you a family? Then you have been highly favoured by the Lord. He has seen fit to entrust you with a responsibility above any other. Do not rest until you know that your children are in the ark of salvation. If you wait until they come under the influence of others, it may be too late. I bear the testimony to the power of a mother's prayers. I never got beyond the reach of my mother's prayers, nor beyond the power of my early training. Next to God, the memory of my name in mother's prayer had more to do with my salvation than any other thing. Are all the children in?

Read: Proverbs 1:8-9; 2:1-8

June 19   FAMILY ALTAR

"The strength of a nation lies in the homes of its people." These are the words of Abraham Lincoln.

Let me introduce and illustrate an interesting verse in Proverbs 22:28: *Do not move an ancient boundary stone set up by your forefathers.*

Among the property owned jointly by two young brothers who were carpenters, was the old tumble-down place of their birth. One of the brothers was soon to be married and the old house was to be torn down and replaced with a new one. For years, neither of the brothers had visited the cottage, as it had been leased. As they entered now and started the work of demolishing the place, floods of tender memories began to sweep over them. By the time they reached the kitchen, they were well-nigh overcome with their emotions. There was the place where the old kitchen table had stood with the family Bible, and there is where the family knelt to pray together. They were recalling now with a pang, how in later years, they had felt a little superior to that time-honored custom carefully observed by their father.

One of the brothers said, "We're 'better off than he was, but we are not 'better men." The other agreed, saying, "I'm going back to the old church and the old ways, and in my new home I'm going to make room for worship as Dad did." Raise up the family altar.

The strength of a nation lies in the homes of its people. *Do not move an ancient boundary stone set up by your forefathers.*

Dr. J.G. Paton said, "No hurry for market, no rush for business, no arrival of friends or guests, no trouble or sorrow, no joy or excitement ever prevented us from kneeling around the family altar while Dad offered himself and his children to God." It was on his father's life in his home, that Dr. Paton based his decision to follow the Lord wholly. "He walked with God, why not I?"

What is home without a Bible?

A home's a mighty precious place,
It's more than floors and walls and space,
More than a place to hang your hat,
Ah, yes, a home is more than that.

A home's a place where children grow,
Where they life's lessons learn to know,
Where love and law together blend,
A place of blessing without end.

And home's a place where God is known,
Where His blest Word in hearts is sown,
Where little lips are taught to pray,
And feet are helped to walk God's way.

Read: Deuteronomy 6:1-9

June 20   FATHER'S DAY

If fathers are like me, their kids may say, "My dad's not the kissing kind." I guess I got that from my father, who wasn't really the kissing kind either. Oh, he might lend his cheek, or lean over for the other person to display his or her affection; but Dad had his own way of letting us know he loved us. Let anyone get into a tight spot, and he was there to help. Dad would share what he had, lend a listening ear or give the shirt off his back. He had a genuine concern.

So, there are different ways of expressing love and affection — sharing, lending, listening, giving and praying. I hope you know a Dad like that! You may say, "My dad's not the kissing kind... but he sure knows how to walk in Christian love!" The Bible says, *Let us not love with words or tongue but with actions and in truth* (1 John 3:18).

DAD'S GREATEST JOB

I may never be as clever as my neighbor down the street,
I may never be as wealthy as some other men I meet;
I may never have the glory that some other men have had,
But I've got to be successful as a little fellow's dad.

There are certain dreams I cherish that I'd like to see come true,
There are things I would accomplish ere my working time is through;
But the task my heart is set on is to guide a little lad,
And to make myself successful as that little fellow's dad.

It is that one job I dream of; it's the task I think of most;
If I'd fail that growing youngster, I'd have nothing else to boast.
For though wealth and fame I'd gather, all my future would be sad,
If I'd failed to be successful as that little fellow's dad.

I may never get earth's glory; I may never gather gold;
Men may count me as a failure when my business life is told;
But if he who follows after is a Christian, I'll be glad —
For I'll know I've been successful as a little fellow's dad.

Read: Galatians 6:1-4

June 21   ROOM FOR THE GOOD

Our inspiration today has its roots in Romans 12:9: *Hate what is evil; cling to what is good.*

All of us have a drawer in the kitchen where everything from recipes and rubber bands to scissors, string and paper clips, is stored. You know what I mean — anything and everything small. Then comes some rainy day when you decide you're going to tidy up that drawer. So you throw out all the stuff you'll never use again and make room for new things.

I think there is a lesson here for all of us. Our lives, particularly our minds, need cleaning out sometimes. We need to make room for new things in our minds. Thoughts of hate, envy, jealousy and greediness are destructive. The sooner we get rid of them the better. And then we can fill up the space with good thoughts! In place of hate, store love; in place of despair, store hope; in place of doubt, store faith.

Let's harbour the thoughts and attitudes that reflect the person of Jesus Christ.

Read: Philippians 4:8

WORDS — LIKE BUTTER

I agree with the statement, "Many people like soft butter." Soft butter is pliable! It spreads easily and goes further than hard butter. It glides across toast with ease and soaks in much more quickly.

Butter reminds me of words. Hard words tear and cause resentments. Hard words may even ruin a friendship. But a soft word is always welcome! It can soothe and bring comfort. It can bring hope to the hopeless. With this in mind, I cannot help but think of Proverbs 15:1: *A gentle answer turns away wrath, but a harsh word stirs up anger.*

Pleasant words are a honeycomb, sweet to the soul and healing to the bones (Prov. 16:24). I hope you are among the many who like soft butter on your toast. Have a good day!

Read: Psalm 141:3

June 22 DON'T BE DISCOURAGED

I say this kindly: "Every woman has the privilege of changing her mind." I wonder if we don't over-do it at times — like the day a lady went into a shoe store. She tried on several pair of shoes, but she couldn't make up her mind about one specific pair. She decided to wait until later. She offered her apologies to the salesman. Smiling, he assured her that it was perfectly alright. "I have been in this business too long to let one customer discourage me." Those words gave the lady a lift for the day.

Discouragement is a tool of the Enemy. It seems to be his master weapon. Listen! Courage is of the Lord! Hold your head high! With Him you can face disappointments and thwarted plans. Be of good courage!

Read: Deuteronomy 1:38

JUST A MINUTE!

All of us have heard the words, "Just a minute." Mom calls, "Pauline, set the table." Pauline says, "Just a minute," and continues to play the piano. Dad calls, "Bring me the hammer." Jack says, "Just a minute," and stays with his project.

I wonder if we are aware of the value of "wasted minutes"? Our "just a minute's" add up to wasted hours. Let me remind you of our stewardship of time. Could we use our "just a minute" to the advantage? Let me suggest something: It takes just a minute to send up a prayer heavenward. Long prayers demand no urgent need. God's ear is alert to hear the weakest, faintest and shortest prayer.

Would you read Psalm 5:1-3 today?

June 23   WHAT IF....?

Children have a way of picking up peculiar expressions. Have you ever heard them say, "Wonder if....? Wonder if it will rain? Wonder if we will move?" I think what they're really saying is, "What if it should rain? What if we should move?"

No doubt we have all asked the question, "What if....?" What if Columbus hadn't discovered America? Where would we be? What if Mr. Bell hadn't discovered the telephone? What would our teenagers do?

Let me zero in on something more serious. What if God had not loved the world enough to send us His Son? What if His Son had refused to die for our sins? What if He had not risen from the dead and given us the hope of eternal life? What if!

The fact is — He did! God so loved that He gave! Jesus Christ gave His life freely! He rose from the dead giving us a glorious prospect. Reflect upon John 3:16 today.

Read: John 14:1-3

EVERY LITTLE BIT ADDS UP

We have all heard it said, "Every little bit adds up." Little things count! Remember when bobby-pins or clothespins were lying around everywhere. Mother would stress the necessity of not losing these simple little things. We might have said, "Mom, what's a bobby-pin? They're cheap, aren't they?"

Every little bit adds up! Every berry can fill the basket. Every penny enlarges our savings. Every person helps to make up the congregation. May I never grow careless with little thoughtless words, little indiscreet actions and little unwholesome attitudes. Every little bit adds up!

"Who despises the day of small things?" (Zech. 4:10).

Read: Mark 9:41. "Because you belong to Christ."

June 24   GOD'S CUPBOARDS ARE FULL

Grandma's kitchen was always full of good things — big crusty loaves of bread, pies and cookies. She kept large raisin-centered sugar cookies in a special corner of the cupboard. They were there for the asking.

Have you ever truly calculated the blessings of the Christian life? GOD'S CUPBOARD IS FULL AND OVERFLOWING! To those who believe, there is peace of heart, soul and mind. There is the gift of a clear, clean conscience, worth more than riches. There is freedom from the bondage of sin. There is contentment in doing His will. There is grace for every trial and testing. God's cupboard is full! It is all there for the asking! *For He satisfies the thirsty and fills the hungry with good things* (Ps. 107:9).

Read: Matthew 7:7 for today.

GET A LIFT — BUY A HAT!

Women's hats have borne the brunt of countless jokes. They have been called many things. But it still can't be denied that a new hat gives a lady a lift. Sometimes the renovation of an old one does the trick too. Everyone needs a lift at times. The monotony of the everyday tasks tax us all alike. A change of scenery, a new piece of furniture or a new hat gives a lift for living.

When we experience that let-down feeling, it's time for renewal. Isaiah said it well: *They that wait upon the LORD shall renew their strength; they shall mount up with wings as eagles; they shall run, and not be weary; and they shall walk, and not faint* (Isa. 40:31, KJV). New courage and strength can be received by waiting in God's presence. We can receive a lift through prayer.

Let's go into today with Isaiah 40:31. Have a good day!

June 25   SMILE, LIFE IS TOO SHORT

I enjoy collecting poetry and, from time to time, will recite or quote from lines that linger in my mind. I am drawing attention to one entitled, "Life is so short."

> *Let's smile and be kind because life is so short*
> *And most of the way is rough.*
> *The times are trying, the road upgrade,*
> *And always trouble enough.*
>
> *Life is too short for spite and revenge,*
> *And paying back wrong for wrong;*
> *Try patience and love and forgiveness,*
> *Meet slights with a smile and a song.*

It goes on to say that this sad world needs the wealth of your love, your gentle care, your word of encouragement and your smile. Smile — it's worth a million dollars and doesn't cost a cent!

Read: Proverbs 17:22 sometime today.

NEW EXPERIENCES

It's fun to travel through new territory, to view new scenery and to see unfamiliar places. Such adventures call for direction, so road maps are essential! They give the guidance we need.

Many times in our lives we are called upon to travel through unfamiliar territory. New experiences come to all of us. There is sorrow over the loss of a loved one. There are disappointments in our plans. There are strange and perplexing situations. There are adjustments to make and new things to be conquered.

All of these experiences call for faith. Without faith, we have nothing to hold us, nothing to steady us, nothing to keep us on the right path. Faith in our Creator, our Maker, faith in His Word which is the road map, faith in His promised Presence.

For today as you travel, read Psalm 19.

June 26   SALVATION — John 3:16

For God so loved the world that He gave His one and only Son, that whoever believes in Him shall not perish but have eternal life (John 3:16).

The golden text of the Bible! If we were to telephone heaven and ask for the way of salvation, we might receive the answer in John 3:16. Enjoy the simple gospel with me today!

1. The Source of Salvation: *For God.* Psalm 68:20 says, *Our God is a God of salvation; and to* GOD, *the Lord, belongs escape from death* (RSV). Salvation means deliverance from the consequences of sin; deliverance through the atoning work of Christ. God in His everlasting mercy supplied a way of salvation.

2. The Reason for Salvation: *so loved.* The very essence of God is love. To be a righteous and loving God, He had to have an equal amount of hatred for sin. God saves people, not *in* their sins, or *with* their sins, but *from* their sins. *God demonstrates His own love for us in this: While we were still sinners, Christ died for us* (Rom. 5:8).

3. The Cost of Salvation: *gave His one and only Son.* God paid the price of redemption! Heaven's best came down to earth to bring salvation to lost humanity. Heaven's treasure for sinful man! It was love that sent the Saviour to this wicked world below. He loved us and gave Himself for us. God gave — it cost Him His Son.

4. The Condition of Salvation: *that whoever believes in Him.* *In* Him, notice, not *about* Him! Many people know and believe *about* Him, but not all believe *in* Him. Faith in Christ secures salvation! Man's part is to accept Him in faith, believing. (Rom. 10:9) (1 John 5:12-13).

5. The Consequences of Rejecting Salvation: *perish.* Not to believe brings with it condemnation. Look at John 3:17,18: *For God did not send His Son into the world to condemn the world, but to save the world through Him. Whoever believes in Him is not condemned, but whoever does not believe stands condemned already because he has not believed in the name of God's one and only Son.*

The greatest sin is unbelief. Life in this world is too short to reject this salvation that God offers to you.

> *Whosoever cometh, need not delay.*
> *Jesus is the true, the only living way....*
> — P.P. Bliss

Read: John 3:1-18

June 27 THE CONDITION & NATURE OF A SINNER

Israel's story is our story! What happened to Israel can happen to us. God can deliver us from this present evil world, save us, keep us and someday take us to be with Him in glory.

The gospel story can well be seen in the pages of Exodus. God wanted Israel to be free from the yoke of bondage and free from slavery. Israel in Egypt portrays a graphic figure of the condition of the sinner. He is bound by sin. The sinner is in the hands of the one who rules him with despotic power. He is sold under sin, led captive by Satan, bound in the chains of lust, passion and temper, and left without strength, without hope and without God. Such is the sinner's condition! He is the slave of another and everything he does is done in the capacity of a slave. God is able to deliver from the clutches of sin and Satan.

The gospel of the grace of God introduced an entirely new condition. The believer in Christ has been taken out of his former condition of guilt and placed absolutely and eternally in a new condition of unspotted righteousness. He is born in a certain condition and, until he is "born again," he cannot be in any other. Self-improvement and turning over a new leaf will not change a sinner's condition. *...In Christ, he is a new creation* (2 Cor. 5:17).

The case is the same for the question of nature. How can a man alter his nature? He may make it undergo a process, he may try to subdue it, he may place it under discipline, but it is nature still. That which is born of flesh is flesh! There must be a new nature. When we are born again by the operation of the Spirit of God, we are made partakers of a new nature.

Now this is eternal life: that they may know You, the only true God, and Jesus Christ, whom You have sent (John 17:3). It all rests on the great truth that Jesus died and rose again. Infinite justice was satisfied, mercy and truth are met together, righteousness and peace have kissed each other, and the sinner has his need met (Ps. 85:10). *Christ died... the righteous for the unrighteous, to bring you to God* (1 Peter 3:18).

Read: Ephesians 2:1-10

June 28   THE SECRET OF HAPPINESS

Since the longing to be happy is universal among man, yet comparatively few have achieved happiness, let us carefully note the conditions for happiness. We will be looking at Psalm 119:1-9. Here, the word, "blessed," means "happy."

[Happy] *are they who keep His statutes and seek Him with all their heart* (119:2). God's Word is God's will for us. Let the Word of God do something for you. We need to submit our will and our conduct to God's Word and God's will.

[The happy people] *do nothing wrong; they walk in His ways* (119:3). They are careful to avoid sin. The godly keep God's Word and walk in His ways, because the Lord has commanded it. Our heart's desire should be that the Lord, by His Word and Holy Spirit, so directs our thoughts, words and actions that they will be in harmony with His Word and His will at all times. Such a man will not be ashamed nor condemned by his heart, accused by his conscience, nor suffer loss at the judgment seat of Christ. He will have a clean record.

The Word of God not only provides the key to true happiness, it also gives the secret of victory in our lives (119:9). Man is beset by many temptations and desires. Here is the way he may be cleansed. Jesus said to His disciples, *"You are already clean because of the word I have spoken to you"* (John 15:3). "The fellow is so full of the Word," was the answer of the man who tried to entice a young Christian boy into drinking; the boy had used the Word to counter-attack temptations. The Lord Himself used the Word three times to keep sin out when He was tempted.

In our homes or in our hands, it may remain unopened;
In our heads it may be forgotten;
But in our hearts it will keep us from sin.

What is your attitude toward the Word of God? Man's response to God is of great importance. Man is a responsible being and decides his spiritual welfare and eternal destiny. If you have neglected the Word, why not get back to it? Take God at His Word! Receive it and believe it! Get to the Word!

Read: Psalm 119:1-9

June 29   A HAPPY MAN — Psalm 1

Psalm 1 is a fitting introduction to the entire book of Psalms. There is a two-fold aspect to consider in the happiness of the man in this passage.

A. HIS NEGATIVE CHARACTER: There are some things he will not do.

1. He does not walk in the counsel of the wicked. He knows that the way of the wicked will perish. The counsel of the wicked is to walk in the broad way that leads to destruction (Matt. 7:13-14).

2. He does not stand in the way of sinners. Sinners are those who deliberately transgress against light. To stand in their way of doing things is to show an attitude that is at home with the way of sinners.

3. He does not sit in the seat of mockers. Those who begin to walk in the counsel of the wicked are in danger of ending up in the seat of mockers. They make a mockery of sin, eternity, heaven and hell. When men live in sin, they go from bad to worse.

B. HIS POSITIVE CHARACTER:

1. He is joyful! His delight is in the law of the Lord. The Christian life is entering into a new and happy inheritance in the Word of God. All who love the Lord will find delight in His Word!

2. He is thoughtful! On His law he mediates day and night. Meditation on the Word of truth is as needful for our spiritual health and strength as food is for the body. These are days when we ought to get literally soaked up in God's Word, like a saturated sponge!

3. He is fruitful! Fruit is forthcoming! The fruit is according to the character of the tree and it is always in season. Fruit-bearing is natural, because there is abundance of life when the roots are in the rivers of God. The outward life will be fresh and green when inward life is pure and full.

4. He is successful! Whatever he does prospers. The bud and the blossom produced by the Holy Spirit will come to fruition. God has the right to look for fruit in your life and mine.

Did you notice the contrast? The wicked are like chaff. The chaff has no power to resist either the wind or the fire. The lawless, like chaff, are driven about with every wind of doctrine, popular opinion and worldly success. The way of the wicked must perish, because it is the way of pride, pleasure, unbelief and rejection of Christ. Consider the contrast and join with those whose delight it is to follow the Lord.

Read: Psalm 1

June 30   PREPARE TO MEET THY GOD!

"Therefore this is what I will do to you, Israel, and because I will do this to you, prepare to meet your God, O Israel" (Amos 4:12).

Charles Wesley said, "A charge to keep I have, a God to glorify; a never dying soul to save and fit it for the sky." We spend many years preparing for life's work. Our schools do much of this preparation. How many years do you spend in school for life's work? Time is spent to prepare for this life! What about our preparation for heaven? Would you be ready to meet God? Life is brief! Just a vapour, a heart-beat! Life is like a weaver's shuttle, Job says. Like water poured on the ground, says David. Like the grass of the field, says Isaiah.

You have heard it said, "Heaven is a prepared place for a prepared people." Those whose sins have been washed away through the blood of Jesus Christ are prepared. If you take Jesus as your Saviour in this life, you will be with Him in the next. It does pay to prepare! If you do not prepare you will spend eternity in hell. The wicked will be thrown into hell and separated from God forever

(Ps. 9:17). Beyond the grave, we will meet God! God has given us a free will. We may choose.

God has loved you from the foundation of the world. It is He who, in the person of Jesus, upon the cross, virtually gave Himself for you. It is He who, through the varying stages and circumstances of your life, tried to win you. It is He whose love would not let you go, in spite of repeated denials. It is He who will be just and righteous at the judgement; for as the Judge of all the earth, He will do right.

The Judge will give full consideration to your case apart from others. You will meet Him personally! He will judge you individually! If you are guilty, then He will pronounce His verdict, and send you to your punishment. If you have been brought to a realization of your lost condition, and have cried out for mercy, then you will face God as the God of compassion and mercy. If you have willingly renounced your sin and taken your stand for Christ, then God will be to you the God of blessing.

I trust that you will meet this God — the God of blessing and mercy. Prepare to meet Him! Be robed in the righteousness of Jesus Christ! Know that by the grace of God, you can be fully prepared.

Read: Amos 5:4-15

July 1   **GOVERNMENTS**

From time to time, we are given the opportunity to vote for national political leaders. I trust you take your right to vote seriously. Christian citizenship includes some responsibility in this area. According to Romans 13:1-7, the believer's relationship to human government is as much a matter of divine revelation as is his relationship to those in the Church. Christians are to recognize the responsibilities and rights of a nation's leaders.

There are responsibilities to both God and man. Human government derives its authority from God. Governments are appointed and approved by God (Rom. 13:1-2). Governments may be weak or strong, just or oppressive, benevolent or cruel, but in each case, God has His way and moves His own plan forward. All of Bible history is intended to reinforce this truth.

Governmental responsibilities are two-fold. First, they are to secure the nation against all forms of lawlessness. They must protect the community and punish the criminal. So, we should not resort to civil disobedience! Secondly, they are to keep the nation financially solvent. They need our taxes. So, we should not be alarmed about paying taxes. Governments must pay for officials and for public services. The Bible teaches that a nation's leaders have the right to our monetary support and our moral support. There is the allegiance to the principle of authority.

In 1 Timothy 2:1-4, Paul says we are to pray for all races of people, for all ranks of people and for all responsibilities of people. As believers, as citizens, we need to help, support and pray for those who give leadership to our country.

Read: Romans 13:1-7

July 2   **IF A MAN DIES, SHALL HE LIVE AGAIN?**

Life is certain, death is sure. Sin is the cause; Christ is the cure.

Death is still claiming a tremendous harvest. Most every newspaper and every news program makes this very apparent. If a man dies, shall he live again? This is the general inquiry and often an inquiry unsatisfied. The question rings in every breast. Man's life is short! Are there any lessons from the brevity of human life that we can learn? The Psalmist cries out, *Teach us to number our days aright, that we may gain a heart of wisdom* (Ps. 90:12). Days lost cannot be recovered! A watchfulness over the moments saves the hours. Diligence prevents waste! The days are numbered! No one has any time to lose. The true preparation for the life to come is to occupy this present one with careful and diligent fidelity.

It is difficult to determine the measure of light Job had on the question of the future life. If a man dies, will he live again? The satisfactory answer to this comes from the lips of our Saviour, and that makes it an entirely satisfactory answer. Christ's teachings all proceed on the assumption that there is a future life. His teachings are constantly supported by an appeal to the future conditions of reward and punishment. His own triumph over death is a great example!

The entire chapter of 1 Corinthians 15 deals with the gospel of the resurrection. Jesus is alive to carry out His purpose of grace in our hearts. The triumph comes through our Lord Jesus Christ! Through Him, we shall conquer! His resurrection was the seal of the power of Calvary. He lives, and through Him, we will live! Without Him, our lives would close in disaster and ruin.

While some friends were talking about death, one old lady said, "I am not looking for the undertaker, but for the uppertaker."

No man is prepared to live until he is prepared to die. Are you ready to die? Come to Christ — now is the day of salvation!

Read: Job 14:1-17

July 3   SEARCH ME, O GOD!

David never penned a more magnificent psalm than Psalm 139. None of us could have written it! There is not one of us who does not willingly acknowledge the need for just such an experience. It was prompted by a desire for cleansing from sin that would be thorough and complete. We are looking at verses 23-24.

Are you glad to know that God knows all about you? If the X-ray could read and the camera record every uncharitable, unchristian and unclean thing about us, we would want to get as far away as possible from these devices. Would we be willing to open the innermost part of our hearts to the gaze of another person? At this point in David's life, he was set on being right with God. The remedy is with God!

Two things emerge. One is the need to be searched. *The heart is deceitful above all things and beyond cure. Who can understand it?* says Jeremiah in Jeremiah 17:9. Did you ever go on a tour of inspection with God? If you ever do, you will never forget the journey. He holds the searchlight! The all-revealing light uncovers a bit of pride, self-ambition, jealousy, rebellion, impurity and anger. Are we like the mighty oak that fell in a storm because worms had eaten away the inside until it was hollow?

The second thing is the need to be cleansed. For the tree that fell, there was no salvation. But there is for you! The remedy is with God! For the one who prays this prayer, there is cleansing. There is hope! The blood of Jesus Christ cleanses us from all sin. The prayer also includes guidance in a person's life. ...*Lead me in the way everlasting* (Ps. 139:24b). ...*In all your ways acknowledge Him and He will make your paths straight* (Prov. 3:6). *The steps of a good man are ordered by the Lord....* (Ps. 37:23, KJV). It may be only one step at a time, but that is enough!

Are you willing to let God search your heart today? He knows you! You are before Him as an open book. Welcome the X-ray of God! The remedy is with Him!

Read: Psalm 139

July 4   SIN — WHAT IS IT?

For the wages of sin is death; but the gift of God is eternal life in Christ Jesus our Lord (Rom. 6:23).

SIN! Just a three letter word and yet, within those three letters we have comprehended all the sorrow and grief of the world and the reason for all the suffering, pain, heartache, disease and death from the beginning of human history until now. As long as there is sin in the world, there will be suffering and death. Sin is an extremely unpopular subject. We may try to make light of it and refer to it as human weakness. We may call it a trifle, but God calls it a tragedy. We may even seek to excuse ourselves of sin.

What does the Bible say about sin?

1. The thought of foolishness is sin (Prov. 24:9). It must be understood that God looks at the heart. He knows our every thought! *For out of the heart come evil thoughts, murder, adultery, sexual immorality, theft, false testimony, slander* (Matt. 15:19).

2. Sin is transgression of the law (1 John 3:4). Sin is missing the mark. Sin is falling short of the goal that God has set. God's goal is Jesus Christ! When we fail to follow His example, we miss the mark and fall short of the Divine standard (Rom. 3:23).

175

Whatsoever is not of faith is sin (Rom. 14:23, KJV). This cuts deep into our self-life.

3. Unbelief is sin! (John 16:9). It is an insult to the truthfulness of God. *Anyone who does not believe God has made Him out to be a liar....* (1 John 5:10) is the word of God. Unbelief shuts the door to heaven and opens it to hell. Unbelief rejects God's Word and refuses Christ as Lord and Saviour. Unbelief causes men to turn a deaf ear to the gospel.

Let me just mention some characteristics of sin. Sin is not always a hideous thing in the eyes of men — it has its pleasures! Moses chose the afflictions of God's people rather than the pleasures of sin for a season. There may be present pleasure, *jellyfish pleasure*. The jellyfish is perhaps the most harmless looking of all inhabitants of the ocean. Small fish may delight for a moment in the sheltering folds of its seemingly soft and tender tentacles, but in a little while, they are paralyzed, captured and devoured. The pleasure of sin is like that — attractive in form, but deadly in character. Jellyfish pleasures are swimming about in abundance in the sea of human life today. Avoid them as you would a monster jellyfish.

Sin is also deceitful. It is constantly promising, but never fulfilling. Thank God, there is a remedy for sin in the person of His Son Jesus. The remedy is the shed blood of the Lord Jesus. The blood of Jesus cleanses us from all sin (1 John 1:9).

Read: 1 John 1

July 5   **THE FEAR OF DEATH!**

Statistics of a survey covering a period of several years among Bible and high school students, from many parts of North America, gave this startling fact: 65 percent were moved to accept Christ through some form of fear. Those moved by love averaged only 6 percent. Others were moved by a desire for peace and joy. The influence of fear is powerful!

In many ways, we do bow the knee to fear. We fear the laws of nature and obey them. We do not step off a high building because we fear the law of gravity. We fear, to some extent, the laws of the land. What do we do when we see that black and white car with flashing lights? Any fear that merely frightens and startles can have no lasting moral effect. Such fear breeds bondage! Only by the fear of the Lord do men depart from evil.

Paul's character sketch of the ungodly applies to our genera-tion: *There is no fear of God before their eyes* (Rom. 3:18). We are not afraid of God's judgement. *...Man is destined to die once, and after that to face judgement* (Heb. 9:27). Death does not end all! If death ended all, there would be no judgement. Death still reigns today! Every grave is a testimony to the truth of God's Word.

Can we be prepared, when dying, to do that which we are not prepared to do while living? It is not what we feel or think or say, so much as what we are, that will determine what we will do in that hour. Those who trust in Jesus Christ *now* will have no difficulty *then*. The question is a personal one, "How will you do?" No one can do the dying for you. The question is an urgent one. Time is short! Life is uncertain! You may be nearer the brink than you think! The only wise thing to do is to yield yourself to the Lord Jesus Christ.You need not be afraid to die. Jesus died that you might live.

Jesus said unto her, "I am the resurrection, and the life. He who believes in me will live, even though he dies...." (John 11:25). Trust in the Saviour and pass from death unto life! There is a prayer that a preacher prayed often — "Help men and women, boys and girls to do now what they will be glad they did when they stand in Your presence."

Read: John 11:25-26; 1 John 5:12-13; Revelation 3:20

July 6 THE STORY OF THE SCARRED HAND

William Dixon was an infidel. He did not believe in God, and if there was a God, he could not forgive Him. Just two years after he was married, his wife and little boy had died. This made him very bitter. He refused to go to church and for ten years he didn't.

About this time, a stirring event took place in the village of Brackenthwaite. Old Peggy Winslow's cottage caught fire and was burned to the ground. The poor old lady was pulled out of the fire, alive, although nearly suffocated by the smoke. At the same time, people standing around heard a child's pitiful voice. It was Dicky Winslow, Peggy's orphan grandchild whom no one had really cared for up until this time.

Was it too late to save him? The stairs had fallen already! Suddenly, William Dixon rushed to the burning cottage, climbed up the tottering wall by means of the iron piping, and took the trembling boy in his arms. Down he came, holding the child with his right arm and supporting himself with the other. Both reached the ground in safety. Little Dicky was not hurt at all, but the hand with which Dixon had held on to the hot pipe was terribly burned. The burn healed but left a deep scar that he would always keep.

Peggy Winslow died soon afterward from the shock of this incident. Then the question came, "What is to become of little Dicky?" Mr. and Mrs. Lovatt wanted to adopt him, because they had lost a little child. To everyone's surprise, William Dixon wanted Dicky too. So how were they going to decide?

A meeting was called in the town. There was the minister, the mill owner and some others. Mr. Haywood, the miller said, "It's very kind of the Lovatts and Dixon to want the little boy, but who was going to have him?" Mr. Lipton, the minister remarked, "A man like Dixon would not be a suitable guardian because he would make the boy an infidel like himself. But the Lovatts are Christians and they would train the boy the better way to go. Dixon was brave in saving his body from the fire, but it rests with us to see that his soul is saved too." With this they turned to ask Mr. Lovatt and Dixon why they wanted the boy. Mr. Lovatt told them that Dicky would replace their little lost son. He would have a mother, learn to say his prayers and be brought up to love the Lord. All were good reasons for wanting the boy. Now it was Dixon's turn.

(Finish the story tomorrow.)

July 7   THE SCARRED HAND (Cont'd)

It was Dixon's turn.

"I have only one thing and that is this," he said. Then he quietly took off his bandage from his left hand and held up the scarred and injured hand. It was quiet in the room. Then they all broke out into loud cheering and some eyes filled with tears. The sight of the scarred hand was more powerful than the Lovatt's good reasoning. The majority voted for Dixon, none could go against. He certainly had a claim on Dicky by reason of what he suffered for him. Dicky never missed a mother's care, for Dixon was both father and mother to him. He taught the boy to read and told him stories. Dicky never forgot how he was saved from the fire.

One summer, there was an exhibition of pictures in the town. Dixon took Dicky to see them. Dicky was impressed by the picture of Jesus' meeting with Thomas and the words, "Put your finger here and see My hands." Dicky then wanted his new daddy to tell him the story illustrated in the picture. Dixon did not want to, but Dicky urged him. Soon they saw their own experience. Dicky said, "It would have been horrid if I had not believed that you saved me from the fire, wouldn't it? Perhaps when Thomas saw the scars of the Good Man, he felt he belonged to Him. I would have believed at once, when I saw your hand." It became Dicky's favourite story.

One evening, Dixon could not sleep. He could not get the picture at the local exhibition out of his thoughts. When he did fall asleep, he dreamt that a scarred hand was reaching out to him. He seemed to hear the words. "These hands were pierced for you, I have a claim on your life." Dixon's love for Dicky had softened his heart. The thing that he had done to make Dicky his own was the same thing that Jesus had done for him. Dixon found out by reading the Word that he belonged to the Saviour who had been wounded for his transgression. He then gave himself to the Saviour, into the keeping of those blessed Hands.

Read: Isaiah 53

July 8   FOUR KINDS OF LISTENERS

The Sower is the Son of Man. The Seed is the Word of God. The Soil is the Human Heart. Everything is in the Seed! The Seed is the same in every case. The difference lies in the soil. How well do we actually hear the Word of God? What kind of soil does your heart represent? Each man is the cultivator of his own heart.

1. There is the beaten path, the hard soil. The heart is like a public foot-path. The heart that is filled with selfish thoughts and the pleasures of sin will be a hard heart. Each refusal to hear and obey is like a hundred steps on the human heart. The human heart can become hard like pavement. The seed falls on, not in. This is the dangerous place and the difficult place for the seed. The seed is exposed to the fowls of the air and devoured. This is the indifferent hearer. The Evil One comes and snatches away what has been sown in the heart. This is stolen seed!

2. There is the rocky soil, stony ground. There is no depth of earth. This is the shallow heart, the emotional hearer. The seed is joyfully received, but there is very little root, so the plant is quickly starved and scorched. With no firm roots there is no enduring quality. This is starved seed!

3. There is the thorny soil, occupied soil. This is the preoccupied heart. There are competing loyalties, preoccupation with material things and the worries of this world. The seed is being choked. Worldly cares make the soil of the heart unfruitful. A thorn is anything that crowds Jesus out of our lives. Other "things" drain our spiritual lives. This is strangled seed!

4. There is the good ground, prepared soil. The ground has been the object of special care. This is the honest hearer. This heart is open to the seed. The seed has liberty in the soil of this heart. The understanding of the Word is the germinating of the seed. This is the fruitful heart. There are degrees of fruitfulness even in good soil. That depends on how well you listen and allow the Word to work in your life. The character of the fruit betrays the nature of the soil. This is successful seed!

The great object of the Sower is fruit! Has the soil of your heart been revealed today? What kind of listener have you been? The Seed is the same in every case; the difference lies in the soil.

Read: Matthew 13:1-8; 18-23

July 9   THIS MATTER OF THE WILL

You will meet people who say, "I wish I had your faith" or "I'd like to believe in Jesus, but I can't." Such statements are not true. God does not withhold His grace from people who want it. The real trouble with people who say they cannot believe is that they do not *want* to believe. God does not tantalize men with salvation and then make it impossible for them to have it. The reason people do not want to believe is because they do not want their lives to be changed by God's power. They want to keep on doing the things they like to do. They love their sin, consciously or not, and want to continue in it. For all their talk, they want nothing to disturb their enjoyment of doing what they themselves want to do.

In the account of the impotent man in John 5, we might see a bit of the above. Jesus challenged the will of this man, *"Do you want to get well? Get up! Pick up your mat and walk."* Take action! Faith steps forward! God enables! Believe Him and act, this is faith! God has given us a will with which to choose His will. It is God's will that you believe — that you believe in the Lord Jesus Christ as your personal Saviour. Believing in Christ is not merely an intellectual matter, or a matter of the emotions; it is a matter of the will, that part of your personality where you make deliberate choices and decisions.

Do you suppose Jesus singled out the most helpless case there was by the pool that day? He was paralyzed for thirty-eight years. It would be like Jesus to help the neediest soul. Jesus knew the man's condition and He knows ours too. The impotent man blamed his condition on what others had not done for him — *"I have no one to help me into the pool when the water is stirred."* So the question was asked, *"Do you want to get well?"* His attention was focused on the Saviour. Would he trust Jesus and obey Him?

Do you let yourself be crushed by inevitable circumstances? Take action! As faith steps forward, God enables! The miracles that Jesus did were only symbols of the greater works that He would do in transforming people spiritually. One of the greater works is His ability to impart eternal life. The life-giving power of God is His! He is Life! He gives Life! He gives it to you as you hear Him and believe Him! Verse 24 is in the present tense: *If you believe in Christ, you have eternal life here and now.* Many times man's extremity is God's opportunity.

Read: John 5:1-15

July 10   SAVED AND SATISFIED

The first few verses of Psalm 40 give us the experience of a soul passing from darkness into light, from the miseries of a lost condition into the joy of salvation. Notice what the Lord did for the author: *Lifted him up out of the slimy pit, out of the mud and mire, set his feet on a rock, gave him a firm place to stand and put a new song in his mouth.* The gospel of salvation is apparent. David's experience has been the experience of many others. This is indeed a testimony.

In a time of confusion and distress, we come to see ourselves as we really are — helpless and unworthy. We are but dust, sinful and lost. Our sins are the cords by which we are let down into the dismal darkness of the pit. All of us have to come to the realization that all have sinned and come short of the glory of God. The repentance of sin finds its answer immediately. God hears the cry of the penitent heart (vs. 1). His arm is not shortened that He cannot save. Only God can bring you out from the chains of sin and the consequences of it. It is a mighty deliverance from the sinking miry clay of our own ideas to the rock of God's eternal truth, and to have our ways so established that we are kept from falling back into our former condition. I want to impress upon you this matter of being kept by the power of God (I Peter 1:5). [God] *is able to keep you from falling* (Jude 24). The Lord is your keeper!

The secret is abiding in Him (John 15). Get into the Word of God daily. Pray every day! Fellowship with God's people! We all need the fellowship of God's children for growth and strength. Witness for Christ and work for Him. Someone has well said, "You never backslide on your knees."

There is a new song. This new song belongs to the new life of faith. It is the song of the Lamb. He is worthy to receive all honour! This overflowing life comes from those who have believed and know Christ as Lord and Saviour. The testimony of a sound, happy, consistent life cannot be hidden. The joy is unspeakable and full of glory. My favorite verse in the Bible is, *Though you have not seen Him, you love Him; and even though you do not see Him now, you believe in Him and are filled with an inexpressible and glorious joy* (1 Peter 1:8).

Read: Psalm 40

July 11   THE SECOND COMING

"Do not let your hearts be troubled. Trust in God, trust also in me. In my Father's house are many rooms; if it were not so, I would have told you. I am going there to prepare a place for you. And if I go and prepare a place for you, I will come back and take you to be with me that you also may be where I am (John 14:1-3).

One of the greatest promises are tucked away in just four words: *"I will come back."* It was first spoken as a word of comfort to the disciples when their hope of the kingdom on earth was shattered. The Lord Jesus was about to leave them, but a bright spot in His leaving was the promise, *"I will come back."*

The hope of His return became the incentive, the power and the action of the early Church. Trials and suffering were nothing in the days when this hope burned bright. The church was on fire, even through days of bitter persecution.

I believe the spiritual life of the Church is determined by its attitude toward the truth of the second coming of Christ. Someone has said, "Show me a Church that believes in the second coming of Christ, and I'll show you a Church that is on fire for God; a soul-winning church; a missionary church." What the Church needs today is a vision of the shortness of the hour.

The impending return of our Lord has inspired great revivals. The second coming of Christ is a great incentive to holiness (1 John 3:2-3). This is a purifying hope! There is little hope for the future down here, but there is a blessed hope for the future up there.

The last promise in the Bible concerns His second coming: *"Yes, I am coming soon."* It's the last prayer as well: *Come, Lord Jesus* (Rev. 22:20). Between the first and the last promise is a mass of prophecy concerning His coming. God's program is running on time! His Word is going into fulfillment. Scoffers are laughing it off (2 Peter 3:3-4), but the end will come! Do not be discouraged! Look up! Heaven is a prepared place for a prepared people. Are you ready for heaven? Are you looking for that blessed hope, the glorious appearing of our great God and Saviour, Jesus Christ? (Titus 2:13).

Read: John 14:1-3; 2 Timothy 4:8; Revelation 22:20

July 12   THE UNCERTAINTY & BREVITY OF LIFE

You have made my days a mere handbreadth; the span of my years is as nothing before You. Each man's life is but a breath (Ps. 39:5).

Life is a mystery — it always has been! Man has been unable to define life, though scientists have tried. But we have to admit that life is real. Man lives! God has given us the breath of life (Gen. 2:7). Because we live, we will spend eternity in one of two places — heaven or hell.

Life is uncertain and life is brief. Life is going at a tremendous rate. We hear of someone's death every day. People are passing away quickly. Life is so uncertain today! (Prov. 27:1). When you go somewhere in your car, you don't know whether you will arrive home alive. We just don't know!

Life is uncertain with respect to the weather. Tornadoes, floods and storms have taken lives. Some have been caught in a burning building. The hatred of a man's heart has caused murder. We are never sure! Life is brief! Job says, *"My days are swifter than a weaver's shuttle."* *Like water spilt upon the ground,* says David. That is why he mentions Psalm 39:4 and Psalm 90:10.

We are not here to stay! We are a pilgrim people, strangers and visitors. This world is not our home, we're just passing through. The shell of our living is here on earth, but the kernel is up in heaven. Our citizenship is in heaven (Phil. 3:20).

What good is it for a man to gain the whole world, yet forfeit his soul? Or what can a man give in exchange for his soul? (Mark 8:36-37). Jesus says, *"I have come that they may have life, and have it to the full"* (John 10:10). Give your life to Christ, He can do more with it than you can!

Read: Psalm 39

July 13   JUSTIFICATION

Therefore, since we have been justified through faith, we have peace with God through our Lord Jesus Christ.... (Rom. 5:1).

Many think of salvation as a sort of fire insurance against the day of judgement — the escape from hell. The thought of heaven is secondary; as long as they could be sure of escaping the lake of fire, they would be content to live here forever. There is more to salvation than merely having your sins forgiven and going to heaven when you die. It includes the redemption of body, soul and spirit.

Justification is an act of God whereby a guilty sinner is declared righteous and just in God's sight, by the imputation of God's righteousness to him on the basis of the satisfactory and completed work of the Lord Jesus Christ. This redemptive work of Christ consists of more than His atoning death on the cross. It includes the resurrection. The fact that Christ died for our sins cannot justify the sinner. The death of Christ paid the penalty of sin; it does not make the sinner righteous. Justification, the act of God declaring us just (righteous) comes through the resurrection of Christ. *He was... raised to life for our justification* (Rom. 4:25).

Justification consists of the forgiveness of sin and the removal of its guilt and punishment. It is difficult for us to understand God's feeling towards sin. To us, forgiveness often seems easy, largely because we are indifferent towards sin. But to a holy God, it is different. Even men find it hard to forgive when wronged (Ps. 130:4).

Negatively speaking, justification is not by the works of the law (Rom. 3:20). The law can open the sinner's eyes to his sin, but it cannot remove it. The law simply defines sin and makes it exceedingly sinful, but it does not free you from sin.

Positively speaking, justification is by God's free grace (Rom. 3:24). The ground of our justification is the blood of Jesus Christ (Rom. 5:9). The condition for justification is believing in Jesus Christ (Gal. 2:16). We are justified by faith! The best of men need to be saved by faith in Jesus Christ, and the worst need only that.

Are you justified and declared righteous? Then you have peace with God (Rom. 5:1).

Read: Romans 4:1-12; 5:1-11

July 14   ETERNAL LIFE

He lives who lives to God alone, and all are dead beside.
For other source than God is none, whence life can be supplied.

Life is certain since God has given us life! Man is a living soul. God is the author of natural life, of physical life that is so short and uncertain.

God is the author and the source of eternal life. He is the living God! He is the Fountain of Life (Ps. 36:9). God promised eternal life from the beginning of the world (Titus 1:2).

Eternal life is in Jesus Christ! *In Him was life, and that life was the light of men* (John 1:4). Jesus Christ gives eternal life (John 10:28). *Christ Jesus... has destroyed death and has brought life and immortality to light through the gospel* (2 Tim. 1:10). *He who has the Son has life, he who does not have the Son of God does not have life* (1 John 5:12).

There is also the witness of the Holy Spirit. The Holy Spirit takes the things of the Word and points to the Saviour. The Holy Spirit is faithful in speaking to our hearts. He convicts and convinces us that we need to accept the gift of eternal life. *The Spirit Himself testifies with our spirit that we are God's children* (Rom. 8:16).

The Word of God is the instrument of this spiritual life (1 Peter 1:23). *The word of God is living and active. Sharper than any double-edged sword....* (Heb. 4:12). The Word of God gives us the assurance of knowing that we have eternal life (1 John 5:13). This has been a source of assurance to me personally!

How do we possess this life? Eternal life is the promise of God! This promise is the Word of life! He that believeth has everlasting life! Eternal life is a gift! It must be given, for it cannot be bought. God is offering eternal life as a gift to all who will receive it. He will never force anyone to take it. The "whosoever will" still stands! Eternal life is the gift of God through Jesus Christ our Lord. This life is received by faith! Believe in child-like faith. Receive Him! (John 1:12). Eternal life is yours for the taking!

Read: John 1: 1-13

July 15   THE ONLY FOUNDATION

For no one can lay any foundation other than the one already laid, which is Jesus Christ (1 Cor. 3:11).

The term "foundation" is architectural and refers to the lowest part of a building. It denotes the beginning of things. The Church is a building, a spiritual edifice, and Jesus is the foundation stone.

a) Christ is the foundation of the gospel. The Word is emphatically the gospel of Jesus Christ. He is its founder, its source, its subject and its glory. All the doctrines, privileges, ordinances and blessings are from Him. He is the Head of the Church, the Chief cornerstone.

b) Christ is the foundation of a sinner's acceptance of God. Jesus is the only access to God. He said, *"I am the way and the truth and the life"* (John 14:6). There is only one mediator between God and man, the man Christ Jesus. *In Him we have redemption through His blood, the forgiveness of sins....* (Eph. 1:7). We who are frail, lost sinners are justified by faith.

c) Christ is the foundation of a believer's hope. *...He has given us new birth into a living hope through the resurrection of Jesus Christ from the dead* (1 Peter 1:3). In Him, we have full and complete salvation. *Everyone who has this hope in him purifies himself, just as He is pure* (1 John 3:3).

d) Christ is the foundation of the whole Church. *...On this rock I will build my church and the gates of Hades will not overcome it* (Matt. 16:18). He is the Head of all things to the Church.

This foundation is distinguished by its strength. We all know how important a foundation is to a building. It is the safety of the building. Jesus Christ is a sure foundation (Isa. 28:16).

This foundation is distinguished by its suitability. Christ is one with the Father. He is the truth! He is Holy! He is Just! God chose Him from the foundation of the world and sent Him to be the propitiation for the sins of the world (1 John 2:2). He became the sinner's Saviour!

This foundation is distinguished by its perpetuity. God says, *"I the LORD do not change"* (Mal. 3:6). Christ remains invariably the same (Heb. 13:8).

In conclusion, we can see the folly of attempting to lay any other foundation. Men have attempted! They have tried to build on their self-righteousness, their good works, their acts of generosity and even their church membership. When we exclude the Lord Jesus Christ, we build on a wrong foundation.

Reflect on the sufficiency of the foundation already laid! Build on a foundation that will last forever (Heb. 7:25).

Read: 1 Corinthians 3:10-15; Isaiah 28:16

July 16   TWO PATHS LIE BEFORE YOU

Which one will you take? There is a choice! The call is to enter through the narrow gate. The narrow gate and the narrow road lead to life. The wide gate and wide road lead to destruction. God is faithful in showing us both ways. He gave us the capacity and freedom to choose. I am a person! Where there is personality, there is intelligence, mind, will, reason, individuality, self-consciousness and self-determination. God does not force us to follow His path; He gives us a choice. The word today is ENTER the way of life!

The wide gate and the wide road lead to destruction. Many are walking on that road. This is the path of sin and the way of unbelief. This is the popular road; many travel here. There seems to be no stop signs. This gate admits anything and everything. The way of sin leads to death (Rom. 6:23). Many just go with the flow; they close their eyes and follow the crowd to a lost eternity.

The narrow gate and the narrow road lead to life. Jesus is calling us to count the cost of choosing the narrow way. Conversion and regeneration are the gate by which we enter. The new birth leads to life! There must be a new heart, a new creation (2 Cor. 5:17). The bent of the soul is changed! We must swim against the stream of worldly ways. We must be willing to forsake all and follow Christ. There will be opposition from within and without. We have to choose to be identified with Jesus Christ.

I know the gospel has been accused of being narrow, but it is narrow because it is the way of truth. It is the way of holiness, humility and obedience. It is the way that leads to life. We want a narrow doctor when we are sick, not just any doctor with any kind of medicine. We want a narrow pilot who knows the way and where to land. We like a narrow coach in sports to guide the game and instruct in the proper rules.

Through the "Haven of Hope" radio broadcast from CJRM, Regina, I realized that I needed to step onto the narrow road to life (1938). I met Christ at the narrow gate, at the cross. He took away my sin and I have never been sorry! I find it sad that, as Jesus said, *"...only few find it"* (Matt. 7:14).

Are you on the path that leads to life?

Read: Matthew 7:13-14

July 17   ONE MINUTE AFTER DEATH!

A man dies — what then? Jesus draws back the curtain and lets us get a glimpse of the beyond. Let's look at the rich man today.

The rich man lived in luxury every day. He was well-dressed and well-fed. In time, the rich man died and was buried. He woke up in a world where not one single desire could be granted. Now, one minute after death, a lifetime had turned into torment. He saw the truth, believed in God, believed in prayer, believed in heaven, believed in missionary work (Luke 16:28), but all too late. He had a new set of values now, but it was too late. He was in a world where things were fixed. He cried out to have it changed, but to no avail. He wanted to get over to the other side, but a great gulf was fixed. He realized that opportunity has value only in the earthly life. He cried out for someone to persuade his brothers in the land of the living to seize the good opportunity of salvation before death brought them where he was. The rich man had a new view of things one minute after death. Everlasting thirst for a drop of water is an awful experience for one who never knew want. He put himself beyond prayer and beyond hope, and now eternally, beyond help.

The value which you set upon Jesus Christ will be eternally fixed one minute after death. If you set no value on prayer and godliness in this life, there will be no value set on them one minute after death. People die as they live! God will place no value on your earnestness one minute after death.

Will you hear the words, "Son, remember....?" Remember the sins, the wasted life, the scorn with which you mocked your faithful parents and your pastor? Remember the selfishness and greed that shut the door of heaven; the times you fought against the voice of the Holy Spirit? Remember the prayers of the ones who sought by every means to bring you into the grace of Jesus Christ?

The clock of life is wound but once and no man has the power to tell just when the hand will stop. Now is the only time you own!

Live, love, toil with will;
Place not faith in "tomorrow," for the clock may then be still.

Read: Luke 16:19-31

July 18   BELIEVING AND RECEIVING

What is salvation? That is the first question of everyone who is honestly inquiring about the way of salvation. Thank the Lord for the simplicity of the gospel!

He then brought them out and asked, "Sirs, what must I do to be saved?" They replied, "Believe in the Lord Jesus, and you will be saved — you and your household." (Acts 16:30-31).

What you really want to know is how to believe. You must believe in the Lord Jesus as your own personal Saviour. *He came to that which was His own, but His own did not receive Him. Yet to all who received Him, to those who believed in His name, He gave the right to become children of God* (John 1:11-12).

It is a Person we must receive. It is not faith in our faith, but faith in the person of Jesus Christ. Believing is receiving, and receiving is believing.

There was a shop girl, a few years ago, who could not have bought a dollar's worth of anything. The next day she could go out to buy a thousand dollar's worth of goods. What made the difference? She married a rich husband, that was all. She received him, and all he had became hers. By receiving Christ, you become a child of God.

I think you should know that it is free! Salvation is free, but it is not cheap; it cost God His Son on Calvary. He is the gift of God to all who will take Him.

A lady in Glasgow came to Moody one day and said, "You are always saying 'Take, take, take.' Is there a place in the Bible where it says, 'Take,' or is it only a word that you use?" Mr. Moody said, "The Bible is sealed with it; it is almost the last word in the Bible."

The Spirit and the bride say, "Come!" And let him who hears say, "Come!" Whoever is thirsty, let him come; and whoever wishes, let him TAKE the free gift of the water of life (Rev. 22:17).

189

The lady said, "I have never seen that before." Then and there, she took Christ as her Saviour.

Are you going to let time slip by and pass up the opportunity to say, "Christ is my Saviour"? Take God at His word TODAY!

Read: Acts 16:22-34

July 19   THE SEEKING SAVIOUR

We will look at one of the three parables in Luke 15, the parable of the Lost Sheep.

Frequently, crowds gathered to hear Jesus teach. In this parable, we have men and women who, through home and family associations or through their occupations, were looked down upon by the Pharisees and Scribes. And they were the ones who wanted to hear Jesus! Sinners make up the majority in any age. The Lord Jesus does not despise them, for among them are many hearts tender and ready to listen. To the publicans and the sinners, the words of Jesus are full of hope.

Two words unlock this entire chapter: "Lost" and "Found"! God sets a high value on the souls of men. When a soul is lost it is lost to Him! The picture is simple! A shepherd is pasturing a flock of one hundred sheep somewhere on the hills of Palestine. One is lost — does the shepherd care? This shepherd cared enough to leave the ninety-nine others in search of the one that was lost. This tells me something: The Good Shepherd is LOOKING! *We all, like sheep, have gone astray, each of us has turned to his own way* (Isa. 53:6). That is our picture! We are not trying to find the Shepherd, the Shepherd is seeking until He finds us. With gracious persistency, the Saviour follows a wandering soul year after year and day after day.

In looking, He LOCATES! He sees you just where you are. Perhaps he has located you in some peculiar circumstance where He can come and help you. That may be the place where the Shepherd and the sheep meet.

When and where He locates you — that is where He LIFTS you! He puts you on His shoulder. He sees that you need Him! Under the dominion of sin, a soul is drawn nearer and nearer to spiritual ruin, often reduced to a state of helplessness. Then Jesus comes! He looks, He locates and He lifts because He LOVES! He desires to restore! He desires to bring you back into fellowship with Him. Jesus loves you! To Him a soul is worth more than the whole world (Mark 8:36). *[He] came to seek and to save what was lost!* (Luke 19:10). *The Son of Man* [came]*... to give His life as a ransom for many* (Matt. 20:28).

There is joy in heaven when a soul is saved! You can make heaven happy today! Jesus said, *"All that the Father gives me will come to me, and whoever comes to me I will never drive away"* (John 6:37).

Read: Luke 15

July 20   BEING AND BECOMING A CHRISTIAN

There are many, many people who claim they are Christians because of some merit of their own. Let me try to respond!

Let us take the negative aspect first:

1. You are not a Christian because you belong to a Christian country. You might be surprised at how many people actually believe this. They claim that they are Christians because they were born in Canada, the British Empire, or the United States.

2. You are not a Christian because you had or have Christian parents. Many count on the merit of their noble birth. Their parents were Christians and so they are too. I've heard people say, "My mother was a Christian, so I'm alright."

3. You are not a Christian because you go or belong to a church. I had that idea for a long time! Go to church, take catechism, be sprinkled, have my name on the church roll and I'd be all set for heaven. Wrong!

4. You are not a Christian because you live and act and are so good. To live a fine moral life is good. To live a clean life is good. But that does not make you a Christian. Doing good, giving to the poor, visiting the sick are all commendable, but God's Word stands — *not by works....* (Eph. 2:9).

If God intended us to get to heaven on our own merit, why do you suppose He sent Jesus Christ into the world? Surely not just to teach us the way to live! There was a greater purpose! Christ came to die for our sins so that we could be forgiven. Salvation is now the gift of God!

Positively speaking now, what is a Christian? The dictionary says, *A Christian is one who believes in the Lord Jesus and the truth taught by Him.* That is good! What does the Bible say? It says, a Christian is one who is born again from above by the operation of the Holy Spirit. God has worked the marvel of the new birth in a person's life (John 3:3-8). This is one of the "must's" in the Word of God. *You must be born again.*

Salvation is found in no one else, for there is no other name under heaven given to men by which we must be saved (Acts 4:12). If you are saved, you are a Christian.

Men and women and boys and girls must realize that they are sinners before God. Man must repent of his sin! There must be a turn about in his life. Man must believe in the Lord Jesus Christ, live for Him and serve Him! He is the greatest Employer! It pays to be a Christian and to serve Him! It is a joy to have His promised presence. He is a Friend!

Someone has said, "Unless you are saved, you sin with every breath." You need Jesus! Turn to Him today!

Read: John 3:1-21

July 21   DISCIPLESHIP

In the same way, any of you who does not give up everything he has cannot be my disciple (Luke 14:33).

The claim was made and many have gladly yielded. Many believers have laid their life on the line.

We notice that large crowds were traveling with Jesus (Luke 14:25). He turns to them and declares the cost of discipleship (vs. 26). This involves crossbearing (vs. 27). Then Jesus illustrates the need for counting the cost (vs. 28,31-32).

What does discipleship mean and what does it involve? We need to see the correct picture of the demands, the standards and the nature of discipleship. There is the call to be identified with a Person. That person is Jesus! There was a day when I decided to accept the Lord Jesus Christ. Then I was identified with Him in baptism. I also saw the need for counting the cost and being committed. Discipleship is commitment! A disciple is recognized in fully following the Lord (see Joshua 14:7,8). God puts a premium upon faithful service. Are we willing to do the humble tasks? Are we faithful in little things? It all boils down to everyday practical Christian living! It's a matter of being "salty" for the Lord Jesus.

Christ had chosen twelve men to become His disciples. They were now part of this teaching. The claims of Christ were being revealed more and more in His teaching. There was no room for half-heartedness. No turning back! (Luke 9:62). There should be whole-heartedness, submission and glad obedience on our part in everything. The obedience of faith covers the whole realm of life!

From the illustrations in this account, can we build a godly life and a godly character? Can we finish the foundation without yielding to the Lord Jesus Christ? Can we wage good warfare without being committed? Can we have victory in our lives? Not without yielding to the Holy Spirit.

I have often said, "The proof of your conversion is continuance." Go with Jude 20:21 today.

Read: Luke 14:25-35

July 22   MAN NEEDS A MASTER!

Who is the Master of your life? In this present world of ours, we get carried away with "things." We get so involved with the tangible that we lose sight of the eternal.

Let's talk about the rich young man in Matthew 19:16-22. This rich young man sensed a lack in his life. He wanted to know how to get eternal life. We know the story! He was a man of wealth, he was reverent, he was enthusiastic, he was courteous, he had a clean record and he had high moral standards. Yet in spite of all that, something was missing. He came asking, "What do I still lack?"

Christ knows the heart of man! He knew where the problem was with this man. Jesus also gave him a chance to arrive at eternal life. His words to this man were: "Go, sell, give, come and follow." That required sacrifice! A costly prize requires a costly price! We can see that riches were this man's master. A complete committal of himself to God was required. This man had a desire, but he was not willing to pay the price. He was unwilling to join in with Jesus. He went away sad.

Christ must become the ideal in our lives. He must be the Master of our lives. Moody once said, "Give your life to God; He can do more with it than you can." We have only one life, not two or three, and I want to live that life for Christ! I want to be prepared for eternity.

The invitation is now! *'Come for everything is now ready'* (Luke 14:17). Salvation is now! *...Now is the day of salvation* (2 Cor. 6:2). Nearness to God is now! *But now in Christ Jesus you who were far away have been brought near through the blood of*

Christ (Eph. 2:13). Sonship is now! *Dear friends, now we are children of God, and what we will be has not yet been made known. But we know that when He appears, we shall be like Him, for we shall see Him as He is* (1 John 3:2).

Read: Matthew 19:16-23

July 23   LESSONS FROM A BANKRUPTCY

Our Lord never lost an opportunity to let the light of truth shine into dark, sin-clouded souls. He had just told the parable of a certain rich man to expose the sin and folly of covetousness. Then He pressed home upon the hearts of the disciples the needlessness of anxiety over worldly and material things. In other words, "Don't Worry!"

Jesus touched base with the value of life. Life is more than food. Do we eat to live or live to eat? Your life is of more value to Him than the food and the raiment needed to sustain that life. Do not worry about your life! Consider the ravens! They have no storerooms or barns, yet God feeds them. You are of more value than birds!

Life is more than clothing! Consider the lilies! They do not labour or spin, yet God dresses them! With regard to supply and adorning, the disciples of Christ must learn to trust and rest in the Lord. Your Father knows what you need.

The word and the promise of Jesus Christ is, *"Seek first His kingdom and His righteousness, and all these things will be given to you as well"* (Matt. 6:33). God will give us the things we need as surely as He gives the sunshine from heaven and the very air that we breathe.

What do you set your heart upon? (Luke 12:29). We are called upon to *set* [our] *minds on things above, not on earthly things* (Col. 3:2). The "things" of this world lack permanence!

"Watch out! Be on your guard against all kinds of greed; a man's life does not consist in the abundance of his possessions (Luke 12:15). Money does not spell success! Thrills do not spell happiness!

Trust God for your every need. *And my God will meet all your needs according to His glorious riches in Christ Jesus* (Phil. 4:19).

Read: Luke 12:22-34

July 24   AN IMPORTANT QUESTION — John 9:35

Jesus heard that they had thrown him out, and when he found him, He said, "Do you believe in the Son of Man?" (John 9:35).

Our text is found in the account of the miraculous cure of the man born blind. In this chapter, we see the malice and envy of the Pharisees and Chief Priests. We notice the fear of the parents, as they are called into question. We see more than anything, the honesty and the testimony of the man who was healed. I like verse 25! *He replied, "Whether he is a sinner or not, I don't know. One thing I do know. I was blind but now I see!"* (John 9:25).

Go to the question in verse 35: *"Do you believe in the Son of Man?"* This question is urgent and important. There are still some who do not believe. You would think that the events of history would lead men to believe in God's Son, Jesus. He is equal with God (John 10:30). Creation and redemption are ascribed to Him (Col. 1:16-17).

The question calls for faith! Do you BELIEVE? Faith is the act of the heart by which we invite Him into our life, the act of the will by which we submit to Him in cheerful obedience. This question relates to our personal faith in Christ. Do YOU believe? Where do you stand in relation to the Son of God?

When we believe, our lives change. Our eyes open to see Jesus. Our spiritual eyes! I have never seen Jesus with my physical eyes, but He is as real to me as you are. Can I share my favorite Bible verse again? *Though you have not seen Him, you love Him; and even though you do not see Him now, you believe in Him and are filled with an inexpressible and glorious joy....* (1 Peter 1:8). Our ears open to hear the truth of God's Word, as well. *The man without the Spirit does not accept the things that come from the Spirit of God, for they are foolishness to him, and he cannot understand them, because they are spiritually discerned* (1 Cor. 2:14).

To them that believe, He is precious!

Read: John 9

July 25   REPENTANCE

Repentance is one of the foundational doctrines of the Bible. How would you define repentance? When is man prepared to repent? He is not prepared to believe and receive the gospel until he is ready to repent of his sins and turn from them.

John the Baptist came preaching repentance (Matt. 3:2). Jesus came with the same message (Mark 1:15). Peter, on the day of Pentecost, raises the same cry (Acts 2:38). Paul went to Athens and uttered these words as well (Acts 17:30).

Let me speak of repentance from the negative side first.

1. Repentance is not fear. Many people are waiting for some kind of fear to come down upon them. But multitudes become scared without really repenting. Profane men have called upon God in a terrible storm or earthquake, but you could not say they repented. When the event was over, they went on the same as before.

2. Repentance is not feeling. Many people are waiting for a certain kind of feeling to come. In times of trials, deep feelings do show. It seems as if the trials are going to result in repentance, but the feeling too, often passes away.

3. Repentance is not fasting and afflicting the body. A man may fast for weeks and months and yet not repent of one sin.

4. Repentance is not remorse. Judas had terrible remorse, but that was not repentance.

5. Repentance is not conviction of sin. That may sound strange, but men could be under deep conviction, such that they could not eat or sleep, and they still might not repent. Do not confuse conviction of sin with repentance.

6. Repentance is not praying. Many will pray and read the Bible and think that will bring about the desired effect. You may read and pray and cry to God and still not repent

What is repentance? In the Irish language, it implies a man walking in one direction, only to turn completely about and begin walking in the exact opposite direction. It is an "ABOUT TURN." Repentance is a "change of mind." Our thinking about God changes. Our thinking about Jesus changes. Our thinking about the Holy Spirit and the Word of God changes. Our thinking about sin changes. It is a change of heart! A change of life-style! A change of language! *The old has gone, the new has come* (2 Cor. 5:17).

So, there is a moment in every man's life when he can stop and say, "By the grace of God, I will repent of my sins and turn from them." Bear in mind that God does not ask any man to do what he has not the capacity or ability to do. God would not command all men to repent if they were not able to do so. Now is the time to turn to God. God is merciful!

Read: Matthew 3:1-12

July 26   FAITH

Faith is being sure of what we hope for and certain of what we do not see (Heb. 11:1). *...Without faith it is impossible to please God, because anyone who comes to Him must believe that He exists and that He rewards those who earnestly seek Him* (Heb. 11:6).

Follow the story in John 4:43-54. Miracles were done to promote and increase faith in Jesus' followers. If this nobleman's heart had not been moved through the sickness of his son, he never would have known the healing power of Jesus Christ through faith. This is the working of an honest heart, with an earnest request. *"Come before my son dies."* The gentle rebuke of Jesus in verse 48 does not defer him. Was Jesus trying to say, "Are you prepared to believe Me without seeing signs and wonders?" The nobleman basically says, "Signs or no signs, come and heal my son." The Lord gave him the word of assurance, *"Your son will live."* The man believed Jesus and went home. He was prepared to believe without signs and wonders. Faith is taking God at His word!

Faith is rewarded! There is the confirmed evidence! The exact time of the word, *"Your son will live,"* was traced to the time of healing. Such faith is confirmed by the providence of God. God is asking you to believe Him and His word! *So then faith cometh by hearing, and hearing by the word of God* (Rom. 10:17, KJV).

When it comes to salvation, FAITH is, (using an acrostic), **F**orsaking **A**ll, **I T**ake **H**im.

But these are written that you may [continue to] *believe that Jesus is the Christ, the Son of God, and that by believing you may have life in His name* (John 20:31).

Read: Hebrews 11; John 4:43-54

July 27   THE NEW BIRTH

In reply, Jesus declared, "I tell you the truth, no one can see the kingdom of God unless he is born again" (John 3:3).

The corruption of human nature requires the new birth. We need to read Romans 1 to see and believe in the total depravity of man. No one can enter heaven without the new birth. Evil is so inwrought into man's constitution and habits that it is necessary to be spiritually reconstructed in order to see as God sees, feel as God feels and act as God wills.

In seeking to understand this most searching truth, let me point out, first of all, that it was spoken by the Lord Jesus Christ. It is strange that most people admit that Christ was the greatest teacher, but so few adhere to His teaching, particularly this great truth of the new birth. "Never did a man speak like this Man," was the testimony even of His enemies. It was He who is the wisdom of God, that said, *"You must be born again."* There is no escape from this — He said it and He means it!

We need also to point out the necessity of the new birth. *No one can see the kingdom of God unless he is born again.* By nature, we are born spiritually blind, we cannot see into that sphere where God alone is King. Satan has so blinded the mind that it is morally impossible for such to enter. Everything that sinful man touches is defiled, and nothing defiled shall enter into the heavenly kingdom. This new kingdom in Christ can only be peopled by a new creation after His likeness. *For the kingdom of God is not a matter of eating and drinking, but of righteousness, peace and joy in the Holy Spirit* (Rom. 14:17). He must be born from above before he can enter into the possessions of those things which are above.

The new birth is a mystery to the natural man. Nicodemus, being still a mere natural man, was not able to grasp this great spiritual truth. *The man without the Spirit does not accept the things that come from the Spirit of God, for they are foolishness to him, and he cannot understand them, because they are spiritually discerned* (1 Cor. 2:14). It is the darkness of unbelief that does not comprehend the true light. Although a man cannot reason out the mysteries of the new birth, that does not make it any the less real or necessary.

The new birth is the work of the Holy Spirit. It is the Spirit that quickens; the flesh profits nothing. The Spirit is sovereign, He moves where He wills. The sword of the Spirit is the Word of God. *For you have been born again, not of perishable seed, but of imperishable, through the living word of God* (1 Peter 1:23).

Read: John 3:1-16

July 28   THE GREAT HELPER — THE HOLY SPIRIT

The Lord Jesus Christ is mighty to save sinners; the Holy Spirit is mighty to help saints. The Holy Spirit is God's executive worker on earth, if we can put it that way.

He is the Comforter and a Counselor! *And I will ask the*

Father, and He will give you another Counselor [Comforter] *to be with you for ever* (John 14:16). He is our Helper! (Rom. 8:26). The Holy Spirit was promised (Acts 1:4). The Holy Spirit could not be given until Jesus was glorified (John 7:39).

The work of the Holy Spirit is three-fold: *When He comes, He will convict the world of guilt in regard to sin and righteousness and judgment: in regard to sin, because men do not believe in me; in regard to righteousness, because I am going to the Father, where you can see me no longer; and in regard to judgment, because the prince of this world now stands condemned* (John 16:8-11).

The greatest sin is unbelief (vs. 9). Christ is righteous! Therefore, God could receive Him back. He has become our righteousness (vs. 10). Satan has been judged. He has been defeated by the death and resurrection of Jesus Christ.

The Holy Spirit continues to guide, teach and show us the Son, the Lord Jesus Christ. *But when He, the Spirit of truth, comes, He will guide you into all truth. He will not speak on His own; He will speak only what He hears, and He will tell you what is yet to come. He will bring glory to me by taking from what is mine and making it known to you* (John 16:13-14).

Has the Holy Spirit been doing His office work in your life? Is He guiding you into the truth? Has He been a comfort to you? Has He been your Counselor?

Thank the Lord for His Holy Spirit today! He is faithful!

Read: John 16:8-14

July 29   FATAL FRUITLESSNESS

In this parable, we see two things: Fatal fruitlessness and the goodness and severity of God.

Israel, the fig tree, was planted in God's vineyard. Time was given for Israel to become fruitful. The three years in this parable may be represented by the three periods: the Judges, the Kings and the Prophets. The three years could be the years of Christ's ministry. Then again, the three years may not be that important.

The thing is this, God has the right to look for fruit. The fruit of faith! We are called upon to believe Him and to obey Him. Israel was faithless, fruitless and disobedient. We could place ourselves into this parable. Believers are to be fruitful! (John 15:1-8). Our witness to Jesus Christ ought to be fresh and current. Our walk needs to be above-board. Our words should reflect a change in our lives. Our daily life needs to show the love of Christ to others, in our homes and in our work place. We need to be spent for others (2 Cor. 12:15).

The fruitless tree keeps a certain energy to itself. It draws the moisture away from the surrounding soil. It takes in but gives nothing. The tree which Jesus saw on His way to Bethany one day, was cursed — not because it was barren, but because it was false. In the fig tree, the fruit should appear before the leaves. He saw the leaves, but no fruit. Appearance before God is not enough. Profession is not enough. Religion is not enough! God desires the real thing! God is looking for fruit!

The tree which produces is the tree that is sound to the core. Christ offers a merciful reprieve. Under His patient rule, He allowed another year — another year of repentance, another year of renewal. Time is a sacred and solemn trust, an opportunity we must not waste.

John the Baptist came warning, *"The axe is already at the root of the trees, and every tree that does not produce good fruit will be cut down and thrown into the fire"* (Luke 3:9). John was calling a people back to God.

Consider the goodness of God in letting you stand another year. Another year when He will work around you, in you and with you to bring fruit that will glorify Him.

Read: Luke 13:6-9; Isaiah 5:1-7; Romans 2:4

July 30   THE GOOD SHEPHERD — Psalm 23

There is perhaps no image of Christ that has so powerfully appealed to the imaginations of men in all the ages as has the "Good Shepherd." Among all the Psalms, the 23rd is a favourite! I would like to briefly enumerate some blessings and benefits.

1. Decision: *The Lord is my Shepherd.* A personal choice has led to personal possession. He is mine! I am His!

2. Assurance: *I shall not want.* I shall lack nothing. *My God will meet all my needs according to His glorious riches in Christ Jesus* (Phil. 4:19).

3. Rest: *He makes me lie down in green pastures, He leads me beside quiet waters.* What a peaceful position! Do we have time for green pastures and quiet waters? George Mueller of

Bristol said, "The first great and primary business to which I ought to attend is to have my soul happy in the Lord." Food for his own soul was the object of his meditation.

4. Restoration: *He restores my soul.* He is gracious to forgive and to restore. So often we stray; become restless and unhappy. He knows our name, our nature and our needs.

5. Guidance: *He guides me in paths of righteousness.* The paths that are right may not always be easy. They may be difficult and different from what we think. He guides for His Name's sake.

6. Comfort: *Even though I walk through the valley of the shadow of death, I will fear no evil.* There is no evil to fear when the Shepherd is near! Though the shadow of death is dreadful, there is comfort. He is with us! He is walking alongside and that is sufficient! The pilgrim is always in good company.

7. Protection: *Your rod and staff, they comfort me.* The rod and staff were the instruments of defence and deliverance. What they were to the sheep, the Word of God is to us.

8. Provision: *You prepare a table before me in the presence of my enemies.* He knows when and how to feed His sheep. He cares for His sheep. The shepherd finds new fields for pasture (away from holes and poisonous grass).

9. Satisfaction: *You anoint my head with oil; my cup overflows.* Luke 6:38 says, *The grace of God gives good measure, pressed down, shaken together, heaped up and running over.*

10. Heaven: A priceless prospect! Heaven! *Surely goodness and mercy will follow me all the days of my life, and I will dwell in the house of the Lord forever.* Goodness to supply, mercy to forgive and a mansion prepared beyond this life. We will be with Him forever.

Do you know the Shepherd?

July 31   LAZARUS — FROM DEATH TO LIFE

The story of Lazarus in John 11 is, in a spiritual sense, the history of all who have passed from death unto life. We will select a few stages:

1. There was sickness! (vs. 1-3). Loved by the Lord, yet smitten with sickness. Jesus said, *"This sickness will not end in death. No, it is for God's glory so that God's Son may be glorified through it"* (vs. 4). Through some cause or other, soul sickness is almost always the prelude to deeper spiritual blessing.

2. There was death! Trying to explain His delay in coming and Lazarus' condition, Jesus said plainly, *"Lazarus is dead."* (vs. 14). Lazarus was a fit subject for the demonstration of God's resurrection power. *As for you, you were dead in your transgressions and sins... but... God, who is rich in mercy, made us alive with Christ....* (Eph. 2:1,4). Christ is the answer to sin's consequences! Here He makes Himself known as the resurrection and the life.

3. There was Life! *He that was dead came out* (vs. 44). The life-giving power of Jesus Christ could only appear in the case of a dead person. Resurrection-life comes only from death. To share Christ's power, we must go to the cross, die to self and rise to newness of life. *...Unless a kernel of wheat fall to the ground and dies, it remains only a single seed. But if it dies, it produces many seeds* (John 12:24).

4. There was faith! *Many of the Jews put their faith in Him* (vs. 45). The fact that Lazarus had been raised from the dead by the word of Jesus Christ, was in itself, a most convincing witness to His divinity. The influence of Christ's risen life in us should be the leading of others to believe in Jesus Christ.

Do you have a living, current testimony? *But in your hearts set apart Christ as Lord. Always be prepared to give an answer to everyone who asks you to give the reason for the hope that you have. But do this with gentleness and respect....* (1 Peter 3:15). *For you died, and your life is now hidden with Christ in God. When Christ, who is your life, appears, then you also will appear with Him in glory* (Col. 3:3-4).

Read: John 11:1-45

August 1   JOB 31 — A Character Sketch

Have you ever welcomed an examination of your life?

You may see yourself in the mirror of this chapter. Follow the list and see the integrity of Job.

1. Purity in the look (vs. 1). *"I made a covenant with my eyes not to look lustfully at a girl."*

2. Cleanliness of hands (vs. 7b). *"...if my hands have been defiled...."* (See Psalm 24:4).

3. Thoughtful of domestic servants (vs. 13). *"If I have denied justice to my menservants and maidservants...."*

4. Justice for the poor (vs. 16). *"If I have denied the desires of the poor...."*

5. Willingness to share (vs. 17). *"If I have kept my bread to myself, not sharing it with the fatherless...."*

6. Clothing for the poor (vs. 19,32). *"If I have seen anyone perishing for lack of clothing, or a needy man without a garment...."*

7. Gave help to the fatherless (vs. 21). *"If I have raised my hand against the fatherless, knowing that I had influence in court...."*

8. Did not love money (vs. 24-25). *"If I have put my trust in gold or said to pure gold, 'You are my security'...."*

9. Refused to turn to idols (vs. 26-27). *"If I have regarded the sun... or the moon... and my hand offered them a kiss of homage...."*

10. Did not rejoice over the misfortune of others (vs. 29). *"If I have rejoiced at my enemy's misfortune or gloated over the trouble that came to him...."*

11. Confession of wrong (vs. 33). *"If I have concealed my sin as men do, by hiding my guilt in my heart...."*

12. Accountable (vs. 37). *"I would give him an account of my every step...."*

Job may be defensive in this chapter, but it still reveals a lot about his character. Are your standards as high as his?

For the believer, the person of Jesus Christ is the standard. *Christ* [left us] *an example, that* [we] *should follow in His steps* (1 Peter 2:21).

Read: Job 31

August 2   PSALM 78 — A Psalm of Instruction

Here are some lessons from history — the makings of a good Bible study! The first verse would have us hear with the ear the words of His mouth.

We will divide the Psalm into two main themes: The sins of Israel and the wonders of God.

There is first of all a challenge to tell the next generation (vs. 1-8). Our children must know the deeds of the Lord. Turn to Judges 2:10 for a startling reinforcement of this.

Four sins of Israel are listed in verses 9-11. [Ephraim was the strongest tribe at the time, but they lost their precedence later (vs. 67)].

See the Wonders of God! (vs. 12-16).

See the sins of Israel (vs. 17-22). Rebellion became Israel's way of life.

See the Wonders of God! (vs. 23-29). Read Exodus 16:13.

See the sins of Israel (vs. 30).

See the Wonders of God! (vs. 31). Read Numbers 11:33-35.

See the sins of Israel (vs. 32). O, the sin of unbelief!

See the Wonders of God! (vs. 33-35). The disciplines of God!

See the sins of Israel (vs. 36-37). Read Isaiah 1:11-13.

See the Wonders of God! (vs. 38-39).

See the sins of Israel (vs. 40-42).

See the Wonders of God! (vs. 43-55).

See the sins of Israel (vs. 56-58).

See the Wonders of God! (vs. 59-72).

Or do you show contempt for the riches of His kindness, toler-ance and patience, not realizing that God's kindness leads you towards repentance? (Rom. 2:4).

God is good! God is gracious! God is great!

August 3   GOD YEARNS FOR SINNERS

"Do I take any pleasure in the death of the wicked? declares the Sovereign LORD. Rather, am I not pleased when they turn from their ways and live?" (Ezek. 18:23). *But if a wicked man turns away from the wickedness he has committed and does what is just and right, he will save his life* (Ezek. 18:27). *For I take no plea-sure in the death of anyone, declares the Sovereign LORD. Repent and live!* (Ezek. 18:32). *What is man that you are mindful of him, the son of man that you care for him?* (Ps. 8:4).

Many do not understand how God, who has the utmost hatred for sin, can have the most tender heart towards sinners. God draws men and women to Himself with cords of infinite love. There are those who know they are sinners, but don't care; there are those who don't know that they are sinners and there are those who do know and who do care. To all of these, the Saviour is offering divine mercy, redemption and everlasting life. The songwriter states a real truth: "Christ receiveth sinful men."

The parable of the lost sheep in Luke 15 is designed to show the pleasure God takes in the conversion of sinners. The God of heaven pursues poor wandering sinners with the call of His Word and the strivings of His Holy Spirit until they turn from their wicked ways. God takes pleasure in repentant, returning sinners. The repentance and conversion of a sinner on earth is a matter of joy and rejoicing in heaven. It is possible for even the greatest sinner to be brought to repentance. While there is life, there is hope. The worst of sinners, if he repents and turns to God, will find mercy. The conversion of a soul from sin to God is the raising of that soul from death to life. It is a great and wonderful and happy change. When sinners repent, it accomplishes God's design. There will be joy in heaven, joy in your home and joy in your heart!

"Come now, let us reason together," says the LORD. *"Though your sins are like scarlet, they shall be as white as snow; though they are red as crimson, they shall be like wool"* (Isa. 1:18).

Read: Luke 15

August 4   THE INFANT CHURCH

The book of Acts is to the gospels what fruit is to the tree. In the gospels, we see the corn of wheat falling into the ground and dying; in Acts, we see the bringing forth of fruit. In the gospels, we see Jesus purchasing the Church with His blood; in Acts, we see the Church, so purchased, rising into actual existence — first among the Jews at home, next to the surrounding Gentiles — until it gains footing in the great capitals of the ancient world, from Jerusalem to Rome and out into the uttermost part of the earth.

The infant Church was mighty in its infancy! The people's child-like trust seemed to be sprinkled with resurrection freshness. They were in fellowship with their risen Lord. The resurrection of Christ was an unquestionable fact to them. He had become their very life! They had each experienced the power of His presence. They were in fellowship with one another. They were together in unity and prayer. They were waiting as instructed for the promise of the Holy Spirit.

Speaking about prayer, E.M. Bounds says, *How feeble, vain and little is* [our] *praying compared with the time and energy devot-*

*ed to praying by holy men in and out of the Bible... No learning...
no earnestness, no diligence, no study, no gifts will supply* [for the
lack of prayer]. *What the Church needs today is... men of prayer,
men mighty in prayer.*[5] Prayer means warfare, and every time we
pray, we possess more of the enemy's territory. A good man's
prayers will climb heaven's heights and bring a blessing down!

The infant Church was inspired and instructed by the Scriptures.
They honoured the Word! The choice of another disciple was dis-
cerned through the Scriptures (Acts 1:15). Just looking ahead,
Pentecost brought about some great characteristics: A learning
Church, a Church of fellowship, a praying Church, a Church where
things happened, a sharing Church, a worshipping Church, a happy
Church and a Church of people whom others could not help liking
(Acts 2:47); a Church of people praising God and enjoying the
favour of all the people.

Read: Acts 1

August 5   THE EMPOWERED CHURCH

A praying Church will always be a powerful Church. The true
influence of a Church does not come from the social standing of
her members, nor the stateliness of the building, but rather it
comes from the presence and power of the Holy Spirit.

Pause to check the "one accord" verses for a moment: Acts
1:14; 2:1; 2:46; 4:24; 5:12; 15:25. *...When brethren live together in
unity... there the Lord bestows His blessing....* (Ps. 133). We could
coin the word, "Togethertiveness."

To be filled with the power of the Holy Spirit, we must be
emptied of all self-seeking and uncharitable attitudes. The Holy
Spirit comes in as we make room for Him!

During the revival back in 1948 at the Prairie Bible Institute,
Mr. Geswein said, "The Holy Spirit is resident in the believer, but
is He president?" As believers, we are sealed with the Holy Spirit.
*And you also were included in Christ when you heard the word of
truth, the gospel of your salvation. Having believed, you were
marked in Him with a seal, the promised Holy Spirit* (Eph. 1:13).
James McConkey once said, "I used to think that a few men had
the monopoly on the Holy Spirit; now I know that the Holy Spirit
has a monopoly on a few men."

Through the sending of the Holy Spirit to empower the

Church, God is going to establish and extend His Kingdom and make known the gospel to the ends of the earth. The Holy Spirit was promised and given as a gift from the Father.

The Holy Spirit came as a *mighty wind* and as *tongues of fire*, symbolic of a personality that cannot be limited or controlled by the mere will of man. The Church was filled with the Holy Spirit. The people were possessed and controlled by the mighty power of God. As earthen vessels, they were charged with heavenly treasure. They were enabled to speak different languages with clear expression and appropriate words. They had the ministry of communication: *...they began to speak.* The effect this had on their community was amazing. The crowds in Jerusalem that day heard the wonders of God declared in their own language!

In our personal lives, we need the infilling of the Holy Spirit. We need to yield to the Holy Spirit! *Be filled with the Spirit,* is Paul's good word to the Church at Ephesus (Eph. 5:18). "Fillings" kept coming to them to replenish the Spirit and power they had received. (See Acts 4:8,31; 13:52). We must continue to live and walk in the Spirit. This happens best when we are full of the Word.

Read: Acts 2:1-13

August 6   THE WITNESSING CHURCH

A praying Church will always be a powerful Church; and then, it will become a real witnessing Church. Peter became the mouthpiece of the Church in its early beginnings. He quotes from the book of Joel, where the promise of the Spirit was given (Joel 2:28-32). He testifies to the Divine approval of Jesus of Nazareth. Jesus' miracles, wonders and signs were incontestable evidence of His holiness and oneness with the Father. Peter had great boldness — he knew no fear in declaring the resurrection. He was a witness to His resurrection! Peter was driving home the things of which the people themselves had read (Acts 2:25-35). The outpouring of the Holy Spirit was promised by the Father after the ascension of Jesus Christ. The Holy Spirit was now at work convicting unbelievers of sin. With conviction came confession! (Acts 2:37). Peter did not leave them in the dark. *Peter replied, "Repent and be baptized, every one of you, in the name of Jesus Christ for the forgiveness of your sins. And you will receive the gift of the Holy Spirit"* (Acts 2:38). Peter did not say, "Reform and be more civilized," but "repent and be baptized." To repent meant to change their minds completely regarding Jesus Christ whom they rejected; and to be baptized implied the renouncing of the old life. It was an open confession of Christ as Lord! In doing this they would receive the gift of the Holy Spirit. This message received a tremendous response. *Those who accepted his message were baptized, and about three thousand were added to their number that day* (Acts 2:41). Being grafted into the living Christ, they became possessed with His Spirit and they grew in the grace and in the knowledge of their Lord and Saviour.

They were glad in their hearts, *praising God and enjoying the favour of all the people. And the Lord added to their number daily those who were being saved* (Acts 2:47).

Read: Acts 2:14-47

August 7   LAME FROM BIRTH

The book of Acts is full of the acts of the power of God. Spirit-filled men were on the cutting edge! Peter and John are the instruments through whom God was working in Acts 3.

First, we see a picture of Need. *Now a man crippled from birth was being carried to the temple gate called Beautiful, where he was put every day to beg from those going into the temple courts* (Acts 3:2). He had never played with other boys. He had never climbed a hill or gone fishing with his father. He had never run an errand for his mother. But one day, that all changed. Out of habit, he stretched out his hand for a gift. How his heart must have filled with hope when he saw Peter and John stop. Then he heard, *"Look at us!"* The door of hope opened! He gave them his attention. *Peter said, "Silver or gold I do not have, but what I have I give you. In the name of Jesus Christ of Nazareth, walk"* (Acts 3:6). Peter and John had faith in the saving name of the risen Christ. They had something infinitely better than silver or gold. *...Instantly, the man's feet and ankles became strong. He jumped to his feet and began to walk.* An unmistakable testimony! He began *walking and jumping and praising God.* (Check in on Isaiah 35:6).

Of course, the people were filled with wonder and amazement. Peter cashes in on the opportunity. What an opportunity to preach the name of Jesus Christ. *"By faith in the name of Jesus, this man whom you see and know was made strong. It is Jesus' name and the faith that comes through Him that has given this complete healing to him, as you can all see"* (Acts 3:16). With all the authority of heaven, Peter calls these people to repentance.

What happened to the lame man is a picture of what happens to the sinner when he comes to the Lord Jesus Christ. Sin makes us crippled in God's sight. We are helpless and hopeless and unable to walk in a way that pleases God. We need to come to Christ! Christ has been raised up and appointed for us. *"When God raised up His servant, He sent Him first to you to bless you by turning each of you from your wicked ways"* (Acts 3:26). Jesus came to give His life, to save the lost and to reconcile us to God.

Read: Acts 3

August 8   A WITNESS

"Yet He has not left Himself without testimony: He has shown kindness by giving you rain from heaven and crops in their seasons; He provides you with plenty of food and... joy" (Acts 14:17).

I want to focus on the words, *"Yet He has not left Himself without testimony [or witnesses]."* Jesus says in Acts 1:8, *"But you will receive power when the Holy Spirit comes on you; and you will be My witnesses in Jerusalem, and in all Judea and Samaria, and to the ends of the earth."*

We are to be witnesses! We witness in the power of the Holy Spirit and leave the results with Him. Witnessing is letting Christ walk into your conversation. The Lord has placed believers in the work place in the real world to be witnesses for Him. We witness by life and by lip to those around us. We are being watched! Our attitude towards our employers and employees will show. Our work ethic should reflect our relationship with our Lord.

The great commission remains: *"Go ye therefore, and teach all nations, baptizing them in the name of the Father, and of the Son, and of the Holy Ghost: Teaching them to observe all things whatsoever I have commanded you: and, lo, I am with you always, even unto the end of the world"* (Matt. 28:19-20, KJV).

We are accountable! *So then, each of us will give an account of himself to God* (Rom. 14:12). Paul speaks about persuasion! *Since, then, we know what it is to fear the Lord, we try to persuade men. What we are is plain to God, and I hope it is also plain to your conscience* (2 Cor. 5:11). In the context of 2 Corinthians 5, we have the responsibility of being ambassadors (vs. 20). The message of reconciliation is what we share (2 Cor. 5:19).

Do your neighbors, your employers and your employees know that you are a Christian? Do we really believe that the gospel is the power of God? Are we ashamed to be identified with Jesus Christ? Can we identify with Paul? *I am not ashamed of the gospel, because it is the power of God for the salvation of everyone who believes: first for the Jew, then for the Gentile* (Rom. 1:16). What we share is superior to anything the world has to offer. May we be gracious, tactful, courteous and friendly. May our lives be consistent and clean.

Lord, lay some soul upon my heart and love that soul through me; and may I nobly do my part to win that soul for Thee.

Proverbs 11:30 says, *He that winneth souls is wise.*

Read: Acts 1:1-11

August 9   A FRIEND — A NEW PARTNER

A man of many companions may come to ruin, but there is a friend who sticks closer than a brother (Prov. 18:24).

The last line of this Proverb is often used in connection with Jesus Christ. He comes nearer to us than any brother can. A human brother can be very close to us in his knowledge of us and his brotherly love for us, but Christ, our Divine Friend, knows and loves even more. His knowledge of us is perfect! Our hopes, fears, struggles and sorrows are all known to Him, and He sympathizes. The sympathy of our friends and loved ones is limited. Their presence is greatly appreciated, but Jesus understands and comes nearer than any person can. Some friendships are temporary, some are shallow. Jesus proved His friendship by doing more than any man ever did for his brother. *Greater love has no one than this, that he lay down his life for his friends* (John 15:13).

Jesus Christ is the same yesterday and today and forever (Heb. 13:8). He is always the same; our brother is not. We can never be quite sure that even our kindest brother will be in a mood or in a position to lend us his ear or his hand. Jesus is always available!

True friendship is independent of time. It does not wear out with years. True friendship is independent of circumstances. It holds on through thick and thin.

Friendship is possible! I would encourage you to seek the lasting friendship of Jesus Christ. He is a Friend you can introduce to others. His friendship is love! It is not our attractiveness, but rather the love of Jesus that makes Him our abiding, faithful Friend. Go with Proverbs 18:24 today!

A friend loves at all times (Prov. 17:17).

Read: John 15:13; Proverbs 17:17; Proverbs 18:24

August 10   JUDAS ISCARIOT

God's book is full of warning! Men of the Scriptures stand there as red lights to make us stop and think. Judas Iscariot is one of them. Think of it! Doesn't it make you shudder? He was with Jesus for approximately three years, yet he chose to go his own way. It's hard to believe that he would betray his Master, but his story shows us some things about our own lives.

It shows that our environment does not necessarily make us true followers of Jesus Christ. Belonging to a Christian home will not make you a Christian. Faith is a very personal thing! We need to decide to make a decision. Our parents cannot make this decision for us. We have to choose!

This is also saying that the human heart is capable of rejecting Christ and all the light we have regarding salvation. Are we rejecting the gospel message because we have heard it so frequently? We go to church, hear the Word of God and still have no intention of ever deciding to accept God's invitation. We may put on a good front yet never know in our heart if we have eternal life.

Judas Iscariot appeared to be good — like the time when Jesus was anointed at Bethany (see John 12:4-5). He seemed to be concerned for the poor, but really covetousness was ruling in his heart the whole time. *He did not say this because he cared about the poor but because he was a thief; as keeper of the money bag, he used to help himself to what was put into it* (John 12:6). He didn't care about the poor.

There did come a moment in time when Judas saw the folly of his sin. But unfortunately, there was only remorse, not repentance. That's not enough for God. He has a place for every man and it will be either heaven or hell. We have this life to prepare for the next.

Have you ever been born again from above by the Spirit of God, through faith in Jesus Christ, who loved you and gave Himself for you? Do you know you are His child? *The Spirit Himself testifies with our spirit that we are God's children* (Rom. 8:16).

Read: John 12:1-8; Acts 1:15-20

August 11   A PERSONAL ENCOUNTER

By faith, you can know Jesus Christ as your personal Saviour! Today, I want to single out four persons in the Bible who had personal experiences with Jesus Christ.

Paul on the road to Damascus made a right turn and his whole life was changed. The Ethiopian eunuch, a man of great authority, read the Scriptures and, with the help of Philip, made a decision for the Lord Jesus Christ. A fortune teller woman with the spirit of divination came to know Christ through the ministry of Paul. The Philippian jailer cried out for salvation after the earthquake set the prisoners free. This hardened jail keeper became a child of God, a changed man because he believed in the Lord Jesus Christ as his personal Saviour (Acts 16:16-34).

In all four people, there was a great change: Paul, a persecutor, became a great preacher; the eunuch, a heathen, became a Christian; the fortune teller, filled with a foul spirit, became clean; and the jailer, a man of cruelty, became a tender servant of God.

Why do men and women turn to Jesus Christ? Is it the desire for peace? We all know the saying, "The heart is restless until it rests in God." The world cannot give peace of heart. The world was never meant to satisfy the human heart! A round world cannot fill a three-cornered heart. The desire to be set free from the slavery of sin is a good reason to turn to Jesus Christ. So is the desire to understand the written Word of God, even the conviction the Word often brings to our hearts. Faith comes by hearing, and hearing by the Word of God.

What happens when men turn to Jesus Christ? First, there is the acknowledgement of sin. We sin because we are sinners. Remember, Paul acknowledged that he was the worst of sinners (1 Tim. 1:15). But there is a remedy for sin! *If we confess our sins, He is faithful and just and will forgive us our sins and purify us from all unrighteousness* (1 John 1:9). Secondly, there is faith in the Lord Jesus. We accept Jesus Christ as our personal Lord and Saviour by faith. With all of the four people mentioned above, faith in the Lord Jesus Christ became very personal. And then a wonderful change takes place. Man leaves the old life and puts on the new. The whole plan of salvation is a work of God's grace!

Read: Ephesians 2:1-10

August 12   CHRIST MY REDEEMER

Two striking thoughts run through the history of mankind: The depravity of man and the redemption of Jesus Christ. The moment sin entered in Eden, the promise of redemption followed. Some have asked, "Why did God permit sin?" The greater question is, "Why did He plan to take it away?" Through Jesus Christ there is redemption from sin. Again there's the verse: *If we confess our sins, He is faithful and just and will forgive us our sins and purify us from all unrighteousness* (1 John 1:9). *All of us have become like one who is unclean, and all our righteous acts are like filthy rags; we all shrivel up like a leaf, and like the wind our sins sweep us away* (Isa. 64:6). Every act of disobedience against God is sin. Sin must be punished! Sin *will* be punished! Being a righteous and holy God, God cannot tolerate sin — it's a contradiction of terms! Sin is evil and God is good!

There is hope! There is redemption! Christ is the Redeemer! He forgives us and saves us from sin! When the Lord God forgives sin, through faith in Jesus Christ, He blots them out and remembers them no more. [He] *will again have compassion on us;* [He] *will tread our sins underfoot and hurl all our iniquities into the depths of the sea* (Micah 7:19).

Jesus also justifies! He declares us righteous! *God presented Him as a sacrifice of atonement, through faith in His blood. He did this to demonstrate His justice, because in His forbearance He had left the sins committed beforehand unpunished — He did it to demonstrate His justice at the present time, so as to be just and the one who justifies those who have faith in Jesus* (Rom. 3: 25-26).

Jesus gives us eternal life! The gift of God is eternal life through Jesus Christ our Lord. We love Him because He first loved us. Our salvation cost Him His life. Have you ever thanked Him for your salvation? Aren't you glad for the invitation of Isaiah 1:18? *"Come now, let us reason together," says the LORD. "Though your sins are like scarlet, they shall be as white as snow; though they are red as crimson, they shall be like wool."* Praise the Lord!

Read: Romans 3

August 13 WHEN GOD FORGIVES HE FORGETS

"I, even I, am He who blots out your transgressions, for my own sake, and remembers your sins no more" (Isa. 43:25).

"I have swept away your offenses like a cloud, your sins like the morning mist. Return to me, for I have redeemed you" (Isa. 44:22). From man's standpoint, let us check in with Colossians 3:13: *Be kind and compassionate to one another, forgiving each other, just as in Christ God forgave you* (Eph. 4:32). *And when you stand praying, if you hold anything against anyone, forgive him, so that your Father in heaven may forgive you your sins* (Mark 11:25). And, remember Peter's question: *"Lord, how many times shall I forgive my brother when he sins against me? Up to seven times?" Jesus answered, "I tell you, not seven times, but seventy-seven times"* (Matt. 18:21-22). Then, the verse on how to forgive: *"This is how my heavenly Father will treat each of you unless you forgive your brother from your heart"* (Matt. 18:35).

When God forgives He forgets. Our sins are blotted out; they are gone; they are cast behind His back and they are remembered no more. God is merciful! Do you know earth's greatest measure? Here it is: *As far as the east is from the west, so far has He removed our transgressions from us* (Ps. 103:12).

Christ died for our sins! "Calvary covers it all" is the thought of a song. A person was once reporting that, at one point, the ocean was seven miles deep when someone suddenly burst out with a spontaneous, "Hallelujah!" Why? What does Micah say? *You will again have compassion on us; you will tread our sins underfoot and hurl all our iniquities into the depths of the sea* (Micah 7:19).

What about forgiving one another? Are we genuinely forgiving? Let me say again, "Never harbour an unforgiving spirit; nothing sours life more." I think Peter's question as to how many times we should forgive finds its answer in forgiving all the time. Love does not compile statistics; it *keeps no record of wrongs* (1 Cor. 13:5).

Remember the African custom, "Forgiveness Week"? Everyone pledged that week to forgive any wrong, real or fancied, that may have caused misunderstanding. The week ended with a joyful festival among the native believers. Could we initiate a week like that?

Let us go into today with Psalm 32:1: *Blessed is he whose transgressions are forgiven, whose sins are covered.* Amen!

Read: Psalm 32

214

August 14   TAKING A STAND FOR CHRIST

Finally, be strong in the Lord and in His mighty power (Eph. 6:10). These are days when God's people ought to take a stand for Christ! How easily we shrink in this matter of sharing our testimony. Have we no reason for the hope that is ours? *But in your hearts set apart Christ as Lord. Always be prepared to give an answer to everyone who asks you to give the reason for the hope that you have. But do this with gentleness and respect* (1 Peter 3:15).

The object of our confession is Jesus Christ! The words of Jesus are stark reminders: *"Whoever acknowledges me before men, I will also acknowledge him before my Father in heaven"* (Matt. 10:32). Paul says *that if you confess with your mouth, "Jesus is Lord," and believe in your heart that God raised Him from the dead, you will be saved* (Rom. 10:9). Your confession may help someone. It is true that our confession of Christ should match our everyday life, our daily walk. What we do sometimes speaks so loud that they cannot hear what we're saying.

> *You are writing a gospel, a chapter each day,*
> *By deeds that you do and the words that you say.*
> *Men read what you write, whether faithful or true;*
> *Say! What is the gospel according to you?*

Why confess Christ? Because Jesus also says, *"Whoever disowns me before men, I will disown him before my Father in heaven"* (Matt. 10:33). We must not disown Jesus Christ. Blessing and strength comes to the believer who takes his stand for Christ.

Take a stand for Christ in baptism. This is a definite step of obedience. One who is born again cannot look at this as trivial, because it is definitely taught in the Scriptures. *Or don't you know that all of us who were baptized into Christ Jesus were baptized into His death?* (Rom. 6:3). I always like the verse in 1 Peter 3:21: *...And this water symbolizes baptism that now saves you also — not the removal of dirt from the body but the pledge of a good conscience towards God. It saves you by the resurrection of Jesus Christ.* Let me add Colossians 2:12: *...having been buried with Him in baptism and raised with Him through your faith in the power of God, who raised Him from the dead.* Verses just keep pouring in: *...For all of you who were baptized into Christ have clothed yourselves with Christ* (Gal. 3:27). Be identified with Jesus Christ!

I just want to say that faith precedes baptism. Take a stand in partaking of the Lord's table. Be identified with believers who belong to the body of Christ.

Read: Romans 6:1-11

August 15   A GREAT FAILURE

The parable of the rich fool was spoken to a man with a greedy eye. He misunderstood the mission of Christ. Christ was not a judge over property and possessions. The warning was, *"Watch out! Be on your guard against all kinds of greed; a man's life does not consist in the abundance of his possessions"* (Luke 12:15).

Then the story follows. The rich man was evidently a land proprietor. He could pull down his barns at will without consulting anyone. The day of prosperity is perhaps a greater test of a man's character than the day of adversity. The vision of lavish abundance is before his eyes. He is thinking! He is asking! The die is cast! *"This is what I'll do. I will tear down my barns and build bigger ones...."* (Luke12:18). He is weighed in the balance and found wanting. There is no recognition of God in all his plans; no acknowledgement of His goodness. God is not in all his thoughts. He built his barns too narrow — for himself. He built his barns too low — without God! This rich pauper's life was entirely absorbed in his own ease and gratification. A self-centered life is forever a lost life! "Plenty of good things" would do nothing for him in eternity. He built his barns too short — for this life only! If riches are your best friends, you will someday have to say good-bye to them.

What a terrible awakening! *"God said to him, 'You fool! This very night your life will be demanded from you'"* (Luke 12:20). This sudden hand-writing of God on the wall of his self-satisfied soul was a fearful interruption of his godless plans. Covetousness is a kind of lunacy that makes men fools in the sight of God. The Lord had this application: *"This is how it will be with anyone who stores up things for himself but is not rich toward God"* (Luke 12:21). Not being rich toward God when He has brought within our reach the unsearchable riches of Christ, the riches of His grace and glory, is to play the fool. Covetousness even in the New Testament is classed with idolatry (Col. 3:5). Let me say again as I've been saying throughout these writings, "Things lack permanence!"

Set your minds on things above, not on earthly things (Col. 3:2). *But store up for yourselves treasures in heaven, where moth*

216

and rust do not destroy, and where thieves do not break in and steal. For where your treasure is, there your heart will be also (Matt. 6:20-21).

Read: Luke 12:13-21

August 16   FROM DARKNESS TO LIGHT

Jesus did not go about the world sight-seeing; He went about doing good. The blind man in John 9 was to Jesus a far more interesting sight than any building. We can be sure that Jesus looks down on this world in the same way today. The Lord Jesus confirms the declaration that He is the Light of the World by giving sight to the blind, as well as light and life to all who believe.

The leading features of this chapter can easily be gathered up. *There was blindness!* This blindness had all the mystery of the origin of sin hanging about it. It was not because he or his parents had sinned in any particularly grievous way that he was born blind, but rather so that the work of God could be manifested. This man was born blind so that the Son of Man might have the opportunity of showing His divine power. Was not sin permitted to enter the world for the same reason — so that the wonderful works of God's love and grace could be made known in the incarnation and the crucifixion of His Son?

There was deliverance! The method of this man's salvation was about as strange and mysterious as was the cause and origin of the blindness. His eyes were anointed with clay made by spittle, and then he was told to go and wash in the pool of Siloam (vs. 6). There was no virtue in the dust, the spittle, the clay, the pool, or the washing to unseal the eyes of this man born blind. The eye-opening power lay in his obedience to the word of Him who spoke. The man was not responsible for being born blind, but he was responsible for accepting or rejecting the word, "Go wash!" Had he not obeyed the word, he would have remained blind.

It is when we believe and obey Him, putting His Word to the test by an actual definite committal, that we come back seeing. The blind man took no credit for himself in the matter, and he was not ashamed to tell all he knew about it (which wasn't very much) (vs. 11). He could only tell of the means; he could not explain the miracle. But there is a joyful ring about the "I know" in verse 25. It is the confidence born of a blessed experience. Although he knew little about the

Man who had opened his eyes, his faith in Him was very great.

It is a sure sign that Jesus Christ has become a blessed Master when a person is anxious for others to become His disciples too (vs. 27). The name of Jesus has little power in our lives if it does not inspire us to fearlessly plead with others to trust and follow Christ as well. When Jesus met the blind man a second time (vs. 35), the blind man believed and worshipped Him (vs. 38). To believe is to have the Light of Life! To reject the Light is to remain in darkness.

Read: John 9

August 17   SIR, WE WANT TO SEE JESUS!

These were the words of some Greek men in John 12. They came with a desire! May that be our desire!

What does this desire imply? It implies that they had some knowledge of Jesus. They had heard about Him and His name was familiar to them. They may have had an idea that He was the Messiah. It implies that they longed for more; they longed for their knowledge to increase. What they knew was not enough — it was too limited. Did they want to know Him in a personal way or in an experimental way? It implies that they came to the right place and the right persons. They came to Philip, Philip told Andrew, and they both went to Jesus.

When have you last seen Jesus? Today we see Him in His Word. Has the song, "More about Jesus" by E. Hewitt, ever spoken to you? Do you know more about Him? I trust you know Him as your personal Saviour.

What reasons do we have for this desire? Do you know what we see when we see Jesus? We see the clearest manifestation of the Father. Jesus came to show us the Father (John 1:18). We see His boundless knowledge, His power, His love and His holiness. In Christ, we see the wisdom of God. We see the "storehouse" of all spiritual blessing (Eph. 1:3). In Christ, we see the fullness of God. We see pardon for the guilty, peace for the restless, joy for the unhappy, salvation for the lost, eternal life for those who believe and an inheritance that never fades (1 Peter 1:4).

What does a "believing sight" of the Lord Jesus do for us? It enlightens the mind. We were in darkness and sin and one day the light shone in, and we became the children of light. It cheers and comforts the heart. It transforms the soul — we are partakers of

His divine nature (2 Peter 1:3-4). *Therefore, if anyone is in Christ, he is a new creation; the old has gone, the new has come!* (2 Cor. 5:17). *And we, who with unveiled faces all reflect the Lord's glory, are being transformed into His likeness with ever-increasing glory, which comes from the Lord, who is the Spirit* (2 Cor. 3:18).

When is the best time to come asking like the Greeks? The best time is NOW! The invitation still stands. *"Come to me, all you who are weary and burdened, and I will give you rest"* (Matt. 11:28). *Salvation is found in no one else, for there is no other name under heaven given to men by which we must be saved.* (Acts 4:12). *Let us fix our eyes on Jesus, the author and perfecter of our faith, who for the joy set before Him endured the cross, scorning its shame, and sat down at the right hand of the throne of God* (Heb. 12:2).

Read: John 12:20-34

August 18   JONAH

Jonah built a little booth,
A shelter from the heat.
A gourd vine grew, protection from
The wind that on him beat.

Jonah rejoiced, exceeding glad
For this convenient gourd —
Espec'lly since this comfort was
Provided by the Lord!

"I thank Thee Lord, Thou hast been good
To my dear wife and me;
We're glad we're in a peaceful land
Of great prosperity.

"It makes us feel so good —
This little bungalow —
The kitchenette, the living room,
The rug, so soft, you know.

"We love our children, every one,
We keep them home for God.
The homeland needs them just as much
As mission fields abroad.

"And fundamentalists are we,
My children, wife and I —
So thankful that we're saved by grace,
Secure until we die!

"What didst Thou say? Oh — Nineveh?
Well, that's another thing.
Right now we want to praise our God
We're sheltered neath His wing!"

Thus fundamental Jonahs to
The Lord their praises tell.
They'll sing, "We're saved and satisfied."
Till Nineveh goes to hell!

— Ted Laskowski

August 19 JONAH, THE RUN-AWAY PROPHET

The book of Jonah stands among the minor prophets as a lesson of the cost of disobedience. Jonah knew the claims of God on his life. He had a mission in the plan and purpose of God. He knew the call of God! He knew the message that he was to bring to Nineveh. However, Jonah ran away from his task. He bought a ticket for a boat ride to end the call and the commission. He tried to get away from the presence of God by changing his geographical location. He was going to get out of his circumstance, but the Lord created another circumstance to hem him in. God sent a violent storm! Fear gripped the crew! Jonah was asleep! The captain came to rebuke him and Jonah had to admit that he was running away from God. This confession set them all into a state of fear. When in trouble, people cry to God.

The word from Jonah was to throw him into the sea, and all would be calm. At first they did not want to do this; they did not want to be guilty of taking a man's life. But the storm did not stop until they threw Jonah overboard. The calm of the storm put the fear of the Lord in the hearts of the sailors.

Have we sensed the call of God upon our lives? Have we shared our faith in the work place? Have we avoided an opportunity to speak for Jesus Christ? Have we found ourselves running away from God? Have we thought that different locations would change our circumstances to witness? Have we fallen asleep on the commission of Jesus Christ? Have you made promises to the Lord that you haven't kept? Have you counted the cost of disobedience?

The book of Jonah offers a challenge!

Read: Jonah 1

August 20   JONAH IN THE BELLY OF A BIG FISH

Two articles appeared in publications stating that a brown and white shark, weighing about five tons, over twenty-five feet in length, was brought to shore by fishermen in Israel. The mouth of the shark was over three feet wide. No such fish had ever been seen in that area before. Critics of the account of Jonah now have to admit that there is a fish large enough to swallow a man.

Japanese newspapers reported that the body of a thirteen year old boy, still clad in a shirt and white linen pants, was found in a two thousand pound shark caught near Nagasaki. This disposes of the argument that there is no fish with a throat large enough to swallow a person.

The Lord provided a great fish (Jonah 1:17). What did Jesus say? *"For as Jonah was three days and three nights in the belly of a huge fish, so the Son of Man will be three days and three nights in the heart of the earth"* (Matt. 12:40).

For Jonah, the fish meant deliverance! God had created circumstances that made his escape impossible! Then Jonah prayed from inside the fish. He did what most of us would do. When afflictions come, we cry to God. When in danger, we cry to God. God is indeed *an ever-present help in trouble* (Ps. 46:1).

Jonah thought he could disobey God and get away with it. He went down to Joppa, down into a ship, down into the sea, and down into a fish's belly. The way of the backslider is down, down, down, and down. The way back up is hard and difficult. The fish became sick of this backslidden preacher and vomited him up. Even a fish does not appreciate a believer out of fellowship! What humiliation for a prophet! Jonah prayed, and deliverance came. When the backslider begins to pray, he is on his way back up.

Is there a lesson here? God has a plan for our lives. We can know His will for us. God's Word is His will! We can pray and talk to God and let His Holy Spirit guide us! We just need to obey.

Read: Jonah 2

August 21   JONAH GOES TO NINEVEH

The call and the commission are still the same. God does not give up! In His gracious way and in His tender mercy, He does His best to make us line up with His will for our lives. God wants our lives to be fruitful. God is patient! God wants us to be channels of blessing.

Jonah had another chance. The word of the Lord came to him a second time. The commission was the same, the place was the same and the message was the same. There is no blessing apart from the will of God. Are we willing to do His will? On the front fly-leaf of one of my Bibles are these words: "Dear Lord, anything, anytime, anywhere!"

Jonah was on his way! He had come to the point of obedience, and obedience stirs to action. Jonah was very sure of what God wanted him to do and God never sends a man out alone! God was with him and also gave him the message. The messenger and the message go together (Jonah 3:4). Jonah walked through the city streets, crying out for all to hear. Judgement was to come! When God has a man set aside for a great task, He begins to work. God was speaking to the people of Nineveh through Jonah. The wickedness of Nineveh was great! Judgement was to come!

Jonah's message struck home (vs. 5). The people of Nineveh believed God, proclaimed a fast and all, from the greatest to the least, put on sackcloth. There were no exceptions in Nineveh; all were guilty and all needed to repent. When God's word strikes home, we come to see our sinfulness. What we need in our day is repentance — genuine repentance. Nineveh gave up their evil ways and their violence.

When did you last cry to God for mercy? Our nation today needs revival and repentance. Would you read 2 Chronicles 7:14, Psalm 33:12, Proverbs 14:34 and 2 Peter 3:9?

Repent and be converted; be saved from all your sin!

Read: Jonah 3

August 22   JONAH'S ANGER AT THE LORD

God had mercy upon the city of Nineveh. Mercy means that God does not give us what we deserve. Grace means that God gives us what we do not deserve. God takes no pleasure in the death of the wicked. *"Do I take any pleasure in the death of the wicked? declares the Sovereign LORD. Rather, am I not pleased when they turn from their ways and live?"* (Ezek. 18:23).

God loves us with an everlasting love. Some men have been defiant in the presence of God, yet God did not strike them dead. Once an atheist, blaspheming in a certain market place, challenged God to show His power by striking him dead within five minutes. The five minutes elapsed, and following the tense delay, the man spoke to his audience. "What did I tell you?" he said. An old lady standing by asked if he had any children. When he answered yes, she said, "If one of your children handed you a knife and said, 'Kill me Daddy,' would you do it?" "Why no!" came the reply, "I love them too much." "That is exactly why God didn't strike you dead — He loves you too much," said the lady.

But now Jonah is displeased! He had brought the message of judgement upon the city as instructed, but now God wasn't doing what He said He was going to do. Jonah wanted to see the city overthrown. He began grumbling, but God had another lesson ready for him. Jonah was the opposite of Abraham, who prayed for God to spare Sodom and Gomorrah (Gen. 18:16-33). But God had to punish them for their wickedness. How different! Jonah sat back *wanting* to see the city destroyed, but God spared them.

God reproves Jonah for his attitude. Jonah was complacent and comfortable in the shade of a vine. But God brought a worm, destroyed the vine and allowed the sun to blaze upon Jonah's head. I can hear God saying, "You feel sorry for yourself and the vine, yet you did nothing to make it grow; it sprang up overnight and died overnight. Should I not feel sorry for these people? Why were you so self-satisfied and self-centered?" I am sure Jonah was more concerned about the souls of men from that day on.

We should ask ourselves from time to time, "What is our attitude toward the wickedness around us?" Should we not have a heart of compassion?

Read: Jonah 4

August 23   AMBASSADORS FOR CHRIST

Christianity is relevant! Jesus Christ is relevant! We are here to present Christ by life and by lip! Christ is more than a biography of one who lived in history. Christ is contemporary! He is here now!

What is an ambassador? An ambassador is a representative of his King in an alien land. We are citizens of another Kingdom walking around in this world. Our primary citizenship is in heaven; we belong to two worlds. We are representatives of Jesus Christ. We are to talk to people about Christ.

What is an ambassador? An ambassador represents his country. It is like a little bit of Canada in another country. An ambassador does not express his own opinions or ideas; he will say what his King wants him to say. He speaks with the authority of the country he represents.

What is an ambassador? An ambassador is one who has direct access to his King. This means involvement! He is involved with the Word of God and prayer. He stands in direct relationship with his King. He is an authority because he is involved with Jesus Christ. He has access to the throne of grace and that brings God very near.

What is an ambassador? An ambassador is one who is motivated by one primary passion: To be true to his King. In an alien land, he is prone to being side-tracked. Many times he may fail to represent his Sovereign Lord. He can become so involved with the material world that he fails to be true.

Have we been true to the heavenly Kingdom to which we belong? Read 2 Kings 5 and discover a young girl from Israel who was an ambassador.

Read: 2 Corinthians 5:17-21

August 24   OUR RELATIONSHIP TO THE WORLD

"They are not of the world, even as I am not of it" (John 17:16). *In* the world, but not *of* the world. The believers are given to Christ *out* of the world (vs. 6). The world is under the control of the evil one (1 John 5:19). The world is coddled by the illusions and guided by the false principles of the god of this world. The believers have, in spirit, been lifted out of the world. Believers are established in Christ, who is our righteousness, peace and joy in the Holy Spirit. They are not of the world, even as Christ is not of it.

In this high priestly prayer, Jesus is praying for the protection of believers (vs. 11,15). Believers will be hated by the world (vs. 14) because the Word cuts across the paths of those who are walking contrary to God's way. The worldly wise cannot receive the precious things of God. *The man without the Spirit does not accept the things that come from the Spirit of God, for they are foolish-ness to him, and he cannot understand them, because they are spiritually discerned* (1 Cor. 2:14). Those whose hearts are filled with the love of God are not concerned about how much they are hated. God is able to keep!

The Lord Jesus saved us for a purpose! *As you sent me into the world, I have sent them into the world* (John 17:18). Those sent by Him will be equipped by Him. He sends no one out alone! We have His promised Presence! The Son has given Himself as freely to us as the Father gave Himself to the Son, so that His great love might triumph in and through us.

Have you noticed the petitions in John 17?

> 1. *Glorify your Son* (vs. 1,5).
> 2. *Protect the disciples* (vs. 9,11).
> 3. *Cleanse and purify them through the Word* (vs. 17).
> 4. *Unify all who will believe* (vs. 20,23).

Remember the song, "I pray that they all may be one."

Read John 17

August 25   PRAYER IS IMPORTANT!

Prayer is as important as breathing. Prayer is the Christian's vital breath. Prayer is talking to God. The Bible is God talking to us. Why do we pray? What does prayer do? Prayer brings us near to God. God's methods are still men; men mighty in prayer. E.M. Bounds said, *Prayer to God the noblest exercise, the loftiest effort of man....*[6] Would to God we did more prayerful praying."

We need to cultivate the spirit of prayer. *You have granted him the desire of his heart and have not withheld the request of his lips* (Ps. 21:2). I have always enjoyed that verse. That is the nature of prayer — "heart's desire."

Prayer includes praise and thanksgiving, petition and interces-sion, as well as confession. Some of the essentials to prevailing prayer are: Truthfulness — *call on Him in truth* (Ps. 145:18); Simplicity — *not... babbling like pagans* (Matt. 6:7); Persistence — *pray and not give up* (Luke 18:1); Belief — *believe that you have received it* (Mark 11:24).

Some of the hindrances to powerful prayer are: Iniquity in the heart (Ps. 66:18); Willful disobedience (Prov. 28:9); Selfishness (James 4:3); An unforgiving spirit (Matt. 18:35); A lack of faith

(Heb. 11:6). Faith shares the omnipotence it dares to trust!

Looking at Psalm 143, we may see the heart that gets answers to prayer: A heart that is dismayed (vs. 4); A heart that is thirsty (vs. 6); A heart that is fainting (vs. 7); A heart that is trusting (vs. 8); A heart that is teachable (vs. 10); A heart that is willing to be led (vs. 10b); A heart that is serving (vs. 12). We learn so much from David. He knows God to be faithful and righteous. His thirst for God is deep and desirous. His prayer is simple: Show me, rescue me, teach me and lead me (vs. 8-10).

> *Prayer is the soul's sincere desire,*
> *Unuttered or expressed,*
> *The motion of a hidden fire*
> *That trembles in the breast.*
>
> *Prayer is the burden of a sigh,*
> *The falling of a tear,*
> *The upward glancing of an eye*
> *When none but God is near.*

Read: 1 Timothy 2:8

August 26   DANIEL — A MAN OF PURPOSE

Character is what you are when you are alone!

The life of Daniel affords a real challenge to anyone in any age. Daniel is among the captives taken to Babylon by King Nebuchadnezzar during the siege of Jerusalem. We know nothing about his parents, but judging from his character as a lad, he must have been nurtured in a God-fearing home, for the soundest of principles of life had been formed early.

It does our hearts good to meet young people who have a well-balanced personality. In many places of the world today, we find young people falling by the wayside; for in many places and instances, we either stand or we fall. A personal knowledge of Jesus Christ is a mighty safeguard for our young people in this world. Testing times will come, and they do come everyday. Testing times are needed for our moral and spiritual development.

In the account of Daniel, the king's command was to select blameless, skillful and wise youths to be students at the Royal College; then they would stand in the king's palace. It was a three-year course. They were to learn the tongue of the Chaldeans. The

Chaldeans were the politicians, philosophers, theologians and teachers of the nation. What an opportunity for a young, bright, hopeful man! Among those chosen were Daniel and his three friends.

They were assigned to a daily amount of food and wine from the king's table. The worldly man sees no difficulty here, rather a grand chance to attain honour and earthly glory. But for the man who is in abiding fellowship with God, it is very different. Here is where Daniel took his stand. He purposed in his heart not to defile himself with food offered to idols. This, in our day, would be called "narrow-mindedness" and "puritanical bigotry." But the man who is not able to stand against popular opinion will soon be swept away. May God help us to have determination and purpose in our lives!

God allowed Daniel to find favour with those around him. He was faithful! Faith in God and plain fare brought victory for both body and soul. They forewent the king's fare and received the favour of God. Godliness is profitable! The wisdom that profited Daniel was not found in the schools of the learned, but in the closet of communion with the God of heaven.

> Dare to be a Daniel!
> Dare to stand alone!
> Dare to have a purpose firm!
> Dare to make it known!

— P.P. Bliss

Read: Daniel 1:1-20

August 27   VINE, BRANCHES AND FRUIT

Jesus is the True Vine! He was true to God, true to His own nature and true to the sons of men. We are the branches! Those who are in Him bear fruit.

The theme of John 15 is ABIDING! The NIV uses the word, "remain." That word is found at least ten times in the first eleven verses. The theme is abiding; the result, fruit-bearing. Having placed your faith in Jesus Christ, you are a branch. There is a command to *remain. "Remain in me, and I will remain in you. No branch can bear fruit by itself; it must remain in the vine. Neither can you bear fruit unless you remain in me"* (John 15:4). Apart from Jesus Christ there is no fruit. *"I am the vine; you are the branches. If a man remains in me and I in him, he will bear much fruit; apart from me you can do nothing"* (John 15:5). God has the right to look for fruit (Isa. 5:1-7).

What is the fruit? It is the very character of Christ! We are to let the very life of Christ flow through us. The apostle Paul had this goal continually. *My little children, of whom I travail in birth again until Christ be formed in you* (Gal. 4:19). We need to be open to the Word of God. The Word has a cleansing effect (John 15:3). The trimming results in more fruit (vs. 2). The riches of the grace of God are seen here as making the fruitful even more fruitful. What is the Word like? *For the word of God is living and active. Sharper than any double-edged sword, it penetrates even to dividing soul and spirit, joints and marrow; it judges the thoughts and attitudes of the heart* (Heb. 4:12). We are the true disciples of Christ when His character is manifest in our lives. What the sap of the vine is to the branch, the Spirit of Christ is to the believer. *The fruit of the Spirit is love, joy, peace, patience, kindness, goodness, faithfulness, gentleness and self-control* (Gal. 5:22-23). When the Spirit has full control of our lives, the characteristics of Christ will appear. The condition of fruitfulness is seen in *abiding*. The results of abiding are answers to prayer (John 15:7), the Father's glory (vs. 8) and the Father's joy (vs. 11).

The life lived in and for Christ is the only God-glorifying life!

Read: John 15:1-11

August 28   LAW AND GRACE

When did you last read the Ten Commandments?

And God spoke all these words:

"I am the LORD your God, who brought you out of Egypt, out of the land of slavery.

"You shall have no other gods before me.

"You shall not make for yourself an idol in the form of anything in heaven above or on the earth beneath or in the waters below. You shall not bow down to them or worship them; for I, the LORD your God, am a jealous God, punishing the children for the sin of the fathers to the third and fourth generation of those who hate me, but showing love to a thousand generations of those who love me and keep my commandments.

"You shall not misuse the name of the LORD your God, for the LORD will not hold anyone guiltless who misuses His name.

"Remember the Sabbath day by keeping it holy. Six days you shall labour and do all your work, but the seventh day is a Sabbath to the LORD your God. On it you shall not do any work, neither you, nor your son or daughter, nor your manservant or maidservant, nor your animals, nor the alien within your gates. For in six days the LORD made the heavens and the earth, the sea, and all that is in them, but He rested on the seventh day. Therefore the LORD blessed the Sabbath day and made it holy.

"Honour your father and your mother, so that you may live long in the land the LORD your God is giving you.

"You shall not murder.

"You shall not commit adultery.

"You shall not steal.

"You shall not give false testimony against your neighbour.

"You shall not covet your neighbour's house. You shall not covet your neighbour's wife, or his manservant or maidservant, his ox or donkey, or anything that belongs to your neighbour" (Exod. 20:1-17).

Is there nothing in the divine character of God but stern requirements and prohibitions? If this is true, then God is law, not love! Bless His name, there is more in His heart than could ever be wrapped up in the Ten Commandments. If you want to see what God is like, take a good look at Jesus Christ. The law was given by Moses, but grace and truth came by Jesus Christ. The law serves to reveal sin; the law shows us the need for a Saviour. There is no way we could keep the Law. *For it is by grace you have been saved, through faith — and this not from yourselves, it is the gift of God — not by works, so that no one can boast* (Eph. 2:8-9).

Read: Galatians 3:1-25

August 29   ARE THE HEATHEN REALLY LOST?

There seems to be a tendency in us to indulge in the wishful thinking that the heathen souls who die without Christ are not lost because they lacked the necessary opportunity to hear and accept the gospel. The command of Christ was and is, *"Go ye into all the world, and preach the gospel to every creature"* (Mark 16:15, KJV). Would Christ have us waste time, money and effort in winning the heathen to Himself if heaven were just as sure to them without hearing the good news? Paul tells us something about the heathen. *The wrath of God is being revealed from heaven against all the godlessness and wickedness of men who suppress the truth by their wickedness, since what may be known about God is plain to them, because God has made it plain to them. For since the creation of the world God's invisible qualities — His eternal power and divine nature — have been clearly seen, being understood from what has been made, so that men are without excuse* (Rom. 1:18-20). Just as they have no excuse for not knowing, we have no excuse for not telling if we know. We notice that the heathen are in fact heathen purely as the result of their own choices and actions. *For although they knew God, they neither glorified Him as God nor gave thanks to Him, but their thinking became futile and their foolish hearts were darkened. Although they claimed to be wise, they became fools and exchanged the glory of the immortal God for images made to look like mortal man and birds and animals and reptiles* (Rom.1:21-23). This is the primary explanation for the countless idols they worship. The heathen are lost and will continue to be lost until we bring them to a saving knowledge of our loving Saviour. We need to go, give and pray! A poem graced the platform of the tabernacle at the Prairie Bible Institute:

> *Is there a soul who died, who died because of me,*
> *Forever shut away from heaven and from Thee,*
> *Because I tightly clutched my little earthly store,*
> *Nor sent Thy messengers unto some distant shore?*

We need to be involved, to move forward in God's plan to win the lost. We need to make every effort to sow the Seed, the Word of God. Perhaps God has placed you beside someone at work, in the hospital, in the neighborhood or even in your own family circle.

Go with 2 Peter 3:9 today!

Read: Romans 1:14-32

August 30   THE BATTLE IS THE LORD'S

The battle is the Lord's and we are in it! Israel's conflict began when they stood in the full power of redemption. Until they met Amalek, they had nothing to do. All the previous conflict had been between Jehovah and the enemy. They had but to "stand still" and see the mighty arm of God fight for them and enjoy the fruits of victory. The battle between Amalek and Israel points out some lessons for us to learn. The battle begins when we receive Jesus

Christ as our personal Saviour. We have an enemy! There is a conflict! However, the believer can exclaim, *But thanks be to God! He gives us the victory through our Lord Jesus Christ* (1 Cor. 15:57). *No, in all these things we are more than conquerors through Him who loved us* (Rom. 8:37).

Amalek stands before us as the flesh, the old man, the carnal mind. The flesh exists in the believer; the old man creeps up from time to time. We are to put off the old man and put on the new (Col. 3:5-14). *Sin shall not be your master* (Rom. 6:14). The word is, *Do not let sin reign in your mortal body.* We do not have to obey our evil desires (Rom. 6:2).

The Christian life is a battle! There is conflict! It is true that Jesus forgives us all our sin, but we must make things right where we have wronged someone. There is restitution to be made sometimes. Many times we need to ask for forgiveness and that is not easy. The battle is real! We stand in victory in Christ! The assurance of victory should be as complete as the sense of forgiveness, since both are founded upon the great fact that Jesus died and rose again. The death of Christ answers all the claims of God in reference to our sins. His resurrection becomes the spring of power in all the details of the conflict. He died for us, and now He lives in us! The former gives us peace, the latter gives us power. Prayer is power!

Can you picture yourself on top of the hill with Moses? (Exod. 17:11). The hands of our great Intercessor can never hang down! His intercession never fluctuates. *Therefore He is able to save completely those who come to God through Him, because He always lives to intercede for them* (Heb. 7:25). *Christ... is at the right hand of God... interceding for us* (Rom. 8:34). Sense the victory! Moses built an altar and called it, "The LORD is my Banner" (Exod. 17:15). *We will shout for joy when you are victorious and will lift up our banners in the name of our God. May the LORD grant all your requests* (Ps. 20:5).

Read: Exodus 17:8-15

August 31   THE GREAT CHANGE — Psalm 51

The penitential language of this Psalm is always appropriate on the lips of a soul passing out of the agonies of conscious guilt into the joy of forgiving grace.

Here we have deep and real confession. There is no attempt to cover it up. He is conscious that his secret sin was an open insult to the name and character of God. God desires truth in the inward parts (vs. 6). He feels keenly that God looks on the heart. Nothing but the mercy of God can meet his case (vs. 1). He pleads for cleansing from sin (vs. 2). The remedy must be as thorough as the disease. The remedy would not be perfect if it only dealt with past sins and present guilt; the heart which is deceitful and wicked must be changed. The pure heart is a new creation. David prays for a pure heart (vs. 10). With the new heart comes the new spirit.

David prays for the restoration of joy (vs. 12). With indwelling sin there is no joy. Sin brings sorrow! There is joy in salvation, a joy that should never be lost. Although we have had the cleansing of His blood, we still need the power of His Spirit to keep us from falling. There is power in the blood!

As Philip P. Bliss wrote, "What a wonderful change has been wrought in my life since Jesus came into my heart!" David sees himself teaching others. He sees sinners turning to God (vs. 13). When, by experience, we have learned to walk in God's ways, we have something to tell and something to teach. David sees himself as a vessel that God can use to speak and sing His praise (vs. 14-15). A broken and a contrite heart God will not despise (vs. 17).

God's infallible cure for the guilt and the pollution of sin is the blood of Jesus Christ. Trust in the saving, keeping power of the Lord Jesus Christ. There is hope and there is deliverance! *So if the Son sets you free, you will be free indeed* (John 8:36).

Read: Psalm 51

September 1   FALL OF MAN

The LORD God formed the man from the dust of the ground, and breathed into his nostrils the breath of life, and man became a living being (Gen. 2:7). *I am just like you before God; I too have been taken from clay* (Job 33:6).

Man was not a helper in the creation of the world. What did God have in mind? *Then God said, "Let us make man in our image, in our likeness, and let them rule over the fish of the sea and the birds of the air, over the livestock, over all the earth, and over all the creatures that move along the ground"* (Gen. 1:26). It is the soul of man that bears God's image. God is a Person, and personality exists where there is intelligence, mind, will, reason, individuality, self-consciousness and self-determination. With these faculties, man was taken and placed into a beautiful garden. God appointed employment to man. *The LORD God took the man and put him in the Garden of Eden to work it and take care of it* (Gen. 2:15). God placed man into the garden with a commandment as well. *And the LORD God commanded the man, "You are free to eat from any tree in the garden; but you must not eat from the tree of the knowledge of good and evil, for when you eat of it you will surely die"* (Gen. 2:16-17). We do not know how much time elapsed between chapters two and three of Genesis, but we do have the account of man's fall.

The real sin was that they, Adam and Eve, disobeyed and doubted God's word. Satan very subtly and craftily created doubt. Eve listened to his suggestion, looked at the fruit and lusted after it. *When the woman saw that the fruit of the tree was good for food and pleasing to the eye, and also desirable for gaining wisdom, she took some and ate it. She also gave some to her husband who was with her, and he ate it* (Gen. 3:6). The moment they ate, they knew they had sinned. They hid themselves from God, and man has been hiding ever since! When God came to them in the garden and called for them, they began making excuses. *Therefore, just as sin entered the world through one man, and death through sin, and in this way death came to all men, because all sinned* (Rom. 5:12).

God came to the rescue! He gave a promise — Genesis 3:15.

The LORD God made garments of skins for Adam and his wife and clothed them (Gen. 3:21). The promise is fulfilled in Jesus (John 10:10).

Read: Genesis 3

September 2   SIN SEPARATES!

And the LORD God made garments of skin for Adam and his wife and clothed them (Gen. 3:21). We have here, in figure, the great doctrine of divine righteousness. The robe which God provided was an effectual covering because He provided it. God's apron was founded on the shedding of blood. Fig leaves are not enough! Today, God's righteousness is set forth in the cross; man's righteousness is set forth in the works of his hands.

Man was banished from the garden to go to work for a living. A sad moment in our history. Basically, sin separates! *But your iniquities have separated you from your God; your sins have hidden His face from you, so that He will not hear* (Isa. 59:2). Dr. Bob Jones is to have said, "You can't win playing the game of sin." Sin leaves its marks. It prevents man from being happy. What happens around us is an eloquent witness to the fact that sin fills our world. All the sorrow, bitterness, violence, tragedy, heartache and shame of man's history are summed up in that little word — SIN.

People don't like to be told they are sinners. But the Bible declares that every person on earth is a sinner in the sight of God. *For all have sinned and fall short of the glory of God....* (Rom. 3:23). A visiting minister was asked not to preach on sin. He was told to say it was just a mistake. The minister walked over and took down a bottle of poison from a shelf. The bottle was plainly marked in big red letters — POISON, DO NOT TOUCH. He said, "Do you feel it would be wise for me to remove this label and put one on that reads, ESSENCE OF PEPPERMINT? Do you not see that the milder you make the label, the more dangerous you make the poison?"

Sin — plain, old-fashioned sin, the same sin that caused Adam to fall is what we are all suffering from today. It will do us more harm than good to try and dress it up with a fancy, more attractive label.

Man's salvation from sin stands on a lonely, barren, skull-shaped hill called Calvary. God demonstrated His own love for us in this: *While we were still sinners, Christ died for us* (Rom. 5:8). *...Christ died for our sins according to the Scriptures... He was buried...* [and] *He was raised on the third day according to the Scriptures....* (1 Cor. 15:3-4). The word for us today is, *Yet to all who received Him, to those who believed in His name, He gave the right to become children of God* (John 1:12).

Read: Genesis 3:17-24

September 3   CAIN AND ABEL

The book of Genesis is the 'seed plot' of the whole Bible and man's entire history. In the persons of Cain and Abel, we have the first examples of a religious man and a man of faith. Born as they were, sons of fallen Adam and outside of Eden, they had nothing, naturally, to keep them both from lives of sin. They were both sinners, both had a fallen nature, neither was innocent. They both came into the world as the partakers of the nature of their father — a fallen, sinful, ruined nature.

The life of Cain and Abel furnish a fair opportunity for the distinctive qualities, capacities, resources and tendencies of nature to manifest themselves. David declares: *Surely I was sinful at birth, sinful from the time my mother conceived me* (Ps. 51:5). Abel was not distinguished from his brother Cain by anything natural. The difference was not in themselves, in their nature or their circumstances; it lay entirely in their sacrifices. It was not a question of the *offerer*, but of his *offering*.

Abel brought of the firstlings of his flock — an offering where the blood of an innocent animal was shed. Cain brought of the fruit of the ground — an offering without the shedding of blood. God had established a divine principle: *Without the shedding of blood, there is no remission.* The shedding of blood affords the acceptance of a sinner before God. Therefore, God was more pleased with Abel's sacrifice than with Cain's, because Cain did not give his best — his all — to God, and seek the remission of his sins.

Cain has millions of followers today who believe in their own works. They want to come in their own way. But God's way, the *only* way, is through Jesus Christ. *For the wages of sin is death, but the gift of God is eternal life in Christ Jesus our Lord* (Rom. 6:23).

Read: Genesis 4:1-15

September 4   ABEL'S SACRIFICE

By faith Abel offered God a better sacrifice than Cain did. By faith he was commended as a righteous man, when God spoke well of his offerings. And by faith he still speaks, even though he is dead (Heb. 11:4). Abel entered by faith into the glorious truth that God could be approached by sacrifice; that there was such a thing as a sinner placing the death of another between himself and the consequences of his sin. The claims of God could be met by the blood of an innocent animal offered to God for the forgiveness of sins. This in short, is the doctrine of the cross.

In the cross, the convicted sinner has divine provision for all his guilt and all his need. Christ has cleared the prospect of death and judgement for the one who believes. *It has now been revealed through the appearing of our Saviour, Christ Jesus, who has destroyed death and has brought life and immortality to light through the gospel* (2 Tim. 1:10). Christ has put away sin by the sacrifice of Himself. This is in type set forth in Abel's "more excellent sacrifice."

There was no attempt on the part of Abel to set aside the truth of his own condition; he found a substitute. Thus it is with every poor lost sinner — Christ is his substitute, his ransom, his "most excellent sacrifice." Nothing but the perfect sacrifice of the Son of God can give ease to the heart and conscience. It is faith which puts the soul in present possession of peace. *Therefore, since we have been justified through faith, we have peace with God through our Lord Jesus Christ* (Rom. 5:1).

It is not a question of feeling. Feeling is not faith! Faith justifies the soul, purifies the heart, works by love and overcomes the world. Faith believes God when He speaks, and takes Him at His word. This life has God as its source, a risen Christ as its channel, the Holy Spirit as its power, heaven as its sphere and eternity as its duration. There is life in a look at the crucified One. *He Himself bore our sins in His body on the tree, so that we might die to sins and live for righteousness; by His wounds you have been healed* (1 Peter 2:24).

Read: Hebrews 11:1-6

September 5   THE WICKEDNESS OF THE WORLD

When the wicked thrive, so does sin, but the righteous will see their downfall (Prov. 29:16).

In the days of Noah, man multiplied and so did wickedness. *The LORD saw how great man's wickedness on the earth had become, and that every inclination of the thoughts of his heart was only evil all the time* (Gen. 6:5). Sin is sin — as it was in Noah's time, so it is today. Wickedness is rampant, sin is a spreading leprosy.

Wickedness is great when great men are wicked. Man is totally depraved, he is naturally corrupt. *As it is written: "There is no one* righteous, not even one.... (Rom. 3:10). *The heart is deceitful above all things and beyond cure. Who can understand it?* (Jer. 17:9).

Notice, *the LORD was grieved that He had made man on the earth, and His heart was filled with pain* (Gen. 6:6). He was sorry that man chose to do evil. *You have not bought any fragrant calamus for me, or lavished on me the fat of your sacrifices. But you have burdened me with your sins and wearied me with your offenses* (Isa. 43:24). Sin must be punished!

Now notice, *But Noah found favour in the eyes of the LORD* (Gen. 6:8). Noah was distinguished from the rest of the world. He did not find favour in the eyes of men, but he did in the eyes of God. When the rest of the world was corrupt and wicked, Noah kept his integrity. He was a just man. He walked with God. *Noah was a righteous man, blameless among the people of his time, and he walked with God* (Gen. 6:9). We are only what we are and where we are by the grace of God. *But where sin increased, grace increased all the more....* (Rom. 5:20). Grace means that God gives us what we do not deserve.

Read: Genesis 6

September 6   THE WORD OF GOD AND FAITH

By faith Noah, when warned about things not yet seen, in holy fear built an ark to save his family. By his faith he condemned the world and became heir of the righteousness that comes by faith (Heb. 11:7). Nature is governed by what it sees and senses. Faith is governed by the pure word of God. When God spoke to Noah of pending judgement, there was no sign of it. But the word of God made it a present reality to the heart that could mix that Word with faith. Faith does not wait to see a thing before it believes. All that the man of faith needs is to know that God has spoken. A single line of Scripture is an abundant answer to all the reasonings and imaginations of the human mind.

It was the word of God which sustained the heart of Noah during his long course of service. The word of God was the ground on which he stood when scoffers sneered at him for building the ark.

How do we stand in a day that's evil? Through God's pure, incorruptible and eternal Word. God's word was the simple resting place of Noah's heart, when all around the thoughts of the hearts of men were only evil all the time. In this story, we find God's judgement of nature with all its evil, and at the same time, we see the revelation of His saving grace in all its fullness.

At Calvary, we see the waters of life set free and the windows of heaven opened. The Lord Jesus has met all that could be against us. He put away sin by the sacrifice of Himself. The triumphant language of Romans 8:31-32 is, *What, then, shall we say in response to this? If God is for us, who can be against us? He who did not spare His own Son, but gave Him up for us all — how will He not also, along with Him, graciously give us all things?*

The Lord shut Noah and his family in. They were safe. Are you in the ark of salvation? Take Christ and be "shut in" for heaven.

Read: Genesis 6:11-22

September 7   BABEL-LANGUAGE

Now the whole world had one language and a common speech. As men moved eastward, they found a plain in Shinar and settled there. They said to each other, "Come, let's make bricks and bake them thoroughly." They used brick instead of stone, and tar for mortar. Then they said, "Come, let us build ourselves a city, with a tower that reaches to the heavens, so that we may make a name for ourselves and not be scattered over the face of the whole earth" (Gen. 11:1-4). We have here a revelation of human ambition and a manifestation of Divine displeasure. Isn't this just like human nature? The human heart ever seeks a name, a portion and a centre in the world. Left to self, it will ever find its objects in this lower world. Man is indeed allied to this earth.

To make a name for himself was man's objective on the plain of Shinar, and such has been his objective ever since. Man is a self-seeking, self-exalting creature who so often leaves God out of his plan. Looking at this Babel confederacy, we also notice man's marked tendency to organize. This organization left God out! Notice: *But the LORD came down to see the city and the tower that the men were building. The Lord said, "If as one people speaking the same language they have begun to do this, then nothing they plan to do will be impossible for them. Come, let us go down and confuse their language so they will not understand each other"* (Gen. 11:5-7). Such was the end of man's first organization.

God's word to mankind was to be fruitful, multiply and fill the earth. In order to spread them out, God confounded [mixed up] their language. Languages come in families today. Have you ever sensed how closely related they are? For example, take the word, *school*; in German, it's *schule*; in Dutch, it's *schol*.

In conclusion today, I want to bring your attention to three Scripture passages which may be read in an interesting and profitable connection: Genesis 11, where God gives various tongues as an expression of His judgment; Acts 2, where He gives various tongues as an expression of His grace; and Revelation 7, where we see all those tongues gathered round the Lamb in glory.

Read: Genesis 11:1-9

September 8   ABRAHAM CALLED!

The life of Abraham, like the course of a river, has a few turns. A life of faith in God will always be fragrant. *The LORD had said to Abram, "Leave your country, your people and your father's household and go to the land I will show you. I will make you into a great nation and I will bless you; I will make your name great, and you will be a blessing"* (Gen. 12:1-2). God had spoken and Abraham believed and obeyed the call. He was to be a special instrument in the hand of God. This speaks of separation. The call was very personal. He alone could answer it.

I borrow the phrase, "I being in the way the Lord led me." You cannot lead anything that does not move. Many of us are far too settled. Compared to the tent-dwellers of Abraham's time, we are *really* settled down. The Christian life is not one of standing still. This life is a life of faith in God and fellowship with God. God promises to instruct us and to guide us (Ps. 32:8). The Word is so precious. There has not failed one word of His good promise.

The promise of being made a blessing was given to Abraham. Messianic prophecies were going to be fulfilled. We can only be a blessing for God after we have been blessed by God.

Is God calling you to some specific task? Are you going to obey? Obey God's call — do as Abraham did! *So Abram left, as the LORD had told him; and Lot went with him. Abram was seventy-five years old when he set out from Haran. He took his wife Sarai, his nephew Lot, all the possessions they had accumulated and the people they had acquired in Haran, and they set out for the land of Canaan, and they arrived there. Abram traveled through the land as far as the site of the great tree of Moreh at Shechem. At that time the Canaanites were in the land. The* LORD *appeared to Abram and said, "To your offspring I will give this land." So he built an altar there to the* LORD, *who had appeared to him. From there he went on towards the hills east of Bethel and pitched his tent, with Bethel on the west and Ai on the east. There he built an altar to the* LORD *and called on the name of the* LORD (Gen. 12:4-8).

Read: Genesis 12:1-9

September 9   ABRAHAM IN EGYPT

In the spiritual world of our Christian experience, as well as in the natural world, changes may come very suddenly. Who would have thought that a man with Abraham's faith would turn aside at the first temptation. At our best and strongest moment, we are in danger of falling, if not kept by the power of God through faith. If faith is to triumph and grow, it must be tested. Peter writes in his epistle that the testing of our faith is precious (1 Peter 1:7). Trials make the promise sweet; there is no discipline of soul without them.

Faith has its trials as well as its answers. It is not to be imagined that the man of faith, having pushed out from the shore of circumstances, finds it all smooth and easy sailing. By no means. Again and again, he is called to encounter rough and stormy skies; but it is all graciously designed to lead him into deeper and more matured experiences of what God is to the heart that confides in Him. Were the sky always without a cloud, and the ocean without a ripple, the believer would not know so well the God with whom we have to do.

We are frequently led to judge the rightness of a path by its exemption from trial; but the path of obedience may often be found most trying to the flesh.

Abraham's experience led to fear. He was afraid they would take his life. He was more concerned about his own safety than the honour and chastity of his wife. It led to hypocrisy! He pretended to be what he was not. Do we show our faith when the presence of a human being is a greater restraint upon our actions than God's all-seeing eye? It is sad when a child of God has to be warned and corrected by a man of the world. Pharaoh knew that Abraham did not belong in Egypt. The world knows better at times and rebukes us. Oh, that our lives might be consistent!

Let us watch against the tendency to slip aside from the narrow way. Let us remember Jesus Christ, *who gave Himself for us to redeem us from all wickedness....* (Titus 2:14). Abraham returned! He came back to the place where he first got side-tracked. Are you in fellowship with the Lord today?

Read: Genesis 12:10-13:4

September 10   ABRAHAM AND LOT SEPARATE

Abram went up from Egypt, back to where he had first built an altar, and he called on the name of the Lord. This is the essential step to take when we have erred in life. We need to go back to the place where our straying began. Abram renewed his fellowship with God. God renews His promise to Abram in chapter 15.

You will notice that Lot always goes along. Lot, however, was living for his own pleasure and profit. The well-watered plains were very attractive, and getting along with Abram was becoming more difficult. Both were rich. The conditions of the country would not permit them to live together. There was strife! Abram took the aggressive and said, *"Let's not have any quarreling between you and me, or between your herdsmen and mine, for we are brothers"* (Gen. 13:8). Then he says, *"Is not the whole land before you? Let's part company. If you go to the left, I'll go to the right; if you go to the right, I'll go to the left"* (Gen. 13:9). The friend of God can easily afford to let others have the first choice.

Stop to look at the selfishness of the worldly-minded. *Lot looked up and saw that the whole plain of the Jordan was well watered, like the garden of the LORD, like the land of Egypt, towards Zoar* (Gen. 13:10). Lot separated himself from the man of faith with a light heart and took the richer land. His mind was set on earthly prosperity. But self-seeking believers bear no testimony for God.

After the separation, Abram receives a message from the Lord: *"Lift up your eyes from where you are and look north and south, east and west. All the land that you see I will give to you and your off-spring forever"* (Gen. 13:14-15). Abram lifted up his eyes at the invitation of the Lord. Herein lies the great distinction between the worldly Christian and the faithful one. One is moved by self-interest, the other by the Word of the Lord. Abram went on leaning on the promises of God. Wherever he went, he set up an altar to the Lord.

Are you concerned about living a separated life? Are you living for the Lord?

Read: Genesis 13:1-18

241

September 11   ABRAHAM'S CHARACTER

Abraham stands out in the story of Lot's captivity. One's character is often revealed when others are in trouble. Lot had taken his abode in Sodom. Now we see him as a captive. He is a prisoner.

We see Abraham as a man of sympathy. He could have said, "He has himself to blame, it serves him right; he should not have gone to Sodom." Instead, Abraham seeks Lot's deliverance. Those who walk in fellowship with God cannot remain indifferent to the plight of others. It has been said, "The claims of a brother's trouble are answered by the affections of a brother's heart." Genuine faith, while it always renders us independent, never renders us indifferent; it will never wrap itself up in its fleece while a brother shivers in the cold. How indifferent we are at times! We ourselves are only where we are and what we are by the grace of God. May we make it our business to go out of our way to lend a helping hand.

We see Abraham as a man of courage. With his handful of servants, he goes against four kings. I'm sure he was in the minority. The man of faith attempts great things. Abraham's faith worked by love; he loved his nephew Lot and dared to do this great deed. This reminds me of the touching story of a little girl who was carrying her baby brother. A passerby remarked, "Isn't he heavy?" She replied, "No, he's my brother." Abraham brought back his nephew. Do we seek to help others return to the fellowship of believers?

We see Abraham as a man of power. He brought back all. Victory was complete. Abraham's power lay in his life of faith. Faith shares the omnipotence it dares to trust. The Lord was his portion, and he wanted to be to the honour and glory of God. He did not ascribe the victory to himself.

We all make choices. Many make choices for honour, fame, prestige, riches and pleasure, but these don't bring real joy. Real joy comes from being set apart for God. Many a battle will need to be fought by the man of God who is fully separated. But thank God for His presence! Some day soon we may hear His, "Well done."

Read: Genesis 14:13-16

September 12   ABRAHAM ENCOURAGED

A man finds joy in giving an apt reply — and how good is a timely word! (Prov. 15:23).

God's words are always in season. His consolations are neither few nor small. Every now and again, God encouraged Abraham. *After this, the word of the LORD came to Abram in a vision: "Do not be afraid, Abram. I am your shield, your very great reward"* (Gen. 15:1). God did not let Abraham down. Abraham was to find his present rest and peace in God.

1. This message contains a revelation of God's love. The admonishment, *"Do not be afraid,"* runs throughout the Bible. It is the language of love and grace. Jesus says it frequently in the gospels. Paul uses the phrase in his epistles.

2. This message contained a revelation of God's power. *"I am your shield."* The Omnipotent, personal God declares Himself the protection of the man who walks by faith. It was infinitely better for Abraham to be hidden behind God's shield than to take refuge beneath the patronage of the King of Sodom. So many have found that God is a very present help in trouble. God is our refuge.

3. This message contains a revelation of God's fullness. *"I am your very great reward."* This promise was given after Abraham refused the unhallowed gifts of the King of Sodom. Abraham did not take that which might hinder him in his life. God had enriched him! It is still the desire and the delight of God that His people be satisfied with Himself. The greatest reward God can give is a fuller acquaintance with Himself. These unsearchable riches are for us today in Christ.

How long have you known Jesus? Does He dwell in your heart by faith? *It is because of Him that you are in Christ Jesus, who has become for us wisdom from God — that is, our righteousness, holiness and redemption* (1 Cor. 1:30). Have you enjoyed all that is yours in Christ? God gave us all when He gave us His son!

Read: Genesis 15:1-7

September 13 ABRAHAM WALKING BEFORE GOD

Age may shut us out from the joys and companionships of youth, but through grace it may ripen our friendship with God. *When Abram was ninety-nine years old, the LORD appeared to him and said, "I am God Almighty; walk before me and be blameless"* (Gen. 17:1). Faith alone can enable a man to walk before an Almighty God. This implies having nothing whatsoever before our hearts save God Himself. If I am basing my expectations upon men and things, I am not walking before God. The only way to get above the world is to walk by faith, because faith so completely fills the scene with God that there is no room for the things of this world. If God fills up my entire range of vision, I can see nothing else. This revelation of God as our all-sufficiency is made known to us in Jesus Christ. There is enough in Him to meet all our need.

Notice the commission: *"Walk before me and be blameless."* This call affected Abraham's life. He was to act as one who lived in the immediate presence of Almighty God. It has always been a real challenge to understand that God sees and knows everything. Just to know that God sees me ought to put a check on my life. It should affect our character. The highest human perfection lies in a whole-hearted life before God. Of course, all perfection comes from Him who alone is perfect. We have that in Jesus Christ!

Notice the submission: *Abram fell facedown* (Gen. 17:3). He bowed his face to the dust, and God talked with Him. It is when man is in the dust that God can talk to him in grace. Abraham's posture is a beautiful expression of entire prostration in the presence of God. The best answer to God's high calling is a humble and broken spirit. God always talks to the heart of the self-abased.

Notice the transformation: *"No longer will you be called Abram; your name will be Abraham, for I have made you a father of many nations"* (Gen. 17:5). Abram, the exalted, is changed into Abraham, the fruitful. He has bowed with his whole heart to the will of God and his character is transformed. Complete surrender brings a complete change of nature. By yielding to the Holy Spirit we are transformed (2 Cor. 3:18).

Read: Genesis 17:1-8

September 14   ABRAHAM SERVING

Many Old Testament incidents yield some New Testament truths. An obedient soul enjoys the communion of the Lord. Obedience refreshes the Lord, as being the fruit of His own grace in our hearts. The life of Abraham bears out some practical lessons. *The LORD appeared to Abraham near the great trees of Mamre while he was sitting at the entrance to his tent in the heat of the day. Abraham looked up and saw three men standing nearby. When he saw them, he hurried from the entrance of his tent to meet them and bowed low to the ground* (Gen. 18:1-2).

1. There is a gracious visit. The Lord appeared. Three men stood nearby. Jehovah manifests Himself in the form of three. Does this suggest the Trinity of God? The Trinity is interested and exercised in seeking to bless and save man. The Trinity is active in the salvation of man. God's gracious visit was visible to Abraham.

2. There is a hearty reception. Abraham hurried to meet them and bowed low to the ground. He had a humble spirit. He was ready to extend hospitality. This led to fellowship with His Lord. The soul that has discovered the Lord yearns to abide in His presence where there is fullness of joy. Is this fellowship still yours today?

3. There is the readiness to serve. *"Let a little water be brought, and then you may all wash your feet and rest under this tree. Let me get you something to eat, so you can be refreshed and then go on your way now that you have come to your servant." "Very well," they answered, "do as you say"* (Gen. 18:4-5). Love lends swiftness to the willing feet.

The devotion of Abraham was rewarded with a revelation of the secret purpose of God. The promise of a son was made. The way into the deeper things of God often lies through self-sacrifice and active service. Open your heart to God, and His heart will be open to you! Would you also ponder the words, *"Is anything too hard for the Lord?"* (Gen. 18:14a).

Read: Genesis 18:1-15

September 15   THE FAITH OF ABRAHAM

The highest test of character often comes directly from the hand of God. Abraham's heart was put to the most severe test: *Then God said, "Take your son, your only son, Isaac, whom you love, and go to the region of Moriah. Sacrifice him there as a burnt offering on one of the mountains I will tell you about"* (Gen. 22:2). God was testing the reality of his faith.This command required something very close to Abraham's heart; it was passing him through a searching crucible indeed. God requires truth in the inward parts. There may be much truth on the lips and in the intellect, but God looks for it in the heart. It is no ordinary proof that God looks for, as to the love of our hearts. Isaac, our greatest love, must be offered as a burnt offering. This surely, is putting faith to the test. Faith is precious to God! (1 Peter 1:7).

God Himself was the living and abiding support of Abraham's

heart, and therefore he was prepared to give up all for Him. Faith never stops at circumstances, or ponders results — it only looks at God. The moment we confer with flesh and blood, our testimony and service are marred, for flesh and blood can never obey. We must rise early and carry out, through grace, the Divine command. Thus we are blessed and God is glorified. When God's own word is the basis of our acting, we will have strength and stability.

Abraham's devotion was fully proven and accepted. *"Do not lay a hand on the boy,"* [God] *said. "Do not do anything to him. Now I know that you fear God, because you have not withheld from me your son, your only son"* (Gen. 22:12). Faith is always proved by action, and the fear of God by the fruits which flow from it.

Are you placing your faith in God? Are you open to the blessed reality of a life of faith?

Read: Genesis 22:1-14

September 16   THE DAY OF SMALL THINGS!

Who despises the day of small things? (Zech. 4:10).

The naturalist doesn't — he throws in his grain and watches it grow and waits for it to ripen. The philosopher doesn't — he knows that the minor must precede larger and more important events. The mother doesn't — the more helpless the baby, the more care she displays; she sees the great potential in the infant God doesn't — He uses small things! (1 Cor. 1:26-29).

1. Moses had a staff! As a shepherd, he always carried it with him (Exod. 4:2-3). The signs before Pharaoh, the parting of the Red Sea and the smiting of the rock to bring out water were all done through Moses' staff. God used this staff as an instrument of His power when Moses and Aaron honoured and obeyed Him.

2. Gideon had 300 men! They had pitchers, torches and trumpets. God won a great victory for Israel against a mighty Midianite army with a hand-full of men (Judg. 6-7).

3. Samson had a jaw bone! He killed a thousand Philistines with the jaw bone of a donkey and then threw it away. We would have framed it! (Judg. 15:15-17).

4. David had a sling! Just a piece of leather with a pocket for a stone. David, just a lad, a shepherd boy with his sling and his faith in God, in whose Name he won a great battle.

5. Mary had some perfume! With a heart of love and gratitude, she entered the house where Jesus was and anointed Him. She broke the alabaster jar and the odour filled the house (Mark 14:3-9).

6. Dorcas had a needle! Dorcas was busy making garments and coats to give to the Lord's work. God honoured her good works by raising her from the dead (Acts 9:36-42).

God is in essence saying, "Use what you have." What is in your hand? Put it to work for God! God will honour every little thing done for Him! *He who is faithful in a very little is faithful also in much* (Luke 16:10a, RSV).

Has God given you a talent? Use it! The day of small things demands from all of us more watchfulness and prayer. Moody once said, "Give your life to God, He can do more with it than you can."

Read: Zechariah 4:10

September 17   REALITY!

The experience of salvation through the work of the Holy Spirit must be a real experience. The things of God are real! The Word of God is real. *For the word of God is living and active. Sharper than any double-edged sword, it penetrates even to dividing soul and spirit, joints and marrow; it judges the thoughts and attitudes of the heart* (Heb. 4:12). Is my life real? I borrow some of the words of 1 Samuel 13:3: *Jonathan defeated the garrison... and Saul blew the trumpet throughout the land.* Saul blew the trumpet as if he was the real man who had fought the battle. Saul appears rather hypocritical here, taking the credit for what he did not do. Am I defeating the Philistines, or am I blowing the trumpet? Is my life real?

Paul's life was real! *Therefore I urge you to imitate me* (1 Cor. 4:16). *Join with others in following my example... and take note of those who live according to the pattern we gave you* (Phil. 3:17).

The Christian life is real! The Christian life is practical! A Christian is a believer in work clothes! Does our walk and our talk match? I need to be real in my talk. Am I a man of my word? Can I be trusted? Am I truthful?

What about our thought life as believers? Is there reality in our thinking? Our minds are so polluted today. Proverbs 23:7 says, *For as he thinketh in his heart, so is he* (KJV). If you had your thought life portrayed on a screen; what would it be like? The Bible says, *The Lord knows the thoughts of men* (Ps. 94:11). What is the exhortation? *Whatever is true, whatever is noble, whatever is right, what-*

ever is pure, whatever is lovely, whatever is admirable — if any-
thing is excellent or praiseworthy — think about such things (Phil.
4:8). Our prayer should be, *Search me, O God, and know my heart;*
test me, and know my... thoughts. See if there is any offensive way in
me, and lead me in the way everlasting (Ps. 139:23-24).

Being real in our work is also necessary. People are not looking for diplomas and certificates — they want to see reality.

God is faithful! Jesus Christ is real!

> *He's real to me, He's real to me; my precious Lord is real to me,*
> *My soul demands reality. My precious Lord is real to me.*

Read: 2 Corinthians 5:11-21

September 18   MISSIONARY MESSAGE

Our twentieth century became blood-stained by martyrdom in
the cause of world missions. You have all heard of the five young
missionaries who laid down their lives in Ecuador. In the truest
possible sense, Peter Fleming, James Elliot, Ed McCully, Nate
Saint and Roger Youderian gave their last full measure of devotion. They considered their lives expendable. Immediately after
their death, however, the five young men were branded as fool-
hardy zealots. People said, "Why this reckless squandermania of
valuable lives?" Cynics asked, "Where was God during this brutality?" Even earnest sincere Christians had their moments of questioning, "Why did God allow this to happen?"

These fearless five went forth to dare, to do and to die. They
furnish a never-to-be-forgotten example of how much it cost a few
because so many allowed it to cost them so little. Did it happen to
stir our lethargic hearts? Did it happen to break us from our
avarice and greed? How else might God stir us from our apathy
and insensibility and cause us to respond to world evangelism?

Many did dedicate their lives to the Lord after that incident.
Missionary replacements were sped up! Many became more
earnest in prayer. We have been prayerless so often. It is granted
that we can not do more than pray until we have prayed, but we
can do more *after* we have prayed. Our greatest weapons against
all odds are prayers.

When martyrs die, it is time for every believer to take a personal inventory. Without question, we have lived too selfishly and
too smugly. Where does giving fit into the big picture? To what

extent do we sacrifice? Are we willing, as parents, to let our children prepare and go into the mission field? The death of these five missionaries must not be forgotten. It must make us think about our stewardship in relation to world missions. Are we going to resolve that, from this day forward, we will do our utmost, at home and abroad, to spread the gospel of Jesus Christ?

Can we whose souls are lighted, with wisdom from on high,
Can we to men benighted, the lamp of life deny?

"Therefore go and make disciples of all nations, baptizing them in the name of the Father and of the Son and of the Holy Spirit, and teaching them to obey everything I have commanded you. And surely I am with you always, to the very end of the age" (Matt. 28:19-20).

Read: 2 Corinthians 8:9; 9:6-15

September 19   THE WORTH OF A SOUL

The LORD God formed the man from the dust of the ground and breathed into his nostrils the breath of life, and man became a living being [or soul] (Gen. 2:7). Man became a living soul! Man is God's crown creation! You are alive today! Have you ever thought about the seriousness of ever having lived? Because you are alive today, you will spend eternity in one of two places — heaven or hell. With this in mind, we want our thoughts to center on the worth of a soul. We must exclaim: *What is man that you are mindful of him, the son of man that you care for him?* (Ps. 8:4).

The worth of a soul, who can count its value? Who can appraise its worth? An immortal soul is beyond all price! In money, one soul is of more value than the wealth of the world (Mark 8:36). In suffering, it is better that all the people in the world should suffer all their lives on earth, if by suffering, one soul could be saved. There is no trouble too great, no humiliation too deep, no suffering too severe, no love too strong, no labour too hard, no expense too large, but that it is worth it, if it occurs in an effort to win a soul.

God loves every soul with an everlasting love, greater and deeper than any human love can possibly be. A soul will never die! When this earth of ours has crumbled to dust and has passed away into the forgotten past, our souls will still be living.

The salvation of a man's soul is the main subject of Scripture. *Concerning this salvation, the prophets, who spoke of the grace that was to come to you, searched intently and with the greatest care....* (1 Peter 1:10). *Even angels long to look into these things* (1 Peter 1:12). The fact that Jesus came is the evidence of the worth of a soul. We must realize the value and the immortality of precious souls (Dan. 12:3). God wants us to pray! *I urge, then, first of all, that requests, prayers, intercession and thanksgiving be made for everyone — for kings and all those in authority, that we may live peaceful and quiet lives in all godliness and holiness. This is good, and pleases God our Saviour, who wants all men to be saved and to come to a knowledge of the truth* (1 Tim. 2:1-4).

Read: Psalm 8

September 20   THREE LAST THINGS

He who testifies to these things says, "Yes, I am coming soon." Amen. Come, Lord Jesus (Rev. 22:20).

1. God's last promise! "*I am coming soon.*" Last words are precious words! Jesus spoke this last promise by the Holy Spirit through John. Jesus knew it was His final message. Five words, "*Yes, I am coming soon.*" *Yes* speaks of the certainty of His coming. *I* speaks of the personality of His coming. *Coming* speaks of His personal return. *Soon* speaks of the time of His coming.

2. The last prayer! *Amen. Come, Lord Jesus.* It is the response of the last promise. It is the prayer for the soon return of our Saviour from heaven. It is not a prayer for world conversion, for world peace or for worldwide revival. It is a prayer for the return of Christ. The final answer to this world's problems is not the United Nations. The very final answer is the return of the King of Glory. We are called upon to wait and watch for His return (Titus 2:11-13).

3. The last invitation! *The Spirit and the Bride say, "Come!" And let him who hears say, "Come!" Whoever is thirsty, let him come; and whoever wishes, let him take the free gift of the water of life* (Rev. 22:17). The presence of the Spirit and the Bride on earth witness to Jesus Christ. This is an urgent call! Whosoever will may come! The word, *come,* is used three times. Do you realize that this might be your last invitation? Tomorrow may be too late!

A.B. Simpson wrote,

Lingering soul, delay no more,
Haste ere life's brief hour is o'er,
Haste, ere mercy shut the door,
Come to Jesus now!

Francis Havergal wrote,

What will you do without Him when He has shut the door;
And you are left outside because you would not come before;
When it is no use knocking, no use to stand and wait;
For the word of doom tolls through your heart, that terrible "too late."
Why will you do without Him? He calls and calls again.
"Come unto Me! Come unto Me!" Oh shall He wait in vain?
He wants to have you with Him: Do you not want Him, too?
You cannot do without Him, And He wants even you!

Read: Matthew 11:28-30; Revelation 22:17-21

September 21   THE LAST DAYS

As it was in the days of Noah, so it will be at the coming of the Son of Man (Matt. 24:37). Noah was a real person! The flood was a great fact! The second coming of Christ as the Son of Man will be an unfailing certainty. What the state and condition of the world will be is clearly revealed. There was great and growing wickedness in the days of Noah, and so it will be when Jesus comes. The world did not grow better and better; it grew worse and worse. *God saw that the wickedness on the earth was great* (Gen. 6:5). Jesus mentions Lot in Luke 17:28: *"It was the same in the days of Lot. People were eating and drinking, buying and selling, planting and building"* (Luke 17:28).

Paul gave warning to Timothy. *But mark this: There will be terrible times in the last days. People will be lovers of themselves, lovers of money, boastful, proud, abusive, disobedient to their parents, ungrateful, unholy, without love, unforgiving, slanderous, without self-control, brutal, not lovers of the good, treacherous, rash, conceited, lovers of pleasure rather than lovers of God* (2 Tim. 3:1-4). There was faithful warning in Noah's day! Noah was a preacher of righteousness for 120 years (Gen. 6:3). In the days of Noah, the people were overtaken suddenly. They did not believe the testimony of Noah. We can see that the habits and sins of society remain unchanged.

Christ shall come suddenly! *For as lightning that comes from the east is visible even in the west, so will be the coming of the Son of Man* (Matt. 24:27). Who shall stand when He appears? All who entered the ark in the days of Noah were saved. The Lord shut them in! Kept by the power of God. All who are in the Kingdom of God's dear Son will be taken away before the judgement of God falls on the disobedient and unbelieving. Our job is to be ready when He comes! Everyone outside the ark was visited with the judgement of God. The flood came and swept them away. The ark was a means of salvation. The ark was beyond reach the moment the door was shut. The day of opportunity was gone forever.

Be ready! Accept Christ as your personal Saviour now!

Read: Matthew 24:36-51

September 22   ATONEMENT

The importance of any news item can be gauged by the amount of space given to it in the newspaper. The same rule may apply to the Bible. Take the subject of death. As we read the Bible, we find that the smallest possible space is given to notices of the death of Bible characters. That impression changes as we come to the New Testament. We find a great deal of space — whole chapters — devoted to the death of Christ. Matthew devotes a chapter of 66 verses; Mark has 47 verses; Luke has 56 verses; and John has 42 verses. How is this? The implication is that the death of Christ was different from all other deaths. The fact is that our Lord's supreme work for the salvation of men was accomplished in His death. We come to live! He came to die! Death was the means of accomplishing the work He came to do.

The great evangelist D.L. Moody was right when he remarked, "You take the great doctrine of substitution and atonement out of the preaching of Paul, Peter, John, James, Philip and all other holy men, and you take out all that they preached. There does not seem any ray of hope for men that ignore the blessed subject of the atonement." On one occasion, when Tennyson the poet was on a holiday in a country place, he asked an old Methodist lady if there was any news. She replied. "Why, there is only one piece of news that I know and that is, 'Christ died for all.'" Tennyson responded, "That is old news and good news and new news." He was right!

The day of atonement was Israel's great day. It was the most solemn day in all the year. It was a day of necessary humiliation, and a day of special sacrifice. The High Priest would enter into the Holy of Holies and sprinkle blood upon and before the mercy seat, signifying that once more God had covered their sins for one more year. How welcome the provision of the Levitical offerings.

The work of Christ was more thorough! Christ's work does not pass over or overlook sin, it takes it away. Christ's death puts away sin completely! Doing your best is not enough! Satan's doctrine is doing. God's work is done! It is ours to accept by faith. Love was and is behind the atonement! Jesus is the atonement! Christ died for us. He is our substitute, the only sacrifice that God could accept for the atonement of sin (Acts 4:12).

Read: Leviticus 16

September 23 PAUL AS A WITNESS FOR CHRIST

Paul had a remarkable conversion! (Acts 9). He spoke of it wherever he went. Paul took a definite stand! The story of his conversion was his apologetic for Christianity. It affected kings and governors. Paul's defense reveals the characteristics of a true Christian.

1. Paul was a changed man! He was known by the Jews. They knew who he was and how he lived. They knew what he did and what he believed. Paul was religious. He had persecuted the Church until, one day, he met the Master face to face. The change was radical and complete.

2. Paul was an empowered man! God had a purpose in saving this man. *"This man is my chosen instrument to carry my name before the Gentiles and their kings and before the people of Israel"* (Acts 9:15). He had a definite call and he was not disobedient. *I was not disobedient to the vision from heaven* (Acts 26:19). Someone has said, "He who offers God second place, offers Him no place." *I have had God's help to this very day,* says Paul, *and so I stand here and testify to small and great alike. I am saying nothing beyond what the prophets and Moses said would happen* (Acts 26:22).

3. Paul was a devoted man! He was devoted to Christ. He preached Christ! He spoke about the death and resurrection of Christ. He upheld the cross of Christ (Gal. 2:20).

4. Paul was a misunderstood man! *To those who are... perishing... the preaching of the cross is foolishness* (1 Cor. 2:14).

253

5. Paul was a faithful man! He was fearless and faithful in the face of kings and governors. Some were "almost" persuaded to believe in Jesus (Acts 26:28). Paul's desire was that all who heard him should become like him, except for his chains. The peace of God was in his heart! The unsearchable riches of Christ were his.

Have you been converted? Has there been a definite change in your life?

Read: Acts 9:1-31; 22:1-21; 26

September 24   LIFE INSURANCE — Psalm 91

The true minister of God is a salesman representing the greatest firm in history. It is the Life Insurance Company of Heaven. Its officers are Father, Son and Holy Spirit. Their main office is in heaven and there are countless branch offices all over the world. This Company offers an absolute life insurance policy free of charge. It guarantees eternal life to every one who will accept it. It is retroactive, taking care of all the past. It cannot be cancelled nor altered, and it contains no conditional or confusing fine print. The policy is signed by God the Father, written with the blood of Jesus Christ and sealed by the witness of the Holy Spirit. *For there are three that* [testify] *in heaven, the Father, the Word and the Holy Ghost: and these three are one* (1 John 5:7, KJV). There are no premiums, the only requirement is your willingness to receive it.

Listen to the story of a dear old saint's experience with an insurance salesman. After the salesman had explained his policy to her, she replied, "But Mister, I have all that and more in an insurance policy I already possess and it doesn't cost all that money you are asking for yours." The salesman, moved by curiosity, requested to see her policy. She produced her Bible and turned to Psalm 91. She said "There it is — every imaginable insurance in the world. In verse one, I have social security: *abiding under the shadow of the Almighty*; in verse two, I have insurance against damage in war: *He is my refuge and my fortress*; in verse three, I have health insurance: *Neither shall any plague come nigh thy dwelling*; in verse twelve, I have collision insurance: *Lest thou dash thy foot against a stone*; in verse fifteen, I have fire insurance: *I will deliver him*; and in verse sixteen, I have life insurance: *With long life I will satisfy him*." The life insurance salesman made no further attempt to sell his policy.

We are talking about everlasting life! God desires that we all have the assurance of everlasting life. Take inventory! Man's existence is compared to grass that is soon cut down, a flower that fades and a vapour that appears for a little moment then vanishes away. We must choose now! We must prepare now!

An unknown author writes:

> *When as a child, I laughed and wept... time crept;*
> *When as a youth, I dreamed and talked... time walked;*
> *When I became a full grown man... time ran;*
> *When older still I daily grew... time flew.*

May God give us wisdom to make each moment count for Him. Live each short hour with God and the long years will take care of themselves.

Read: 1 John 5:1-15

September 25   PRACTICAL FAITH

Paul was always glad and thankful to hear of the faith and love of believers everywhere he went (Eph. 1:15). Faith and love need to be practical. Faith and works are inseparably connected. A faith which does not work is useless, and work without faith is equally dead. There are three kinds of works in the Bible: Wicked works, dead works and good works (James 2:17).

1. Wicked works are works of darkness. They refer to the grosser, overt sins of the irreligious, also called the works of the flesh. They are enumerated by Paul in Galatians 5:19, such things as adultery, idolatry, hatred, strife, heresy, envy, murder, drunkenness and so on.

2. Dead works are religious works. They refer to man's effort to gain salvation through ritual, sacrifice, behaviour, morality, education and piousness. The acts of joining a church, being baptized, praying, reading the Bible and living a moral life as attempts to get to heaven are dead works. The people of Paul's day who kept the letter of the law and rejected Christ were guilty of dead works.

3. Good works are the natural results of our salvation. Good works are proof of our faith before men. Faith is the root, works are the fruit! God sees the root, but men can only see the fruit. James says, *...A person is justified by what he does and not by faith alone* (James 2:24). Paul says, *...A man is justified by faith apart from observing the law* (Rom. 3:28). This seems like a flat contradiction. The contradiction is not real. Paul wrote about justification of a sinner in the sight of God. This is faith! James is dealing with the question, "How can the saved sinner be justified in the sight of men?" This is by works! Men will not know what happened until they see the evidence in our lives (James 2:18).

Jesus said, *"Let your light shine before men, that they may see your good deeds and praise your Father in heaven"* (Matt. 5:16). The greatest sermons ever preached are through godly lives. The most eloquent sermons are in homes and offices and shops and factories by those who show in themselves in all things a pattern of good works adorning the doctrine of God our Saviour (Titus 2:10).

Christianity is not a way of talking but a way of walking!

Read: Ephesians 1:15-23

September 26   DEAD AND MADE ALIVE

Paul reminds us in Ephesians 2 that there was a past condition. We were dead! We lived in the ways of the world. We had no life, we had no hope. Remember who you were? Remember how you obeyed the forces of evil, obeying its unseen ruler? We all lived like that! It's so easy to drift along on the stream of this world's ideas of living. It is the path of least resistance. Read Romans 1 and see how corrupt human nature is.

There is a present position! *But because of His great love for us, God, who is rich in mercy, made us alive with Christ even when we were dead in transgressions — it is by grace you have been saved* (Eph. 2:4-5). God has lifted us right out of the old life. Enjoy David's testimony. *He lifted me out of the slimy pit, out of the mud and mire; He set my feet on a rock and gave me a firm place to stand. He put a new song in my mouth, a hymn of praise to our God. Many will see and fear and put their trust in the LORD* (Ps. 40:1-3). God made us alive with Christ! God has seated us with Him in the heavenly realms. *Praise be to the God and Father of our Lord Jesus Christ, who has blessed us in the heavenly realms with every spiritual blessing in Christ* (Eph. 1:3).

For it is by grace you have been saved, through faith — and this not from yourselves, it is the gift of God — not by works, so that no one can boast. For we are God's workmanship, created in Christ Jesus to do good works, which God prepared in advance for us to do (Eph. 2:8-10).

Does the past condition describe your life? Are you living in sin and only for yourself? Let me encourage you to come to Christ in simple faith. Trust Him for your salvation! Your present position will then be in Christ. God loves you and has a wonderful plan for your life. Be alive in Christ! Be ready for heaven! Make your reservations today!

Read: Ephesians 2:1-10

September 27 WHO YOU WERE – WHAT YOU ARE

Again, Paul gives us a good reminder. Repetition is the mother of all wisdom!

We were Gentiles by birth. *Remember that at that time you were separate from Christ, excluded from citizenship in Israel and foreigners to the covenants of the promise, without hope and without God in the world* (Eph. 2:12). Indeed a helpless condition. Across the pages of your life would be written "hopeless and helpless." *But now in Christ Jesus you who once were far away have been brought near through the blood of Christ* (Eph. 2:13). Christ has unified the conflicting elements of Jew and Gentile. *For He Himself is our peace, who has made the two one and has destroyed the barrier, the dividing wall of hostility....* (Eph. 2:14). Christ is our living peace. In Christ, there is love and unity. God has drawn us into the circle of His love and purpose. The conflict is over!

The blood of Christ reaches every single member, no matter how far apart they may be. To every believer, this is the only source of life. We are all one in Christ on the ground of His shed blood. The war is over and Christ is the Victor!

Through Christ, we have access to the Father (Eph. 2:18). We can approach the throne of grace. *Let us then approach the throne of grace with confidence, so that we may receive mercy, and find grace to help us in our time of need* (Heb. 4:16). Fellowship has been restored!

Through Christ, we are fellow-citizens — born into God's family through faith in Him! *Our citizenship is in heaven. And we eagerly await a Saviour from there, the Lord Jesus Christ* (Phil. 3:20). I still have to show my citizenship papers at the border when I cross over from Canada to the United States. I have, however, made reservations for heaven. Heaven is my home!

Remember the chorus,

One door and only one, and yet its sides are two,
Inside and outside, on which side are you?
I'm on the inside, on which side are you?

Choose to follow Jesus Christ and enjoy the benefits and the blessings of being a fellow-citizen bound for heaven.

Read: Ephesians 2:11-22

September 28   SHEEP TALK — Psalm 23

If sheep could talk, and a wise and a foolish sheep were speaking together, I fancy the foolish one would sound like this: "I know where the crystal brook babbles, and I shall never want for drink. I know where the great oak spreads its leafy branches, and I shall not want for shade. I know where the green pastures of tender grass grow, and I shall never want for food. I know where the door of the fold stands wide open, and I shall never want for refuge."

Then I hear the wise sheep answering, "O foolish sheep! I have a better reason than yours for not wanting. I have the best Shepherd in the world, therefore, I shall not want. If the brook dries up He will find another for me. If the tree is cut down by the woodsman's axe, He will lead me to the shadow of a great rock. If the pastures dry up under the summer's sun, He knows how to find others. And when the wolf comes, He will lay down his life, if need be, for his sheep. O foolish sheep! I shall never want, because I trust not in things that may change, or in men that prove false, but I trust in the Shepherd who does not change, nor does He fail."

Men and women argue after this fashion. They say, "I am keen of brain and skillful of hand, therefore I shall not want. The balance in my bank account is comfortable, therefore I shall not want. I have influential friends at court, therefore I shall not want. I am strong in body and able to make a good living, therefore I shall not want."

But the bank may fail, the skillful hands lose their cunning, friends may prove false, health may end, and wealth may disappear. When all these are gone, where will we be? That is when we need this supreme truth: "It is not the favourableness of our circumstances, but the fact of the Lord's Shepherdship which is the perpetual pledge that we shall not want!" (James H. McConkey, from *Beside Still Waters,* p. 19).

Read: Psalm 23

September 29   SALVATION IS NOT....

Salvation is not reformation, nor imitation, nor education, nor confirmation, nor is it imagination. But it is regeneration — that is becoming a new creation, by the Spirit's operation, through blood redemption, at cost beyond conception, and it's found in God's revelation which is for every nation.

Paul wrote, *Therefore, if anyone is in Christ, he is a new creation; the old has gone, the new has come!* (2 Cor. 5:17). Regeneration, or the new birth, is the impartation of a *new* life, not just the old one fixed up. It is a spiritual quickening being made alive by the Holy Spirit. It is a supernatural act of God, whereby He imparts a new life and a new divine nature. The sinful condition of man demands it, the holiness of God demands it and the need for it is universal. *Jesus declared, "I tell you the truth, unless a man is born again, he cannot see the kingdom of God "* (John 3:3).

It is a divine work of God, with the Holy Spirit as the divine agent, which brings about regeneration. God is faithful! The Holy Spirit takes the things of God's Word which are instrumental in regeneration, and He applies them to our hearts.

We must accept the message of the gospel and apply it to our lives. The condition is so simple: *"I tell you the truth, he who believes has everlasting life"* (John 6:47). Whosoever will may come! *Everyone who calls on the name of the Lord will be saved.* (Rom. 10:13). No one is forced into the Kingdom of God. *Yet to all who received Him, to those who believed in His name, He gave the right to become children of God* (John 1:12). It is He, who is the wisdom of God, that said, "You must be born again." Christ said it and Christ means it!

This new life is marked by a changed life. A man who used to hitch his horse in front of the saloon each day, was seen hitching his horse in front of the church one Sunday morning. The saloon keeper called out, "Say, why is your horse hitched in front of the church this morning?" The man turned around and said, "Last night I was converted, and I've changed hitching posts."

Read: John 3:1-8

September 30   THE POWER OF TOUCH

Think of the touch of an artist, a surgeon, a musician, a gardener, a mother, a carpenter, a seamstress. The hands of Jesus touched many lives!

1. The Corrective Touch (Luke 22:51).

Jesus corrected something Peter had done.
All of us need Jesus to touch our ears.
We need to hear with the inner ear of our hearts.

2. The Quieting Touch (Matt. 8:15).

Peter's mother-in-law was healed of a fever.
She was set free to serve.
We need to serve with our hands.

3. The Illuminating Touch (Matt. 9:29-30).

Two blind men received their sight.
Blindness is symbolic of a soul in darkness.
We need Jesus to touch our eyes (Eph. 1:18).

4. The Restoring Touch (Mark 7:33).

A deaf and dumb man was freed to hear and speak.
The tongue is to be used for praise, not profanity.
We need Jesus to touch our tongues to confess His name.

5. The Blessed Touch (Mark 10:13).

Children were brought to be blessed.
Parents brought them, disciples barred them,
Jesus blessed them.
Our children and grandchildren need Jesus!

6. The Healing Touch (Luke 5:13).

A man covered with leprosy came begging.
Leprosy represents sin.
We need spiritual healing, the forgiveness of sin.

7. The Life-Giving Touch (Luke 7:14).

A widow's son was being carried to his burial.
We were dead in our sins (Eph. 2:1).
We are born in sin, blind in sin and bound by sin.
We need the life-giving touch of Jesus!

Remember the song, "He Touched Me."
Remember the poem, "The Touch of the Master's Hand."

October 1   THE PASSOVER

The story of the Passover is just an early edition of the Gospel of Christ. Life is in the blood (Lev. 17:11). What a grand promise given that night in Egypt, *"...when I see the blood, I will pass over you"* (Exod. 12:13b).

The Passover story affords some relevant applications:

1) Condemnation (Exod. 12:12). The sentence of death passed upon all the firstborn. There was no difference between Jew or Egyptian. *All have sinned* (Rom. 3:23). This condemnation rests upon all who are outside of Christ. The Bible says, *"Whoever does not believe stands condemned already"* (John 3:18).

2) Substitution. Either the firstborn or an innocent substitute must die. Each man is to take a lamb for his house. Christ is the Lamb of God! (John 1:29). *Christ, our Passover, has been sacrificed* (1 Cor. 5:7).

3) Appropriation. *...Take some of the blood and put it on the sides and tops of the doorframes....* (Exod. 12:7). Only the blood on the door posts was between the firstborn and the avenger. By faith, we lift up the sacrifice of Christ. The blood that flowed on Calvary is between our guilty souls and a sin-avenging God. The precious blood of Jesus Christ still avails for us! God looks down upon us, as it were, through the blood of Christ.

The blood is the ground for our atonement. The Hebrew word *atonement* means "to cover" with regard to sin; it means that sin is so covered that God regards it as gone.

The blood is the ground for our redemption. The blood was the price that was paid for our redemption (1 Peter 1:18-19).

The blood is the ground for our peace (Col. 1:20).

The blood is the ground for our forgiveness. *In Him we have redemption through His blood, the forgiveness of sins, in accordance with the riches of God's grace* (Eph. 1:7).

The blood is the ground for our drawing near. *But now in Christ Jesus you who once were far away have been brought near through the blood of Christ* (Eph. 2:13).

Hunger makes bread precious, thirst makes water precious, poverty makes riches precious. Sin and condemnation make the blood of Christ precious.

The love of sin leads away from God. What sin does, the blood of Christ undoes. *But if we walk in the light, as He is in the*

light, we have fellowship with one another, and the blood of Jesus,
His Son, purifies us from all sin (1 John 1:7).

Read: Exodus 12:1-29

October 2   THE MANNA TYPE OF CHRIST

Then the LORD said to Moses, "I will rain down bread from
heaven for you. The people are to go out each day and gather
enough for that day. In this way I will test them and see whether
they will follow my instructions" (Exod. 16:4). *"Our forefathers*
ate the manna in the desert; as it is written: 'He gave them bread
from heaven to eat.'" Jesus said to them, "I tell you the truth, it is
not Moses who has given you the bread from heaven, but it is my
Father who gives you the true bread from heaven. For the bread of
God is He who comes down from heaven and gives life to the
world" (John 6:31-33). God supplied His people in the desert with
manna from heaven. It was a provision of His bounty. It was the
staff of their lives. We do not envy the people of Israel who were
fed with angel's food; we rather rejoice with the Jews and Gentiles
that we have the true Bread from heaven.

Christ is a type of manna! Manna was food from heaven! It
came from the storehouse of God. Israel was in need and God met
that need. Christ as the Bread of Life is the free gift of God. He
came down from heaven to supply the need of our spiritual life. In
Christ, there is an abundance of mercy and grace.

The manna was received daily! *Each one gathered as much as*
he needed (Exod. 16:18b). The manna was designed for the body,
a temporary provision. Jesus is the Bread of Life! He gives everlasting life! The manna was limited to Israel. Jesus is given and
freely offered to the whole world. *Jesus declared, "I am the bread*
of life. He who comes to me will never go hungry, and he who
believes in me will never be thirsty" (John 6:35). The Bread of
Life lasts forever! Manna was only for a short time. *"I tell you the*
truth, he who believes has everlasting life. I am the bread of life.
Your forefathers ate the manna in the desert, yet they died. But
here is the bread that comes down from heaven, which a man may
eat and not die. I am the living bread that came down from heaven.
If anyone eats of this bread, he will live for ever. This bread is my
flesh, which I will give for the life of the world" (John 6:47-51).

Wherever you travel, almost any time of the day, even through the night, people are eating, satisfying the desires of the body. What are they doing about feeding their souls? Are their spiritual lives starved? Is your life spiritually starved? *Taste and see that the* LORD *is good* (Ps. 34:8).

Read: John 6:25-59

October 3   THE SMITTEN-ROCK TYPE OF CHRIST

"I will stand there before you by the rock at Horeb. Strike the rock, and water will come out of it for the people to drink." So Moses did this in the sight of the elders of Israel (Exod. 17:6). *They all ate the same spiritual food and drank the same spiritual drink; for they drank from the spiritual rock that accompanied them, and that rock was Christ* (1 Cor. 10:3-4).

Water in the wilderness! The smitten rock typified Christ! The rock is an emblem of strength, an emblem of stability. Jesus is immutable! He is strong and stable!

The rock was smitten at God's command. The smiting was typical of the sufferings of Christ. Christ suffered by the will and appointment of God. *This man was handed over to you by God's set purpose and foreknowledge; and you, with the help of wicked men, put Him to death by nailing Him to the cross* (Acts 2:23).

The rock was smitten by Moses. The Law-giver smiting the rock is a striking representation of Jesus meeting the claims of the law, bearing its penalties on His own Person.

The rock was smitten in the presence of the elders of Israel. Christ suffered publicly! He was tried, condemned, mocked, beaten, scourged and crucified before the elders of Israel. His sufferings were open and manifest, not done in a corner secretly. The stream of water did not flow until the rock was smitten. The gushing stream was typical of the water of life. Jesus is the Water of Life!

On the last and greatest day of the Feast, Jesus stood and said in a loud voice, "If anyone is thirsty, let him come to me and drink. Whoever believes in me, as the Scripture has said, streams of living water will flow from within him" (John 7:37-38). The blessings of grace come to us through the merits of the Mediator. The benefits of Christ's death meet all the sinner's needs. The stream was free to all of Israel. Christ is free to all who receive Him.

Can you hear the last invitation? *The Spirit and the Bride say, "Come!" And let him who hears say, "Come!" Whoever is thirsty, let him come; and whoever wishes, let him take the free gift of the water of life* (Rev. 22:17).

Read: Exodus 17:1-7

October 4   WORDS!

What is a word? Webster tells us it is that which is said. It is a declaration, a promise, a means of communication, a source of information, and it can be an order or a command. The plural is talk — an articulated sound which symbolizes and communicates an idea.

Do our words have meaning? Do we think before we speak? What did Jesus say about words? *"But I tell you that men will have to give account on the day of judgment for every careless word they have spoken. For by your words you will be acquitted, and by your words you will be condemned"* (Matt. 12:36-37). Before Jesus said those words, He said, *"For out of the overflow of the heart the mouth speaks. The good man brings good things out of the good stored up in him, and the evil man brings evil things out of the evil stored up in him"* (Matt. 12:34-35). Paul said, *Nor should there be obscenity, foolish talk or coarse joking, which are out of place, but rather thanksgiving* (Eph. 5:4). What is your heart full of right now?

Proverbs is full of the subject! *When words are many, sin is not absent, but he who holds his tongue is wise* (Prov. 10:19). *He who guards his lips guards his life, but he who speaks rashly will come to ruin* (Prov. 13:3). *The tongue has the power of life and death, and those who love it will eat its fruit* (Prov. 18:21). Then there is Ecclesiastes 5:2, written on my heart by an English teacher at Prairie Bible Institute: *Do not be quick with your mouth, do not be hasty in your heart to utter anything before God. God is in heaven and you are on earth, so let your words be few*. That is good advice! Remember, God has given you *two* ears and *one* mouth; He intends for you to do twice as much listening as talking. Be *swift to hear and slow to speak* (James 1:19-20). Words are wonderful things and we could not do without them. We use words to express ourselves. We use words to communicate ideas. Good ideas! *A man finds joy in giving an apt reply — and how good is a timely word!* (Prov. 15:23). *Pleasant words are a honeycomb, sweet to the soul and healing to the bones* (Prov. 16:24). *A word aptly spoken is like apples of gold in settings of silver* (Prov. 25:11).

Paul says, *Let your conversation be always full of grace, seasoned with salt, so that you may know how to answer everyone* (Col. 4:6). Mix a little salt with your conversation!

Two prayers: *Set a guard over my mouth, O LORD; keep watch over the door of my lips* (Ps. 141:3). *May the words of my mouth and the meditation of my heart be pleasing in your sight, O LORD, my Rock and my Redeemer* (Ps. 19:14).

Read: Matthew 12:32-37

October 5   LIGHT

This is the message we have heard from Him and declare to you: God is light; in Him there is no darkness at all (1 John 1:5). *And God said, "Let there be light," and there was light* (Gen. 1:3). He spoke and it was done. Unbelief asks, how, where and when? The answer — *By faith we understand that the universe was formed at God's command, so that what is seen was not made out of what was visible* (Heb. 11:3). This is the teachable spirit!

God called the light day and the darkness night. The presence of light makes the day; the absence of light makes the night. In the history of mankind, we soon learn that there are sons of light and sons of darkness. Believers receive the Light of Life and the Son of Righteousness shines upon them. Unbelievers remain in darkness; they are still wrapped in the shades of spiritual night. You belong to either one or the other. You may be poor, despised, and uneducated, but if, through the grace of God, you have come to Christ, the Light of the World, you are indeed a son of the day. If you are a total stranger to the Light of the World, you are a son of the night.

God made two great lights — the greater light to govern the day and the lesser light to govern the night (Gen. 1:16). The sun is the great light, the center of our system. It is a beautiful and appropriate symbol of Christ. The moon strikingly reminds us of the Church. The moon reflects the light of the sun. The Church is to reflect the Light of Christ. It should watch against everything that would hinder that reflection. The Church walking in the Light of Christ will reflect that Light! Will the world around us see the traits of Christ's character in us? *"You are the light of the world. A city on a hill cannot be hidden. Neither do people light a lamp and put it under a bowl. Instead they put it on its stand, and it gives light to everyone in the house. In the same way, let your light shine before men, that they may see your good deeds and praise your Father in heaven"* (Matt. 5:14-16). Our relationship and responsibility to God and men are clearly revealed. Jesus said, *"I am the light of the world. Whoever follows me will never walk in darkness, but will have the light of life"* (John 8:12).

Read: Genesis 1:1-19

October 6   I AM A PILGRIM

The pilgrimage of Abraham is one of my favorite themes! *By faith Abraham, when called to go to a place he would later receive as his inheritance, obeyed and went, even though he did not know where he was going. By faith he made his home in the promised land like a stranger in a foreign country; he lived in tents, as did Isaac and Jacob, who were heirs with him of the same promise* (Heb. 11:8-9).

What is a pilgrim? A pilgrim is one who has no fixed habitation; one who is journeying through a strange and foreign land. I would like to share three features of a pilgrim.

1. A pilgrim's attitude! The attitude of a visitor! We are not here to stay. Consider the tent dwellers of the Old Testament saints over against our modern homes today. The picture is obvious! They were not so settled as we are today. Pitch a tent, pull up the stakes and move on. The patriarchs had the shell of their longing here on earth, but the kernel was in heaven. *But our citizenship is in heaven. And we eagerly await a Saviour from there, the Lord Jesus Christ* (Phil. 3:20). The song writer says, "I'm a pilgrim, I can tarry but a night."

2. A pilgrim's appetite! Speaking of appetites, what makes your mouth water? People are continually feeding on something. They go after their desires. Israel wanted to have meat one day, as well as a king. *So* [God] *gave them what they asked for, but sent a wasting disease upon them* (Ps. 106:15). Israel also desired to go back to Egypt where they had onions, leeks, garlic and cucumbers. A pilgrim should have no desire to return to this world of sin. Nor should they be attached to possessions. "THINGS" lack permanence! Jesus taught us to sit lightly on earthly possessions.

3. A pilgrim's activity! His is a living active faith. A pilgrim goes on from stage to stage, from experience to experience, from faith to faith. He advances in the knowledge of God, in love, in obedience and in holiness. Sometimes we see nothing but impossibilities (the Red Sea).

> *Got any rivers you think are uncrossable?*
> *Got any mountains you cannot tunnel through?*
> *God specializes in things thought impossible;*
> *He does the things others cannot do.*
>
> — Oscar Eliason

Is there anything too hard for God? He would have us act on His promises.

Our lives need to be devoted to Him! Whitefield said one day, "Lord, if you see me nestling in pity, put a thorn in my nest."

> *Only one life, 'twill soon be past.*
> *Only what's done for Christ will last.*

Life is a journey to be taken but once!

Read: Hebrews 11:8-19

October 7   ESSENTIALS TO PREVAILING PRAYER

"Men are God's method. The Church is looking for better methods; God is looking for better men... What the Church needs today is not more machinery or better, not new organizations... but men whom the Holy Ghost can use — men of prayer, men mighty in prayer. The Holy Ghost does not flow through methods, but through men. He does not come on machinery, but on men. He does not anoint plans, but men — men of prayer." — *E.M. Bounds.*[7]

1. Pray sincerely! *The LORD is near to all who call on Him, to all who call on Him in truth* (Ps. 145:18). *"And when you pray, do not be like the hypocrites, for they love to pray standing in the synagogues and on the street corners to be seen by men. I tell you the truth, they have received their reward in full"* (Matt. 6:5). Some have given testimony later in life that their prayers never got past the ceiling of the church because they were not sincere and truthful; they wanted to be acknowledged for their much praying.

2. Pray simply! Blessed simplicity! *"And when you pray, do not keep on babbling like pagans, for they think they will be heard because of their many words"* (Matt. 6:7). Two things make up fruitless prayers: vain repetitions and many words. Long, drawn-out prayers are not needed. Prayer is simple; it's like quietly opening a door and slipping into the presence of God. There in the stillness, we listen for His voice, perhaps petitioning Him or perhaps only listening; it matters not — just being there in His presence is prayer.

3. Pray earnestly! *Elijah was a man just like us. He prayed earnestly that it would not rain, and it did not rain on the land for three and a half years* (James 5:17). Prayer moved the hand of God! The Church prayed earnestly. *So Peter was kept in prison, but the church was earnestly praying to God for him* (Acts 12:5). You know about his release from prison.

4. Pray persistently! Be persistent in your prayers. *Then Jesus told His disciples a parable to show them that they should always pray and not give up* (Luke 18:1). Do not quit! Never give up! Keep on praying!

5. Pray believing! Faith will climb heaven's heights and bring a blessing down. Faith to lay hold of God! *But when he asks, he must believe and not doubt, because he who doubts is like a wave of the sea, blown and tossed by the wind* (James 1:6).

6. Pray agreeing! Agree with others! *"Again, I tell you that if two of you on earth agree about anything you ask for, it will be done for you by my Father in heaven. For where two or three come together in my name, there am I with them"* (Matt. 18:19-20). God blesses the unity of His people.

7. Pray in the Name of Jesus! *"And I will do whatever you ask in My name, so that the Son may bring glory to the Father. You may ask Me for anything in My name, and I will do it"* (John 14:13-14).

October 8   THANKSGIVING — Psalm 103

If your heart is full, it needs no priming! I wonder sometimes whether our praise to God is really whole-hearted — often we do things so half-heartedly. We owe our best to God! He made us! We are the work of His hands! Thank Him for the very air that you breathe!

David gives vent to his soul. He expresses his heart-felt gratitude! David says, "Forget not" the blessings of God. What are some of these blessings?

1. He forgives all my sin. Psalm 32:1-2 would endorse this. *Blessed is he whose transgressions are forgiven, whose sins are covered. Blessed is the man whose sin the LORD does not count against him and in whose spirit is no deceit.*

2. He heals all my diseases. The soul is subject to many spiritual maladies. Pride, anger, lust and slothfulness are among the many. Spiritually, we are daily under His care. No disease baffles His skill. When physical illness overtakes us, He sustains us with His grace. Remember what God said to Paul: *My grace is sufficient for you, for my power is made perfect in weakness.* Then Paul said, *I will boast all the more gladly about my weaknesses, so that Christ's power may rest on me* (2 Cor. 12:9).

3. He redeems my life from the pit. He has removed the sentence of death! He has defeated the enemy of our soul! David says, *He lifted me out of the slimy pit, out of the mud and mire; he set my feet on a rock and gave me a firm place to stand. He put a new song in my mouth, a hymn of praise to our God. Many will see and fear and put their trust in the LORD* (Ps. 40:2-3). Job has this testimony: *I know that my Redeemer lives, and that in the end He will stand upon the earth* (Job 19:25).

4. He crowns me with love and compassion. We enjoy the favour of God daily. His love and mercy surround us. *His mercies are new every morning* (Lam. 3:22-23). We have His promised presence! *He loves us with an everlasting love* (Jer. 31:3).

5. He satisfies my desires with good things. Only God Himself can satisfy! *He satisfies the thirsty and fills the hungry with good things* (Ps. 107:9). The Lord works marvelous changes. My youth (the inner man) is renewed. From a sparrow to an eagle, that is the picture. You were meant to fly. Earth was never meant to satisfy the human heart!

Read: Psalm 103:1-5

October 9   **THANKSGIVING**

From coast to coast, we set aside a day for Thanksgiving. A day to bring to mind the mercies of God. Every day should be Thanksgiving Day!

Thanksgiving glorifies God! (Ps. 50:23). The call to thanksgiving is numerous in the Bible (Ps. 50:14; 100:4; 107:1).

Gratitude should be the logical response for all the benefits and blessings we enjoy (Ps.103:2). There are manifold and manifest reasons for thanksgiving:

1. Our Surroundings! We can thank God for the land in which we live. Remember the hands of steel, the hearts of gold and the years of toil that pioneers have rendered for this country. We can be thankful for our homes, where we experienced the care and concern of our parents; for the schools, at which we received our early childhood training and development; for our friends, who were there when we needed them.

2. Our Spiritual Heritage! We can also thank God for the church where we worshipped, where we were fed spiritually, where we had fellowship and where we were able to grow; for the Bible which was the instrument of our new birth, the nourishment for our soul, the comfort in times of sorrow and the weapon to fight the foe. How we should prize the Bible, use it frequently, follow its teaching, love its laws, abide by its principles and serve its Christ.

3. Our Salvation! Thank God for Christ who has become our salvation; for God's provision; for the forgiveness of sin; for the Holy Spirit, our Comforter and Guide; for the prospect of heaven! Let me say here, "True thanksgiving is making proper preparation for heaven." David asks in Psalm 116:12, *How can I repay the Lord for all His goodness to me?* Then he says, *I will lift up* [take] *the cup of salvation and call on the name of the Lord* (vs. 13). God is pleased when we take His offer of salvation. He is pleased when we call on Him!

A long time ago, on a classroom door in a public school, I read these lines:

> *Hearts, like doors, will open with ease*
> *To very, very little keys.*
> *And don't forget that two of these*
> *Are "I thank you" and "If you please."*

May we all have an attitude of gratitude every day of the year! May we all wear the garment of gratitude! Gratitude exalts God, dispels gloom and encourages graciousness. Thanksgiving is the politeness of the soul!

Read: Psalm 116

October 10   MORE THANKSGIVING!

Thanksgiving is one of the happy days of the year. To mother and grandmother, it means hours of preparing turkey dressing, baking pumpkin pies and setting the table. The tiring labour is forgotten, however, when they hear the exclamations of delight from children, grandchildren, family members and friends. After the meal, the adults visit and the children run outside to play in the leaves.

But Thanksgiving is more than a reunion with loved ones, lively conversation and football games. It's a day to count your blessings and offer thanks to the ONE who has provided them all and more. To God we offer praise for the freedom we enjoy. We thank Him for our health and our homes, our family and our friends. I'm sure you are grateful for many things! The list could be long.

Every day ought to be filled with thanksgiving! It has been said, "A grateful mind is a great mind." The Bible says, *It is a good thing to give thanks to the Lord* (Ps. 92:1). *It is a time to bless the Lord* (Ps. 103).

Gratitude is the memory of the heart, the homage of the heart
Rendered to God for His goodness.

Psalm 100 says, *Shout for joy to the LORD, all the earth. Worship the LORD with gladness; come before Him with joyful songs. Know that the LORD is God. It is He who made us, and we are His; we are His people, the sheep of His pasture. Enter His gates with thanksgiving and His courts with praise; give thanks to Him and praise His name. For the LORD is good and His love endures for ever; His faithfulness continues through all generations.*

Read: 1 Thessalonians 5:18

October 11   THANKSGIVING — Psalm 116

How can I repay the LORD for all His goodness to me? (Ps. 116:12). This is a deeply personal and sensible consideration. When we speak of God's goodness, we should magnify and speak highly of Him. How can I repay the Lord? Can I give anything proportionate? I can no more pretend to give a recompence to God than I can merit any favour from Him. What would God be pleased with as the acknowledgement of a grateful mind?

First, what are some of the good things He does? He hears us (vs. 1). He has bent His ear to listen (vs. 2). What a privilege to have the sympathetic ear of God. God hears and answers prayer! He delivers from death (vs. 3, vs. 8). We have this victory through our Lord Jesus Christ who loved us and gave Himself for us. He saves us (vs. 4). He protects us (vs. 6). He is bountiful (vs. 7). *And my God will meet all your needs according to His glorious riches in Christ Jesus* (Phil. 4:19). Innumerable things could be listed as our minds recall the bountiful blessings. He provides health and strength, food, clothing and shelter. Oh, that men would praise the Lord for His goodness!

It is the feeling, the ever-growing feeling of the deepening experience, that no fitting return can be made to God. The only possible return we can make is to let Him do all His work of grace in our lives. Are there some returns? Can we repay the Lord? We can respond in love (vs. 1). We can yield to God the affection of our heart. We can call on Him (vs. 2). This is an expressive way of showing our gratitude. We can rest in Him (vs. 7). We can show our confidence in Him by resting our souls entirely in Him. This He desires! (Matt. 11:28). There is rest in Jesus! We can walk with Him (vs. 9). *I urge you to live a life worthy of the calling you have received* (Eph. 4:1). God considers our lives precious, so we can offer Him the expressions of our devotion (vs. 15,16). We can be His servants (vs. 16). We can be thankful (vs. 17). *Through Jesus, therefore, let us continually offer to God a sacrifice of praise — the fruit of lips that confess His name. And do not forget to do good and to share with others, for with such sacrifices God is pleased* (Heb. 13:15-16).

How can I repay the Lord? I can lift up the cup of salvation, I can call on the name of the Lord, I can fulfill my vows to the Lord. Be a man or woman of your word. Be trustworthy!

Read: Psalm 116

October 12   THE BIBLE

The Bible is God speaking! The Bible is not God, but it is God speaking. He spoke to men through the Holy Spirit and the Bible is the result. *For prophecy never had its origin in the will of man, but men spoke from God as they were carried along by the Holy Spirit* (2 Peter 1:21). The Bible is a revelation from God to man. Divine revelation, in this sense, is the communication by God to man of those truths concerning Himself, His plans, His will and His concern for man's redemption, which could not have been known through nature, nor intuition, nor any process of reasoning apart from supernatural aid. God is! He created the universe, He created man in His image for His companionship, His glory and His pleasure. The Bible is a revelation from God to His intelligent creatures.

1. A revelation is possible! With God, all things are possible!

Surely the infinitely wise and powerful God can and will reveal Himself, His plans, and His will to man.

2. A revelation is necessary! Sinful man might, to a certain extent, be able to realize and reason from intuition something about sin and its consequences, but he could know nothing of God's love, His provision for pardon, reconciliation and salvation, or the blessings of the new life in Christ. These truths must come through revelation.

3. A revelation is probable! God longs for His creatures, He yearns over them to bring them into fellowship with Himself. Surely a revelation is pre-eminently probable.

4. A revelation is credible! If it is possible, necessary, and probable, it is overwhelmingly credible. In fact, it would be most difficult to believe that such a revelation would not be given.

5. A revelation is reasonable! It would seem strange indeed if the Author of our being, who has enabled us to communicate with one another in so many ways, would not communicate with us at all.

6. A revelation is certain! The claims are fully substantiated by the miracles, the fulfilled prophecies, the propagation of Christianity, the fruits of Christianity and the satisfaction that has come to hearts all over the world as a result.

This is a great BOOK! Law, history, poetry, prophecy, doctrine, worship, exhortations, stories and drama all combined in one book, making the story of redemption the most fascinating and up-to-date of all literature. Wherever the gospel goes, sinners are saved, churches are built and spiritual food is craved. This is a great BOOK!

This book will keep you from sin, or sin will keep you from this book!

Read: Psalm 19

October 13   THE SECOND COMING OF CHRIST

After He said this, He was taken up before their very eyes, and a cloud hid Him from their sight. They were looking intently up into the sky as he was going, when suddenly two men dressed in white stood beside them. "Men of Galilee," they said, "why do you stand here looking into the sky? This same Jesus, who has been taken from you into heaven, will come back in the same way you have seen him go into heaven" (Acts 1:9-11).

It will be the very same Jesus, the One who was born of a virgin, who taught among men, died on a cross, arose from the dead, and ascended into heaven. This same Jesus in body, with the scars of the nails in His hands, is coming back again. *Look, He is coming with the clouds, and every eye will see Him, even those who pierced Him; and all the peoples of the earth will mourn because of Him. So shall it be! Amen* (Rev. 1:7). He will come back in the same manner in which He left. He went away visibly, He will return visibly! He left them from the Mount of Olives, He will return to the Mount of Olives (Zech. 14:4).

"Do not let your hearts be troubled. Trust in God; trust also in me. In my Father's house are many rooms; if it were not so, I would have told you. I am going there to prepare a place for you. And if I go and prepare a place for you, I will come back and take you to be with me that you also may be where I am" (John 14:1-3).

Jesus is coming again! He may return today! Perhaps tonight!

> Lord, we wait for Thine appearing;
> Even so, Thy people say;
> Bright the prospect is and cheering,
> Of beholding Thee that day.

Paul commended the Church at Thessalonica. *For they themselves report what kind of reception you gave us. They tell how you turned to God from idols to serve the living and true God, and to wait for His Son from heaven, whom He raised from the dead — Jesus, who rescues us from the coming wrath* (1 Thess. 1:9-10). Our waiting is not to be marked by passive, stagnant, complacent attitudes, but rather attitudes of keen anticipation which incite us to new heights of spiritual activity. Those who are truly waiting are witnessing! *For the grace of God that brings salvation has appeared to all men. It teaches us to say "No" to ungodliness and worldly passions, and to live self-controlled, upright and godly lives in this present age, while we wait for the blessed hope — the glorious appearing of our great God and Saviour, Jesus Christ, who gave Himself for us to redeem us from all wickedness and to purify for Himself a people that are His very own, eager to do what is good* (Titus 2:11-14).

> Some golden daybreak Jesus will come.
> Some golden daybreak battles all won.
> He'll shout the victory, break through the blue;
> Some golden daybreak for me, for you.

Will you be ready for that moment? Prepare yourself now — Jesus is coming back!

Read: John 14:1-6; 1 Thessalonians 1:9-10; Titus 2:11-14

October 14   THE SABBATH

By the seventh day God had finished the work He had been doing; so on the seventh day He rested from all His work. And God blessed the seventh day and made it holy, because on it He rested from all the work of creating that He had done (Gen. 2:2-3).

The principle that God had in mind was simple: One in seven days was to be a day of rest. The command to keep it came later. This is the only Sabbath which God celebrated. When man sinned in the garden, and later did not keep the law, God did not rest. The word now is, *"My Father is always at His work to this very day, and I, too, am working"* (John 5:17). God can have no rest where there is sin. Thorns, thistles, sighs, tears, groans, sorrows, sickness, death, degradation, guilt and a ruined world — can God rest with that? Jesus justified His actions on the Sabbath in close relation with His Father. Jesus exemplified the way the Sabbath should be observed. God does not stop His deeds of compassion on that day and neither did Jesus. From the fall to the incarnation, from the incarnation to the cross, God the Son was working. He is still working today!

Today we have a new day, the day after the Sabbath. The day Jesus rose from the dead (Matt. 28.1; Mark 16:1). The first day of the week is not the Sabbath changed, but altogether a new day. It is the first day of a new period, and not the last day of the old. The seventh day stands connected with earth and earthly rest; the first day of the week introduces us to heaven and heavenly rest. The seventh day pertained to Israel; the first day pertains to the Church. Israel was commanded to observe the Sabbath; the Church is privileged to enjoy the first day. The former was the test of Israel's moral condition; the latter is the significant proof of the Church's eternal acceptance. This was the day on which Christ rose from the dead and set forth the triumph of redemption.

The Sabbath day is well and good, but it belongs to Israel. It was given as a covenant sign along with circumcision. *Then God said to Abraham, "As for you, you must keep My covenant, you and your descendants after you for the generations to come. This is My covenant with you and your descendants after you, the covenant you are to keep: Every male among you shall be circumcised. You are to undergo circumcision, and it will be the sign of the covenant between Me and you* (Gen. 17:9-11). *"Say to the Israelites, 'You must observe my Sabbaths. This will be a sign between Me and you for the generations to come, so that you may know that I am the LORD, who makes you holy'"* (Exod. 31:13). It would be difficult to carry out the Sabbath day law due to climactic conditions in the cold north, as well (Exod. 35:3).

For the people of God today, there is a Sabbath rest (Heb. 4:9-10). Do you have the rest of faith? What did Jesus say? (Matt. 11:28).

Read: Deuteronomy 5:15; 6:1; Acts 7:8

October 15 THE CURE FOR HEART TROUBLE

"Do not let your hearts be troubled. Trust in God; trust also in me. In my Father's house are many rooms; if it were not so, I would have told you. I am going there to prepare a place for you. And if I go and prepare a place for you, I will come back and take you to be with me that you also may be where I am" (John 14:1-3).

Our hearts may often be troubled when we look within ourselves, when we see our sins and our failures. Heart trouble is a common malady. Jesus is the perfect remedy! He came to bind up the broken-hearted. What is the Great Physician's prescription for a troubled heart? *"Trust in God; trust also in Me,"* are the words of Jesus. What a comfort to a sinful, sorrowful soul, that He who suffered and died for sinners has all the authority and the power of Almighty God.

For the future, there is the promise of a place. There is plenty of room! This will be a prepared place, a perfect place and a permanent place. Jesus went to the cross, died for our sins, was buried and rose again after three days. He came out of the grave so that we might have eternal life. He ascended into heaven so that He might appear in the presence of God for us (Rom. 8:34). Heaven is a prepared place for a prepared people!

The promise of His return is comforting! *For the Lord Himself will come down from heaven, with a loud command, with the voice of the archangel and with the trumpet call of God, and the dead in Christ will rise first. After that, we who are still alive and are left will be caught up together with them in the clouds to meet the Lord* in the air. And so we will be with the Lord for ever. Therefore encourage each other with these words (1 Thess. 4:16-18).

Will you be at the reception? Jesus had this to say to His Father: *"Father, I want those You have given Me to be with Me where I am, and to see My glory, the glory You have given Me because You loved Me before the creation of the world"* (John 17:24). There is a glorious reception awaiting you at the coming of the Lord! I am looking forward to that day! What a blessed assurance! The way to where He is, is the way of Faith; faith in the Lord Jesus Christ! *Jesus answered, "I am the way and the truth and the life. No one comes to the Father except through Me"* (John 14:6).

Read: John 14:1-6

October 16   CHRIST IN THE OLD TESTAMENT

The coming of Christ was foretold in many Old Testament Scriptures. Even Jesus asserted that Moses wrote of Him. *"I will raise up for them a prophet like you from among their brothers; I will put my words in his mouth, and he will tell them everything I command him"* (Deut. 18:18). Christ frequently applied Old Testament Scriptures to Himself. Look at Isaiah 61:1-2. Jesus read this on the Sabbath day in Luke's gospel. *"The Spirit of the Lord is on Me, because He has anointed Me to preach good news to the poor. He has sent Me to proclaim freedom for the prisoners and recovery of sight for the blind, to release the oppressed, to proclaim the year of the Lord's favour."* A whole chapter spoke of Him in Isaiah 53.

Some of the Old Testament saints looked forward to His coming. Christ Himself said, *"Your father Abraham rejoiced at the thought of seeing My day; he saw it and was glad"* (John 8:56). I always enjoy Abraham in Hebrews 11:10: *For he was looking forward to the city with foundations, whose architect and builder is God.*

Let me mention a few Old Testament titles given to the Lord Jesus. He is known as the Seed of the Woman in Genesis 3:15. He is known as the Star of Jacob in Numbers 24:17. Job said of Him, *"I know that my Redeemer lives"* (Job 19:25). Isaiah's title for Jesus was Emmanuel in Isaiah 7:14.

One day Philip said, *"We have found the one Moses wrote about in the Law, and about whom the prophets also wrote — Jesus of Nazareth, the son of Joseph"* (John 1:45). Jesus constantly appealed to the Old Testament to support His claim that He was the Christ. Jesus said, *"You diligently study the Scriptures because you think that by them you possess eternal life. These are the Scriptures that testify about Me"* (John 5:39).

Sometimes the question has been asked, "Could you win a soul to Christ with the Old Testament?" The answer is, "Yes!" Read Psalm 32:1-5. Think of the Passover in Exodus 12. *Christ our Passover lamb has been sacrificed* (1 Cor. 5:7).

Our hearts should respond in love and gratitude. Thirst makes water precious. Hunger makes bread precious. Sin makes the blood of Jesus Christ precious (1 John 1:7-9).

Read: Luke 4:14-21

October 17   QUESTIONS ABOUT MY PRAYER LIFE

Search your heart and challenge yourself with these questions regarding prayer:

1. Has my prayer life been powerless because of some besetting sin?

2. Has my prayer life been hindered by haste, irregularity, lack of system, unpreparedness of spirit or unbelief?

3. Has my prayer life been fruitless? Have I had such power with God that I can have power with souls?

4. Has my prayer life been limited to my own life, to my own work, to my own service for God?

5. Has my prayer life been intermittent and starved?

6. Has my prayer life been growing? Do I daily know more of the meaning and power of prayer?

7. Has my prayer life been sacrificial? What has it cost me in time, strength, vitality and love?

8. Is prayer still just an emergency, or is it a habit, an attitude of mind and a daily companion?

9. Is thanksgiving for definite answers to prayer having an increasing place in my prayer life?

10. Do I do most of the speaking in the dialogue of prayer, or do I give God ample time to speak to me by His still small voice and through His Word?

11. Do I have new evidence each week of the supernatural power and guidance of God's Holy Spirit for the duties of everyday?

12. Am I growing in grace and spiritual perception to know God's will and to appropriate His fullness in Christ?

Such is the responsibility of prevailing prayer!

Read: John 17

October 18   **A SATISFYING SIGHT**

Dear friends, now we are children of God, and what we will be has not yet been made known. But we know that when He appears, we shall be like Him, for we shall see Him as He is (1 John 3:2).

Five questions:

1. Who shall see Him? We shall see Him! Today we see Him in His Word. A day is coming when we shall see Him more. Jesus is coming again as He promised, to receive us to Himself. When He prayed in John 17:24, we see His desire. Do we have a desire to be with Him?

2. Who shall see Him? We shall! All who have their sins washed in the blood of the Lamb of God shall see Him; all who by faith have accepted Him as their Saviour; all who are born again into the family of God by faith in Jesus Christ. Are you looking forward to seeing Him? (Titus 2:13).

3. How shall we see Him? As He is! In all His glory! *"And now, Father, glorify Me in Your presence with the glory I had with You before the world began"* (John 17:5). Fanny Crosby wrote, "I shall see Him face to face." That is going to be a great moment. Will you be in that number?

4. What will be the effect? We shall be like Him! As a pilgrim people, we are to be Christ-like in our walk and in our talk. A day is coming when we will leave this earthly tent and be clothed in our "heavenly dwelling" (2 Cor. 5:2). We all enjoy 1 Corinthians 15:52-53. It will be a body of glory like His own.

5. Is this quite certain? Yes! We *shall*! This is going to be a reality! In view of eternity, my soul demands reality. Jesus is real! He lives! We serve a living Saviour! Because He lives, we too will live. Assurance! Yes, blessed assurance! All of this may be yours if you will place your faith and trust in the Lord Jesus Christ.

Read: 1 John 3:1-10

October 19   I AM THE BREAD OF LIFE

As bread satisfies the physical appetite of all who feed upon it, so Jesus Christ the Bread of Life satisfies the deeper appetite of all who feed upon Him. Let us look at two kinds of bread.

1. Material Bread! Jesus saw that the multitude was famished for lack of food that was not readily available. A great multitude followed Him because they saw the miracles He did. Jesus, knowing what He would do, asks Philip where they could buy bread for this crowd of people. Philip's arithmetic was perfect perhaps, but he failed to take Jesus' power into account. Andrew did a bit better. He had faith enough to report the little lad's lunch, but not enough faith to believe that with so small a supply the need could be met.

Jesus knew what He would do. The people were seated. Jesus gave thanks and the distribution began. Five barley loaves and two small fish multiplied throughout the crowd. There were even left-overs. The intention of the people then turned to making Him their king. But Jesus knew that it was not God's time for Him to reign. He did not want a loyalty merely based on full stomachs. He withdrew from them.

2. Spiritual Bread! *"Do not work for food that spoils, but for food that endures to eternal life, which the Son of Man will give you. On Him God the Father has placed His seal of approval"* (John 6:27). *Then Jesus declared, "I am the bread of life. He who comes to Me will never go hungry, and he who believes in Me will never be thirsty"* (John 6:35). Spiritual things are paramount! *"Watch out! Be on your guard against all kinds of greed; a man's life does not consist in the abundance of his possessions"* (Luke 12:15). Things of this world lack permanence! The people's response in John 6 is: *"What must we do to do the works God requires?" Jesus answered, "The work of God is this: to believe in the one He has sent"* (vs. 28, 29). *"For the bread of God is He who comes down from heaven and gives life to the world"* (John 6:33). The Bread of Life is able to satisfy your spiritual hunger perfectly and quench forever your spiritual thirst.

Go with John 6:37 today.

Read: John 6:1-15; 25-40

October 20   PHILIP AND THE ETHIOPIAN

1. An Earnest Worker. That's Philip! During the persecution of the Christians by Saul (later Paul), we see Philip in Samaria preaching the gospel with great results. This is evident by the statement, "And there was great joy in that city."

Philip was quick to receive divine direction. He was obedient and self-denying. He was prompt to go wherever he was sent. He was ready to exchange a large field of service for a small one — ready to exchange Samaria for a desert. He made no excuses. He was eager to follow the leading of the Holy Spirit. We see him running to meet the one to whom he was to speak. He began at once to speak to the man about the Word that he was reading. Philip was skillful and kind and he was Scriptural. He took the passage from Isaiah 53 and showed the man Jesus. Philip is practical. He leads this man to a personal knowledge of Jesus Christ, and what is more, he administers baptism. Believers need to be baptized! This is not optional!

2. A Sincere Seeker. That's the Ethiopian. He was a man of high rank and authority. He was a noble seeker. He was a diligent seeker. He was a teachable seeker. We find him returning from Jerusalem, reading from the Word of God. He was eager to learn the truth and willing to be instructed. He desired Philip to come and explain the Scriptures to him. When he saw that the Scriptures spoke of Jesus, he became a believer. He received Christ as his Saviour. He was a confessing believer. He was not ashamed to profess Christ in the presence of others. I am sure others were with him as escorts. Then we see him leaving with joy.

This is always a good sign when believers come to know that Christ is their Saviour. There is joy!

Faith is the greatest difficulty for seekers, yet, when it is won, it seems strange that so simple a matter should have hindered. Remember the acrostic for FAITH: Forsaking All, I Take Him.

Read: Acts 8:26-40

October 21   PETER AND CORNELIUS

At Caesarea there was a man named Cornelius, a centurion in what was known as the Italian Regiment. He and all his family were devout and God-fearing; he gave generously to those in need and prayed to God regularly (Acts 10:1-2). Here lay the great excellence of his character. God had made Himself known to him. God is the God of the individual, Jew or Gentile. Cornelius was not saved however, until Peter came with the gospel (Acts 10:24-48).

God is at work all the time! God was preparing Peter at the same time He was preparing Cornelius. The Lord was teaching Peter that He loves all men the same. When the messengers of Cornelius arrived, Peter was still wondering what the vision he had seen could mean, but he went. Cornelius was over-joyed at the presence of Peter. He had his house full and ready to hear what Peter had to say. This was new for Peter. They were Gentiles to whom he was speaking. Peter's ministry had only been among the Jews, now he had a new audience. But Peter had learned the lesson that God has no favourites. This has always been true, but Peter had to learn this and he did.

The gospel is universal! The gospel is for everyone! The gospel is for you! Do you believe with all your heart that Jesus is God's Son and that He died to take away your sin? Your faith in Him should be a life-changing faith. God prescribes the terms of salvation. *He who has the Son has life; he who does not have the Son of God does not have life* (1 John 5:12). Here is the answer to your spiritual need. Faith in Christ spells salvation and deliverance from the consequences of sin.

The effect of Peter's message that day was the water baptism of an entire household (vs. 47). That is the step of obedience every believer should take. Seal your faith in the waters of baptism. Baptism is the pledge of a good conscience toward God (1 Peter 3:21). Baptism is the symbol of an altered life, the symbol of complete fellowship with Christ. The Christian life is a new life in Christ, an active life of joy and triumph in Christ.

Read: Acts 10-11:18

October 22   THE EAGLE

Once in the Old Testament and once in the New Testament, God and Christ are compared to a bird (Deut. 32:11; Matt. 23:37). In each case, the comparison suggests thoughts of motherhood and love.

In the Old Testament the bird is an eagle. There are four outstanding references to this noble bird. The first is in Exodus where it speaks of REDEMPTION. The second is in Deuteronomy where it speaks of EQUIPMENT. The third is in Isaiah where it speaks of POWER and the fourth is in Psalms and it speaks of RENEWAL.

1. REDEMPTION! *"'You yourselves have seen what I did to Egypt, and how I carried you on eagles' wings and brought you to myself'"* (Exod. 19:4). Israel was in bondage in the grip of the Egyptian taskmasters. The Lord's redeeming love reached down and lifted them clear out of slavery and brought them into fellowship with Himself. This is the picture of the greater redemption that God did for us on Calvary through our Lord Jesus Christ.

2. EQUIPMENT! *...Like an eagle that stirs up its nest and hovers over its young, that spreads its wings to catch them and carries them on its pinions* (Deut. 32:11). The training which the mother bird gives her young to equip them for life sets forth the discipline by which God strengthens and develops the faith of His people. God's divine disturbances are summons to the heights. God is there to help us. *...Underneath are the everlasting arms* (Deut. 33:27). God's ways are there to equip us for greater things.

3. EMPOWERED! *But they who wait for the LORD shall renew their strength, they shall mount up with wings like eagles, they shall run, and not be weary, they shall walk, and not faint* (Isa. 40:31, RSV). When a storm strikes, the eagle sets its wings in such a way that the air currents lift it above the fury of the storm. Those who wait, those who hope, will soar! *"In quietness and trust is your strength"* (Isa. 30:15). Wait on the Lord, be of good courage — He will strengthen you.

4. RENEWED! *Who satisfies your desires with good things so that your youth is renewed like the eagle's* (Ps. 103:5). The poets have attributed to the eagle miraculous powers of becoming young again through the moulting time that characterizes all birds. The plumage returns and the flight is renewed. It is the picture of the renewal of the Holy Spirit that Paul talks about in Titus 3:5.

With these spiritual resources, let us take heart as we face the days that are ahead.

> *Though your way be long and dreary,*
> *Eagle strength He'll still renew,*
> *Garments fresh and foot unweary,*
> *Tell how God has brought you through.*

Read: Isaiah 40:21-31

October 23   AWAKENING FAITH — Acts 16

In Acts 16, we have the record of the early converts of the Church at Philippi. There was Lydia, whose heart the Lord opened. She believed and was baptized. Then the poor slave girl, possessed with an evil spirit. She was delivered and experienced salvation. This led to persecution from her masters, who had Paul and Silas put in prison. Were Paul and Silas disheartened and discouraged? About midnight, they began praying and singing hymns to God, and the other prisoners were listening to them (Acts 16:25). These men were not ashamed of the gospel. This brings us to the jailer!

The earthquake must have been quite a shock. The jailer saw the prison doors open and he supposed the prisoners were gone — and he knew the consequences. Paul had to prevent him from taking his own life and this made an impression on the jailer. He witnessed reality. God was at work on behalf of these men and the gospel. Paul was able to speak freely to the jailer.

This jailer came with man's greatest question: *"What must I do to be saved?"* He was now concerned about his salvation. This is nearest to his heart. Notice the clear cut answer that Paul gives to this man: *"Believe in the Lord Jesus, and you will be saved — you and your household"* (Acts 16:31). We must approve the method God has taken to reconcile the world to Himself. Christ is the answer! Christ is the way! Christ is the only mediator. *"Salvation is found in no one else, for there is no other name under heaven given to men by which we must be saved"* (Acts 4:12). The answer is the same for every member of the family.

Was the man really converted? What do you think? *The jailer brought them into his house and set a meal before them; he was filled with joy because he had come to believe in God — he and his whole family* (Acts 16:34). Faith produces joy! The gospel is the power of God to everyone that believes. *I am not ashamed of the gospel, because it is the power of God for the salvation of everyone who believes: first for the Jew, then for the Gentile* (Rom. 1:16).

Read: Acts 16:11-34

October 24   WORSHIP

When you go to God's house, what do you expect, what do you experience and what do you exercise? When you worship, do you really worship? Using an acrostic, I'd like to share what worship might include.

W — Wanting to know God better. Does Psalm 84:2 describe my longing? *My soul yearns, even faints, for the courts of the LORD; my heart and my flesh cry out for the living God.* I believe worship has in it this desire. God desires to give spiritual blessing when we desire to know Him and desire to follow Him.

O — Obeying His Word. God desires an obedient heart! *"Take to heart all the words I have solemnly declared to you this day, so that you may command your children to obey carefully all the words of this law"* (Deut. 32:46). You get more light on the things of God's Word as you obey.

R — Realizing His holiness and greatness. *Exalt the LORD our God and worship at His holy mountain, for the LORD our God is holy* (Ps. 99:9). When we worship, we come into the presence of a Holy God. If you want to see how great God is, read Isaiah 40 sometime and see.

S — Seeking His will. *I desire to do Your will, O my God; Your law is within my heart* (Ps. 40:8). We know that prayer is essential and we come praying. *Teach me to do Your will, for You are my God; may Your good Spirit lead me on level ground* (Ps. 143:10).

H — Honouring Him with our substance. Giving is a part of worship. *Honour the LORD with your wealth, with the firstfruits of all your crops* (Prov. 3:9). *Each man should give what he has decided in his heart to give, not reluctantly or under compulsion, for God loves a cheerful giver* (2 Cor. 9:7).

I — Inviting Him to control all our thoughts and actions. We're like a carburetor on a car that needs cleaning and tuning up. *Finally, brothers, whatever is true, whatever is noble, whatever is right, whatever is pure, whatever is lovely, whatever is admirable — if anything is excellent or praiseworthy — think about such things* (Phil. 4:8).

P — Praising Him with all our heart. *He put a new song in my mouth, a hymn of praise to our God. Many will see and fear and put their trust in the LORD* (Ps. 40:3). *The prayer of a righteous man is powerful and effective* (James 5:16).

What is your definition of worship?

Read all the references again.

SPIRITUAL SURVIVAL!

People want to know if we are in the last days. Will there be peace in this world? Will we see the return of Christ? In other words, what about the future? The future in the Word of God is made known for practical purposes and not for mental enjoyment. The Bible says, *What kind of people ought we to be?* (2 Peter 3:11).

1. Be attentive to the word of prophecy (2 Peter 3:1,2). Be a man or a woman of the Book! Peter reminds his readers of the prophets and the command of Christ. Prophetic photographs of coming events are brought into focus in the New Testament. The prophetic word did and will give us knowledge of what will happen in the future (2 Peter 3:3-7).

2. Be acquainted with the ways of God (2 Peter 3:8). We are not to be ignorant. We are not only to increase our knowledge, we are to dispel ignorance. We are not to be ignorant as to the divine estimation of time (vs. 8). We are not to be ignorant as to the desire of the Lord (vs. 9). We are not to be ignorant as to the characteristics of that day (vs. 10). The Day of the Lord will come! This world is marked for destruction. Acquaintance with the ways of God will save us from panic and fear.

3. Be active in the work of purity. Peter presses home the moral application (2 Peter 3:11-15). Be engaged in the work of holiness. Our life is to line up with the Lord Jesus. We are to fear sin more than bombs. In the new heaven and the new earth dwells righteousness. We need to become acclimatized!

4. Be alert to the wiles of the Enemy (2 Peter 3:17). Be on your guard! Peter gives us two aspects of the wiles of the Enemy.

>   *a. False teachers distort the Word of God.*
>   *b. False teachers seek to mislead the saints.*

Let nothing move you from Jesus Christ! *But grow in the grace and knowledge of our Lord and Saviour Jesus Christ. To Him be glory both now and for ever! Amen* (2 Peter 3:18).

Read: 2 Peter 3:1-18

October 26   A LOOK AT DAVID — Psalm 5

David was a man of God. He had real spiritual aspirations and a real thirst for God. Let's study him briefly in Psalm 5.

1. He has contact with God. In the first three verses, we see a

286

prayerful invocation. It is a reminder of a consistent devotional life. Prayer is personal conversation with God. Prayer brings the soul near to God. Prayer is a blessed privilege. We need to practice unhurried communion with God.

2. He considers God. In the next three verses (vs. 4-6), we see a prayerful contemplation. We see what God is like. God's hatred of sin is inseparable from His holiness. To be a Holy God, He must have an equal amount of hatred for sin. He does not sympathize with sin. Sin chokes the channel of communion with God. Calvary is God's answer for the sin question.

3. He comes to God. The next two verses are a prayer of supplication (vs. 7-8). We have confidence in God! Do you love to be in God's house? Here is a heart that is in sympathy with God. We can ask for guidance. Here we learn to trust in His love and we are strengthened to go out and face the Enemy.

4. He counts on God. We can leave the Enemy in His hands (vs. 9-12). The enemies of the psalmist are the enemies of God, and his prayer is a prayer of righteous retribution. A day is coming when there will be a casting away from God. Trust awakens joy, trust calls for praise. Our refuge is in God!

Count upon God in your life. Do not leave Him out. It is good to have God's favour upon our lives. His Divine protection is our portion day by day.

Read: Psalm 5

October 27   JESUS IS COMING SOON

What was true in Noah's day was true in Lot's day. Noah's testimony was largely unheeded and so was Lot's testimony in Sodom. There was no great revival before the flood. And there was no great turning to God in Lot's day. There were less than ten believers in the whole district of Sodom and Gomorrah (Gen. 18:32). Today, the company of true Bible-believing, born again Christians is pitiably small in comparison to the host of unbelievers. Judgement is pending! Jesus is coming!

An unknown author writes,

Quite suddenly, it may be as I lie in dreamless sleep,
God's gifts to many a sorrowing heart, with no more tears to weep;
That a call shall break the slumber, and a Voice sound in my ear,
"Rise up, my love, and come away; behold the Bridegroom's here."

Hope is the ballast of the soul! Hope will keep the soul from rolling and tumbling in the great storm.

We are living in a day when the world is thoroughly shaken by the tremendous breath-taking strides that history has taken. Men pant with unutterable fatigue as they endeavor to keep up with the mad whirl of our space-age. Few realize, however, that just beyond the horizon, there is an event greater than any the passing ages have ever seen. Jesus is coming! Our Enemy would keep us from believing in the truth of His coming. Satan knows and recognizes what this belief teaches us (Titus 2:11-14). If we are occupied with the second coming, Satan's clutches upon our souls will be broken.

Jesus must come again if Calvary is to be vindicated and His infallible word verified. In view of the sudden, imminent return of the Lord, the Scriptural injunction is not, "Get ready," but, "Be ready"!

The fig tree is budding today! Israel is back in the Land! Spiritual fruit among them will come after Messiah returns. This is promising! We await the coming of the Lord! We do not wait in vain!

God makes a promise, faith believes it, hope anticipates it and patience quietly awaits it!

Read: Luke 17:20-37

October 28   LAUGHTER!

A cheerful heart is good medicine (Prov. 17:22).

Laughter is a sign of health! What we need today is a good sense of humour. God gave us the power to weep, and He also gave us the power to laugh. We can respond to the gloom of life and to the humour of life. So we have the gift of mirth!

Humour is mirth compounded with tender compassion for all that is frail, and profound reverence for all that is sublime.

In life, we must see both: solemn truths which come to us, and the lighter touches of life. He who has never smiled at the antics of a kitten or a puppy has lost touch with certain basic realities of life.

Each person has the right to own his or her own feelings, but I feel that our humour ought to be clean and free from any trace of irreverence. It should not be off-colour, nor malicious.

God gave us humour as an outlet for our emotions. How often the irritations of life can be resolved in moments of cheer and pleasantry. Frequently tensions are broken when there is a burst of laughter. Often the tensions in our own hearts can be resolved if we could sit down and laugh at ourselves a bit more.

Do you have the ability to smile even when the going is a bit rough? A cheerful heart is good medicine! For some people, I know it is the best medicine.

Humour is one of the important allies of faith! Be of good cheer today! Let me add two more verses: *A happy heart makes the face cheerful, but heartache crushes the spirit* (Prov. 15:13). *A cheerful look brings joy to the heart, and good news gives health to the bones* (Prov. 15:30).

Read: Proverbs 15:1-13,30

October 29   HURT FEELINGS!

Today, I may step on your toes! I'm sure that all of us have friends and acquaintances whose feelings are very easily hurt. We have to always be on our guard since they are overly sensitive. We can never feel quite comfortable in their presence.

Sometimes, husbands and wives are overly sensitive. Both are saying, "Don't you dare step on my toes." This leads to conflict and triggers "hurt feelings."

Why are some people so sensitive? Is there a feeling of inner insecurity and inferiority? That may be the reason. One who is strong and confident will not be easily threatened by others. But when people are uncertain about themselves and not too confident about their own abilities, they will be easily hurt by the criticism and remarks of others. Such people live on the defensive. There is a feeling of uneasy pride, for they too want to succeed in life.

This spirit is learned in childhood, sometimes when parents say things like, "That boy or girl does things much better; why can't you be like that?" This helps to develop a feeling of inferiority.

How do you remove "hurt feelings"? What is the remedy? One way is to go to the person who hurt you and tell him or her about it. Tell them how you feel. You may find out that no insult was intended. The other way is to sit down and carefully examine yourself. Try to find out why you are on the defensive. Why are you so easily threatened? Try to get at the source of the matter. Talk it over with some trusted friend. You may discover in your relationships with others that others are human too. You may also discover, if you are really honest with yourself, that many things that gave you "hurt feelings" are things that are true.

So, the real solution may be self-examination. Be willing to admit shortcomings. Pray with David in Psalm 139:23: *Search me, O God and know my heart; test me and know my anxious thoughts.* If you think someone has hurt you, pray the prayer of David earnestly and see if you don't rise to find the "hurt feeling" gone.

Read: Galatians 6:1-10

October 30   PRETENDING!

All of us are aware of what the word "camouflage" means. Men and machines can be disguised to make them blend in or look harmless. There is a lot of mental and emotional camouflage today. We try to conceal what actually goes on within. We use masks to hide our true identities, to hide our inner feelings. We cover up our inner motives and desires so that they will appear acceptable.

Pretense is very common in everyday life! We say, "How nice to see you" when we are actually thinking, "I wish I could have avoided you." Naturally, social graces require that we do not say everything that comes into our minds.

But there may be some dangers to pretending. In most cases, we put ourselves in the best possible light with regard to our accomplishments. We even pretend that we know more than we really do. We use fancy terms to cover up our ignorance about a subject. Often when a minister is present, people will pretend to be very religious — more than they actually are. This is a form of spiritual camouflage. Others parade as humble souls to hide their inner pride. And some take on a boastful attitude to hide their feelings of insecurity.

When we pretend, we can't relax; we're always threatened. We must keep up a front. All of this produces unnecessary tensions.

Why do we build up an elaborate front? Do we want others to think well of us? Can we not face ourselves as we really are? Who are we trying to impress? The word to all of us today is, "STOP PRETENDING."

Learn to face reality. All of us have fears and weaknesses. All of us have emotional highs and lows. All of us have sin. But God has also given all of us certain resources — don't minimize these. Put God at the centre of your life! Be yourself! Be honest with yourself! God loves you! Make a contribution with your life.

Read: James 1:22-27

October 31   PREJUDICE!

Prejudice is an evil that has plagued mankind for many centuries. The Romans and Greeks viewed all other nations, including our fore-fathers, as barbarians. In the days of Jesus, there was a strong racial conflict between the Jews and the Samaritans. Today there are large barriers of prejudice between the races in our country. I'm sure a certain amount is in all of us.

The word "prejudice" finds its root meaning in the act of "pre-judging." That is forming an opinion about someone else in the absence of all the facts. It is forming judgements of people based on factors other than who they are as persons.

Prejudice is something that grows in the developing personality. For example, as children, we grow and learn to get along with people. As our circle grows, we begin to relate to acquaintances outside the home, and then to strangers and those of different races, religions and languages.

Today there is a high demand for social growth. Today we must be able to meet the strangers and relate to them. Many of us are not ready for this.

Have you ever thought of pride as being the back of all our individual prejudice? Have we not harboured an attitude that says we are better than others? Do we not tend to draw lines of distinction between various groups?

I'm wondering if we need to read Romans 12:3. *For by the grace given me I say to every one of you: Do not think of yourself more highly than you ought, but rather think of yourself with sober judgment, in accordance with the measure of faith God has given you.*

We should never let our prejudices against certain people prejudice us against their ideas and their accomplishments.

Read: Romans 12:3-21

November 1   ALONE!

In a world of over-population, we get the feeling that we are not very important. We are just a person lost in the crowd. Many times we stand alone. There is an inescapable aloneness in life!

It is true, each of us is alone in many of life's relationships. Through heredity and environment, we have acquired certain qualities that make us different from any other person. There is also the factor of personal responsibility. No one can live your life for you. There are responsibilities that only you can meet. There are decisions and choices that no one else can make for you. No one can believe for you. Each person must believe for himself or herself. No one can really do your work for you; only you can do it.

We are aware that friends and relatives can give support. A doctor can alleviate pain. But still, there are the things that we face ALONE. The times when we stand alone put us to a real test.

Many people are afraid to be alone. It is not surprising that many people surround themselves with the sound of a radio or a television. You see, silence is terrifying!

We become very conscious of being alone. We feel like Elijah who said, *"I am left alone"* (1 Kings 19:9-14). Do you share this feeling sometimes? You are thinking and saying, "I am the only Christian in this office, I am the only Christian in my department, I am the only Christian in this factory." A nurse may be alone with a dying patient. But that means that you may be the only one who can touch another life and help.

I believe you can draw upon the resources of heaven. Practice the presence of God in your life. You are not alone! He is nearer than breathing! There is a Friend that sticketh closer than a brother. Take the words of that great hymn with you today: "What a Friend we have in Jesus." You need not be lonely when Jesus is your Saviour and Friend. Christ's friendship is open to every believer.

Read: Psalm 46

November 2   TIRED FEELING!

So many people suffer from fatigue. We all talk about being tired at times. A hard-working labourer, a mother in a home, a secretary at a desk and a man in his office — all feel tired from time to time. Some say they're always tired. The lazy man will say he was born tired. Would you believe that much of our fatigue is not physical, but functional? Often it grows out of an attitude toward work, rather than the physical exertion required to do something. It is not so much the muscles, as the mind. Your fatigue may require a change in your mental attitude towards your work.

Tired feelings often arise from discontentment. You dislike your work or it's boring, and that will make you weary. Remember when you were a boy or girl and your parents said, "Would you please mow the lawn or wash the floor?" and you suddenly became extremely tired. When, on the other hand, someone called you to come and play ball (which requires more physical energy), that did not bother you at all.

To be sure, our bodies do get tired. Even Jesus was weary at times. This is a call to rest! The Lord has graciously provided sleep and rest to overcome it.

Just to talk about tensions, grief, depression and disappointments can cause extreme fatigue. A pessimistic outlook on life does the same. A worrisome approach can make the day seem long, and the nights even longer.

Do you know what we need? A higher perspective in life! We must learn to see our work as means to higher goals. For example, a father and mother providing a home for those they love.

The highest goal and the greatest rest are found in the words of Jesus: *"Come to me, all you who are weary and burdened, and I will give you rest"* (Matt. 11:28). Jesus is saying, "I will ease and relieve and refresh your soul." You will find rest!

Is this a good time to remind you of the Lord's day, the day of rest? You need this rest physically, mentally and spiritually (Heb. 10:25).

Read: Matthew 11:25-30

November 3   FEELINGS OF GUILT!

We are confronted by many conflicts in life. One of the greatest of these is the conflict between good and evil, or right and wrong. This struggle has been going on ever since the fall of man in the Garden of Eden. Living in the stream of humanity, none of us can really escape it.

Sin is very real! It is in our lives, our actions and our attitudes, as well as in our hearts and our minds. Feelings of guilt arise as we become aware of sin in our lives.

There are two kinds of guilt: Healthy guilt and unhealthy guilt. Generally, when we speak of a guilt complex, we are referring to unhealthy guilt. A person with this may feel there is no room for forgiveness. Then there are those (like David) who, when they see their guilt, acknowledge their sin and find forgiveness. *Then I acknowledged my sin to You and did not cover up my iniquity. I said, "I will confess my transgressions to the LORD" — and You forgave the guilt of my sin* (Ps. 32:5). This is the result of healthy guilt. David discovered that there was no point in hiding his sin from God (Ps. 32, 51, 139).

Psychiatrists and pastoral counselors are saying today that confession can often be the turning point in a person's recovery. For all that has ever happened there is forgiveness. *Blessed is he whose transgressions are forgiven, whose sins are covered* (Ps. 32:1). No one needs to live with a guilt complex (Ps. 51). You can accept God's love and forgiveness! You can have the assurance of sins forgiven!

Let me add this: In my own experience, I have met people who find it hard to forgive themselves. Do not punish yourself for past sins and continue to feel guilty. If God is able to forgive us, should we not also learn to forgive ourselves? Forgiveness must be practiced, as well as received. Forgiveness is the gift of God's love. Remember the return of the prodigal son? He was fully forgiven and fully re-instated. You will find your wholeness in Jesus Christ!

Read all the references above.

November 4   MEMORY

Memory is a wonderful thing — one of the most priceless gifts of a bountiful Creator. Memory enriches our lives! By it, we live in the present and in the past. As we move through life, the vast storehouse of memories increases. We cherish memories!

Unfortunately, not all memories are happy ones. There are some that we blot out from consciousness, for they haunt us and make us miserable. All of us are aware that the mind can retain only so much, and the trivial things soon drop out in order to make room for more important things. This is passive forgetting. At times this can be annoying, like when we forget a name we should have remembered.

Our memories may be determined by our attitudes. Tell me

what things you remember best and I will tell you what kind of person you are. The comedian has a mind full of jokes and anecdotes. The philosopher has a mind full of systematic reasonings. The cheerful man remembers the joyful, happy experiences. The person who is easily offended will remember hurts inflicted upon him. Therefore, your memory could very well reveal your temperament and character.

May I mention in passing that some things will need to be forgotten. Especially some past wrongs. These tend to turn hatred into bitterness and you are only hurting yourself. I can hear you say, "That's easier said than done." You cannot just tell your mind to forget. You cannot just wipe memory away.

What can you do? Fill your mind with other thoughts, so that one memory will crowd out another. Place a lofty thought in its place. Lay aside past hurts and insults by replacing them with feelings of love and sympathetic concern for those who hurt you. Above all, experience God's forgiving love first and then you will be able to forgive others as well as yourself. When God blots the record, He forgives and forgets (Micah 7:18, 19). Paul says, *But one thing I do: Forgetting what is behind and straining towards what is ahead* (Phil. 3:13). I want to be the kind of person God wants me to be.

Read: Philippians 3:12-21

November 5   LIFE IS...!

It is good to be alive!

1. Life is the gift of God! God is the source of life! *The LORD God formed the man from the dust of the ground and breathed into his nostrils the breath of life, and man became a living being* [soul] (Gen. 2:7). You are a living soul. You do not just *have* a soul, you *are* a soul. Wesley wrote,

> *A charge to keep I have, a God to glorify,*
> *A never dying soul to save and fit it for the sky.*

A biology teacher said to a class one day, "I am a soul. My body is not the real me. It's not that my body has a soul, but rather that my soul has a temporary body." "I *am* a soul." Earthly life is the gift of God, and so is eternal life through faith in Jesus Christ.

2. Life is the target of sin! *Therefore, just as sin entered the world through one man, and death through sin, and in this way* *death came to all men, because all sinned* (Rom. 5:12). Oh, the heartache, the sorrow, the suffering in this world as a result of sin. The word **SIN** spells: **S**elf, **I**niquity and **N**o satisfaction. There is, however, good news! *Christ... appeared... to do away with sin by the sacrifice of Himself* (Heb. 9:26).

3. Life is the object of redemption! *"For God so loved the world that He gave His one and only Son, that whoever believes in Him shall not perish but have eternal life* (John 3:16). Christ came to give us life (John 10:10). There is a spiritual dimension to living that is very real. *And this is the testimony: God has given us eternal life, and this life is in His Son. He who has the Son has life; he who does not have the Son of God does not have life. I write these things to you who believe in the name of the Son of God so that you may know that you have eternal life* (1 John 5:11-13).

4. Life is the prelude to eternity! Life is a journey to be taken but once! The minor prophet Amos writes, *Prepare to meet your God* (Amos 4:12). Death being so solemn, so final, so uncontrollable, are we prepared to face it?

> *Life is certain, death is sure;*
> *Sin is the cause, Christ is the cure.*

Salvation is in a Person! That Person is Jesus Christ. Do you know Him in a personal way?

Read: 1 John 5:1-12

November 6   **FRIENDSHIP!**

One of the most beautiful descriptions of friendship in literature is the Bible's own account of the friendship between David and Jonathan. The story is a classic! These two men might well have been rivals, yet here we have the shepherd and the prince knit together in close friendship.

To be a friend we must be willing to pay the price of being a friend. We need friends! I often meet people who say, "I haven't a friend in the world." There is the feeling of complete aloneness. We need friends! We need others to stand by our side, to give support and to be our companions.

A deeper need for friendship reaches into our inner emotional life. We all need to have a feeling of personal worth. A friend is one who thinks well of us and considers us to be worthy. He will make us think well of ourselves. He will also give of himself to us. Basic to our lives is not only the need *to* love, but also the need to *be* loved. It is important to cultivate the art of friendship. Try to find someone with similar interests and then share them. Be a friend! Remain loyal in spite of the cost! There are far too many "fair-weather" friends.

Do you want an example of whole-hearted friendship? Have you heard the words of Jesus? *"Greater love has no one than this, that he lay down his life for his friends"* (John 15:13). Be willing to pay the price of being a friend.

Albrecht Durer, a renowned painter, had a true friend. When they were young men and both interested in art, it was decided that Durer would paint while his friend worked to support him. It took many years for the artist to make a name for himself, and by that time his friend's hands were calloused and hardened by toil. To express his thanks to his friend, Durer painted a picture of these hands, and it became his most famous work of art. It was a tribute to a friend who was willing to sacrifice for friendship.

We need friends! Cultivate the art of friendship!

Read: 1 Samuel 18:1-5

November 7   CHANNELS!

Our lives ought to be fresh, fragrant and fruitful! We need to maintain a healthy outlook on life. In other words, my life and yours ought to be a channel through which blessings flow. I want to be a channel of blessing! Blessings are benefits! (Ps. 103). We need an inlet and an outlet in our lives to remain healthy and fresh. We do not want to become like the Dead Sea.

For starters, we need open minds. We should be open to new ideas. We should not be opposed to change. We should welcome fresh discoveries so that life doesn't become static.

We also need stable minds. We need convictions based on the Word of God. We need to share them. Today, I am calling for consistency. A Bible School teacher said, "Consistency, thou art a jewel," and I have never forgotten that. Are you a man or woman of conviction?

We need constructive minds. A constructive mind thinks clearly and expresses itself freely. I'm calling for a balance that may not be easy. If the mind is viewed as a channel, it must take in a fresh stream of ideas and impressions if it is to pass them on again to others. Man must have his inlets and his outlets.

Now we ask, "What are some of the things that replenish your mind?" So many things make inroads today. Television, magazines, newspapers, etc. The big question is, "Are you coming back to the Bible for some input?" Faith needs nourishment! Feed your mind with the truth of God. Are you furnishing the chamber of your mind with the things of God? Is God central in your life? We must bring in the apostle Paul's injunction here again: *Whatever is true, whatever is noble, whatever is right, whatever is pure, whatever is lovely, whatever is admirable — if anything is excellent or praiseworthy — think about such things* (Phil. 4:8).

Read: 2 Timothy 2:20-21

November 8   FEELINGS OF LONELINESS

This world is a busy place! Thousands of people rush from place to place. Our highways are over-crowded. Many feet beat upon the sidewalks of our cities. There are always people. And there are those who feel alone in the middle of it all. There is possibly no feeling that is more disheartening than that of loneliness.

Today's songs speak of this feeling. Much romantic music, negro spirituals, even the crooning of western songs sing out the cry of loneliness. It may sound like a strange paradox in the light of today's discussion about overpopulation.

To be sure, there are real feelings of being alone. The loss of a loved one would be a good example, where no one comes to share the sorrow. In some situations, no one comes to share the joys of life either. So there are real feelings of loneliness.

But there can be loneliness even in a crowd or in a busy family. There are people who live together and yet walk alone. It is a reaction to life that is not healthy.

What can we do? Begin by taking a healthy attitude toward yourself and your relationship with others. You see, a solitary person often takes a sour attitude toward life as a whole. He or she is unhappy and not even friendly to him or herself. Sometimes you may ask people, "Are you ever lonely?" And some will say, "No, I have so many friends that I never get a chance to feel lonely." On the other hand, there are those who say, "I feel so lonely, no one ever pays attention to me." One has learned the art of friendship and the other has not. To have a friend, you must be a friend. Cultivate friendship! Take an interest in helping others and you will not live in solitude.

One of the best answers and means to overcoming the feeling of loneliness is to practice the companionship of God. Our Lord Jesus often reached out His Hand of blessing to those who walked alone. Cultivate a living personal friendship with the Lord Jesus Christ and you will find that you never walk alone. Part of Proverbs 18:24 says, *There is a Friend who sticks closer than a brother.* You are never alone!

Read: Matthew 28:20; Psalm 8

November 9   **PATIENCE!**

You have all heard the words, "Patience is a virtue!" How patient are we? Can we wait for things to happen in their own good time, or are we so eager that we hurry them? Often through impatience, we spoil the very thing we are seeking to achieve.

The word "patience" suggests two ideas: forbearance and endurance. Patience may mean a willingness to wait. Patience may include continuance in our endeavor to achieve. Both of these elements should be present in our lives.

A person is not born with patience — it is something we must learn. For example, a child would rather have a dime right now than wait a week for five dollars. For everything in life, we must learn to practice patience.

Worthwhile accomplishments require a certain amount of time. When you plant a seed in the ground you must wait for it to grow. God usually works in the realm of nature with calm leisure. He has no need to hurry.

Then, of course, there are many things that test our patience. A period of illness can be very trying. Waiting for someone at a pre-arranged corner can be frustrating — fifteen minutes can seem like an hour. Driving on the highway in rush-hour traffic, bending a nail as you hammer, hitting a golf ball into the rough can all strain our patience. Often we blame the objects or persons that frustrate us, but the real difficulty lies within ourselves. We must learn to conquer our natures if we are to learn the art of patience.

Patience is not a passive virtue! Patience is dynamic! The

Bible says, *Let us run with patience* (Heb. 12:1, KJV). It is the patient struggle that helps us win in the battle of life. When you are tempted to be impatient, look to the Author and Finisher of your faith. He revealed great patience in all that He did and He still has patience with us today.

Learn to be patient and exercise patience. Keep climbing!

God is faithful; He will not let you be tempted beyond what you can bear. But when you are tempted, He will also provide a way out so that you can stand up under it (1 Cor. 10:13).

Read: Hebrews 12:1-13

November 10   THINGS!

We live in a world of "THINGS"! From morning till evening, we are surrounded by "things." The clothes we wear, the home we occupy, the food we eat, the car we drive, the tools we use and the equipment we handle. Each of us must come to terms with our environment. Surroundings may play a part and make a difference. Attitudes will make a difference. Our society is overly concerned about "things." This material world plays a tremendous role in our lives. People are more interested in making a living than making a life. Our primary concern in life is the paycheque and the "things" it will buy. In this highly commercialized society, we are driven to buy. The urge is so strong. Credit terms are so easy to get.

Here is some information that I read: One hundred years ago, the average person had seventy-two wants and sixteen needs. Today, there are five hundred and ninety-four wants and one hundred and eight articles regarded as necessary. The pressure of the material is far greater than it was one hundred years ago. In 1860, there were 6,000 articles made and sold; in 1960, there were 425,000 articles made and sold. The result of this is a restless striving for "things" — a yearning that can never be fully satisfied. The more we have, the more we want. This leads to discontentment. A spirit of discontentment is most unhealthy, emotionally, mentally and spiritually. We have allowed the material world to dominate us, rather than us ruling over it, as God intended.

The apostle Paul displays a marvelous spirit of detachment when he says, *I have learned to be content* (Phil. 4:12). This kind of spirit is a bit scarce today. Do not allow yourself to come under the tyranny of "things." The Bible says, *Seek first His kingdom and*

*His righteousness, and all these **things** will be given to you as well* (Matt. 6:33). *"Watch out! Be on your guard against all kinds of greed; a man's life does not consist in the abundance of his possessions"* (Luke 12:15).

> *Turn your eyes upon Jesus,*
> *Look full in His wonderful face,*
> *And the things of earth will grow strangely dim*
> *In the light of His glory and grace.*

— Helen H. Lemmel

Read: Matthew 6:25-34

November 11   ARMISTICE!

There was once a small city with only a few people in it. And a powerful king came against it, surrounded it and built huge siegeworks against it. Now there lived in that city a man poor but wise, and he saved the city by his wisdom. But nobody remembered that poor man (Eccl. 9:14-15).

Here is a city, hemmed in by a powerful enemy, with starvation and death staring it in the face. A council is called and no answer is found. Then a poor man unfolds a plan to deliver the city. But nobody remembered that poor man. How soon we forget those who did us a great service. Little wonder we quote the well-known poem, "Lest We Forget."

Remembrance Day is a Canadian holiday that honors the memory of the men and women who died in World War I, World War II and the Korean War. Do you recall the dates? World War I was June 28, 1914 to November 11, 1918. World War II was September 1, 1939 to September 2, 1945. The Korean War was June 25, 1950 to July 27, 1953.

The red poppy of Flander's Field serves as the symbol of Remembrance Day. Each year a ceremony is held by veterans who place wreaths at a cenotaph on this national holiday. The day commemorates the courage and patriotism of all the men and women who served our country. Do we fail to see the courage and devotion and service they rendered to their country?

Three words sum up this day in my mind:

1. Commemoration. We remember with proud thanksgiving and deep affection the men and women who, by their wisdom, saved our cities of yesterday.

2. Emulation. This means to copy or to imitate. We too must exercise the faith and the courage of these men and women.

3. Dedication. We re-affirm our allegiance to the goal of peace. We dedicate ourselves against all brutality, cruelty, tyranny and evil, and we dedicate ourselves to God, who gives us the right life.

Read: Romans 12:9-21

November 12   ADAPTABILITY!

Do you have a high level of adaptability? Or are you the kind of person who thinks he is always right? The kind of person for whom there are only two sides to any issue — the one you hold and the wrong one. In our personal relationships with others, we need to be flexible. When two people meet, there are bound to be differences. No two people will ever think exactly alike on every issue, and that's normal. Each person has the right to his or her own opinions. The person who has nothing to feel threatened about will not go around with a chip on his shoulder trying to defend his viewpoint. He is confident that his views will stand on their own merit.

Some people feel that there is just one side to a question, and they prefer not to hear the other side. We tend to classify people as either "with us" or "outsiders." In such a view, the "I — We" relationship has weakened. There is too much of the "I" and too little of the "we." We need a balanced viewpoint.

We need people who think for themselves, people of conviction. We need standards by which we can live, but we must be willing to give and take. In other words, we need to be a bit more adaptable.

Many differences can be reconciled if we are adaptable. Paul's view of life was put into these words, *I have become all things to all men* (1 Cor. 9:22). His goal was to win men to Jesus Christ. Paul had learned to be at home in all levels of society. Effective Christian living requires adaptability. We must learn to understand others and practice that understanding. This may well involve humility and unselfishness. Adaptability is a Christian virtue. Let's practice it!

Remember, Jesus Christ came not to please Himself; He came for others (Rom. 15:3a). The song goes,

> *Others, Lord, yes others. Let this my motto be,*
> *Help me to live for others, that I might live like Thee.*

Read: Philippians 4:10-13

302

November 13   LIVING WITH YOURSELF

There are some people who are hard to get along with. They have certain traits that make it unpleasant for us to be with them. So, we usually spend very little time with them. But the fact remains that such people have to live with themselves twenty-four hours a day.

A person with a hot temper does not make a pleasant companion. A person with a jealous disposition does not make a good friend. Have you ever thought how hard it must be for such a person to live with him or herself? Do I need to examine my own life? What kind of person am I?

I suppose all of us have tried some kind of personality test at one point in our lives. It could be a good beginning. These tests may tell us a good deal about ourselves if we reflect on them.

What kind of a person am I? Ask yourself, "Am I the kind of person I would like to live with for the rest of my life?" Are you capable of this kind of reflection? It is good for us to meet ourselves as we really are. This could be the first step in character and personality growth. This is essential.

There is another dimension which goes even deeper. What about my spiritual life? Would I welcome the X-ray of God? Am I willing to place myself in the presence of God and pray? *Search me, O God, and know my heart; test me and know my anxious thoughts* (Ps. 139:23). There is no better way to learn about yourself than to be alone with God. With Him there is no room for sham or hypocrisy. An all-seeing eye is present. With this attitude, we begin to know ourselves in depth.

All of this leads to one conclusion: Living with ourselves requires that we live as in the presence of God. In His presence we see our sins and our failures, but we also see the joy of His forgiving love. This is found in the Person of Jesus Christ. Man in Christ is man at his best!

Read: Psalm 139

November 14   SMILE!

Our facial expressions are the most important things we wear. They surely affect those who are looking at and watching us. *A happy heart makes the face cheerful, but heartache crushes the spirit* (Prov. 15:13). *A cheerful look brings joy to the heart, and good news gives health to the bones* (Prov. 15:30). *A cheerful heart is good medicine, but a crushed spirit dries up the bones* (Prov. 17:22).

I have always enjoyed those verses. I believe we can detect an artificial smile easily. Our smile should spring from our inner resources, from the heart. *Rejoice in the Lord always. I will say it again: Rejoice!* This is Paul's injunction. Let him continue: *Let your gentleness be evident to all. The Lord is near. Do not be anxious about anything, but in everything, by prayer and petition, with thanksgiving, present your requests to God. And the peace of God, which transcends all understanding, will guard your hearts and your minds in Christ Jesus* (Phil. 4:5-7). That is good advice. Don't worry, pray about everything and don't forget to thank Him. You will experience God's peace, which is far more wonderful than the human mind can understand. His peace will keep your thoughts and your hearts quiet and at rest as you trust in Christ Jesus.

Adverse circumstances, frustrating experiences, sorrow and disappointment cannot alter the heart that is at peace and rest in God. *Thou dost keep him in perfect peace, whose mind is stayed on Thee, because he trusts in Thee* (Isa. 26:3, RSV).

Back to the above verses. A smile can add a great deal to one's face value. What is a smile? A smile is a window in the happy heart to show that your heart is at home. A smile is a curve that sets things straight. Did you know that it takes seventy-two muscles to frown and only fourteen to smile? Smiles are wrinkles that shouldn't be removed. Smiles give birth to smiles. If someone doesn't have a smile today, give them one of yours.

> *The world is like a mirror, reflecting what you do:*
> *And if your face is smiling, it smiles right back at you.*

Keep smiling! It's worth a million dollars and doesn't cost a cent.

Read: Hebrews 8:10; John 15:11

November 15   LOOKING UP!

The Christian faith is a joyous and happy faith. You may smile at the following illustration because it indicates the exact opposite of what I want to say. William Feather, a well-known writer, tells the story about a young man who found a five-dollar bill on the street. From that time on, he never lifted his eyes when walking. In the course of the years, he accumulated 29,516 buttons, 54,172 pins, 12 cents, a bent back and a miserable disposition. He lost the glory of the sunlight, the sheen of the stars, the smile of friends, tree blossoms in the spring, the blue sky and the entire joy of living. How foolish you say, but look how often we keep our eyes on human temporal scenes without "looking up" in worship.

We live in a busy world where we're always in a hurry. What do you think is the cure for hurry? My answer (based on the story of Zacchaeus) is more hurry. Hurry away from the wrong goals in life. Jesus knew that Zacchaeus had spent much of his life pursuing earthly gain. Jesus slowed him down by inviting him to hurry. *Jesus... said to him, "Zacchaeus, make haste and come down; for I must stay at your house today." So he made haste and came down, and received Him joyfully* (Luke 19:5-6, RSV). He finally slowed down.

In his own way, he was asking ultimate questions. What is the meaning of life? Who am I? Where did I come from? Where am I going in such a hurry? Here is a simple lesson in hurry: Hurry away from the pursuit of possessions. There is another dimension in life which is very real.

Start climbing! Zacchaeus had a desire to see Jesus. When you meet Jesus, you will experience a dimension of height that will make you a whole person. A little man suddenly grew tall!

All men are apt to increase in stature when they respond to Jesus Christ. Look up! Hurry up in the right direction.

Read: Luke 19:1-10

November 16   FRUSTRATION AND SELF-CONTROL

An automobile out of control is a dangerous bit of equipment on our highways. A fire burning out of control leads to great destruction of property. Even more tragic and dangerous is the life of a man out of control. Some tragic pages of history have been written about people who had not learned to control themselves. Alexander the Great lost his temper and killed one of his best generals and most trusted friend. Peter the Great confessed, "I have conquered an empire, but I have not been able to control myself." Lack of self-control cost Moses the right to enter the promised land. The examples are multiplied.

Today there are tragedies in many homes, communities, minds and bodies due to the lack of self-control and the absence of true restraint.

Life is full of frustrating experiences. All of us have them at times — minor or major. It may be what people say about us. It may be driving in heavy traffic. It could be long periods of illness. Disappointments come in our business or work.

We may respond to these frustrations with repression. We may press them into the background of our subconscious mind. Such repressions are not healthy. The sore remains and at a convenient time it will boil over. Repression is the failure to face up to the reality of our inner feelings. This does not lead to proper self-control.

There is a better way! Like going up a steep stairway, the climb is not easy, but there is real satisfaction when you reach the top. The discipline of the soul is never easy, but it is always worthwhile.

First of all, admit that these frustrations exist. We are frustrated (hostile, angry, resentful)! We must be aware of the thing we are trying to conquer. Secondly, ask yourself, "Why do I feel this way?" Learn to be honest with yourself! Thirdly, exercise your will to overcome the attitude you have developed. The conquest of the self-life is not easy, but it is important.

How often I have said, "I need Another to help me to live my Christian life." I cannot do it on my own. I have to look to Jesus Christ, my Lord and Saviour for His direction. I ask myself some simple questions: What would Jesus do? How would Jesus react in the circumstances that I am in at this time? *Christ...* [left us] *an example, that* [we] *should follow in His steps* (1 Peter 2:21). He is with us today to help us surrender our selves to Him.

Read: James 1:1-12

November 17   DEEP CALLS TO DEEP

Deep calls to deep in the roar of your waterfalls; all your waves and breakers have swept over me (Ps. 42:7). This is a verse that caught my attention one morning.

Deep calls to deep. There are wonderful harmonies in nature. Science has discovered so much for us. Voices call to one another across vast spaces. The deep of the ocean calls to the deep of the azure sky. Sound is all around us!

Tune in to the frequency of heaven for a few moments! The deep of divine redemption calls to the deep of human need. God is always first! He sees the longing, the yearning of the heart for Himself. Do you know why that is? Because He has set eternity in our hearts. *He has made everything beautiful in its time. He has also set eternity in the hearts of men; yet they cannot fathom what God has done from beginning to end* (Eccl. 3:11). Man has a bent toward God! To be made for eternity yet forced to dwell in time is for mankind a huge tragedy. Everything within us cries for life and permanence, but everything around us reminds us of mortality and change.

Listen! The depth of HIS heart appeals to the depth of man's heart. "Thou hast made us for Thyself and the heart is restless until it rests in God." Would that we might answer back!

Often we go through life miserable, poor and blind when all the time we could be rich. The depth of Christ's wealth can be ours. In Jesus Christ there is a resource that is measureless. His love knows no limit, His grace knows no measure. We need to tap into that by faith! Take the pitcher of faith — the well is deep. *With joy you will draw water from the wells of salvation* (Isa. 12:3).

God's eternity and man's mortality join to persuade us that faith in Jesus Christ is not optional. Make HIM the object of your faith today. The deep in us calls to an unchanging relationship of love and joy that we have in Jesus Christ.

Read: Psalm 42

November 18   PARADOXES

A paradox is an apparent contradiction which in reality may conceal a profound and great truth. There are a number of them in the Bible which the Lord has designed for the believer. Only the Holy Spirit can enlighten us to enjoy these hidden truths. Notice a few:

1. We see unseen things (2 Cor. 4:18). *So we fix our eyes not on what is seen, but on what is unseen. For what is seen is temporary, but what is unseen is eternal.*

2. We conquer by yielding (Rom. 6:18). *You have been set free from sin and have become slaves to righteousness.*

3. We find rest under a yoke (Matt. 11:28-29). *"Come to Me, all you who are weary and burdened, and I will give you rest. Take My yoke upon you and learn from Me, for I am gentle and humble in heart, and you will find rest for your souls."*

4. We are made great by becoming little (Luke 9:48). *Then He said to them, "Whoever welcomes this little child in My name welcomes Me; and whoever welcomes Me welcomes the one who sent Me. For he who is least among you all — he is the greatest."*

5. We are exalted by being humble (Matt. 23:12). *"For whoever exalts himself will be humbled, and whoever humbles himself will be exalted."*

6. We become wise by being made fools for Christ's sake (1 Cor. 1:20). *Where is the wise man? Where is the scholar? Where is the philosopher of this age? Has not God made foolish the wisdom of the world?*

7. We are made free by becoming His bond servant (Rom. 8:2). *Through Christ Jesus the law of the Spirit of life set me free from the law of sin and death.* (See also Rom. 6:17-29).

8. We possess all things by having nothing (2 Cor 6:10). *Sorrowful, yet always rejoicing; poor, yet making many rich; having nothing, and yet possessing everything.*

9. We wax strong by being weak (2 Cor. 12:10). *That is why, for Christ's sake, I delight in weaknesses, in insults, in hardships, in persecutions, in difficulties. For when I am weak, then I am strong.*

10. We live by dying (John 12:24-25). *"I tell you the truth, unless a grain of wheat falls to the ground and dies, it remains only a single seed. But if it dies, it produces many seeds. The man who loves his life will lose it, while the man who hates his life in this world will keep it for eternal life."*

(Gleaned from Henry G. Bosch, *Our Daily Bread*, © 1973 by Radio Bible Class, Grand Rapids, Michigan. Used by permiossion).

Read: Isaiah 55:8

November 19   "LEAVE THE MIRACLE TO HIM" (I)

A radio broadcast based on the following poem had to be included in this book. The text is, *His mother said to the servants, "Do whatever He tells you"* (John 2:5).

> 1. "Whatsoe'er He bids you — do it!"
>   Though you may not understand;
>   Yield to Him complete obedience,
>   Then you'll see His mighty Hand
>   "Fill the waterpots with water,"
>   Fill them to the very brim;
>   He will honor all your trusting —
>   Leave the Miracle to Him!

Play the song: Trust and Obey.

2. Bind your Isaac to the altar,
    Bind him there with many a cord;
    Oh, my brother, do not falter,
    Can't you fully trust your Lord?
    He it is who watches o'er you,
    Though your faith may oft be dim;
    He will bring new life to Isaac —
    Leave the Miracle to Him!

Play the song: Is Your All On The Altar?

3. See them march around the city,
    Scarce a sound from day to day;
    Scoffers from the walls deride them —
    "Jericho can stand such play!"
    But the Lord's time cometh swiftly,
    Then they shout out with a vim;
    Look, the walls are tottering, falling —
    Leave the Miracle to Him!

Play the song: Dare To Be A Joshua.

Read: John 2:1-11 (To be continued tomorrow)

November 20   "LEAVE THE MIRACLE TO HIM" (II)

4. Face to face with hosts of Midian,
    Gideon's men are sifted out;
    Forth they go, these chosen heroes,
    With no sword, the foe to rout.
    Do you wonder if the vict'ry
    Can be gained by band so slim?
    See! Jehovah's sword is gleaming —
    Leave the Miracle to Him!

Play the song: Faith is the Victory.

5. Watch that scene on plains of Dura;
    See the Hebrew martyr band
    Firmly standing for Jehovah,
    Trusting in His hidden Hand.
    He is mighty to deliver
    From the power of death so grim;
    Fiery furnace cannot harm them —
    Leave the Miracle to Him!

Play the song: Dare To Be A Daniel.

6. Bring to Christ your loaves and fishes,
Though they be both few and small;
He will use the weakest vessels —
Give to Him your little all.
Do you ask how many thousands
Can be fed with food so slim?
Listen to the Master's blessing —
Leave the Miracle to Him!

Play the song: All For Jesus.

7. Oh, ye Christians, learn the lesson!
Are you struggling all the way?
Cease your trying, change to trusting,
Then you'll triumph every day!
"Whatsoe'er He bids you — do it!"
Fill the waterpots to brim;
But, remember, 'tis His battle —
Leave the Miracle to Him!

Play the song: True-Hearted,
Whole-Hearted.

8. Christian worker, looking forward
To the ripened harvest field,
Does the task seem great before you?
Think how rich will be the yield!
Bravely enter with your Master,
Though the prospect may seem dim;
Teach the Word with holy fervor —
Leave the Miracle to Him!

Play the song: Throw Out The Lifeline.

November 21   WE PREACH CHRIST CRUCIFIED

The apostle Paul said, *But we preach Christ crucified* (1 Cor. 1:23). *For we do not preach ourselves, but Jesus Christ as Lord, and ourselves as your servants for Jesus' sake* (2 Cor. 4:5). Jesus said, *"These are the Scriptures that testify about Me"* (John 5:39). *"When I am lifted up from the earth,* [I] *will draw all men to Myself"* (John 12:32).

1. Christ is our Saviour — 2 Timothy 1:8-10.
The exhortation is to BELIEVE HIM! (Rom. 10:16-17; John 6:28-29).

2. Christ is our Example — John 13:15.
The exhortation is to FOLLOW HIM! (1 Peter 2:21).
3. Christ is our Way — John 14:6.
The exhortation is to WALK IN HIM! (Micah 6:8; 1 John 2:6).
4. Christ is our Priest — Hebrews 7:24-26; Romans 8:34.
The exhortation is to CONFESS TO HIM! (1 John 1:9).
5. Christ is our Rock — 1 Corinthians 10:4.
The exhortation is to BUILD ON HIM! (1 Cor. 3:11-12; Matt. 7:24-27).
6. Christ is our Light — John 8:12.
The exhortation is to REFLECT HIM! (Matt. 5:14-16; Ps. 40:10).
7. Christ is our King — Revelation 19:16.
The exhortation is to WAIT FOR HIM! (Titus 2:13; Micah 7:7).

Until I come, devote yourself to the public reading of Scripture, to preaching [exhortation] *and to teaching* (1 Tim. 4:13). *But encourage* [exhort] *one another daily, as long as it is called Today, so that none of you may be hardened by sin's deceitfulness* (Heb. 3:13).

Are you looking forward to HIS coming? Are you ready?

A Christless cross no refuge were for me;
A crossless Christ my Saviour could not be.
But O, Christ crucified, I rest in Thee!

Read all the above Scriptures!

November 22   CHRISTIAN DILIGENCE

Diligence is a constant and earnest effort to accomplish what is undertaken. It is to be attentive and persistent in doing anything. Diligence is required in the Christian life!

1. *Wherefore the rather, brethren, give diligence to make your calling and election sure: for if ye do these things, ye shall never fall* (2 Peter 1:10, KJV). We are to make progress. Through diligence you will have more assurance.

2. *We want each of you to show the same diligence to the very end, in order to make your hope sure. We do not want you to become lazy* [slothful]*, but to imitate those who through faith and patience inherit what has been promised* (Heb. 6:11-12). Diligence is opposed to slothfulness and sluggishness. We are to show sincerity throughout life. We are not to grow disinterested.

3. *If it is encouraging, let him encourage; if it is contributing to the needs of others, let him give generously; if it is leadership, let*

311

him govern diligently; if it is showing mercy, let him do it cheerfully (Rom. 12:8). In the church, we are to exercise our gifts. Believers have a ministry to one another. We are to lead with diligence.

4. *Let us labour* [diligently] *therefore to enter into that rest, lest any man fall after the same example of unbelief* (Heb. 4:11, KJV). We do struggle with unbelief from time to time. But there is the rest of faith, the rest from "myself."

5. *Do your best to present yourself to God as one approved, a workman who does not need to be ashamed and who correctly handles the word of truth* (2 Tim. 2:15). Be diligent in seeking the approval of God. This is for all Christian workers. Paul's great ambition was to please God (Eph. 5:10).

6. *And we have sent with them our brother, whom we have often tested and found diligent in many things, but now even more diligent, because of his great confidence in you* (2 Cor. 8:22, KJV). Titus was found diligent in many things. "He shares my work," Paul says, "and I'm sending him." The diligent will be used in the service of God and the Church. The result of diligent service is more opportunities for service.

7. *Therefore, beloved, since you look for these things, be diligent to be found by Him in peace, spotless and blameless* (2 Peter 3:14, KJV). This has to do with His coming! To be found spotless and in peace. Keep your eyes, speech and feet from all scenes of defiling influence. We should not be ashamed before Him when He comes (1 John 2:28).

Read all the references!
Read: Colossians 3:12-17 (Some good advice!)

November 23   OUT-OF-SEASON FRUIT

Out-of-season fruit is a rare commodity (ie. strawberries in winter). Some fruit is produced in the most unlikely places and at the most unexpected times. Today we want to see three seemingly out-of-season fruits of the Spirit in the words and actions of Jesus.

1. *"Peace I leave with you; My peace I give you. I do not give to you as the world gives. Do not let your hearts be troubled and do not be afraid"* (John 14:27). It seems inconsistent for Jesus to be speaking about peace when men were planning to kill Him. Treachery of the worst type was about to happen. Yet anxiety was banished from His mind and hatred did not exist in His heart. He

was unruffled by malice. He was restful in His walk with God. Fruit produced in pre-Calvary conditions!

2. *"As the Father has loved Me, so have I loved you. Now remain in My love"* (John 15:9). Throughout His life and ministry, Jesus had opposition. The Pharisees hated Him, the disciples were going to forsake Him, Judas Iscariot was about to sell Him and the crowds would soon cry, "Crucify Him!" Could any person produce the fruit of love in such biting conditions? Could love overcome hatred? This love is real! Love produced in the climate of the cross!

3. *"I have told you this so that My joy may be in you and that your joy may be complete"* (John 15:11). Calvary's horizon had already appeared. It was just around the corner. The spikes were already forged in a blacksmith's shop. The wood was already cut in a lumber yard. The hill called Calvary would soon be stained by blood. It seemed like everything had gone wrong! Christ knew His hour would come. But that was not the end! His death would lead to life! How could He be talking about joy? He knew that the cross was not the end, but only the means to the end. His joy defied the terrors of the crucifixion! (Heb. 12:2).

Fruit produced in the cold of Calvary! This fruit is rare and costly! When the conditions of winter come into your life, will your life produce this kind of fruit? Peace that passes all understanding (Phil. 4:7), love that is everlasting, joy that runs deep!

Love is the soil in which we must grow and the foundation on which we must build.

Read: John 15:1-17

November 24   DISCOURAGEMENT IN THE N.T.

Discouragement is the master wedge of our Enemy. A surprising number of discouraged people appear in the gospel stories.

1. *John the Baptist* (Matt. 11:2-6). John is in prison, puzzled and despondent. He wonders, "Can this be the Christ?" He sends two of his disciples to find out.

2. *A sick woman pushing her way through a crowd* (Mark 5:25-34). She is desperate! She longs for her health after so many failures. She has been sick and searching for cures for twelve years and her money is all gone.

3. *The man by the pool of Bethesda* (John 5:1-9). He has been

there for thirty-eight years and he can't get in. He is dependent on others, but no one helps him.

4. *Peter* (John 21:3-8). After a night of fruitless fishing, he says, "What's the use." He caught nothing all night! The "fisherman's luck" was not with him.

5. *The disciples* (John 6:66-69). They became gloomy as they saw the crowds dwindling. The discourse on the bread and the blood was too much, and many of Jesus' followers were leaving.

6. *Mary* (John 11:32). Sitting sad and hopeless in her house because of her brother's death. She comes to Jesus with a reproachful greeting, "Why did you not get here earlier?"

7. *Jairus* (Luke 8:41-56). His only daughter is dying. As he goes to Jesus, the news comes that his daughter is dead. It is too late.

8. *The couple* (Luke 24:17). The Emmaus travellers are most disheartened at Jesus' death. "We thought He would redeem Israel but He's been dead for three days."

Not everyone has earned the right to be discouraged. But these had! John had preached so courageously. The sick woman had spent everything seeking a cure. The man by the pool had waited thirty-eight years. Peter had been fishing all night. The disciples had left so much behind. Mary had waited so bravely with her sister. Jarius had pleaded so hard. The Emmaus disciples had been so hopeful. Yet each is despondent, doubting and discouraged. All their sincere efforts seemed to go unrewarded.

Read all the above references. (We will continue tomorrow.)

November 25   DISCOURAGEMENT — ANSWERED

How did Jesus deal with discouragement? You will notice that His methods vary.

1. To John the Baptist, He sent a report: "Tell John what is happening. The Scriptures are being fulfilled! The gospel is being preached."

2. To the sick woman, He released His powerful energy to heal her. Jesus sensed that some power had gone out from Him.

3. To the paralyzed man at the pool, He gave the command to take up his bed and walk. His commandments are His enabling!

4. To Peter, He said to try again: "Let down your net on the other side of the boat." Here is a fisherman believing a carpenter.

5. To the disciples who were disheartened, He gave assurance: "I have chosen you." The teachings of Jesus and the cost of following Him were being gradually understood.

6. To Mary, He gave comfort: "Only believe and you will see the glory of God." Then the stone was rolled away and Lazarus came forth — alive again!

7. To Jairus, He gave His word: "Do not be afraid, only believe, your daughter will live!" What comfort!

8. To the Emmaus travelers, He gave a Bible exposition on the prophecies of Messiah; He opened up the Scriptures to them.

It is wonderful what a little reasonable explanation or a little assurance will do to dispel despondency. Let me add this about discouragement: Discouragement hides us from the face of God; discouragement disarms us when there are battles to be fought; discouragement burdens us with complaints against our fellow-workers; discouragement plunges us into moody idleness when there is work waiting to be done; discouragement is infectious; discouragement is dangerous.

We need to encourage each other!

Read: Joshua 1
How many times do you read, "Be strong and courageous"?

November 26   DISCOURAGEMENT IN THE O.T.

Discouragement is a miserable mood! Today we step into some of the Old Testament situations.

1. The impatient discouragement of Israel as a nation. They had travelled the long journey with much murmuring and complaining. As a result, thirty-eight more years were added to their wilderness wandering (Deut. 2:14).

2. The faithless discouragement of the ten spies almost cost Israel its opportunity to enter the Promised Land. "We cannot do it — they are giants and we are like grasshoppers" (Num. 13, 14).

3. The frightened discouragement of Elijah made him flee from Jezebel to idle in Horeb. There he wished to die (1Kings 19:1-18).

4. The self-pitying discouragement of Gideon almost blinded him to the personal challenge of his time (Judges 6:13).

In Proverbs 13:12 we read, *Hope deferred makes the heart sick, but a longing fulfilled is a tree of life.*

For Israel, their wanderings were a time of testing and teaching (Deut. 8:2). Think of the disciplines of God. God can change hearts and control events.

In response to the faithless spies, Joshua and Caleb testified certainty that they would succeed. And they did. We need people who will encourage and say, "We can do it!" (Num. 13:30).

To Elijah, there came a word of rebuke for thinking he was alone. Seven thousand people had not bowed to Baal (1 Kings 19:14-18).

To Gideon came the promised word, "I will be with you, I have sent you, go fight Midian." Three hundred men with pitchers, torches and trumpets put the enemy to flight (Judg. 6:14).

Listen! Discouragement is so much an emotional indulgence that a common-sense assessment of a situation is almost impossible. But, when analyzed and explained, it quickly regains proportion.

We must remember that FAITH has already outlived fierce assaults. We must not let discouragement disturb or distort our thinking and our judgement. We must not leave God out! God can! God remains! Be of good courage!

Read: Deuteronomy 1:38 "Encourage him [her]."

November 27   COURAGE

Do you have a healthy attitude towards life? Are you in a good mood today? Mind and feeling have a great influence in our lives. We need healthy emotions, thoughts and values! The human personality is a unity. Body, soul and spirit are elements of the same person. These work together in man. Sometimes though, we have the Dr. Jekyll and Mr. Hyde syndrome.

In Abraham, we have a brave pioneer, the father of faith, but we also have a "dark streak" of timidity and evasiveness. Abraham becomes a mirror of us all; we alternate between cowardice and courage. We need to be unified in our personalities so we can speak with the voice of courage.

The first step in the direction of courage is to believe God! *Abraham believed God* (Gen. 15:6). Abraham went forth! (Gen.12:1-9) We see faith responding! Faith involves separation, but it inherits divine promises. Faith makes a man whole; it moves him towards unity and makes him the man he ought to be.

The second step in the pilgrimage toward courage is to learn from failure. *Abraham went down to Egypt* (Gen. 12:10-20). Faith was receding. Circumstances now led to cowardice, which is lack of courage. He took things into his own hands. God's grace, thankfully, was still at work in man's weakness. God moved in to protect Sarah. Pharaoh was instrumental in checking Abraham and escorting him away. No failure need be final!

The third step is the practice of special courage. *Abraham went up from Egypt* (Gen. 13:1-4). Abraham went back to the place of the altar. He called on the name of the Lord and received courage to go back and start again. There was victory from the lesson of failure. It takes courage to learn from failure!

For many years there was a poster in my office with these words: "The men who try to do something and fail are infinitely better than those who try to do nothing and succeed."

Have you found yourself with many things knocking at your door? Things like fear, anxiety, worry, defeatism, the uncertain future and discouragement to name a few? Would you begin again to listen to God in and through His Word? (Josh. 1:6,7,9,18b).

Read: Genesis 12, 13:1-4

November 28   COURAGE (Cont'd)

Today we reflect on what you read yesterday. We saw Abraham responding in faith — he went forth. We saw his faith receding — he went down to Egypt. And then we saw him returning — he went up from Egypt to build an altar. So we have faith responding, receding and returning.

The word for us today is, *"Be strong and courageous. Do not be terrified; do not be discouraged"* (Josh. 1:9).

"Be strong!" The Hebrew word is *chazag*. It means to be hard. Be hard in the attack on evil. Be hard in the expectation of faith. We need to go back to the requirements of a living faith. Get back on track, leaving the world's way of doing things behind.

"Be courageous!" The Hebrew word is *amats*. It means to be sharp, to learn to master difficult situations — like Joshua at the Jordan, David before Goliath or Daniel in the den. Be courageous in your present crisis, be it physical, emotional, social or spiritual. Courage comes from God in retail quantities, not wholesale.

"Do not be terrified!" The Hebrew word for this is *chathath*. The idea here is being broken or cast down. The test of a man is his resistance to dismay. Dismay means to depress courage, to dishearten. God brings his reassurance alongside: "I will be with you, I will not forsake you, I will not fail." Courage is of the Lord!

It has been said that what has been attributed as ferocity to the tiger is due to its incredible audacity and courage — it simply sees no danger, knows no fear, brooks no delay, uses no artifice, and abandons no object of attack. Are these the elements of Christian courage? If we were filled with a deep sense of God's presence and power and aware of our privileges and responsibilities, would this not blind us to many things that disturb and terrify, and inspire us to do many things that we dread?

Read: Deuteronomy 31:1-8. Be strong and courageous.

November 29   WEARY AND WAVERING

DON'T QUIT

When things go wrong, as they sometimes will,
When the road you're trudging seems all uphill,
When funds are low and the debts are high,
And you want to smile, but you have to sigh,
When care is pressing you down a bit,
Rest, if you must — but don't YOU quit.

> *Life is queer with its twists and turns,*
> *As everyone of us sometimes learns,*
> *And many a failure turns about*
> *When he might have won had he stuck it out;*
> *Don't give up, though the pace seems slow —*
> *You may succeed with another blow.*

Often the goal is nearer than
It seems to a faint and faltering man,
Often the struggler has given up
When he might have captured the victor's cup.
And he learned too late, when the night slipped down,
How close he was to the golden crown.

> *Success is failure turned inside out —*
> *The silver tint of the clouds of doubt —*
> *And you never can tell how close you are,*
> *It may be near when it seems afar;*
> *So stick to the fight when you're hardest hit —*
> *It's when things seem worst that you mustn't quit.*

— Edgar A. Guest

The word "discouragement" should never be found in the dictionary of faith!

I've taught a class for many years,
Borne many burdens — toiled through tears;
But folks don't notice me a bit,
I'm so discouraged — I'll just quit.

Sometime ago I joined the choir,
That many folks I might inspire;
But folks don't seem moved a bit.
And I won't stand it — I'll just quit.

I've led young people day and night,
And sacrificed to lead them right;
But folks won't help me out a bit,
And I'm so tired — I think I'll quit.

Christ's cause is hindered everywhere,
And folks are dying in despair;
The reason why? Just think a bit —
The Church is full of folks who quit.

— Author unknown.

Read: 1 Corinthians 9:24-27; 15:58

November 30   WHY DID HE COME?

1. He came to put away sin. *He appeared to put away sin by the sacrifice of Himself* (Heb. 9:26). *God made Him who had no sin to be sin for us, so that in Him we might become the righteousness of God* (2 Cor. 5:21). *He Himself bore our sins in His body on the tree, so that we might die to sins and live for righteousness* (1 Peter 2:24). We are clothed in the righteousness of Jesus Christ. John said one day, *"Behold, the Lamb of God, who takes away the sin of the world!"* (John 1:29, RSV).

2. He came to seek and to save. *For the Son of man is come to seek and to save that which was lost* (Luke 19:10). The story of Zacchaeus reminds us of a great discovery. Salvation! We have a seeking Saviour! In looking, He locates; in locating, He lifts, because He loves us (Luke 15).

3. He came to give His life a ransom. *"The Son of Man did not come to be served, but to serve, and to give his life as a ransom for many"* (Matt. 20:28). Man is captured by sin and Satan.

Jesus paid the price and set us free. He gave his life as a ransom! Jesus paid it all!

4. He came to destroy the devil's work. *The reason the Son of God appeared was to destroy the devil's work* (1 John 3:8). The devil comes to defeat, destroy and discourage. He is the Tempter, *the father of lies* (John 8:44). At Calvary, Satan was defeated!

5. He came to bring us back to God. *For Christ died for sins once for all, the righteous for the unrighteous, to bring you to God. He was put to death in the body but made alive by the Spirit* (1 Peter 3:18). He came to bring us back to God. *All we like sheep had gone astray* (Isa. 53:6). Peter talks about the Shepherd of our souls (1 Peter 2:25).

Salvation is in a Person! Salvation is in the finished work of Christ! We are invited to believe Him and to receive Him! Believing is a choice! It has nothing to do with feeling. I choose to believe in Jesus Christ, God's Son and my Saviour.

Notice what the Bible says about a Person and a Name. Would you look at Matthew 1:21, John 1:12, Acts 4:12 and Romans 10:9?

Read: Philippians 2:1-11

December 1   WHAT IS MAN? (Part 1)

Man is the least and the greatest of God's creatures; lower than the angels in creature position, but immensely higher in redemption privileges. Man lives one life on earth, consisting of a few years, and a second life in another sphere that will last forever. He has a body that allies him to the ground on which he walks, and a spirit that connects him to God who made him (Eccl. 12:7). Pascal said, "[Man is] a reed, but a reed that thinks; a worm, but a worm capable of measuring the distances of the stars and grasping the universe."

What is man that You are mindful of him, the son of man that You care for him? (Ps. 8:4). *"What is man that You make so much of him, that You give him so much attention"* (Job 7:17).

I'd like to look at two things:
1. The Insignificance of Man.
2. The Greatness of Man.

1. THE INSIGNIFICANCE OF MAN.

a. In origin, allied to dust. *For He knows how we are formed, He remembers that we are dust* (Ps. 103:14). *"...Those who live in houses of clay, whose foundations are in the dust, who are crushed more readily than a moth!"* (Job 4:19).

b. In character, defiled by sin. *Surely I was sinful at birth, sinful from the time my mother conceived me* (Ps. 51:5). *"But how can a mortal be righteous before God?"* (Job 9:2). We are all sinners.

c. In experience, weighted with misery. *"It is all the same; that is why I say, 'He destroys both the blameless and the wicked.' When a scourge brings sudden death, he mocks the despair of the innocent"* (Job 9:22-23). Suffering and death is the lot of all of us.

d. In duration, short-lived and evanescent. *"My days are swifter than a runner; they fly away without a glimpse of joy. They skim past like boats of papyrus, like eagles swooping down on their prey"* (Job 9:25-26). Life is brief! Like a weaver's shuttle! (Job 7:6-7). Like a vapour! (James 4:14). Like a handbreadth! (Ps. 39:5). Like a flower and grass! (Isa. 40:6-8).

e. In destiny, doomed to dissolution (extinction of life). *"If a man dies, will he live again?"* (Job 14:14). *"But man dies and is laid low; he breathes his last and is no more"* (Job 14:10). Death is all around us! There was no written revelation on the subject in Job's day. The insignificance of man!

Read: Psalm 8 (To be continued tomorrow.)

December 2   WHAT IS MAN? (Part 2)

To David, God appeared available as a Father, delighting to bless. To Job, God appeared as a stern Judge, examining men's actions. To us, God's visitation of grace and mercy should impart comfort and awaken praise. Today we look at:

2. THE GREATNESS OF MAN.

a. Created in the image of God. *The Lord God formed the man from the dust of the ground and breathed into his nostrils the breath of life, and the man became a living being* (Gen. 2:7). Man is a living soul, a person with a personality! Man is God's crown creation!

b. Preserved by Divine care. *"What is man that You make so much of him, that You give him so much attention?"* (Job 7:17). *The Lord has been mindful of us; He will bless us* (Ps. 115:12, RSV). *"...I am with you; do not be dismayed, for I am your God. I will strengthen you and help you; I will uphold you with My righteous right hand"* (Isa. 41:10). God cares! He knows all about us! (Ps. 139).

c. Redeemed by Divine Love. *"For God so loved the world, that He gave His one and only Son, that whoever believes in Him shall not perish, but have eternal life"* (John 3:16). *"I have loved you with an everlasting love; I have drawn you with loving-kindness"* (Jer. 31:3). It was love that sent the Saviour!

d. May be renewed by Divine grace. *As for you, you were dead in your transgressions and sins* (Eph. 2:1). *For it is by grace you have been saved, through faith — and this not from yourselves, it is the gift of God* (Eph. 2:8). Paul speaks of the renewing of your mind. *Be transformed by the renewing of your mind. Then you will be able to test and approve what God's will is — his good, pleasing and perfect will* (Rom. 12:2). Paul speaks of being renewed day by day (2 Cor. 4:16). Isaiah invites us to wait upon the Lord (Isa. 40:31).

e. May be immortalized by Divine life and crowned with Divine glory. *Listen, I tell you a mystery: We will not all sleep, but we will all be changed in a flash, in the twinkling of an eye, at the last trumpet. For the trumpet will sound, the dead will be raised imperishable, and we will be changed. For the perishable must clothe itself with the imperishable, and the mortal with immortality* (1 Cor. 15:51-53).

Since man is so insignificant — be humble!
Since man is so great — trust God!

Read: Micah 6:8

December 3   A NEW CREATION

All of us enjoy new things! The marvel of the Christian faith is the "miracle-working" power of the gospel of Jesus Christ (Rom. 1:16). The highest level of this power is the regeneration of men, making them new creatures. Bad men become good, deceivers become honest, liars become truthful, the unlovely become lovely, despisers of God become lovers of God, drunkards become sober, the immoral become pure and the proud become humble.

1. The Condition of this new creation is found "in Christ." We have come to Christ for forgiveness. We have come to Him for shelter and salvation. We have come to Him for strength and supply. We have come to Him for sympathy and service. By grace, we are His! He has redeemed us!

2. The Nature of this new creation is "change." There is a new life! We are born of God (John 1:13). There is a new mind! (Rom. 12:3; Eph. 4:23). There is a new heart with a new focus! (Col. 3:1). There is a new spirit! (Rom. 8:16; Eph. 1:13). There is a new song! (Ps. 40:1-3).

3. The Results of this new creation are that "old things are passed away." The new has come! We have a new view of sin — sin is now seen as "missing the mark," we come up short of the glory of God (Rom. 3:23). There is a new view of self — where selfish attitudes once prevailed, others now come first; we live for Him! A new view of Christ and His love has come into our lives — Christ is a living reality! (1 Peter 1:8). A new influence is evident — there is a change of behaviour. New energy is put into the practice of faith — *we live and move and have our being* [in Him] (Acts 17:28).

Listen to this analogy: Longfellow could take a piece of cheap paper, write a poem on it and make it worth $6,000.00 — that's genius. A mechanic can take material worth $5.00 and make it worth $50.00 — that's skill. An artist can take a 50 cent piece of canvass, paint a picture on it and make it worth $1,000.00 — that's art. God can take a worthless life, put His Spirit in that life and make that life a blessing to humanity — that's salvation.

Therefore, if anyone is in Christ, he is a new creation; the old has gone, the new has come! (2 Cor. 5:17).

Read: 2 Corinthians 5

December 4　　CHRISTIANITY IS LIFE!

...God will credit righteousness [to] *us who believe in Him who raised Jesus our Lord from the dead. He was delivered over to death for our sins and was raised to life for our justification* (Rom. 4:24-25). That is the bridge into chapter five.

Therefore, since we are justified, acquitted, set free, declared righteous, and given a right standing before God through faith, let us grasp the fact that we have the peace of reconciliation to hold and to enjoy — peace with God through our Lord Jesus Christ.

We have peace! Peace is the peculiar benediction of Christianity. No other religion can promise you that. *You will keep in perfect peace him whose mind is steadfast, because he trusts in You* (Isa. 26:3). "With Christ in the vessel you can smile at the storm" are the words of a song. We have been brought into harmony with God. We have been reconciled; we who were enemies of God have now become friends with God.

We have access! Through Him, we, by faith, have access, entrance and, introduction into this grace — the state of God's favour in which we firmly and safely stand. *For there is one God and one mediator between God and men, the man Christ Jesus, who gave Himself as a ransom for all men — the testimony given in its proper time* (1 Tim. 2:5-6).

We have joy! Let us rejoice and exult in our hope of one day experiencing and enjoying the glory of God. Some day we will be in His presence! Moreover, let us also be full of joy "now"! Let us exult and triumph in our troubles and rejoice in our sufferings, knowing that pressure and affliction and hardship produce patient and unswerving endurance. Wesley's favourite word was "now." We have cleansing *now*, we have power *now*, we have victory *now*.

We have hope! Such hope never disappoints, deludes or shames us, for God's love has been poured out in our hearts through the Holy Spirit who has been given to us. Endurance develops maturity of character, approved faith and tried integrity. Character of this sort produces the habit of joyful and confident hope — the hope of heaven.

Your faith is precious to God! Read 1 Peter 1:3-7.

A believer is not exempt from the hardships, heartaches and hurts of life! Joseph, too, was tested, as steel is tested (Ps. 105:18).

Read: Romans 5:1-11

December 5 — GIFT GIVING

Christmas is a time for gift giving. We plan and think about gifts! We dream about the gifts we hope to receive. Our biggest problem is buying a gift for someone who has everything.

God did not have that problem. God is never indifferent to human need. God never forgot His people. *When the time had fully come, God sent His Son* (Gal. 4:4). The person of Jesus Christ is God's greatest gift. You see, Jesus is God's answer to human need.

That which is great attracts our attention, and the golden text of the Bible (John 3:16) speaks of God's greatest gift.

God	The Greatest Lover
So loved	The Greatest Degree
The world	The Greatest Company
That He gave	The Greatest Act
His one and only Son	The Greatest Gift
That whoever	The Greatest Opportunity
Believes	The Greatest Simplicity
In Him	The Greatest Attraction
Shall not perish	The Greatest Promise
But	The Greatest Difference
Have	The Greatest Certainty
Eternal life	The Greatest Possession

Christ is Christmas or Christmas is Christ! *"For to you is born this day... a Saviour, who is Christ the Lord"* (Luke 2:11, RSV).

To you	That is personal
This day	That is present
A Saviour	That is precious

Read: 1 Peter 1:8 (My favorite verse in the Bible!)

December 6 — CHRISTMAS ACROSTIC

If you are like me, it's difficult to express adequately what we feel in our hearts about Christmas. I would like to spell out some of the things we could be mindful of when we think about Christmas. Here you have an acrostic devotional Bible study:

C — Comfort. *The Father of our Lord Jesus Christ is the God of all comfort* (2 Cor. 1:3-5).

H — Holiness. *Christ was the sinless Son of God* (1 Peter 2:22).

R — Redemption. *In Christ we have redemption even the forgiveness of sin* (Eph. 1:7).

I — Inheritance. *We have an inheritance reserved in heaven* (1 Peter 1:4).

S — Salvation. *Christ is our salvation, there is no other* (Acts 4:12).

T — Truth. Jesus is *"the way, the truth and the life"* (John 14:6).

M— Mercy. God forgives me when I admit my sinfulness (Ps. 51).

A — Assurance. *These things* [are] *written... that you may know....* (1 John 5:13, RSV).

S — Satisfaction. *He satisfies the thirsty and fills the hungry with good things* (Ps. 107:9).

The hymn writer says,

> *All that I want is in Jesus, He satisfies,*
> *Joy He supplies;*
> *Life would be worthless without Him,*
> *All things in Jesus I find.*

At Christmas, God came to us in the person of His Son. If you have Jesus you have everything; without Him you have nothing!

Read: Matthew 1:18-25

December 7   THE NAMES OF GOD

What's in a name? Names connect us with people, places and things. They attract us or turn us away. The names of God are not without significance. They tell us something about Him. One of the happiest concepts of God was given to us by Jesus when He said, "Our Father." God is a Person. *God is love* (1 John 4:8). *God is light* (1 John 1:5). [God] *is holy* (1 Peter 1:15). *God is spirit* (John 4:24).

The names of God express different aspects of His being. What one name could be adequate to describe God's greatness? Let us walk through the Bible a bit and see how God reveals Himself through His names more and more as Scriptures unfold.

1. Elohim! The One who is mighty! The Lord who creates! (Gen. 1:1). He is known throughout the Bible as the Maker of heaven and earth. He remembers Abraham (Gen. 17:1). He comforts Israel (Isa. 40:1). He controls the operation of nature (Job 38-41). God is! There is no place He is not! (Ps. 139:7-18).

2. Jehovah-jireh! The One who redeems! The One who provides! (Gen. 22:14). Jehovah represents God in His special relationship with His chosen people. Our pulse begins to beat when we think of Abraham — his call, the promise, his son, Isaac and the test of his faith. Isaac, the heir, is redeemed by God's provision of a ram.

3. Jehovah-nissi! The Lord our Banner! The One who fights for us! (Exod. 17:15). The enemy comes to oppose Israel in her journey. Three men are praying on a hill with the staff in Moses' hands. The Lord gives victory! In the name of the Lord, they set up a banner. If God be for us, who can be against us?

4. Jehovah-Shalom! The Lord is our peace! The One who gives peace! (Judg. 6:24). We are all familiar with Gideon — Israel is in trouble, an army is selected and whittled down to 300 men and the weapons are pitchers, torches and trumpets. The point is this: Gideon is at peace and becomes instrumental in the deliverance of Israel from Midian.

5. Jehovah-Zidkenu! The Lord our Righteousness! The One who is justifying! (Jer. 23:6). The prophet promises a righteous Branch, a ruling King, salvation and safety for Israel.

6. Jehovah-Shammah! The Lord is There! The One who is present! (Ezek. 48:35). This was a message of hope for Israel, her restoration from captivity. The fullness of God's presence was the hope and end of all prophetic expectation. The final and eternal fulfillment will be in Revelation 21:3.

Read: Genesis 22:1-14

December 8   SEVEN LINKS OF FELLOWSHIP

Let's look at the Church *as* a fellowship and the Church *in* fellowship! There are several aspects or links of fellowship.

1. The first link: GATHERED TOGETHER (Matt. 18:20). Gathered together in His name. The presence of Christ drawing us together. Two can have fellowship! There can be friendship and companionship. We have His promised presence!

2. The second link: FRAMED TOGETHER (Eph. 2:21). Another way of saying fitted together. A house has a frame, and the frame needs a foundation. Christ is our Foundation! In the context here, we are fitted into a holy temple in the Lord. There is a common recovery, reconciliation and relationship.

3. The third link: BUILT TOGETHER (Eph. 2:22). God wants to live in this building. He does so through the Holy Spirit. The word was *"I will be their God and they shall be My people."*

The temple in 1 Kings 6:7 was put together in silence. The mightiest works of God are the fruits of silence. God does the placing!

4. The fourth link: JOINED TOGETHER (Eph. 4:15-16). Love seems to be the paramount thought here. We are to speak the truth in love. We need to edify, not tear down. Learn to live in the climate of love! Would 1 Corinthians 1:10 fit in here somewhere?

5. The fifth link: KNIT TOGETHER (Col. 2:2). Interwoven! In weaving, we speak of the warp and the woof. We need each other! We sing, "Blest be the tie that binds our hearts in Christian love." Is ours the fellowship of kindred minds?

6. The sixth link: STRIVING TOGETHER (Phil. 1:27). How we need the united front and the united spirit today! Working and walking side by side for the sake of the gospel. The term here may well be taken from the military. We are one! We stand shoulder to shoulder to make a solid front. Evangelism is a way of life!

7. The seventh link: CAUGHT UP TOGETHER (1 Thess. 4:17). Fellowship down here will prepare us for fellowship up there. Together forever! Christians never see each other for the last time! I heard a trio sing one day in the light of the rapture, "Going Special Delivery Wrapped Up In Love."

Let us make the chain strong!

Read: Ephesians 2:11-22

December 9   SEVEN FELLOWSHIPS!

The root of fellowship is "fellow," giving the idea of being a sharer, a partner, an associate and an equal. It includes the linking of interests, activities and feelings. It has in it the thought of friendship and communion. Here are seven fellowships:

1. Fellowship with the Father (1 John 1:1-4). Fellowship is that communion we have with the Father. Are we at home with God? Is God at home with us? Are you meeting Him in His Word? *Acquaint now thyself with Him, and be at peace: thereby good shall come unto thee* (Job 22:21, KJV). The peace of God comes from knowing Him. God desires and longs for our fellowship!

2. Fellowship with the Son (1 Cor. 1:9). God is faithful! God gave His Son with whom we are called into fellowship! To know Christ is to have this fellowship. Cultivate the friendship of the Lord!

3. Fellowship of the Spirit (Phil. 2:1). The Good News translation says, *You have fellowship with the Spirit.* In this context, the call to fellowship is the call to harmony and humility. The Holy Spirit will make Christ real to you, He will reproduce Christ's life in you and He will re-enact Christ's life and power in your life.

4. Fellowship with one another (1 John 1:7). Notice the condition "if": *If we walk in the Light!* This involves living and practicing the truth, knowing His Word, and admitting and confessing sin. Washers are made shiny by being rubbed against each other in a churning barrel of solution. Again, we need each other.

5. Fellowship in service (Col. 4:7). Fellowship in service calls for cooperation and unity. This is essential to success! Cooperation to "nerve up" for the conflict (1 Sam. 14:6-7). Cooperation to inspire men to improve their conditions (2 Kings 6:1-3). Cooperation to carry through great undertakings (Neh. 4:16-17). Cooperation to bring men to Christ (Mark 2:3).

6. Fellowship of suffering (Phil. 3:10). Suffering for Christ! Christianity is a doctrine of the cross! The purpose is found in 1 Peter 5:10: *To establish, strengthen and to settle you.* Would you read Acts 5:41, Romans 8:17, Hebrews 11:25 and James 5:10?

7. Fellowship in the gospel (Phil. 1:5). Partnership in the gospel is the thrust here — making a contribution for the sake of the gospel. It is just this that creates fellowship among believers. We have a common goal — the desire that others might come to know Jesus Christ.

Unity tends to give fellowship, love tends to bind this fellowship and work tends to extend this fellowship.

Read: 1 John 1

December 10   CHRISTIAN WORKERS!

You are in the work of the Lord! You are a worker! (1 Cor. 15:58).

Christian workers need to be stable. STABILITY! Steadfastness! We are to stand fast in the Lord (Eph. 6:13-14). Satan is on the move. Therefore, we are to resist him, standing firm in the faith (1 Peter 5:9). Christ set His face like a flint to go to Jerusalem (Luke 9:51). Paul was not moved until he had finished his course (Acts 20:24). The three in the fiery furnace would not bow, budge nor burn (Dan. 3).

Christian workers need to be dependable. DEPENDABILITY! How do you know a dependable person? They are honest, faithful, and upright; they are men and women of integrity; they carry out the work entrusted to them; they have foresight and see things that need to be done; they have concern and a sense of obligation. Paul would say, "I am ready" (Rom. 1:16). Am I dependable? Can the Lord, the Church, the pastor depend on you?

Christian workers need to be flexible. FLEXIBILITY! Can I adapt myself to any situation? This involves the knowledge of human nature and the discernment of conditions, differences of opinion and the limitations of a given circumstance. It may mean we have to go against our feelings in a situation. It may mean we need to commend and encourage someone else. In other words, "Take a real interest in ordinary people."

Christian workers need to be available! AVAILABILITY! Here is the attitude of, "Speak, Lord, your servant is listening. Whatever it is, wherever, I'm available." Promptly, without delay. Not putting it off to the last minute. Available with utmost strength, humble submission and fixed determination. It is amazing what God can do in and through and with a man wholly yielded to God. Are you available?

Christian workers are accountable. ACCOUNTABILITY! *So then, each of us will give an account of himself to God* (Rom. 14:12). Our purpose is to please Him! (2 Tim. 2:1-5; Eph. 5:10). We are living in a day of pleasure (2 Tim. 3:1-4). The point is this: *Do your best to present yourself to God as one approved, a workman who does not need to be ashamed and who correctly handles the word of truth* (2 Timothy 2:15). Live with the stamp of God's approval! The charge is in 2 Timothy 4:1-5.

Go with the five big words: STABILITY, DEPENDABILITY, ADAPTABILITY, AVAILABILITY and ACCOUNTABILITY.

Read: 2 Timothy 2:1-5

December 11   GRACE!

Grace is perhaps one of the greatest words in the Bible. We read of the "God of all grace," "the grace of our Lord Jesus" and "the gospel of the grace of God."

Grace includes two things: First of all, it means God's character in relation to man, indicating His favour and graciousness. He gives us what we do not deserve. Secondly, it implies that this gracious attitude is proven by a divine gift — the gift of His Son. We may speak of grace as expressing God's heart and hand. *The LORD is compassionate and gracious, slow to anger, abounding in love*

(Ps. 103:8). *But you, O Lord, are a compassionate and gracious God, slow to anger, abounding in love and faithfulness* (Ps. 86:15).

The grace of God is intended to be realized; it is essential for us to know it works.

First, there is Saving grace! Sin involves condemnation, separation and helplessness. Man cannot deliver himself through his own works, merit or strength. God alone can save, and salvation is by grace. *For it is by grace you have been saved, through faith — and this not from yourselves, it is the gift of God — not by works, so that no one can boast* (Eph. 2:8-9). God's grace is free and it is generous! It is ours through faith — all we have to do is reach out a hand to receive it from God. It's the act and attitude of dependence.

Secondly, there is Sanctifying grace! Grace is not only for the commencement of new life, it is for the present life. Grace is sufficient for the struggles, the spiritual warfare and the realization of all there is in this new life. Grace, first of all, consecrates the soul to God, and then it cleanses and controls our lives. We are set apart for God by the grace of God!

Thirdly, there is Sustaining grace! Grace works moment by moment in the believer's life. We learn how to face temptation. We stand in victory through Christ. Victory is realized by a conscious and decisive appeal to Him. We are in union with the Conqueror. *For it is God who works in you to will and to act according to His good purpose* (Phil. 2:13). Our Captain and Commander goes before. In view of the future, it is the same: *"My grace is sufficient for you, for My power is made perfect in weakness"* (2 Cor. 12:9).

Read: Ephesians 2:1-10

December 12   WONDERFUL COUNSELOR

Today we glibly say, "What's in a name?" We use them so superficially sometimes, merely to label one person in contrast to another. But our names really are meaningful — to us, our family and our friends.

The names of Jesus are very intriguing. From the well-known Christmas text, Isaiah 9:6, we have the name, "Wonderful Counselor." Let me summarize this briefly as two names:

He is *wonderful* in His grace, as well as His greatness;
He is *wonderful* in His mercy, as well as His majesty;
He is *wonderful* in His patience, as well as in His power;

As a *Counselor*, He is compassionate,
He is consistent,
He is confidential.

A counselor needs to be close and accessible. Christ is as close as the whisper of a prayer. He is always available, never away or busy. He is confidential — to Him you can take the most intimate matters of your heart. He is the specialist of the human heart. He is capable. He has all the resources of power and help. He will always guide our steps in the right way (Ps. 37:23). He communicates with the gentle stirring of the Holy Spirit and the inspired Word. You can trust Him!

Read: Isaiah 9:6,7; John 2:24-25; Psalm 37:23

December 13   CHRIST IS A GIFT

Thanks be to God for His indescribable gift (2 Cor. 9:15). Language fails to describe God's amazing gift! God so loved that HE GAVE. Ponder those words once more. What is our normal response to receiving a gift? Do we pay for it? Do we work for it? Do we beg for it? Do we wait for it? NO! We TAKE IT — eagerly and joyfully! If then, Jesus is God's gift to us, should we not simply and gratefully take it and receive Him? In receiving Him, we become saved. How sad that many, many people treat God's gift with an attitude that they would never display toward any other gift. Some are still trying to pay for it. Others don't believe it's for real. And so they don't take it.

Taking is the evidence of believing! If I should start thanking a friend for his gift, praising him for his kindness, assuring him that it will be most useful, and then not take the gift, my friend would think, "He either does not really want it, or else he does not really believe that I am giving it to him."

Yes, taking is the evidence of believing! The words of John 1:11-12 are so suitable for today: *He came to His own, but His own did not receive Him. Yet to all who received Him, to those who believed in His name, He gave the right to become the children of God.* Receiving is believing and believing is receiving.

I'm reminded of what was printed on the pens a certain shoe salesman in London, Ontario was giving away. They said, "If you ever get a chance to become a Christian, take it!" How true!

Read: John 3:1-15

December 14   TEN THINGS ABOUT FAITH

What is your definition of faith? How would you illustrate it? What is it worth? Is your faith genuine?

Now faith is being sure of what we hope for and certain of what we do not see (Heb. 11:1). *These have come so that your faith — of greater worth than gold, which perishes even though refined by fire — may be proved genuine and may result in praise, glory and honour when Jesus Christ is revealed* (1 Peter 1:7).

1. We are saved by faith! *For it is by grace you have been saved, through faith — and this not from yourselves, it is the gift of God* (Eph. 2:8; See also Acts 16:31).

2. We are justified by faith! *Therefore, since we have been justified through faith, we have peace with God through our Lord Jesus Christ* (Rom. 5:1; See also Gal. 3:6; Rom. 4:3,13).

3. We live by faith! *For in the gospel a righteousness from God is revealed, a righteousness that is by faith from first to last, just as it is written: "The righteous will live by faith"* (Rom. 1:17; See also Heb. 11:23-28 — Moses).

4. We walk by faith! *We live by faith, not by sight* (2 Cor. 5:7; See also Heb. 11:8-10; Rom. 4:12 — Abraham).

5. We please God by faith! *And without faith it is impossible to please God, because anyone who comes to Him must believe that He exists and that He rewards those who earnestly seek Him* (Heb. 11:6; See also Heb. 11:3,5 — Enoch).

6. We overcome the world by faith! *For everyone born of God overcomes the world. This is the victory that has overcome the world, even our faith* (1 John 5:4; See also Heb. 24-27 — Moses).

7. We resist the Devil by faith! *Resist him, standing firm in the faith, because you know that your brothers throughout the world are undergoing the same kind of sufferings* (1 Peter 5:9; See also James 4:7; Heb. 11:32-38 — Sample list).

8. We increase our faith by the Scriptures! *Consequently, faith comes from hearing the message, and the message is heard through the word of Christ* (Rom. 10:17; 2 Tim. 3:15-17).

9. We are kept by faith! *Who through faith are shielded by God's power until the coming of the salvation that is ready to be revealed in the last time* (1 Peter 1:5; Heb. 11:29).

10. We pray in faith! *But when he asks, he must believe and not doubt....* (James 1:6).

Four times Jesus scolded his disciples with the words, *"O ye of little faith"* (Matt. 6:30; 8:26; 14:31; 16:8). Two times Jesus commended "great faith" (Matt. 8:5-13; Matt. 15:28).

Our prayer today: Luke 17:5; Mark 9:24

December 15   THE WRITTEN WORD IS:

1. PROFITABLE —

As an agent in conviction. The Ethiopian was convicted when he read the words of Isaiah. When Peter preached on Pentecost people were convicted (Acts 8:28,32; Acts 2:16).

As an aid to teaching. God called Moses, gave him the commandments and they were to be taught (Deut. 6:4-12). Jesus used the Scriptures in teaching His disciples. Later, He commanded them to teach all nations (Matt. 28:19-20).

As an avenue to understanding. Philip recognized the Messiah from what he had read (John 1:45; John 2:17). We have the assurance of faith through the written word (1 John 5:13).

2. POWERFUL —

It is authoritative. Jesus used it against Satan in His hour of temptation (Luke 4:4,8,12). The writer of Hebrews says it is living and active (Heb. 4:12).

It is effective. John says, *But these are written that you may* [continue to] *believe that Jesus is the Christ, the Son of God, and that by believing you may have life in His name* (John 20:31). Words of men carry stronger evidence and authority when written.

3. PRACTICAL —

Paul was a practical theologian. He wrote with repetition (Phil. 3:1). He wrote to express the commandments of the Lord (1 Cor. 14:37). He wrote to warn the believers (1 Cor. 4:14), to test their obedience (2 Cor. 2:9), to bear greetings (Col. 4:14-15). He communicated countless words of counsel, comfort and courage.

4. PERMANENT!

"Heaven and earth will pass away, but My words will never pass away" (Mark 13:31). *For you have been born again, not of perishable seed, but of imperishable, through the living and enduring word of God* (1 Peter 1:23). All literature has a permanence that the spoken message cannot have. Eventually the voice must stop, but the marvel of literature goes on.

5. PRESCRIBED!

Men of old were enjoined to write. Moses was told to write (Deut. 27:2-3); Jeremiah was told to write (Jer. 30:2); John was told to write (Rev. 1:11,19); Paul warned Timothy to give attention to reading (1Tim. 4:13); John encouraged men to search the Scriptures (John 5:39).

Go with 2 Timothy 3:16 today!

December 16   ZACCHAEUS

Jesus Christ went about doing good (Acts 10:38). One of His tours took Him through Jericho. The first mention of Jericho is in the book of Joshua — the spies going in (Josh. 2) and the walls tumbling down (Josh. 6) are both familiar stories to us. Today, Jericho is a beautiful place, with palm trees, flowers and gardens.

In Bible days, Jericho was a great taxation centre. That is where the story of Zacchaeus comes in. Three things about Zacchaeus:

1. The Efforts of Zacchaeus—Efforts that triumph over hindrances. The hindrances arise from: his social position — he is a tax collector; his wealth — he is rich; and his personal stature — he is short. Socially speaking, he was a man who was looked down upon. Tax collectors did not have good reputations. Financially speaking, he was wealthy — wealthy, but not happy. How come? You'd think money would make him happy. But riches are apt to put a serious obstacle in the way. What did Jesus say? (Luke 18:24) What did Moses say? (Deut.7:25). Physically speaking, he was short. He did not venture to solicit an interview; he found even a view to be difficult. He ran the risk of being made fun of by running and climbing a tree. But the necessity of the soul made him quick to invention and oblivious to others. I wonder how much effort we put into overcoming hindrances. Faith carries an "I must" in its bosom. He wanted to see Jesus! The dwarf with a great desire was led to a great discovery.

2. The Encounter with Zacchaeus. *When Jesus reached the spot, He looked up and said to him, "Zacchaeus, come down immediately. I must stay at your house today" So he came down at once and welcomed him gladly* (Luke 19:5-6). His home and his heart were open to the Master. There was no asking, "Who is He?" His heart had answered that. The question often asked is, "Can a person really know God?" Yes! He is knowable! That day the poor and the rich were embraced with the love of God (Luke 18:35). Jesus will have fellowship with both the rich and the poor. There can be a friendship and a fellowship that nothing can separate.

3. The Effect this had on Zacchaeus. From here on in, selfishness and wrongness is renounced and restitution is made. Voluntary confession and voluntary restitution! His character and life are changed (Luke 19:9).

Why did Jesus come? Look at Luke 19:10 and 1Peter 3:18.

Read: Luke 19:1-10

December 17   BROKEN THINGS IN THE BIBLE

We live in a broken world — broken homes, broken hearts, broken promises and broken toys. Broken things are common in life. But to the believer, broken things can be the assurance that God is making something whole. God uses broken things to gain victory.

1. The Broken Law (Exod. 32:19). God used the broken law to show man his need for salvation. Salvation is not found in keeping the law; rather, the law shows us our sin and that we need forgiveness (Gal. 3:24).

2. The Broken Pitchers (Judg. 7:19-20). God used a small army of men with strange weapons to deliver Israel. The pitchers were broken to produce the sound and to let the light of the torches shine into the night. We too are known as vessels (2 Tim. 2:20-21).

3. The Broken Roof (Mark 2:1-12). God saw the faith of four men and honoured their efforts to bring a needy man to Christ. The message of forgiveness was loud and clear. It brought astonishment and glory to God.

4. The Broken Alabaster Jar (Mark 14:3-9). God honoured the cost and the sacrifice of a woman whose gratitude was expressed that day on Jesus Christ. She did what she could, and it was a beautiful thing! That memorial continues to this day.

5. The Broken Loaves and Fishes (Matt. 14:15-21). Jesus provided for a hungry crowd. Through Him there was sustenance for all. He is the Bread of Life! The loaves and fishes had to be broken before they could benefit the people. Could Jesus feed someone through me?

6. The Broken Nets (Luke 5:1-11). The Lord wanted Peter! Peter saw himself as unworthy, but he was called to be a servant of Christ. Men were to become more important than fish. You could call it being "broken for service."

7. The Broken Ship (Acts 27:44). God chose to use a storm and a broken boat to enhance the testimony of His servant Paul. Paul could say on the deck, "I believe in God, we will all be safe." Paul was not ashamed of the gospel.

8. The Broken Body of Jesus (Luke 22:19; 1 Cor. 11:24). His body was literally scourged, pierced and nailed. He was wounded — and it was for us! (Isa. 53:5). The Lord's Table is our reminder!

Are we broken for Him? Is your all on the altar? Are you a slave of Jesus Christ? (Rom. 6:11-14). *In Him we have redemption through His blood, the forgiveness of sins, in accordance with the riches of God's grace* (Eph. 1:7).

Read: Psalm 51:17

December 18   WHY OBSERVE SUNDAY?

Let me bring in Isaiah 58:13: *"If you keep your feet from breaking the Sabbath and from doing as you please on My holy day, if you call the Sabbath a delight and the LORD's holy day honorable, and if you honor it by not going your own way and not doing as you please or speaking idle words, then you will find your joy in the Lord."*

Many passages in the gospels show strict Sabbatarians with their traditions and taboos. Pharisees were prone to legalism, rules and regulations that were stiff, narrow and rigid. Jesus crashed through all of this and went straight to the persons in need. Jesus claimed that human need must take precedence over religious laws. He sought to renew depleted energies and frayed spirits.

The Lord's Day Alliance does safe-guard a day of rest. However, if our puritanical fathers were too strict, our society today is likely to err to the opposite extreme. What does it mean to do good on the Sabbath? We distort the meaning of the day if we think solely in terms of restrictions, rather than the beneficent uses to which the day should be put. This day can be wholesome, joyous and recreative.

The woman who was healed of a crooked back on the Sabbath glorified God! That is what the day is for!

1. It is to straighten us out physically. Six days of work leave a kink in our backs. Rest is part of God's structure in life. If we do not rest consistently each week, we will end up needing more rest for longer periods of time. We need rest and so do others around us. Isaiah says we are not to do as we please.

2. It is to straighten us out spiritually. There are kinks in our minds and souls that need to be relieved as well. Attention must be given to our souls. Our spirits need stretching to new heights. We need instruction and inspiration. Listen! Worship is not a luxury, it is a necessity. Worship is fellowship with others. We need other believers in our lives. We can be instrumental in brightening someone's life. We all need a lift for living!

The place of worship is still the place to be on the Lord's Day!

Read: Matthew 12:10-23, Luke 13:10-17

December 19   THE MIGHTY GOD

In every age, men have stood in awe of those who possess great power. This is true in every area of life — politics, finances, science and sports.

We've been looking at the names of Christ through the eyes of Isaiah (Isa. 9:6). Today, let's study "the Mighty God"!

Christ is the Mighty God as we see Him overcome the world and Satan by a sinless life. He overcame sin on the cross, and death and the grave in the resurrection. This is the greatest demonstration of God's power in the New Testament. The Mighty God!

It was Charles Lamb who said, "If Shakespeare were to come into your home you would rise to honour him; but if Christ were to come into your home you would bow down and worship Him."

Jesus has been declared the Agent of Creation. Before He ever came to earth, His hands tumbled solar systems and galaxies into space. He set the stars on their courses. He kindled the fires of the sun. He scooped out the giant beds of our mighty oceans.

He was mighty in His ministry and miracles. He was mighty in His teaching. I am so glad that the Mighty God became my Saviour. The great Creator became my Saviour!

The Bible has this beautiful invitation: *To all who received Him, to those who believed in His name, He gave the right to become children of God* (John 1:12). The hymn writer says, "Only Believe!"

Read: John 1:1-18; Proverbs 8:22-31

December 20 GOOD THINGS – SMALL PACKAGES

Today we look at an Old Testament Bible character. A young Israelite girl who was taken captive during a time of war. War separates families. She could have been among many missing children. Three things about this captive maiden.

1. Her Initiative! *She said to her mistress, "If only my master would see the prophet who is in Samaria! He would cure him of his leprosy"* (2 Kings 5:3). She was serving Naaman's wife and she seized the opportunity. An army officer in that home had leprosy, and she had sympathy. She had fond memories of a godly upbringing and she did not forget her faith even when far away from home. What a child-like and timely testimony! Good wishes are seeds that often take root and grow and blossom and bear fruit.

2. Her Information! She told of Israel's God. She told of the prophet Elisha. She had the assurance of God's power. She knew a cure! This little girl did not render evil for evil, though she could have, being a captive. She did not wait for some great thing to do. She simply spoke! Solace and help comes to us from the most unexpected sources. Good things come in small packages! (Can I remind you of the fable where a little mouse helped a big lion by chewing at the ropes and setting him free?)

3. Her Influence! Have you read the story? It moved a captain to go, making all kinds of preparations. It moved a king to send a letter to another king. It set in motion a lot of reaction until the news came to the prophet Elisha. Then, it resulted in a cleansed leper. The officer went to dip in the Jordan seven times. Now it was Naaman's turn to say, "Now I know that there is no God in all the world except in Israel."

None of us are too young to do something for Jesus. He has some work for every one of us. Sometimes, we may need to just stand and show our colours. Other times, we may be able to tell people where blessing is to be found. Be an instrument of His joy and peace. Be an example of His goodness and gentleness. Do the work that is nearest to you! This little slave girl's secret was her faithfulness, her usefulness and her strong and simple faith.

Would you write these three words in the fly-leaf of your Bible: ANYTHING! ANYTIME! ANYWHERE!

Read : 2 Kings 5

December 21   WHY I GO TO CHURCH (Part 1)

I rejoiced with those who said to me, "Let us go to the house of the LORD" (Ps. 122:1). Such joy is rare! Is there gladness when you go to church? Or are you glad when it's over? Do you go out of a sense of duty, the desire to please a friend, the force of habit, the necessity of upholding a religious reputation, the fear of a condemning conscience or some other motive? Or do you have spiritual delight? Listen to the psalmist when he says, *Glorify the LORD with me; let us exalt His name together* (Ps. 34:3).

We have the example of Jesus. *He went to Nazareth, where He had been brought up, and on the Sabbath day He went into the synagogue, as was His custom* (Luke 4:16). We have the exhortation of an apostle. *Let us not give up meeting together, as some are in the habit of doing, but let us encourage one another — and all the more as you see the Day approaching* (Heb. 10:25). Have you been able to encourage someone?

Why do I go to church?

1. I go to church to worship! There is joy in worship! Some say they can worship outside of church. That's true, but do they? Fellowship in worship cannot be experienced alone. It requires the gathering of people. Think of the Tabernacle and the Temple. Fire made of two sticks does not give as much warmth as fire made of many sticks. Radio and television preaching can never take the place of real worship. I want to worship God in the best possible way.

2. I go to church to satisfy the hunger in my soul. *Blessed are those who hunger and thirst for righteousness, for they will be filled* (Matt. 5:6). Earth was never meant to satisfy the human heart. Only God can do that. *He satisfies the thirsty and fills the hungry with good things* (Ps. 107:9). Hungry souls do not go away without a blessing. When you are hungry, food is more fulfilling. Have you ever noticed that you eat more and better in the company of others? When I'm alone, it's a piece of toast or a bowl of cereal. I'm sure you can identify with me!

Read: Psalm 122 (More tomorrow!)

December 22   WHY I GO TO CHURCH (Part 2)

3. I go to church to hear the gospel, the Word of God. Both are powerful! (Rom. 1:16; Heb. 4:12). I need this energy, this spiritual instruction! I need exhortation and correction (2 Tim. 3:16). I need a spiritual check-up! I ask myself, "Do I love the Lord's Day, His Word, His Table? Do I find time for Bible study, unhurried prayer and quiet listening to God?" Ask yourself the same questions.

4. I go to church to help further the Kingdom of God. The commission has not changed, and it is best fulfilled through the Church. Most missionary work is done through churches. The Church is the means through which God can reach out to the world. I want to be a part of that Kingdom work, wherever He puts me. What joy awaits the sower and the reaper! (John 4:36-37; Ps. 126:6).

5. I go to church to set an example. Parents whose lives centre around the Church will influence their children. Think of children in godless homes — they miss so much. Regular attendance gives us an influence that nothing else can. In our home, it was a way of life! A right attitude will also be a great influence. Do I love to go, do I prepare myself in heart and mind and do I realize that the adoration of God is my most important, blessed activity?

6. I go to church to receive strength and inspiration for my daily living. A clock needs winding! Fire needs fuel! A car needs gas! My soul needs refreshing! My soul needs food! God is wise — He made the Sabbath (Sunday) so that we might rest and be restored, physically, mentally and spiritually. Listen! There are 156 hours between the close of one Sunday night service and the opening of the next; surely we ought to take one hour in the middle of that to renew our strength, don't you think? (That was a plug for the mid-week prayer meeting. I had to throw it in!).

7. I go to church to enjoy the fellowship. Where will you find better fellowship? God's people are friendly! God's people love each other! I need their fellowship. I need their prayers! Let us make church a place where we can fellowship with each other. Your presence is important! It is always an encouragement. I want my life to be linked with the Church. I believe you do too!

Are you at home in your church?

Read: Psalm 84

December 23 THE EVERLASTING FATHER

A little boy looking at his father's picture (the father having been away from home for a long time) said, "I wish Father would step out of the picture." That's exactly what happened at

Christmas. What the prophets had foretold and the people were waiting for, happened at Christmas. A baby was born and they named Him Jesus.

To continue with the names of Christ in Isaiah 9:6, we now have the name, "The Everlasting Father." This title speaks of His eternity. He came from the Father and as such, has all the characteristics of God the Father. *He is before all things* (Col. 1:17). He is Lord of the past and the present. He holds the future in His hands. *He has set eternity in the hearts of men* (Eccl. 3:11). That is a great verse! Think of it! Eternal forces ripple in our blood. Because Jesus Christ is Eternal, we shall share eternity with Him.

Today, He continues to care for us. The Eternal Father clothed Himself in the garments of human flesh so that we might understand the nature and character of God. Jesus came to show us the Father (John 1:18). He introduced God to us as "our Father."

Jesus Christ ever lives to love, to lift us out of our sinful condition and to give us the gift of eternal life. He has the ability to meet our deepest need and He is always available.

Jesus — the Everlasting Father! Did you talk to Him today?

Read: John 1:1-14; Isaiah 9:6; Colossians 1:16,17

December 24   THE PRINCE OF PEACE

Every newscast seems to include some quest for peace. We hear it and see it on the faces of people everywhere. The human heart hungers for peace. I think it's universal among men. It makes you wonder why we have failed to achieve it when we want it so much. Our search for peace has taken us everywhere, from education, wealth and military might to fame, fortune and fashion. Yet it still eludes us. The world is still searching.

The Prince of Peace makes it possible for man to be at peace with God and for men to live at peace with one another. Jesus Christ is the source of peace! The peace He gives is not won on a battlefield, purchased with money, nor secured by medicine.

The heart of the problem is the problem of the heart! Peace is an inward experience. The peace that He gives is the peace of surrender to the rule of love; the peace of fellowship with God our heavenly Father; the peace of knowing that our sins are forgiven. Read Psalm 32:1-5 sometime. Bear in mind, even at Christmas, that the cradle and the cross are eternally linked together.

Paul says, *He Himself is our peace* (Eph. 2:14). Through Him we have access to the Father by one Spirit.

Peace rules the day when Christ rules the mind!

Read: Isaiah 26:3,4; John 14:27; 16:33; Philippians 4:7

December 25   GOD IS THE GREATEST GIVER

Let's look at some propositional truths today. A proposition is an expression of anything that is capable of being believed; it is a point to be discussed or maintained.

1. If Christ is the gift of God, then see the Father's love. *This is love: not that we loved God, but that He loved us and sent His Son as an atoning sacrifice for our sins* (1 John 4:10). I see here redeeming love! We did not deserve it; we had no right to expect it. It was the expression of purest love.

2. If Christ is the gift of God, then see the Father's grace. *By grace you have been saved through faith — and this not from yourselves, it is the gift of God* (Eph. 2:8). Grace means that God gives us what we do not deserve. The acrostic for GRACE would read: **G**od's **R**iches **A**t **C**hrist's **E**xpense.

3. If Christ is the gift of God, then see the Father's mercy. *He did not spare His own Son, but gave Him up for us all* (Rom. 8:32). Mercy means that God does *not* give us what we *do* deserve. As Wm. R. Newell puts it in his hymn, "At Calvary,"

> *Mercy there was great, and grace was free;*
> *Pardon there was multiplied to me....*

4. If Christ is the gift of God, then He is meant to be received. *To all who received Him, to those who believed in His name, He gave the right to become children of God* (John 1:12). We receive Him by faith! *Being justified through faith, we have peace with God through our Lord Jesus Christ* (Rom. 5:1). He is meant to be received NOW. NOW is the day of salvation!

5. If Christ is the gift of God, then He may also be refused. A gift is never forced! God will not violate the responsible freedom of the human will. It's a GIFT! A gift is never complete until it is received.

Christ has brought forgiveness, reconciliation, justification and sonship to all who believe. Welcome Him into your life!

Read: Romans 5:1-11

December 26   AN EPILOGUE TO CHRISTMAS

Christmas is over! The festivities are over! We are back to a less thrilling road of everyday living. The preparations had their thrills and excitement. You all know now what you got for Christmas.

Christmas is over! Wait just a minute! Is it over? Think of the love that was expressed through giving, sharing and fellowship. This continues throughout the year.

Go with me now to Luke 2:20: *The shepherds returned, glorifying and praising God for all the things they had heard and seen, which were just as they had been told.* The shepherds returned with a new vision before their eyes and a new power in their lives. Gazing on the Babe, they had beheld a mystery — God in the likeness of human flesh. Their souls were thrilled!

The shepherds returned to the complexities of earning a living, to the daily routine of looking after sheep.

We must return from Christmas to the commonplace. It is unavoidable! The shepherds returned with something of the spell of Christmas still upon them. Insights had been gained! It was an unforgettable night! They discovered God in humanity and humanity in God. Hope had been kindled in their lives. The shepherds found ONE who was to make commonplace living a blessing. Christ cast a halo of glory over common toil. He Himself underwent toil and pain, sorrow and adversity. He identified Himself with us so that we may identify ourselves with Him.

Life is routine. The old road lies ahead. There is the hill to climb. There are the burdens to face. But the ONE who came at Christmas is still with us! He is beside us, before us and behind us. Will we return like the shepherds, glorifying and praising God? Every day can and should mean what the essence of Christmas means. Around Christmas we develop some qualities of mind and spirit that should belong with us all the time. Faith in Jesus Christ makes all the difference!

Read: Luke 2:8-20

December 27   SPEND A DAY IN PRAYER (Part 1)

This day could make a difference in your life! You could choose to make it different, to make it a Special Day!

Along the way we need helpful hints to make it meaningful and worthwhile. The Bible gives us some special guidelines for personal prayer. Prayer is the state of the heart, an attitude. It is being in tune with God, with our frequency on heaven (1 Thess. 5:17).

May I suggest a threefold argument for praying?

1. Christ commands it (Matt. 7:7).
2. Experience commends it (Matt. 7:8).
3. Logic defends it (Matt. 7:9-11).

Keeping in time with God is also a part of it. I want a sense of rhythm in my soul — a spirit of prayer. I need to practice a "quiet time" — time set aside for the Word and prayer.

For David, the time was early in the morning (Ps. 5:3). For Daniel, it was three times a day (Dan. 6:10). For Joshua, it was early in the morning (Josh. 3:1). For Jesus, it was in the early morning while it was still dark (Mark 1:35). For you... what's your time? I believe quiet times are indispensable for the growing, healthy believer. These are times when God speaks to us and makes His ways and His plans known to us. Special days can become "anchor points" in your life.

Now you are asking, "Why a *day* of prayer? Why take such a long time? What's it for?" Let me share about five reasons:

1. For extended fellowship with God, beyond your personal private devotions. Just plain "being with" and "thinking about" God. God has called us into fellowship with His Son (1 Cor. 1:9). Fellowship is nurtured by spending time together. God takes special note of those who think upon His name (Mal. 3:16).

2. For a renewed perspective. Like a plane flying over a certain territory to make some discovery. It's to think of our lives from God's viewpoint. How does God look at me? What does He think about me? We need this perspective to sharpen our vision of the unseen and to let the tangible things drop into proper place (2 Cor. 4:17-18). Spiritual things are paramount and permanent!

3. For catching up on intercession. There are non-christian friends and loved ones to bring before the Lord. There are missionaries, neighbors and governments to pray for. Christians know that events can be changed through prayer.

Read: 1 Thessalonians 5:17; Pray continually.
(More tomorrow!)

December 28 SPEND A DAY IN PRAYER (Part 2)

We continue today to answer the question, "Why spend a day in prayer?"

4. For adequate preparation. Nehemiah affords a good illustration: He prays first before he makes a plan (Neh. 1:4;.2:3-5); and then God puts the plan into his heart (Neh. 2:12). Preparations become clear when we get alone with God. We may be dead to opportunities simply because we are not prepared. Who knows, God may want to prepare us for something special.

5. For prayerful consideration of our own lives before God. The Bible says, *Examine yourself* (2 Cor. 13:5). Take inventory! May I name a few areas that need examination? The first area is our personal relationship with the Lord. Ask yourself, "Am I living in a vital relationship? Is my relationship current?" And then we need to examine our love and submission to the Word of God. Do we have a longing and a love for the Word, with the desire to obey it? (Ps. 119). We need to examine our relationships with our brothers and sisters in Christ. This also determines the quality of our relationship with the Lord (Rom. 14:7). Are we patient and loving and forgiving? (Eph. 4:31). We need to examine our attitude towards sin. Do we need cleansing? (1 John 1:7; 3:3). We need to examine our attitude towards the perishable things of the world (1 John 2:15-17). Are temporal things really that important? We need to examine our concern and love for the lost. Do we have a burden for souls? This is one burden that needs to grow in my life.

Renewals in history have usually begun with a few individuals who were willing to pay the price to go all the way with God.

Let us look at how we might go about setting aside a day for prayer. The first thing we need to do is actually *set aside* some time! We all have the same time, though we don't all have the same circumstances. Find a place for some quiet. If this is impossible at home, go for a drive or a walk. Forget about food! Try it — it's a good discipline! Food is secondary and you may learn to value it more. Be free to help your children if they are small and need attention. Take a Bible, a book on Prayer, a pencil and some paper. Thank God for the ability to read and write.

Great peace have they who love Your law, and nothing can make them stumble (Ps. 119:165).

(Some more tomorrow!)

December 29 SPEND A DAY IN PRAYER (Part 3)

We continue today to look at how we might go about setting aside a day for prayer.

Divide the time you've set aside into three parts:

1. Wait on the Lord! Do not hurry! (Isa. 40:31; Ps. 27:14; 62:5). Wait to realize His presence (Ps. 139). Wait for cleansing (Ps. 139:23-24). Stand firm on 1 John 1:9. Wait to worship Him! (Ps. 146-150).

2. Pray for yourself! Ask for understanding (Ps. 119:18). Read the prayer of Jabez (1 Chron. 4:10). The attitude of this time ought to be, "Lord, what do you think of my life?" Think about your life in the light of what you know to be God's will for you. What is pleasing to God? (2 Tim. 2:4; Eph. 5:10). Ask, "What was Jesus' attitude?" *"My food," said Jesus, "is to do the will of him who sent me and to finish his work* (John 4:34). Consider your activities! What are you doing in your service for God? Your use of time? God may speak to you about your schedule, about cutting out some of your activities. There may be some entanglements that rob you of your spiritual progress. Come to some conclusion! Drive some stakes if God reveals something to you! But don't be discouraged if God does not pinpoint an area in your life to work on — it may not be His time for that. He may instead give you a new revelation of Himself if that is what you need. Whatever it is that God shows you, be sure to write it down or mark it in your Bible!

3. Pray for others! Now you have time for unhurried prayer. Pray about specific things for them. You may remember a missionary letter. Pray for their spiritual and physical strength, for courage and mental alertness. Pray some of the Pauline prayers (Phil. 1:9; Col. 1:9; Eph. 3:14-21). Desire for them what the Lord has shown you He desires for them.

Variety is important during the day. Read for a while. Pray for a while. Walk for a while. As things pop into your mind, simply incorporate them into your prayer. Some items may be jotted down and attended to later. Summarize in your notebook the things God said to you, the new insights! The test of such a day is not how exhilarated you are when the day is over, but how well your experiences work into your life the next day. Your daily life will change.

A day of prayer doesn't just happen. The Enemy will attempt to keep you from it. Satan trembles when he sees the weakest

Christian on his knees. So we must take the time! And, who knows, after a day like this you may find yourself saying, "Why didn't I do this long ago?"

Can you make a day like this meaningful in your life?

December 30   CLOSING THE DOOR (Part 1)

As we close the door on the old year, I am not so concerned about reviewing the past year or predicting the year to come; I am concerned about having the proper attitude as we look both ways. So much depends upon our attitudes!

The account in Exodus 14:5-31 may help us to fashion some good attitudes. Israel had reached the Red Sea and it was blocking their way forward. The Egyptians were in hot pursuit from behind. It was a bad situation! They were literally trapped between desperation and the deep, and they began to complain loudly (vs. 10-12).

Don't we find ourselves in bad situations from time to time? We are sometimes caught (like Israel) between the Red Sea (something blocking our advance) and the the Egyptians (something blocking our retreat). Perhaps we rushed stormily through this past year, wanting to get ahead. And then, just when we were in the most hurry, an emergency arose. Things came to a halt! We were called to a stand still. Reflection can be a good exercise!

Several truths begin to surface from this account. The first truth I wish to mention is this: Some of our greatest enemies are not those that confront us, but those that pursue us. It wasn't so much the Red Sea in front that was terrifying as the host of Egypt behind (vs. 10). The enemy behind created the panic. Is this a parable of our situation? Some of us are being pursued by "fear." Fear creates havoc in our minds. Children have fears — ie. fear of failure. Young people have fears — ie. fear of the future. Adults have fears — and frustrations and phobias and perplexities. Life is full of problems! Some people are pursued by grief. Others are pursued by old besetting sins that haven't been laid at the cross. "Selfishness still throbs like an engine at the center of a man's life." The Bible lists a few things that we struggle with in Galatians 5:19-21. Egypt, representing the flesh, is in pursuit. The flesh is out to get you back. The old nature and the world really tug! Is there something that is pursuing you? Something that is hindering your progress toward maturity? How is your spiritual journey? How would you describe your Christian walk this past year? I trust there will be no "carry over" from one year to the next to keep you from beginning afresh in the New Year.

Read: Galatians 5:7; Hebrews 2:1

December 31   CLOSING THE DOOR (Part 2)

A second truth comes from the story in Exodus 14. We see more than the pursuit of the enemy; we see God becoming our rear guard (vs. 19). God not only goes before, He is also behind! The God who was their Leader now also becomes their Protector! Read Psalm 34:7. God is for us! As we begin the New Year, God is before us, behind us, beside us, above us, around us and in us! Hymns flood my mind: "He Leadeth Me!" "Lead on O King Eternal!" "Guide Me, O Thou Great Jehovah!" Read Psalm 139:5 and Isaiah 52:12b. We can close the door on this past year and then trust God to make sure it *stays* shut on anything that pursues us. He can take care of the enemy — our fears, our grief and our sin.

A third truth: Every experience of life has two sides, depending on whom the experience comes. Look at verse 20! The pillar of cloud brought darkness to the Egyptians and light to Israel. The Egyptians saw only darkness; Israel had light. To the persons without God or even without faith, things look pretty dark. For many, it is very dark. To be "Egypt-like" is to see nothing but darkness, confusion and chaos. Sin is on the rampage these days! There is crime, violence, permissiveness and perversion. Even the G.S.T. (Goods and Services Tax) is frightening! To the man of faith, however, the cloud is not all darkness. He sees God in history! He knows God is Sovereign and is in control! He sees God at work! Doors of evangelism have opened in many countries. Some dark periods have brought creative change. Some beautiful pictures come out of the dark room. The disciplines of darkness, detour, disappointments and delay come to my mind. Romans 8:28 fits in here somewhere. The severity of a situation tells me that God is in it. To the man of faith, there is light shining in these dark experiences. Read: Proverbs 4:18.

Let us go to Calvary! The Light of Life seems to be snuffed out. To the natural man it is all darkness. It does not make sense (1 Cor. 1:23). But the light of the resurrection streams across the darkness of the cross. As we close the door on this past year, we can ask God to give us the grace to close the door on all the Egyptians — the temptations, evil habits, old grudges and sins. Join Paul in taking off the old and putting on the new. We can take courage and go on. Go forward! (Exod. 14:15). The past is God's! The present is God's! And the future is God's! His power is greater than all! Let Jesus Christ be everything to you! Live in Him!

Are you going to close a few doors on the old year? How about a New You for a New Year?

Read: Colossians 2:6-7

NOTES

[1]E.M. Bounds, *Power Through Prayer* (Grand Rapids: Zondervan Publishing House, 1965) p. 23.

[2]Bounds, p. 23.

[3]*Springs in the Valley,* comp., Mrs. Charles E. Cowman (Grand Rapids: Zondervan Publishing House, 1939, 1968) pp. 4-5.

[4]*Springs*, p. 262.

[5]Bounds, pp. 12, 27, 30-31.

[6]Bounds, p. 23.

[7]Bounds, pp. 11, 12.

INDEX OF TITLES

Order Form

Ordered By: (please print)

Name: _____

Address: _____

City: _____ Prov./State: _____

Postal/Zip Code: _____ Telephone: _____

Please send me the following book(s): (All Prices in Cdn. Dollars.)

Qty.	Title	Unit Price	Total
_____	*A Lift for Living*	$16.95	$_____
_____	*Setting the Captives Free*	$9.95	$_____
_____	*To Have & To Hold*	$7.50	$_____
_____	*A Voice Behind You*	$9.95	$_____
_____	*Handling Stress*	$9.95	$_____
_____	*And the Pink Snow Fell*	$14.95	$_____
_____	*Protestant Church Growth in Korea*	$24.95	$_____
_____	*Binder of Wounds*	$Call	$_____

Shipping ($2.00 first book - $1.00 each add. book): $_____

G.S.T. @ 7%: $_____

Total: $_____

Payable by Cheque, Money Order or VISA

VISA #:_____ Expiry:_____

Signature:_____

To order by phone, call our toll-free number,
1-800-238-6376
and have your credit card handy.